Electing Congress

Electing Congress

CQ Press
A Division of Congressional Quarterly Inc.
Washington, D.C.

CQ Press
2300 N Street, NW, Suite 800
Washington, DC 20037

Phone: 202-729-1900; toll-free, 1-866-4CQ-PRESS (1-866-427-7737)

Web: www.cqpress.com

Cover design: www.thedesignfarm.com
Cover photos: Scott J. Ferrell, Congressional Quarterly
Interior design and composition: Judy Myers, graphic designer

♾ The paper used in this publication exceeds the requirements of the American National Standard for Information Sciences—Permanence of Paper for Printed Library Materials, ANSI Z39.48-1992.

Printed and bound in the United States of America

12 11 10 09 08 1 2 3 4 5

Library of Congress Cataloging-in-Publication Data

Electing Congress.
p. cm.
Includes bibliographical references and index.
ISBN 978-0-87289-956-8 (pbk. : alk. paper) 1. United States. Congress—Elections. 2. Political campaigns—United States. 3. United States—Politics and government.

JK1976.E43 2008
324.973—dc22

2008008425

TABLE OF CONTENTS

Preface vii

CHAPTER 1 WHO ELECTS CONGRESS 1
More Voters, Changing Voter Patterns 1
The Black Vote: A Long, Painful Struggle 7
Women's Vote: A Victory in Stages 17
The Eighteen-year-old Vote 19
Removing Obstacles to Voting 19

CHAPTER 2 POLITICAL PARTIES AND ELECTIONS 25
Functions of Parties 25
Party System: Unforeseen Development 28
Divided Government 32
Election of Members: Evolving Process 36

CHAPTER 3 WHO GETS ELECTED 45
Characteristics of Members 46
Women in Congress 49
Blacks in Congress 52
Hispanics in Congress 55
Turnover in Membership 56
Shifts between Chambers 62

CHAPTER 4 CAMPAIGN FINANCING 65
Uncertainties, Controversies Surround System 65
Congressional Candidates' Contributions and Expenditures 69
Campaign Finance Issues and Controversies 75
Financing Campaigns: Historical Development 84
Major Reform Laws Enacted in the 1970s 89
Overhaul after Decades of Stalemates 99

CHAPTER 5 REAPPORTIONMENT AND REDISTRICTING 107
Early History of Reapportionment 108
Reapportionment: The Number of Seats 110
Redistricting: Drawing the Lines 116

Major Supreme Court Cases on Redistricting 124
Practical Results of Court's Rulings 129
Mid-Decade Redistricting and Partisan Gerrymandering 134

REFERENCE MATERIALS 141
Political Party Affiliations in Congress and the Presidency, 1789–2007 143
Election Results, Congress and the Presidency, 1860–2006 146
Women Members of Congress, 1917–2007 148
African American Members of Congress, 1870–2007 151
Hispanic Members of Congress, 1877–2007 153
Congressional Information on the Internet 154
Constitution of the United States 156

ILLUSTRATION CREDITS AND ACKNOWLEDGMENTS 165

Index 167

★ PREFACE

In the preface to *How Congress Gets Elected,* the previous edition of *Electing Congress,* CQ Press editors predicted that the 2000 national election might "be one of the most important elections in modern times." The six years that followed proved this a prescient observation.

The 2000 election sent George W. Bush to the White House in the closest presidential race ever, after the Supreme Court in a 5–4 vote halted a recount of disputed ballots in Florida, awarding the state's electoral votes to the former Texas governor. The outcome enraged Democrats and tainted the legitimacy of Bush's presidency, although he would win reelection by a comfortable margin in 2004. Nevertheless, the 2000 election—and the three that followed it through the midterm congressional election in 2006—pushed the nation into a kind of electoral bungee jump that is still playing out in the run-up to the national elections in 2008.

During the six years that followed 2000, Americans witnessed two major historic events: the 2001 al-Qaida attacks on the World Trade Center and the Pentagon and the 2003 U.S.-led invasion and occupation of Iraq. The response to the attacks and conduct of the Iraq war continue to dominate the nation's politics in 2008. Americans also watched as control of the Senate, initially held by the Republicans after the 2000 election, shifted to Democrats in 2001 after a disaffected Republican left the party and threw his support to the opposition. After the 2004 election, Republicans, riding on Bush's coattails, firmly controlled Congress and proceeded to enact important parts of the party's agenda. In 2006, however, Bush's plummeting popularity and the growing national opposition to the Iraq war gave Democrats control of the Senate (by a narrow margin) and the House (by a comfortable margin). The 2008 election resembles the 2000 contest in some ways: there is no incumbent presidential candidate, control of Congress is hotly contested, and the nation's voters are divided, and according to polls, deeply concerned about the country's direction.

Electing Congress is designed to help citizens understand how the U.S. electoral system works, covering its strong points and its flaws. Although focused on elections to Congress, the five chapters also touch on all aspects of elections, including an expanding franchise, paying for elections, the role of political parties, and the process of redistricting.

Who Elects Congress. At the base of understanding U.S. elections is the electorate. Although the franchise was originally limited to upper economic classes, today virtually every adult citizen age eighteen and older has the right to vote. Struggles over the franchise nevertheless continue, as different groups promote or challenge the inclusion of some classes of individuals, often minorities or immigrants, whose legal credentials to vote are in question or whose political allegiance is likely to favor one or the other national political party.

Political Parties and Elections. Since the earliest days of the nation, political parties have been vital elements in the structure and operation of elections at all levels of government. Broadly viewed, the parties are coalitions of people who join together to try to gain governmental power by winning elections and thereby further their social, economic, and ideological goals. The dominant parties—Republican and Democratic—have for more than a century faced only sporadic challenges from independents and third parties.

Who Gets Elected. Americans go to the polls every two years to elect a new Congress and every four years to elect a president. Although the 110th Congress that began in 2007 is an institution primarily of white men, typically in their fifties and sixties, the composition of the national legislature continues to evolve as more minorities and women win election. The most dramatic evidence of change is the election of California Democrat Nancy Pelosi to the post of House Speaker, making her the first woman to hold the job. At the presidential level, the two Democratic frontrunners in 2008 are a woman, Sen. Hillary Rodham Clinton of New York, and an African American, Sen. Barack Obama of Illinois.

Campaign Financing. The most arcane, most complicated, and arguably most controversial dimension of elections is how to pay for them. *Electing Congress* addresses the issue of raising campaign money, which is always in the forefront of a candidate's mind, by making the complicated understandable. The cost of elections spiraled upward by the early twenty-first century. Congressional candidates spent $1.4 billion in the 2006 elections. Members were under relentless pressure to raise funds for their campaigns; many retiring members said that the demands of campaign fund-raising were among their reasons for leaving Congress.

Reapportionment and Redistricting. At the center of national elections for Congress are the twin processes of reapportionment and redistricting. These two activities play important roles in determining control of the House of Representatives. After each national census, the number of House members awarded the states is reapportioned using a mathematical process that reflects population changes among the states. It is largely, but not entirely, noncontroversial. Redistricting, however, is a highly political process that sometimes elicits the pejorative "gerrymandering." After reapportionment, state legislatures or commissions carve out the districts in which House members run for election, often producing districts comprised of like-minded voters who give a political party a high probability of winning the district's seat. As a result, most House seats are largely non-competitive in normal times. Some redistricting plans remains in doubt, but its effect on control of the House is unquestionable.

These discussions in *Electing Congress* are supplemented by anecdotes and sidebar narratives that provide historical detail. An appendix includes tabular data about political parties in Congress, congressional election results, the demographic makeup of Congress, and congressional information on the Internet.

CQ Press Editors

Electing Congress

chapter 1

Who Elects Congress

Few elements of the American political system have changed so markedly over the years as has the electorate. Since the early days of the nation, when the voting privilege was limited to the upper economic classes, one voting barrier after another has fallen to pressures for wider suffrage. First, men who did not own property, then women, then African Americans, and finally young people obtained the franchise. By the early 1970s virtually every adult citizen eighteen and older had won the right to vote.

But by the end of the 1990s only about half of those eligible to vote were exercising that right in high-profile presidential elections, and only between 30 percent and 40 percent of those eligible were bothering to vote in midterm congressional elections. Despite the highly charged partisanship that characterized American politics and the closely fought elections after the turn of the twentieth century, which brought more voters to the polling booth, the turnout rate was not radically altered in either presidential or congressional election years.

The actual turnout rate was difficult to determine because of different ways of measuring the size of the voting population, which was driven in large part by an increasing influx of immigrants, who were not American citizens and therefore could not vote. Census Bureau surveys asking persons if they had voted tended to show higher turnout rates than examinations of actual voting data by scholars and voting analysts. *(See box Measuring Voter Turnout, p. 4 Tables 1-1 and 1-2, pp. 2, 6.)*

The comparatively low turnout led some observers to speculate that people stayed away from the polls because they were disillusioned with the political process. Others said concern about low turnout was overblown, often pointing to voter registration, which—in spite of questions about its accuracy—suggested that a substantial portion of citizens who cared enough about participating in the election process did in fact go to the polls.

MORE VOTERS, CHANGING VOTER PATTERNS

What was indisputably true was that over the course of more than two centuries, the United States brought increasingly more citizens into the election process. During the nation's first decades, all thirteen of the original states restricted voting to adult male property holders and taxpayers. The framers of the Constitution apparently were content to continue this time-honored practice. The Constitutional Convention adopted without dissent the recommendation of its Committee of Detail that qualifications for the electors of the House of Representatives "shall be the same . . . as those of the electors in the several states of the most numerous branch of their own legislatures." [1]

Under this provision fewer than half of the adult white men in the United States were eligible to vote in federal elections. With women and indentured servants disqualified, fewer than one of every four white adults could cast a ballot. Slaves also were ineligible to vote, although freed slaves could vote in some states if they met whatever other qualifications the state placed on its voters.

Those practices actually represented a liberalization of restrictions on voting that had prevailed at one time in the colonial period. Roman Catholics had been disenfranchised in almost every colony; Jews in most colonies; Quakers and Baptists in some. Not until 1842 did Rhode Island permit Jews to vote.

For half a century before the Civil War, the electorate was steadily broadened. The new western settlements supplied a stimulus for allowing all men to vote, and Jacksonian democracy encouraged its acceptance. Gradually, seven states that had limited voting strictly to men who owned property substituted a taxpaying qualification, and by the middle of the century most states had removed even that requirement.

The Fourteenth Amendment, ratified in 1868, made everyone born or naturalized in the United States a citizen and directed Congress to reduce the number of representatives from any state that disenfranchised adult male citizens for any reason other than commission of a crime. Although no such reduction was ever made, that amendment—together with the Fifteenth Amendment, which said that the right to vote could not be denied on the basis of "race, color, or previous condition of servitude"—legally opened the polling booths to black men.

Former slaves did vote in the years immediately following the Civil War, but by the turn of the twentieth century, most southern states had in place laws and election practices that effectively barred blacks from voting. Not until passage of the Voting Rights Act of 1965 would the promise held out by the Fifteenth Amendment begin to be fulfilled.

Women fought for nearly ninety years to win their right to vote; success came with ratification of the Nineteenth Amendment in 1920. In 1971 the Twenty-sixth Amendment lowered the voting age to eighteen for federal, state, and local elections. A Supreme Court ruling in 1972 effectively required states to reduce the time citizens had to live there to be eligible to vote; no state now requires more than a thirty-day residency. By the beginning of the 1990s, only insanity, a felony conviction, or failure to meet a residency requirement barred voting-age citizens from going to the polls, and there was growing controversy over whether the vote should be denied to felons—especially those who had completed their sentences.

Residents of the District of Columbia were given the right to vote in presidential elections with ratification of the Twenty-third Amendment in 1961. And in 1970 Congress authorized residents of the nation's capital to elect a nonvoting delegate to the House of Representatives. This became controversial when the Democrats in 1993, at the beginning of the 103rd Congress, amended House rules to allow the D.C. representative, along with the Puerto Rican commissioner and delegates from Guam, American Samoa, and the Virgin Islands, to cast floor votes under certain parliamentary procedures so long as their votes did not alter the outcome of the vote. Republicans, when they took control of the House in 1995, rescinded this procedure. It was reinstated in 2007 by Democrats, who had regained the majority. In early 2007 District voting advocates were also pushing a plan to enlarge the House by two seats, with one seat going to the District, a Democratic stronghold, and the other to Utah, a Republican state. This would give the District true representation and voting rights, and Utah would gain a nearly assured GOP seat that it was not expected to receive until after reapportionment from population growth after 2010. However, in March 2007 the White House said it opposed the legislation because of constitutional concerns over whether the District met the constitutional definition of a state. This opposition cast serious doubt on the proposal's immediate future.

Turnout Trends

Most significant liberalizations of election law have resulted in a sharp increase in voting. From 1824 to 1856, a period of gradual relaxation in the states' property and taxpaying qualifications for voting, voter participation in presidential

TABLE 1-1 **Eligible Voter Turnout Rates**

Scholars, journalists, and voting analysts have for years lamented what appeared to be a declining rate of voter turnout in elections, which they feared showed a national lack of interest in politics and in deciding which party would control governmental powers. Not everyone agrees.

Declining turnout analyses have traditionally used actual vote counts compared to the voting age population (VAP), persons eighteen years and older. But the VAP number increasingly came under scrutiny as one of its components—immigrants of age but not U.S. citizens and therefore not eligible to vote—grew rapidly in the 1990s and after 2000. Scholars began to look at a turnout rate that showed votes cast in terms of the voter eligible population (VEP). To get a VEP analysts removed from the VAP persons of legal age but who are not eligible to vote because they are not citizens. Increasingly, the largest group was immigrants but included others in prison, on probation, or mentally incapacitated. With this approach the turnout rate is higher than calculations using VAP.[1]

The figures in the table below were prepared by Prof. Michael P. McDonald of George Mason University. He estimates that the average midterm turnout rate from 1974 to 2002 was 39.4 percent. His calculations include votes for House and Senate seats and for governor depending on which drew the highest number of votes.

Presidential election years		Congressional election years	
2004	60.3	2006	40.5
2000	54.2	2002	39.5
1996	51.7	1998	38.1
1992	58.1	1994	41.1
1988	52.8	1990	38.4
1984	55.2	1986	38.1
1980	54.2	1982	42.1

1. Another often quoted measure of turnout came from Census Bureau surveys that asked a representative sample of Americans if they had voted. The bureau's numbers showed a higher turnout rate than analyses using actual votes cast and either VAP or VEP. See Figure 1-1, p. 5, and Table 1-2, p. 6.

SOURCE: United States Elections Project, George Mason University, http://elections.gmu.edu.

elections increased from 3.8 percent to 16.7 percent of the population. In 1920, when the Nineteenth Amendment gave women the franchise, it rose to 25.1 percent.

Between 1932 and 1976 both the voting-age population and the number of voters in presidential elections roughly doubled. Except for the 1948 presidential election, when barely half the people of voting age went to the polls, the turnout in the postwar years through 1968 was approximately 60 percent, according to Census Bureau surveys. This relatively high figure was attributed to a high sense of civic duty that permeated American society in the immediate postwar years, a population more rooted than it was to be later in the century, and to new civil rights laws encouraging blacks to vote.

Despite larger numbers of people voting, the rate of voter participation slumped after 1968. In that year's presidential election, 61 percent of the voting-age population went to the polls. Through successive stages, that mark fell below 50 percent in the 1996 election, as measured against the voting age population standard then widely in use. This was the lowest level of voter turnout since 1924. The 1996 race, however, was widely viewed by political analysts as a relatively easy contest for the popular incumbent president, Bill Clinton, against a relatively weak challenger, Senator Bob Dole, R-Kan. Voting in the midterm elections, always lower than in presidential years, also declined.

The famous postwar baby boom, together with a lower voting age, had produced by the early 1970s a disproportionate number of young voters—those who are the least likely to vote. In the 1972 presidential election, the first in which eighteen-year-olds could vote nationwide, some 11 million young voters entered the electorate. But the actual number of voting participants was only 4.4 million greater than in 1968, resulting in a five-point drop in the ratio of eligible to actual voters. *(See Chapter 2, Political Parties and Elections.)*

Voting participation continued to decrease throughout the rest of the twentieth century even as the baby boomers grew older. There were a few upticks in turnout in both the 1980s and 1990s, most notably in the election of 1992—when the excitement of the nation's first baby-boom ticket (Democrats Bill Clinton and Al Gore), a well-financed independent candidate (H. Ross Perot), and the widespread perception of recession pushed the turnout above 100 million for the first time in the nation's history. By the late 1990s, however, turnout was again on the wane, with the presidential election of 1996 and the midterm congressional contests of 1998 posting the lowest turnout rates for elections of their type since the end of World War II. The first two presidential elections in the twenty-first century showed this trend reversing, with more than a 60 percent turnout in 2004, according to one calculation.

Many reasons for the declining turnouts have been offered. Mark Mellman, a Democratic campaign consultant, has been among those who said they have detected public cynicism about the political process. "There's a sense that the political system is out of their control on one hand and not responsive on the other," Mellman has said. Campaigns that once thrived at the grassroots level—with storefront political headquarters manned by volunteers and stocked with buttons and stickers—were being waged through the more impersonal medium of television.

But another school of thought has contended that low turnout might be overrated as an indicator of voter apathy and cynicism. As expressed by Richard Scammon, former director of the U.S. Bureau of the Census: "Peace and prosperity can generally operate to keep the vote down. . . . In a sense, a low voter turnout is consent. A pool of disinterest may be valuable for a democracy." [2]

Others who have studied voter turnout doubt there has been a real decline. Prof. Michael P. McDonald of George Mason University, who has done extensive examinations of voter eligibility, wrote that declining turnout rates after 1971 were "entirely explained by the increase in the ineligible population." [3] McDonald and other scholars, and even the U.S. Census Bureau, note that the voting age population has increasingly been skewed by the presence of persons of legal age but who are not citizens or otherwise entitled to vote, largely immigrants but also including prison felons, individuals on probation, and mentally incapacitated persons. McDonald contended that in 1972 the number of non-citizens in the United States was under 2 percent of the voting age population, but had increased to nearly 8.5 percent by 2004.

Even so, McDonald noted that his calculations showed an average national midterm turnout rate from 1974 to 2002 of 39.4 percent, which meant that six out of ten potential voters chose not to go to the polls. His calculations for presidential election years showed higher turnout, but still rarely above 55 percent starting in 1972. *(See Table 1-1, p. 2.)*

Public opinion polls have long detected public disenchantment with politics. But the Scammon view was given new impetus in the elections of the first decade of the twenty-first century, at least through 2006.

The 2000 election with no incumbent drew 105.4 million people to the polls, creating a voter turnout of 51 percent, as measured by the traditional all-inclusive standard of voting age population. (McDonald calculated the turnout at 54.2 percent.) But the 2000 presidential race was as contentious as any in the last half century, with the winner—George W. Bush—losing the popular vote and winning the electoral vote, and the White House, only after the Supreme Court decided against ballot recounts in the contested state of Florida. The anger over this election, combined with Bush administration policies and decisions, set the stage for ever-higher public interest in public issues over the next six years.

Traumatic national events—particularly the 2001 terrorist attacks on the United States but also the Bush administration's decision to invade Iraq in a war that was still continuing in 2007—fueled partisan fervor that pointed to the converse of Scammon's argument.

Bush won reelection in 2004—both the electoral and popular votes—but the controversy that surrounded him and his policies helped push voter turnout to over 122 million, with a turnout rate of at least 60 percent and more by some calculations.

The swirling controversies of this period carried into the 2006 midterm elections, in which the Democrats recaptured control of both houses of Congress—for the House, this was the first time Republicans had lost control since 1994. Most analysts attributed the Republican defeat to popular disapproval of the Iraq war, which was reinforced by various other GOP woes, including a series of ethics and lobbying corruption scandals. The 2006 elections set new records for voter participation. Political analyst Rhodes Cook wrote that the turnout rate for the U.S. House was the highest since 1982. "Then, 39.5 percent of the citizen voting age population took part. This time the rate was 39 percent of the eligible citizen voting-age population," Cook wrote.[4]

Outside the issue of how many Americans voted, one other question persistently asked is whether the results would be different if everyone voted. In a paper that they wrote in 1998, two University of California political scientists, Benjamin Highton and Raymond E. Wolfinger,

MEASURING VOTER TURNOUT

Calculating the number and the percentage of citizens who vote in U.S. elections is a commonly used measure of the political involvement of American citizens. Increasingly, the numbers are in dispute because there are different ways to define the universe of citizens who make up the voting population. Most calculations show the turnout rate in midterm congressional elections is dismally low, about 33 percent to 40 percent of potential voters. The turnout rate for presidential elections is higher, sometimes reaching 60 percent, but even that level means a substantial slice of voters could not vote or did not care enough to vote.

The controversy that has arisen in the late twentieth and early twenty-first centuries is rooted in identifying the correct number of citizens of voting age—eighteen years since 1972—who are eligible. A sizeable number of persons over eighteen are not eligible to vote because they are—in the largest numbers—immigrants who are not citizens or persons who are otherwise barred from voting because they are in prison or on parole or mentally incapacitated, conditions that are barriers in most states.

The largest and all inclusive group of people who meet the age standard is called the voting *age* population (VAP) and historically has been based on Census Bureau surveys done near election days. As scholars have taken a closer look at the component of VAP that cannot vote, thereby creating a voter *eligible* population (VEP), accurate measurement has become more possible, almost always resulting in a higher voter turnout number. However, there is no single authority for a VEP number and the historical VAP framework has continued to be used in many analyses.

For the 2004 election, the Census Bureau calculated that 58.3 percent of the VAP voted. But it also calculated what it called the citizen population, removing noncitizens from the base. By this measure 63.8 percent of eligible voters went to the polls. The bureau also noted a third criterion: registration, which is required in every state except North Dakota before a person can vote. The bureau, using its survey results, calculated that 88.5 percent of registered voters went to the polls, but noted that some 55 million persons who said they were citizens were not registered.

Care should be taken with these numbers as well. When states report turnout rates, they calculate the participation based upon the numbers of voters on their rolls, though some states differentiate between active and inactive voters. For 2004 there were only a handful of states with turnout rates below 60 percent or over 80 percent. It is likely that many political observers have access to these numbers when they compare turnout figures over time. This comparison reflects so-called "list inflation," which means many names remain on the voter rolls after ineligibility occurs, normally by people simply moving to a new address or another jurisdiction. The bureau survey approach attempts to minimize this impact.

Some students of voting behavior note that Census Bureau numbers are based on survey techniques and not actual nose counts, as is done—in effect—with ballots that when tallied provide a definitive number. But the bureau clearly states that its surveys ask if a respondent voted, not the specific election contest in which he or she voted. Still others may have responded positively reflecting the societal norm that voting is a "good" thing for an American citizen to do.

Many scholars have spent considerable effort trying to sort out the issues involved in measuring turnout rates as part of the larger academic goal of determining whether the American electorate really is as disinterested in politics as many observers, such as editorial writers, have long lamented.

Generally, efforts to fine-tune the numbers at the state and national level, mostly by excluding persons of age who cannot vote, have shown modestly higher voting rates than ascribed to the electorate in most popular renditions. One such scholar, Michael P. McDonald at George Mason University, calculated the 2004 presidential VAP rate at 55.3 percent and the VEP rate at 60.3 percent, still lower than the Census Bureau's estimates. *(See Table 1-1, p. 2.)* But other scholars and organizations, including the Center for the Study of the American Electorate at the American University, have produced different turnout estimates.

In addition, many estimates historically have been calculated using the vote for the highest office. In presidential years, that is the vote for White House candidates. But in midterm elections in a state it usually is a race for governor or senator, if such an office is up for election. For national purposes, however, the better measurement has usually been the total vote for House candidates, even though that number may be skewed by two factors: 1) several states do not report voting totals in individual races where there was only one candidate even though voters actually went to the polls; and 2) even in states that do report voting totals for all congressional races, many voters just do not cast any ballot in these uncontested races.

In sum, the basic problem confronting any analysis of turnout behavior is not how many persons cast ballots, but rather which rate is used and how the universe of eligible persons is calculated.

FIGURE 1-1 **Voter Turnout Rates, Presidential and Midterm Elections, 1789–2006**

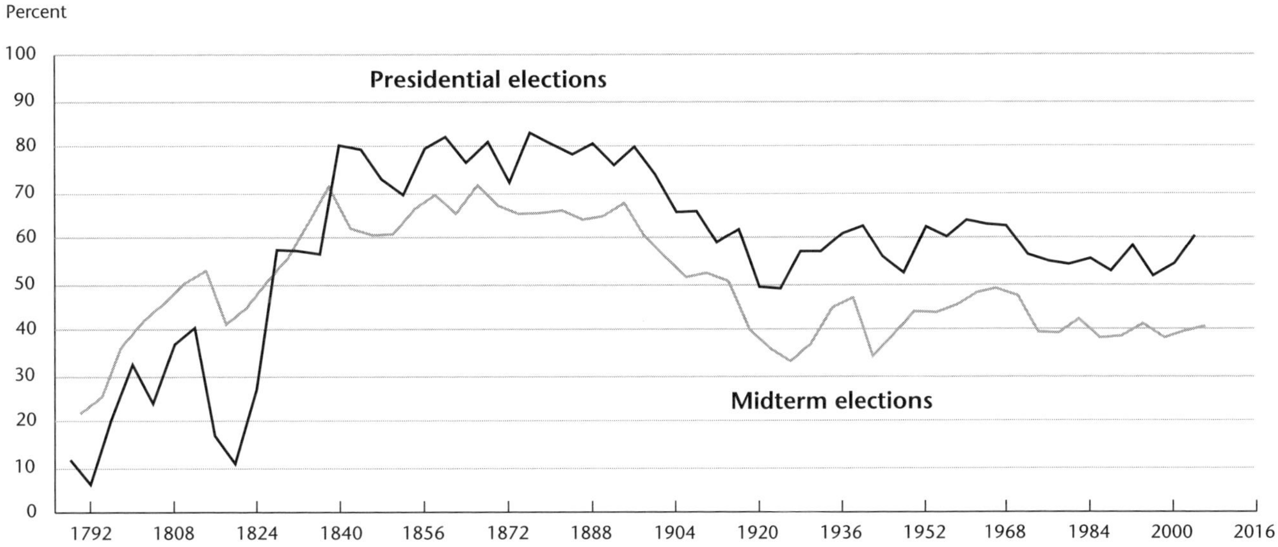

SOURCE: Harold W. Stanley and Richard G. Niemi, *Vital Statistics on American Politics 2007–2008* (Washington, D.C.: CQ Press, 2008).

answered: probably not. "The two most common demographic features of nonvoters are their residential mobility and youth, two characteristics that do not suggest political distinctiveness," they wrote. "To be sure, the poor, less educated, and minorities are overrepresented among nonvoters. But the young and the transient are even more numerous. . . . What our findings have demonstrated is that the 'party of nonvoters' is truly heterogeneous. Taken as a whole, nonvoters appear well represented by those who vote." [5]

Nonetheless, studies by the Census Bureau have shown marked differences in participation among various classes of voters. Older voters tend to vote at a higher rate than younger voters. Well-educated voters tend to vote at a higher rate than those less educated. Whites tend to vote at a higher rate than blacks and Hispanics. *(See Table 1-2, p. 6.)*

Growth of Independents

Although more people identify themselves as Democrats than Republicans, there has been a steady rise over the last half century in voters who do not identify with either party. The American National Election Studies (ANES), a long-running detailed record of voting behavior, recorded for 2004 that 49 percent of voters identified themselves as Democrats, 41 percent as Republicans, and 10 percent as independents. (The figures for 1952, the first year of ANES data, were 57, 34 and 6.) But when the ANES survey data were broken into finer parts, the 2004 results showed 33 percent of respondents said they were Democrats, 28 percent said they were Republicans, and 39 percent said they were independents. The latter category included persons who said they were either an independent Democrat or an independent Republican. In 1952 this larger grouping showed 23 percent of respondents identifying themselves as independent.

The impact of an expanding independent political population was seen in the dramatic midterm elections of 2006, in which Democrats won control of both the House and the Senate after being in the minority in the House every year since 1994 and most of the time in the Senate. Exit polls in 2006 showed that Democratic candidates were favored by 57 percent of voters who claimed they were not affiliated with their major party. Moreover, this group made up 26 percent of all voters, a huge target population that many analysts believe will hold the balance of power in future elections.

Yet when it comes to the act of voter registration, most voters still sign up with one of the two major parties; at least that is the case in the twenty-nine states (and the District of Columbia) where there is such a choice to be made. According to a compilation by the political newsletter *Ballot Access News,* prepared by Richard Winger, in early 2007, Democrats had the registration advantage in thirteen states plus the District of Columbia (a total that included the four most populous states where voters can register by party—California, Florida, New York, and Pennsylvania). Republicans led in seven states (all in the Plains or Rocky Mountain region), and independents had the edge in nine states, five of them in the Northeast (Connecticut, Maine, Massachusetts, New Hampshire and New Jersey). The distribution was roughly the same as a decade earlier. Winger's

TABLE 1-2 **The Nation's Voters, 1980–2004**

This table is based on figures reported by the Census Bureau from its periodic survey of voters. The totals shown at the bottom are higher than compilations using voting totals compared to the number of persons eligible to vote in an election. One reason for the difference may be the social norm that holds voting as an appropriate action for a citizen. This may prompt some respondents to say they voted even if they did not. The bureau also notes that its questions ask only if a respondent voted, not the contest in which the ballot was cast. For a comparison of total turnout rates using actual votes and an estimate of eligible voters, see Table 1-1, p. 2, and box—Measuring Voter Turnout, p. 4.
(Percentages of voting-age populations who said they had voted.)

	Presidential election years							Congressional election years					
	1980	1984	1988	1992	1996	2000	2004	1982	1986	1990	1994	1998	2002
Race/ethnicity													
White	61	61	59	64	56	56	60	50	47	47	47	43	44
Black	51	56	52	54	51	54	56	43	43	39	37	40	40
Hispanic	30	33	29	29	27	28	28	25	24	21	20	20	19
Gender													
Male	59	59	56	60	53	53	56	49	46	45	45	41	41
Female	59	61	58	58	56	56	60	48	46	45	45	42	43
Age													
18–24	36	37	33	39	31	32	42	20	19	18	17	17	17
25–44	59	58	54	58	49	50	52	45	41	41	39	35	34
45–64	69	70	68	70	64	64	67	62	59	56	57	54	53
65 and older	65	68	69	70	67	68	69	60	61	60	61	60	61
Education													
8 years or less	43	43	37	35	30	27	30	36	33	28	24	24	30
4 years high school	59	59	55	58	49	49	52	47	44	42	41	37	40
1–3 years college	67	68	65	69	61	60	66	53	50	50	50	46	48
4 or more years college	80	79	78	81	73	72	74	67	63	63	64	57	69
Total	**59**	**60**	**57**	**61**	**54**	**55**	**58**	**49**	**46**	**45**	**45**	**42**	**42**

SOURCE: U.S. Bureau of the Census, Current Population Survey (CPS) on voting and registration in general elections, 1980–2004.

compilation showed 42 percent of the registrants were Democrats and 32 percent were Republicans. Significantly, a quarter of the registrants identified themselves as independent, a finding in keeping with other measurements of the voting population that showed the continued growth in this segment.[6]

A slightly different measurement was taken by political analyst Curtis Gans, who compiled registration numbers from thirteen states that had comparable numbers since 1962. He reported that in 2006, 37 percent registered as Democrats, 31 percent as Republicans, and 17 percent as "other," a category made up largely of persons claiming independent status. In 1962 the same set of states reported 48 percent Democratic registration, 25 percent Republican, and only 1.4 percent "other." This time snapshot reflected measurements by other scholars and polling organizations that recorded the steady strengthening of the Republican Party to increasing parity with Democrats, who had dominated since the New Deal days of the 1930s. (The difference between Winger's and Gans's numbers appeared to derive from the states that Gans could use because they had consistent historic numbers. Inclusion of states with heavy registration of one party or the other would necessarily produce an outcome different from the more comprehensive numbers used by Winger. But both sets of data show much the same situation by 2006: near parity between the parties—as shown in fact in actual voting—and the growth of independent voters.)

However, the number of registered voters nationwide at any given time is impossible to calculate. States have different registration deadlines; people who move may be registered in more than one state at the same time, or temporarily may not be recorded in any state; and some states do not require preregistration before voting, while others do not require towns and municipalities to keep registration records. *(See box Measuring Voter Turnout, p. 4.)*

Competitive Election Changes

After years of lackluster election competition in the latter decades of the twentieth century, a more robust political scene appeared to be underway starting with the 2000

FIGURE 1-2 **Partisan Identification, 1952–2004**

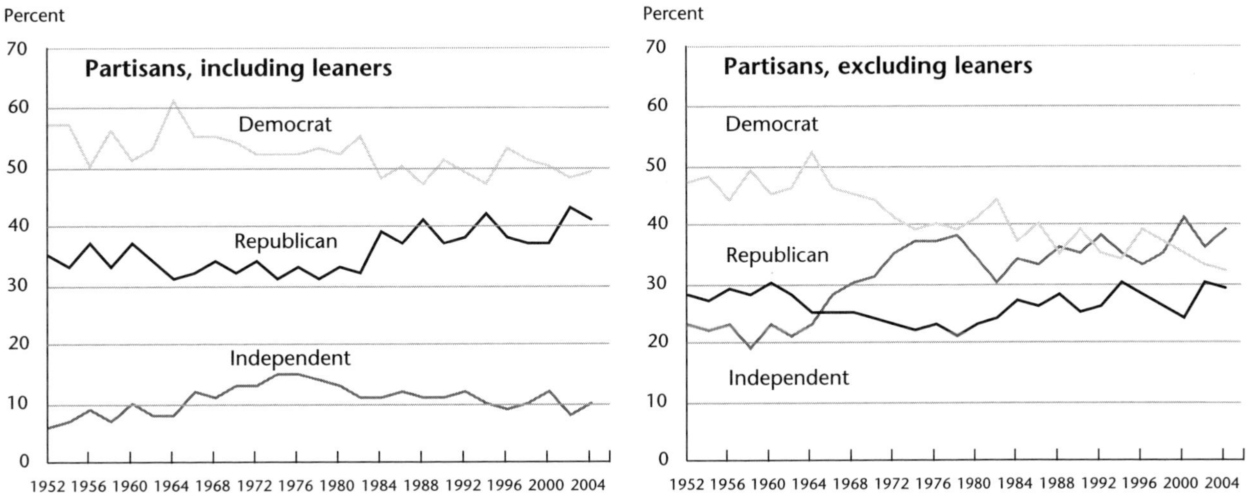

NOTE: "Leaners" are independents who consider themselves closer to one party.

SOURCES: Harold W. Stanley and Richard G. Niemi, *Vital Statistics on American Politics 2007–2008* (Washington, D.C.: CQ Press, 2008). Calculated by the authors from National Election Studies data, Center for Political Studies, University of Michigan, Ann Arbor (www.electionstudies.org/).

national elections. The presidential election that year was essentially a draw with the Democratic candidate, Al Gore, capturing the popular vote by more than a half-million ballots, while the Republican, George W. Bush, won the electoral vote and the White House. Four years later Bush improved slightly on his first election by winning both the popular and electoral counts, but by narrow margins that had been seen only rarely in the twentieth century. Most analysts said the parties at that level were in a nearly dead heat with the outcomes heavily dependent on issues of the day and the organizational strengths of each candidate.

The midterm congressional elections showed a continuing pattern of largely noncompetitive House races, at least until 2006, when voter anger on several issues cost Republican incumbents more than in recent past elections. Senate contests also showed the value of incumbency, although that too suffered in 2006, but the peculiarities of contests for that chamber—especially the election of only a third of the members each time—made senatorial contests less useful as a national measure of political competitiveness in Congress.

On the other hand, all members of the House are elected every two years. Scholars for years noted that most of the 435 races do not involve serious competition between the two major parties. In 1994, the year the GOP won control of Congress for the first time since 1952, there were nearly one hundred competitive districts, measured by a winning percentage of less than 55 percent of the total vote. In 2002 the number was less than fifty seats; in 2004 it was just thirty-two seats. But in 2006 the number of districts with winners below 55 percent of the vote jumped to sixty-eight, the highest in a decade. Political analyst Rhodes Cook noted that the Democratic victory was national in scope, with Democrats gaining in all regions, that two-thirds came in states or districts carried by President Bush in 2004, that most defeated Republicans were not newcomers but veterans with the advantage of incumbency, and that most of the losing GOP members did not have close races in 2004. These dramatic changes were interpreted largely as voter anger over an unpopular war in Iraq, a variety of GOP ethics scandals, and a bungled federal government response to the devastation wrought by Hurricane Katrina in a number of southern states in 2005. Whether the Democratic surge would hold up in future elections was less certain, but the 2006 outcome did demonstrate that the GOP was not in the overall commanding position that it had appeared to occupy during the 1990s and early 2000s.

THE BLACK VOTE: A LONG, PAINFUL STRUGGLE

In no period of American history were all black people excluded from the polls. At the time of the Constitutional Convention, free blacks had the right of suffrage in all the original states except Georgia, South Carolina, and Virginia. Their right to vote stemmed from the fact that the first black people were brought to America not as slaves but as indentured servants, who could expect freedom after a fixed number of years' service to a master. By 1800, however, the majority of black people were held in slavery. As it grew, so did disenfranchisement. At the outbreak of the Civil War, black Americans were disfranchised, solely on the basis of their race, in all except six of the thirty-three states.

President Abraham Lincoln's Emancipation Proclamation of 1863 freed the slaves but did not accord them voting rights. To ease the impact of change on the South, Lincoln preferred to move cautiously in expanding the black electorate. After the Civil War several southern states promptly enacted "Black Codes" barring the newly liberated slaves from voting or holding office. Radical Republicans in Congress responded by passing the Reconstruction Act of 1867, which established provisional military governments in the Southern states. The return of civilian control was conditioned on their ratification of the Fourteenth Amendment, which buttressed individual liberty with "due process" and "equal protection" under the law. The amendment's second section threatened to reduce any state's representation in Congress for denying the vote to any male citizen twenty-one years of age or older.

The Reconstruction Act further stated that a secessionist state could not be readmitted to the Union unless it extended the franchise to all adult males, white and black. Congress followed in February 1869 by submitting the Fifteenth Amendment, prohibiting racial discrimination in voting, to the states. It was ratified twelve months later.

The Radical Republican majority in Congress feared that unless blacks were allowed to vote, Democrats and ex-rebels would quickly regain control of the national government. In the presidential election of 1868, in fact, Gen. Ulysses S. Grant defeated his Democratic opponent, Horatio Seymour, by fewer than 305,000 votes; the new black vote probably decided the election.

CONGRESSIONAL ELECTORAL ANOMALIES

Congressional elections have produced a number of anomalies, particularly in the South, where slavery, the Civil War, Reconstruction, and racial antagonisms created special problems in the electoral process. The counting of slaves for the apportionment of House seats posed an especially difficult problem.

Under a compromise adopted in the Constitution (Article I, section 2) every five slaves would be counted as three persons. After the Civil War and the emancipation of slaves, the Fourteenth Amendment required that blacks be fully counted for apportionment purposes. On this basis, several southern states tried to claim additional representation on readmission to the Union. Tennessee, for example, elected an extra U.S. representative in 1868, claiming that adding the full slave population entitled the state to nine instead of eight House members. Virginia and South Carolina followed suit. But the House refused to seat the additional representatives, requiring the states to wait for the regular reapportionment after the 1870 census for any changes in their representation.

A formula in the Fourteenth Amendment, designed to coerce southern states to accept black voting participation by reducing House seats wherever voting rights were abridged, was, because of its complexity, never implemented. Instead, the Republican-controlled House unseated Democrats from districts in former Confederate states, where abuses of the right to vote were charged. Between 1881 and 1897 the House unseated eighteen Democrats on this basis.

An anomaly of a different sort arose from the 1930 midterm election, when the early stages of the Great Depression threatened to end the Republicans' seventeen-year domination of the House. On election night in November it appeared that the Republicans nevertheless retained the House by a narrow margin. The tally showed 218 Republicans elected, against 216 Democrats and one independent. But in those days, before the Twentieth Amendment moved up the convening date, thirteen months elapsed between the election and the convening of the new Congress. During that interval, an unusually large number of deaths (fourteen) occurred among the newly elected representatives.

In special elections to fill the vacancies, several had no effect on the political balance because the same party retained the seat. But in three cases Republicans who died were replaced by Democrats, tipping the balance to the Democrats' favor in time for them to organize the new Congress in December 1931. A fourth Republican vacancy went to the Democrats in early 1932.

When the Seventy-second Congress convened on December 7, 1931, House Democrats held the edge, 219 to 215, with one independent. As the majority, they were able to elect as Speaker John Nance Garner of Texas. In 1932 Garner was elected as Franklin D. Roosevelt's first vice president.

Even without the special election gains, control of the House likely would have passed to the Democrats in 1931. Immediately after the 1930 general election, a group of Farm Belt Republicans announced that they would withhold their votes from veteran Speaker Nicholas Longworth of Ohio and allow the Democrats to organize the House, which they did. The vote for Garner as Speaker was 218 to 207, a margin greater than the three seats the Democrats gained during the preceding thirteen months.

The 1972 House election oddity resulted from the preelection disappearance of two House Democrats, Majority Leader Hale Boggs of Louisiana and Nick Begich of Alaska, during an Alaskan airplane trip. Despite their absence, both were reelected. Boggs's wife, Lindy, was elected to succeed him after he was declared legally dead in 1973. Begich was declared legally dead after the 1972 election, and a special election to replace him was held in 1973.

Similarly, a dead man was elected to the U.S. Senate for the first time in 2000. Running for a Senate seat, Democratic governor Mel Carnahan of Missouri was killed in an airplane crash three weeks before the November election. As it was too late for officials to remove his name from the ballot, Carnahan polled 50.5 percent of the vote to defeat Republican incumbent John Ashcroft. Although some in his party thought Ashcroft could make a strong case in challenging the result, Ashcroft did not. Democrat Roger B. Wilson, who succeeded to the office of Missouri governor, appointed Carnahan's widow, Jean, to the seat until a special election could be held in 2002, which she lost. Alongside this Senate oddity was another unique occurrence in 2000: Hillary Rodham Clinton became the first first lady to win elective office when she captured a New York Senate seat.

Former slaves obtained important positions in the governments formed under the Reconstruction Act of 1867. P. B. S. Pinchback served briefly as acting governor of Louisiana; Mississippi, South Carolina, and Louisiana had black lieutenant governors. Between 1870 and 1900, southern states sent twenty-two black men to Congress—two of them, Hiram R. Revels and Blanche Kelso Bruce, represented Mississippi as senators. Bruce served a full six-year term (1875–1881) and was a presiding officer of the Republican National Convention of 1880.

Blacks, including a Union soldier, are depicted casting their first ballots in an image published November 16, 1867. In fact, it would take another one hundred years to secure voting rights for African Americans.

The white South did not yield gracefully to this turn of events. Gunnar Myrdal noted in his landmark study of black people in America, *An American Dilemma,* that: "The Fourteenth and Fifteenth Amendments were . . . looked upon as the supreme foolishness of the North and, worse still, as an expression of ill-will of the Yankees toward the defeated South. The Negro franchise became the symbol of the humiliation of the South." [7]

After Reconstruction

Congress in 1870 passed an enforcement act to protect black voting rights in the South, but the Supreme Court in 1876 ruled that Congress had exceeded its authority. In the case of *United States v. Reese,* the Court held that the Fifteenth Amendment did not give anyone the right to vote; it simply guaranteed the right to be free from racial discrimination in exercising that right. The extension of the right to vote itself, the Court said, was up to the states, not the federal government. Therefore, the Court said, Congress had overreached its power to enforce the Fifteenth Amendment when it enacted the 1870 law that penalized state officials who denied blacks the right to vote, or refused to count their votes, or obstructed their voting.

At the same time, the North clearly was growing weary of the crusade for betterment of the condition of blacks. When the first federal troops were withdrawn in April 1877, the remaining Radical Reconstruction governments in the South quickly disintegrated. Some of the newly enfranchised citizens continued to vote, but by 1900, according to historian Paul Lewinson in his book *Race, Class and Party,* "all factions united in a white man's party once more, to put the Negro finally beyond the pale of political activity." [8]

Mississippi led the way in prohibiting black political activity. A new state constitution drawn up in 1890 required prospective voters to pay a poll tax of two dollars and to demonstrate their ability to read any section of the state constitution or to interpret it when read to them.

Literacy Tests for Voters

In Mississippi and other southern states that adopted voter literacy tests, care was taken not to disfranchise illiterate whites. Five states exempted white voters from literacy and some other requirements by "grandfather clauses"—regulations allowing prospective voters, if not otherwise qualified, to register if they were descended from persons who had voted, or served in the state's military forces, before 1867. Other provisions allowed illiterates to register if they owned a certain amount of property or could show themselves to be of good moral character—requirements easily twisted to exclude only blacks.

At one time or another, twenty-one states imposed literacy requirements as a condition for voting. The first to do so, Connecticut in 1855 and Massachusetts in 1857, sought to disqualify a flood of European immigrants. Between 1890 and 1910, Mississippi, South Carolina, Louisiana, North Carolina, Alabama, Virginia, Georgia, and Oklahoma adopted literacy tests—primarily to restrict the black vote.

Nineteen of the twenty-one states demanded that voters be able to read English, and all but four of them (New York, Washington, Alaska, and Hawaii) required the reading of some legal document or passage from the state or federal

Constitution. Either in lieu of or in addition to the reading requirements, fourteen states required an ability to write.

As applied in the South, literacy tests and other voting restrictions virtually disenfranchised black citizens. Outside the South the New York test was by far the most stringent, although there were seldom any complaints that it was applied in a discriminatory way. Despite pressures by civil libertarians, Congress declined for years to void literacy tests on grounds that to do so would violate a state's right to impose its own voting requirements.

Reports of extreme voter discrimination in the South gradually moved Congress to search for remedial legislation. In 1965 it passed a sweeping Voting Rights Act that suspended literacy tests in seven southern states and parts of another. Five years later Congress expanded the law to bar all voter-literacy tests. The landmark legislation was extended repeatedly in the following years, becoming the foundation for a transformation of the political structure of the Southern states.

Poll-Tax Barrier to Voting

The first poll taxes in America were substitutes for property ownership and were intended to enlarge the voting franchise. But only a few states retained them at the time of the Civil War. They were afterward revived for a far different purpose—to restrict the franchise—in all eleven states of the old Confederacy: Florida (1889), Mississippi and Tennessee (1890), Arkansas (1892), South Carolina (1895), Louisiana (1898), North Carolina (1900), Alabama (1901), Virginia and Texas (1902), and Georgia (1908).

The ostensible purpose was to "cleanse" elections of mass abuses, but the records of constitutional conventions held in five southern states during the period revealed statements praising the poll tax as a measure to bar blacks and poor whites from the polls. Some historians have asserted that the main intent of these measures was to limit the popular base of a so-called agrarian revolt inspired by the Populist Party against the existing political structure.[9]

After the Populist era many states voluntarily dropped use of the poll tax, including six southern states—North Carolina (1920), Louisiana (1934), Florida (1937), Georgia (1945), South Carolina (1951), and Tennessee (1953). Proposals to abolish the poll tax were introduced in every Congress from 1939 to 1962. By 1960 only four states still required its payment by voters. In August 1962 the House approved a constitutional amendment—already accepted by the Senate—that outlawed poll taxes in federal elections, and that amendment, the Twenty-fourth, was ratified in January 1964. In 1966 the Supreme Court held that the poll tax was an unconstitutional requirement for voting in state and local elections as well. "Voter qualifications have no relation to wealth nor to paying or not paying this or any other tax. Wealth, like race, creed, or color, is not germane to one's ability to participate intelligently in the electoral process," Justice William O. Douglas wrote for the majority in *Harper v. Virginia Board of Elections.*

White Primaries

Even more than literacy tests or poll taxes, perhaps the most effective disfranchisement of southern blacks was their exclusion from the Democratic Party's primary elections. In the solidly Democratic South of the post–Reconstruction era, winning the party's nomination virtually assured election. Being excluded from voting in the primary was equivalent to being excluded from voting altogether.

Not until 1941 did the Supreme Court make clear that Congress had the power to regulate primary, as well as general, elections. Indeed, in a 1921 decision involving campaign spending, *Newberry v. United States*, the Court seemed to say that Congress lacked power to regulate primary elections. This doubt about the reach of federal power encouraged the eleven states that had composed the Confederacy to begin systematic exclusion of black voters from the primary. The Democratic Party was often organized on a statewide or county basis as a private club or association that could freely exclude blacks.

The effort of Texas to use the white primary to shut blacks out of the political process came before the Supreme Court in five cases, brought over a span of twenty-five years. In 1923 the Texas Legislature passed a law forbidding blacks to vote in the state Democratic primary. Dr. L. A. Nixon, a black resident of El Paso, challenged the law, arguing that it clearly violated the Fourteenth and Fifteenth Amendments. In the case of *Nixon v. Herndon*, decided in 1927, the Supreme Court agreed with Nixon's Fourteenth Amendment claim.

After the 1927 *Herndon* decision, the Texas Legislature authorized the executive committees of state political parties to establish their own qualifications for voting in the primary. Dr. Nixon again sued, challenging the law as racially discriminatory. Attorneys for the state argued that the Fourteenth Amendment's equal protection clause did not apply because the party, not state officials, set up the allegedly discriminatory standards.

With Justice Benjamin N. Cardozo writing for a five-man majority, the Court held in 1932 that the executive committee of the Democratic Party acted as a delegate of the state in setting voter qualifications and that its action was equivalent to state action and was thus within the scope of the equal protection guarantee, which it violated *(Nixon v. Condon)*.

The Texas Democratic Party responded by acting without state authorization to put itself off-limits to black voters. Confronted with this situation, the Court in 1935 retreated to its *Newberry* reasoning and ruled, in *Grovey v. Townsend,* that in this instance the party had acted not as a creature of the state but as a voluntary association of individuals. As such, its actions—even in controlling access to the vote—were not restricted by the Constitution.

In 1941 the Court switched signals again, discarding the *Newberry* doctrine in the case of *United States v. Classic. Classic* was not a racial discrimination case but instead concerned a man convicted of falsifying election returns. His conviction was based on a federal law that made it a crime "to injure, oppress, threaten, or intimidate any citizen in the free exercise or enjoyment of any right or privilege secured to him by the Constitution." He challenged his conviction, arguing that the right to vote in a primary election was not a right secured by the Constitution.

But the Court upheld the conviction, ruling that the primary was an integral part of the election process. The authority of Congress under Article I, Section 4, to regulate elections included the authority to regulate primary elections, wrote Justice Stone, "when, as in this case, they are a step in the exercise by the people of their choice of representatives in Congress."

Three years later, in 1944, the Court overturned *Grovey* and held the all-white primary unconstitutional. This case, *Smith v. Allwright,* arose out of the refusal of S. S. Allwright, a county election official, to permit Lonnie E. Smith, a black man, to vote in the 1940 Texas Democratic primary. Smith sued, saying Allwright had deprived him of his civil rights. Smith was represented by two attorneys for the National Association for the Advancement of Colored People (NAACP), William H. Hastie and Thurgood Marshall. Both were later made judges, with Marshall becoming the first black member of the Supreme Court.

The relentless effort of Texas Democrats to maintain the white primary at last came to an end in 1953 with another Supreme Court decision. In one Texas county an all-white Democratic organization conducted all-white primary elections under the name of Jaybird Club, a self-declared private club. In *Terry v. Adams* the Court declared this a ploy in violation of the Fifteenth Amendment.

Physical and Psychic Coercion

Throughout this period legal devices to curtail black political activity were buttressed by physical and economic intimidation. As Myrdal wrote: "Physical coercion is not so often practiced against the Negro, but the mere fact that it can be used with impunity . . . creates a psychic coercion that exists nearly everywhere in the South. . . . [I]t is no wonder that the great majority of Negroes in the South make no attempt to vote and—if they make attempts which are rebuffed—seldom demand their full rights under the federal Constitution." [10]

Any who summoned up the courage to try to register encountered various delays and harassment. The scornful question "What do you want here, nigger?" often sufficed to send a black person away. If the applicants persisted, the registrar was likely to ignore them, tell them that there were no more registration forms, or direct them to another place of registration, which, if it existed, was usually closed. Southern registrars also displayed a tendency to lose registration forms filled out by black applicants.

More subtle practices limited black political participation in the North as well. With the exception of Chicago, white-controlled city machines excluded black people from any significant role in politics for the first half of the twentieth century. During that time, Congress did virtually nothing to encourage black voting.

Civil Rights Legislation

Not until the 1950s, when the civil rights movement began to gather force, did Congress, at the urging of the executive branch, begin to reassert federal power to ensure the right of black citizens to vote. Its first action was passage of the Civil Rights Act of 1957, which was intended to enforce the voting guarantee set out in the Fifteenth Amendment.

The 1957 act authorized the attorney general to bring lawsuits to halt public and private interference with the right of black people to vote, and expanded federal jurisdiction over such suits. The law also created the Civil Rights Commission to investigate and publicly disclose problems of racial discrimination, including voting problems. The investigatory procedures of the commission and the authorization of the federal lawsuits were upheld by the Supreme Court in 1960, in *United States v. Raines.*

Responding to reports that progress in securing voting rights for blacks still was slow even under the provisions of the 1957 act, Congress in 1960 passed a measure that permitted the U.S. attorney general to sue a state for deprivation of voting rights even if the individuals named initially as defendants—usually voting registrars—had left office. This provision remedied a situation that had arisen in a suit brought by the United States against Alabama voting officials. In addition, Title VI of the 1960 law authorized the appointment of special federal "voting referees" to oversee voter registration in counties where a federal court detected a pattern of voter discrimination.

The Civil Rights Act of 1964 mandated state adoption of standard procedures and requirements for all persons seeking to register to vote. The law also required local officials to justify rejecting an applicant who had completed the sixth grade or had equivalent evidence of intellectual competence. Other provisions of the 1964 law expedited the movement of voting rights cases to the Supreme Court.

In two cases brought under the 1964 act, *United States v. Louisiana* and *United States v. Mississippi,* the Supreme Court in 1965 sanctioned the government's efforts to break the pattern of case-by-case litigation of voting rights violations. The Court upheld federal power to challenge a state's

State troopers in Selma, Alabama, swing billy clubs at marchers in a civil rights voting march in March 1965. On the ground, at right, is John Lewis, a marcher who went on to represent Georgia as a member of the U.S. House of Representatives.

entire constitutional legal framework for voter registration and conduct of elections.

The Voting Rights Act

But progress still was slow. In Dallas County, Alabama, three new federal laws and four years of litigation had produced the registration of only 383 black voters out of a potential pool of fifteen thousand. On March 8, 1965, the Rev. Martin Luther King Jr. led a "Walk for Freedom" to dramatize the need for additional efforts in behalf of registering black voters in Selma, the county seat, and elsewhere in the South. The violence of the reaction of local white law enforcement officers and white bystanders to the peaceful demonstration drew nationwide attention to the dimensions of the problem.

A week later, President Lyndon B. Johnson addressed a joint session of Congress to ask for passage of a new voting rights measure to close legal loopholes that enabled local officials to stall black voter registration. Johnson explained that "no law that we now have on the books . . . can ensure the right to vote when local officials are determined to deny it." Later that month, NAACP official Roy Wilkins appeared before a Senate committee on behalf of the Leadership Conference on Civil Rights to urge Congress to "transform this retail litigation method of registration into a wholesale administration procedure registering all who seek to exercise their democratic birthright." Within five months Congress had approved the sweeping Voting Rights Act of 1965.

The law suspended literacy tests and provided for the appointment of federal supervisors of voter registration in all states and counties where literacy tests or similar qualifying devices were in effect on November 1, 1964, and where fewer than 50 percent of the voting-age residents had registered to vote or voted in the 1964 presidential election.

The law established criminal penalties for persons found guilty of interfering with the voting rights of others. State or county governments in areas of low voter registration were required to obtain federal approval of any new voting laws, standards, practices, or procedures before implementing them. A state or county covered by the act could escape from the law's provisions if it could persuade a three-judge federal court in the District of Columbia that no racial discrimination in registration or voting had occurred in the previous five years.

The act placed federal registration machinery in six southern states (Alabama, Georgia, Mississippi, South

CONSTITUTIONAL PROVISIONS FOR HOUSE AND SENATE ELECTIONS

ARTICLE I, SECTION 2

The House of Representatives shall be composed of Members chosen every second Year by the People of the several States, and the Electors in each State shall have the Qualifications requisite for Electors of the most numerous Branch of the State Legislature.

No Person shall be a Representative who shall not have attained to the age of twenty five Years, and been seven Years a Citizen of the United States, and who shall not, when elected, be an Inhabitant of that State in which he shall be chosen.

Representatives and direct Taxes shall be apportioned among the several States which may be included within this Union, according to their respective Numbers, which shall be determined By adding to the whole Number of free Persons, including those bound to Service for a Term of Years, and excluding Indians not taxed, three fifths of all other Persons. The actual Enumeration shall be made within three Years after the first Meeting of the Congress of the United States, and within every subsequent Term of ten Years, in such Manner as they shall by Law direct. The Number of Representatives shall not exceed one for every thirty Thousand, but each State shall have at Least one Representative; and until such enumeration shall be made, the State of New Hampshire shall be entitled to chuse three, Massachusetts eight, Rhode-Island and Providence Plantations one, Connecticut five, New York six, New Jersey four, Pennsylvania eight, Delaware one, Maryland six, Virginia ten, North Carolina five, South Carolina five, and Georgia three.

When vacancies happen in the Representation from any State, the Executive Authority thereof shall issue Writs of Election to fill such Vacancies.

ARTICLE I, SECTION 3

The Senate of the United States shall be composed of two Senators from each State, chosen by the Legislature thereof, for six years; and each Senator shall have one Vote.

Immediately after they shall be assembled in Consequence of the first Election, they shall be divided as equally as may be into three Classes. The Seats of the Senators of the first Class shall be vacated at the Expiration of the second Year, of the second class at the Expiration of the fourth Year, and of the third class at the Expiration of the sixth Year, so that one third may be chosen every second Year; and if Vacancies happen by Resignation, or otherwise, during the Recess of the Legislature of any State, the Executive thereof may make temporary Appointments until the next Meeting of the Legislature, which shall then fill such Vacancies.

No Person shall be a Senator who shall not have attained the Age of thirty Years, and been nine Years a Citizen of the United States, and who shall not, when elected, be an Inhabitant of that State for which he shall be chosen.

ARTICLE I, SECTION 4

The Times, Places and Manner of holding Elections for Senators and Representatives, shall be prescribed in each State by the Legislature thereof; but the Congress may at any time by Law make or alter such Regulations, except as to the Places of chusing Senators.

The Congress shall assemble at least once in every Year, and such Meeting shall be on the first Monday in December, unless they shall by Law appoint a different day.

ARTICLE I, SECTION 5

Each House shall be the Judge of the Elections, Returns and Qualifications of its own Members, and a Majority of each shall constitute a Quorum to do Business; but a smaller Number may adjourn from day to day, and may be authorized to compel the Attendance of absent Members in such Manner, and under such Penalties as each House may provide.

AMENDMENT XIV

(RATIFIED JULY 28, 1868)

Section 2. Representatives shall be apportioned among the several States according to their respective numbers, counting the whole number of persons in each State, excluding Indians not taxed. But when the right to vote at any election for the choice of electors for President and Vice President of the United States, Representatives in Congress, the Executive and Judicial officers of a State, or the members of the Legislature thereof, is denied to any of the male inhabitants of such State, being twenty-one years of age, and citizens of the United States, or in any way abridged, except for participation in rebellion, or other crime, the basis of representation therein shall be reduced in the proportion which the number of such male citizens shall bear to the whole number of male citizens twenty-one years of age in such State.

AMENDMENT XVII

(RATIFIED MAY 31, 1913)

The Senate of the United States shall be composed of two Senators from each State, elected by the people thereof, for six years; and each Senator shall have one vote. The electors in each State shall have the qualifications requisite for electors of the most numerous branch of the State legislatures.

When vacancies happen in the representation of any State in the Senate, the executive authority of such State shall issue writs of election to fill such vacancies: *Provided,* That the legislature of any State may empower the executive thereof to make temporary appointments until the people fill the vacancies by election as the legislature may direct.

This amendment shall not be so construed as to affect the election or term of any Senator chosen before it becomes valid as part of the Constitution.

AMENDMENT XX

(RATIFIED JANUARY 23, 1933)

Section 1. The terms of the President and Vice President shall end at noon on the 20th day of January, and the terms of Senators and Representatives at noon on the 3d day of January, of the years in which such terms would have ended if this article had not been ratified; and the terms of their successors shall then begin.

Section 2. The Congress shall assemble at least once in every year, and such meeting shall begin at noon on the 3d day of January, unless they shall by law appoint a different day.

Carolina, Louisiana, and Virginia), Alaska, twenty-eight counties in North Carolina, three counties in Arizona, and one in Idaho.

Passage of the Voting Rights Act heralded a significant increase in the number of blacks registered to vote. Within four years, almost a million blacks had registered to vote under its provisions. The Civil Rights Commission reported in 1968 that registration of blacks had climbed to more than 50 percent of the black voting-age population in every southern state. Before the act, black registration had exceeded 50 percent in only three: Florida, Tennessee, and Texas. The most dramatic increase occurred in Mississippi, where black registration rose from 6.7 percent to 59.8 percent of the voting-age population.[11]

Voting Law Extended

In renewing the act in 1970 for an additional five years, its supporters turned back the efforts of southern senators to dilute key provisions. State and local governments were forbidden to use literacy tests or other voter-qualifying devices, and the triggering formula was altered to apply to any state or county that used a literacy test for voting and where less than 50 percent of the voting-age residents were registered on November 1, 1968, or had voted in the 1968 general election.

Under the 1970 law, the preclearance requirement applied to those areas affected by the 1965 law and ten more: three Alaska districts; Apache County, Arizona; Imperial County, California; Elmore County, Idaho; the Bronx, Kings (Brooklyn), and New York (Manhattan) counties, New York; and Wheeler County, Oregon.

By the time the act was due for its second extension in 1975, an estimated 2 million black people had been added to the voting rolls in the South, more than doubling the previous total. The number of blacks holding elective office also increased. The Joint Center for Political Studies reported that the number of black elected officials in the seven southern states covered by the Voting Rights act had gone up from fewer than one hundred in 1964 to 963 in just ten years. The total included one member of the House of Representatives, thirty-six state legislators, and 927 county and municipal officials.

The Voting Rights Act was renewed for seven years and substantially expanded in 1975. The triggering formula was amended to bring under coverage of the law any state or county that was using a literacy test in 1972 and where less than 50 percent of the residents eligible to vote had registered as of November 1, 1972. Two additional provisions gave greater protection to certain language minorities, defined as persons of Spanish heritage, Native Americans, Asian Americans, and Alaska Natives.

The federal preclearance provisions were expanded to apply to any jurisdiction where:

- The Census Bureau determined that more than 5 percent of the voting-age citizens were of a single language minority.
- Election materials had been printed only in English for the 1972 presidential election.
- Fewer than 50 percent of the voting-age citizens had registered for or voted in the 1972 presidential election.

These amendments significantly expanded coverage of the act, bringing in all of Alaska, Texas, and Arizona, and selected counties in several other states, including California and Florida. In addition, provisions were added requiring certain parts of the country to provide bilingual voting materials.

Congress approved a third extension of the act on June 23, 1982, two months before the law was due to expire. The 1982 legislation represented a major victory for a coalition of civil rights groups that included black, Hispanic, labor, religious, and civic organizations. Many of them had criticized President Ronald Reagan's administration for its hesitation and reservations about earlier versions and certain features of the measure.

However, the bill received widespread bipartisan support and strong backing from members of both chambers, including southerners. More than twice as many southern Democrats in both the Senate and House voted for passage in 1982 than in 1965 when the law was first approved. The steady upward trend in southern support for the act reflected changing social and political mores, and a great increase in black voting in the South.

The 1982 law had four main elements. First, it extended for twenty-five years provisions that required nine states and portions of thirteen others to obtain Justice Department approval for any changes in their election laws and procedures. Second, starting in 1984, a jurisdiction could be released from the restrictions by showing a clean voting rights record for the previous ten years. Third, it overturned a 1980 Supreme Court ruling that "intent to discriminate" must be shown to prove a violation. Fourth, it extended the bilingual election provisions through 1992.

The requirement for Justice Department approval of election-law changes figured prominently in redistricting being carried out in the affected states on the basis of the 1990 census. While that proved to be a matter of considerable controversy, which continued even after the next census in 2000, there is little doubt that the Voting Rights Act has had a positive effect on the numbers of blacks winning elective office. According to the most recent compilation by the Joint Center for Political Studies as of early 2007, the number of black elected officials nationwide totaled 9,101. By comparison the number in 1970 was 1,469. The total included thirty-nine members of Congress, all in the House (which had increased to forty-one with the 2006 elections, including one senator). The total in 2001 also included nearly 597 state legislators and one governor, more than 900 positions at the county level, just over 4,000 in municipal offices, 1,044 in judicial or law enforcement positions, and 1,937 in education offices. (These totals were from the fifty states, the District of Columbia, and the Virgin Islands.)

Black Voting Patterns

In the modern era, beginning with the New Deal, blacks have voted heavily for Democratic candidates in spite of continuing efforts by the Republican Party to win them to the GOP flag. The pattern continued in the 2006 midterm election: exit polls showed that 89 percent of the black vote went to Democratic candidates. The 2006 black vote was 10 percent of the total, the same as in 1998 (flawed exit polls in 2002 were not made public). Census Bureau surveys showed that black turnout declined modestly over the twenty-five years from the 1982 midterm elections to 2006. From a high of 43 percent in 1982 the rate declined to 40 percent in 2002, according to the Census Bureau. Exit polls in 2006 indicated the turnout rate was 40.4 percent

Judicial Support

Not surprisingly, the unprecedented assertion of federal power over electoral and voting matters embodied in the Voting Rights Act was immediately challenged as exceeding the constitutional authority of Congress and encroaching on states' rights. But in 1966, in direct contrast to its post–Civil War rulings, the Supreme Court firmly backed the power of Congress to pass such a law. In that case, *South Carolina v. Katzenbach,* the state argued that Congress had exceeded its authority in suspending South Carolina voting standards, permitting the use of federal election examiners, and adopting a "triggering" formula that affected some states but not others. At the Court's invitation, Alabama, Georgia, Louisiana, Mississippi, and Virginia filed briefs in support of South Carolina's challenge. Twenty other states filed briefs in support of the law.

Strong Court Backing

The Supreme Court rejected all constitutional challenges to the act. "Congress," wrote Chief Justice Earl Warren for the decision's 8–1 majority, "has full remedial powers [under the Fifteenth Amendment] to effectuate the constitutional prohibition against racial discrimination in voting." The federal approval requirement for new voting rules in the states covered by the act, Warren observed, "may have been an uncommon exercise of congressional power, as South Carolina contends, but the Court has recognized that exceptional conditions can justify legislative measures not otherwise appropriate."

Also in 1966, in *Katzenbach v. Morgan,* the Court upheld the portion of the Voting Rights Act that permitted persons educated in accredited "American-flag" schools to vote even if they were unable to read and write English. The provision was aimed at enfranchising Puerto Ricans educated in such schools, living in the United States, but unable to demonstrate literacy in English.

Although the basic constitutionality of the Voting Rights Act was now settled, a steady stream of voting rights cases came to the Court in the late 1960s and the 1970s, testing the scope and application of the law. But the Court continued to back and broadly interpret the act. In the 1969 case of *Gaston County v. United States,* for example, the Court refused to let a North Carolina county reinstate a literacy test.

Some Exceptions Allowed

In 1975, however, the Court held in *Richmond v. United States* that a federally approved annexation plan did not violate the Voting Rights Act—even if it reduced the percentage of black voters in the city's population—so long as there were legitimate reasons for the annexation. Despite its willingness to affirm the sweeping provisions of the 1965 law, the Court refused to interpret it as forbidding all use of racial criteria in legislative redistricting or as requiring that blacks be given proportional representation on elected bodies.

In a 1976 decision, *Beer v. United States,* the Court upheld a city's reapportionment of the districts from which city council members were chosen. The change resulted in an increase in the number of black council members, but not in a proportional representation of black voters among the council members. The Court held that the Voting Rights Act was satisfied so long as such changes did not reduce the voting strength of racial minorities.

The next year, in *United Jewish Organizations of Williamsburgh v. Cary,* the Court upheld New York's 1974 redistricting law, which purposely redrew certain districts to give them nonwhite majorities. The county (Kings) affected in the case was one of three in New York that had been brought under the coverage of the Voting Rights Act by the 1970 amendments to that law. The Hasidic Jewish community of the Williamsburgh section of Brooklyn objected that the new boundaries divided their voting strength between two districts. The objectors argued that such use of racial criteria in the redistricting deprived them of equal protection guaranteed by the Fourteenth Amendment and diluted their voting strength in violation of the Fifteenth Amendment.

The Constitution did not prevent all use of racial criteria in districting and apportionment, wrote Justice Byron R. White for the seven-member Supreme Court majority in that case. Nor, he continued, did it "prevent a State subject to the Voting Rights Act from deliberately creating or preserving black majorities in particular districts in order to ensure that its reapportionment plan complies with [the act]. . . ."

"There is no doubt," White continued, that the state, in drawing new district lines, "deliberately used race in a purposeful manner. But its plan represented no racial slur or stigma with respect to whites or any other race, and we discern no discrimination violative of the Fourteenth Amendment nor any abridgment of the right to vote on account of race within the meaning of the Fifteenth Amendment."

In the 1980 case of *Mobile v. Bolden,* the Court for the first time narrowed the reach of the Voting Rights Act. Justice Potter Stewart wrote on behalf of a 6–3 majority that the fact that no black person had ever been elected city commissioner in Mobile, Alabama, under the city's challenged system of at-large elections was not enough to prove the system was in violation of the Voting Rights Act and the Constitution. "The Fifteenth Amendment does not entail the right to have Negro candidates elected," Stewart wrote, but only guaranteed that blacks would be able to "register and vote without hindrance."

Mobile Decision Overturned

The decision set off a reaction in Congress that resulted in specific language being written into the 1982 extension of the Voting Rights Act declaring that a voting practice or law that had the effect of discriminating was in violation of the federal law, whatever the local intent might have been. In 1986 the Court applied the new test to *Thornburg v. Gingles,* ruling that six of North Carolina's multimember legislative districts impermissibly diluted the strength of black votes in the state. The fact that very few black candidates had been elected from those districts was enough to prove that the system was in violation of the law, the Court held.

In 1991 the Supreme Court relied on the 1982 revisions of the Voting Rights Act to rule that the act applied to the election of judges.

Later Court Decisions

Entering the 1990s, blacks and Hispanics were still underrepresented in Congress. To remedy this situation, the Justice Department sought to use the "preclearance" provision of the Voting Rights Act to encourage states with histories of minority voting rights violations to create so-called majority-minority districts—districts where black or Hispanic populations were in the majority. *(See "Minority Representation," p. 133.)*

With newly drawn majority-minority districts, the 1992 election produced a large increase in the total of black and Hispanic House members. The number of blacks jumped from twenty-six to thirty-nine, the number of Hispanics from eleven to seventeen. But some of the districts were sharply criticized as a form of racial gerrymandering because of their irregular shapes, and the Supreme Court in 1993 demonstrated that these districts would come under tough legal scrutiny.

At issue in 1993 was a district that wound its way in a snakelike fashion through central North Carolina, picking up black neighborhoods in four metropolitan areas. The district, drawn at the urging of the Justice Department, was challenged by a group of white voters who alleged that North Carolina had set up "a racially discriminatory voting process" and deprived them of the right to vote in "a color-blind" election. Their suit was dismissed by a federal district court but reinstated by the Supreme Court in a 5–4 decision, *Shaw v. Reno* (1993).

In her opinion for the Court, Justice Sandra Day O'Connor acknowledged that racial considerations could not be excluded from the redistricting process. But she said that in "some exceptional cases" a plan could be "so highly irregular that, on its face, it rationally cannot be understood as anything other than an effort to segregate voters on the basis of race." To justify such a plan, O'Connor said, the government must show that it is narrowly tailored to serve a compelling government interest.[12]

The *Shaw v. Reno* decision returned the case to a lower court for further hearings. Meanwhile, challenges to racially drawn redistricting plans were proceeding in other states, which the Court used to refine its position on racial redistricting. In 1995 the Court struck down a Georgia plan that had created three black-majority districts, including one that stretched from the Atlanta suburbs across half the state to the coastal city of Savannah. The 5–4 vote in *Miller v. Johnson* was the same as in the North Carolina case, but the Court made clear that challenges were not limited to plans with irregularly shaped districts.

Writing for the majority, Justice Anthony M. Kennedy argued that government should not treat citizens as members of a racial class, and he said that the Georgia map could not be justified on the grounds that it was necessary to comply with the Voting Rights Act because the Justice Department had incorrectly interpreted the law to require the maximum number of majority-black districts be created. Redistricting plans were subject to challenge, Kennedy said, if race was "the predominant factor motivating the legislature's decision to place a significant number of voters within or without a particular district."

The decision was widely criticized. President Bill Clinton called the ruling "a setback in the struggle to ensure that all Americans participate fully in the electoral process." But the criticism did not sway the Court's majority. In 1996 the same five-justice majority in *Shaw v. Hunt* rejected the serpentine North Carolina district that it had scrutinized in 1993, arguing that the state had neglected traditional districting criteria, such as compactness, while overemphasizing the importance of race. The Court in *Bush v. Vera* (1996) also found that Texas had improperly used racial considerations in the drawing of three congressional districts. District maps in parts of Florida, Louisiana, New York, and Virginia were also successfully challenged on the basis of race. The Court, however, let stand Illinois' Hispanic majority-minority district after the state argued successfully that it had a "compelling state interest" in it.

Civil rights groups complained that the effect of the rulings would make it more difficult for minorities to be elected to Congress. But their warnings were tempered by the election results. In 1999 there were thirty-seven blacks in the House (down two from 1993) and eighteen Hispanics (up one from 1993). Similar results were seen in the elections in the first decade of the twenty-first century. At the beginning of the 110th Congress in 2007 there were forty-one blacks and twenty-six Hispanics. *(See Chapter 3, Who Gets Elected.)*

In a setback for civil rights organizations the Court ruled in January 2000 that governments covered by the Voting Rights Act can obtain federal approval for election law changes as long as the revisions do not leave minorities worse off than before. In an earlier related decision, in 1997 the Court said the Justice Department could not withhold approval solely because an election law change diluted minority voting strength. At issue was the law's section requiring localities with a history of discrimination to obtain prior approval from Justice before making any change in voting practices or procedures.

In a 2003 case, however, the Court gave states subject to the law discretion to move blacks out of majority-minority districts if they offset the reduced voting strength with gains in minority groups' political influence elsewhere. The ruling upheld a legislative districting plan in Georgia, written by Democrats, that moved blacks out of majority-minority districts to increase Democratic voting strength in adjoining districts.

WOMEN'S VOTE: A VICTORY IN STAGES

The drive for women's suffrage, which began in the late 1830s, was closely related in the beginning to the movement for abolition of slavery. Women, because of their extensive legal disadvantages under the common law, often compared their lot to that of slaves and thus directed the bulk of their political activity against proposals for extending slavery. Women were disfranchised at every level of government. Only in New Jersey did they have a theoretical right to vote. That right had been included inadvertently in the state constitutions of 1776 and 1797, but the state legislature repealed the provision at the outset of the nineteenth century when some women actually attempted to vote.

Early victories for the women's suffrage movement came mostly in connection with school elections. Kentucky in 1838 gave the right to vote in such elections to widows and unmarried women with property that was subject to taxation for school purposes. Kansas in 1861 gave women the vote on all school questions, and by 1880 Michigan, Utah, Minnesota, Colorado, New Hampshire, and Massachusetts had followed suit.

The Woman's Rights Convention at Seneca Falls, New York, in July 1848 is generally cited as the beginning of the women's suffrage movement in the United States. But the Declaration of Principles, which Elizabeth Cady Stanton read at that meeting and which thereafter became a sacred text for the movement, was a much broader and more revolutionary document than a simple claim for the franchise.

Steps Toward the Vote

Direct-action tactics first were applied by suffragists shortly after the Civil War, when Susan B. Anthony urged women to go to the polls and claim the right to vote under terms of the newly adopted Fourteenth Amendment. In the national elections of 1872, Anthony voted in her home city of Rochester, New York; she subsequently was tried and convicted of the crime of "voting without having a lawful right to vote." For almost a quarter of a century, Anthony and her followers pressed Congress for a constitutional amendment granting women's suffrage. On January 25, 1887, the Senate finally considered the proposal but rejected it by a 16–34 vote.

The suffrage forces had more success in some western states. As a territory, Wyoming extended full suffrage to women in 1869 and retained it upon becoming a state in 1890. Colorado, Utah, and Idaho granted women voting rights before the turn of the century. But after that the advocates of suffrage for women encountered stronger opposition, and it was not until the height of the Progressive movement that other states, mostly in the West, gave women full voting rights. Washington granted equal suffrage in 1910, California in 1911, Arizona, Kansas, and Oregon in 1912, Montana and Nevada in 1914, and New York in 1917.

Opponents argued that women were the "weaker sex," that their temperament was unsuited to make the kinds of decisions necessary in casting a ballot, and that suffrage might alter the relationship between the sexes. In the two decades preceding women's enfranchisement, extravagant claims were made by extremists on both sides. Radical feminists often insisted that women voters would be able to cleanse American politics of its corruption and usher in some ill-defined, utopian golden age. Antifranchise forces were as far-reaching in their claims. During World War I, Henry A. Wise Wood, president of the Aero Club of America, told the House Committee on Woman Suffrage that giving women the vote would mean "the dilution with the qualities of the cow of the qualities of the bull upon which all the herd's safety must depend." And the January 1917 issue of *Remonstrance,* an antisuffrage journal, cautioned that women's suffrage would lead to the nationalization of women, free love, and communism.[13]

Supporters of the Nineteenth Amendment, which gave women the right to vote, picket the White House in 1917. The Nineteenth Amendment was ratified in 1920.

Constitutional Amendment

On the eve of World War I, the advocates of militant tactics took the lead in a national campaign for women's rights. In the congressional elections of 1914, they set out to defeat all Democratic candidates in the nine states (which had increased to eleven by election day) where women had the right to vote. They held the majority Democrats in Congress responsible for not submitting a constitutional amendment to the states for their approval of women's voting rights. Only twenty of the forty-three challenged candidates were elected. However, this showing of electoral strength did not move President Woodrow Wilson to take up their cause.

President Wilson's opposition to a constitutional amendment prompted a series of stormy demonstrations by the suffragettes around the White House and other sites in Washington after the United States had entered World War I. The demonstrators insisted that it was unconscionable for this country to be denying its own female citizens a right to participate in government while at the same time it was fighting a war on the premise of "making the world safe for democracy."

At the direction of the administration, thousands of the women demonstrators were arrested and brought to trial. Some were beaten by hostile crowds—often made up of soldiers and sailors who viewed the demonstrations as unpatriotic. At their trials, many of the women stood mute or made speeches advocating suffrage and attacking President Wilson for his refusal to endorse the constitutional amendment.

The jailing of many of these women caused a severe housing problem for District of Columbia penal authorities and created a wave of sympathy for the suffragettes. Public support for their position was heightened by the prisoners' claims that they had been treated inhumanely and had been subjected to unsanitary conditions in prison. To protest these conditions, some of the prisoners went on a hunger strike, and the authorities resorted to forced feeding, an action that aroused even greater public sympathy.

President Wilson capitulated, announcing on January 9, 1918, his support for the proposed suffrage amendment. The House approved it the next day by a 274–136 vote, one vote more than the necessary two-thirds majority. But the Senate fell short of the two-thirds majority in October 1918 and again in February 1919. However, when the Congress elected in November 1918 met for the first time on May 19, 1919, it took little more than two weeks to gain the required majorities in both chambers.

On August 18, 1920, Tennessee became the thirty-sixth state to approve the amendment, enough for ratification. On August 26, Secretary of State Bainbridge Colby signed a proclamation formally adding the Nineteenth Amendment to the Constitution. It stated simply that "The right of citizens of the United States to vote shall not be denied or abridged by the United States or any state on account of sex."

In the 1920 presidential election, the first in which women could vote, it was estimated that only about 30 percent of those who were eligible actually voted. Analyses of the 1924 election indicated that scarcely one-third of all eligible women voted while more than two-thirds of the eligible men had done so. The women's electoral performance came as a bitter blow to the suffragists. In more recent national elections, however, surveys by the Census Bureau have found that voting participation by women is about the same as that of men. *(See Table 1-2, p. 6.)*

Even so, by 2006 women's representation in Congress was well below half, although their numbers continued to increase: in the 110th Congress, which began in 2007, seventy-one women served in the House and sixteen in the Senate. In addition, three additional women represented Guam, the Virgin Islands, and the District of Columbia.

The 110th Congress also saw a historic first: Rep. Nancy Pelosi, a Democratic representative from the San Francisco area of California, was elected Speaker of the House, the first time in history that a woman had risen to that position.

THE EIGHTEEN-YEAR-OLD VOTE

Twenty-one was the minimum voting age in every state until 1943, when Georgia lowered it to eighteen—the age at which young men were being drafted to fight in World War II. The slogan "Old enough to fight, old enough to vote" had a certain logic and public appeal. But no other state followed Georgia's lead until after the war. In 1946 South Carolina Democrats authorized eighteen-year-olds to vote in party primaries but later withdrew that privilege. In 1955 Kentucky voters lowered the voting age to eighteen. Alaska and Hawaii, upon entering the Union in 1959, adopted minimum voting ages of nineteen and twenty, respectively.

Meanwhile, in 1954, President Dwight D. Eisenhower had proposed a constitutional amendment granting eighteen-year-olds the right to vote nationwide, but the proposal was rejected by the Senate. Eventually Congress was persuaded—perhaps by the demographics of America's fast-expanding youth population, which during the 1960s had begun to capture the nation's attention; perhaps by the separate hopes of Republicans and Democrats to win new voters; perhaps by the Vietnam War in which the young were called on to fight again. In the Voting Rights Act of 1970, Congress added a provision to lower the voting age to eighteen in all federal, state, and local elections, effective January 1, 1971.

On signing the bill into law, President Richard M. Nixon restated his belief that the provision was unconstitutional because Congress had no power to extend suffrage by statute and directed Attorney General John N. Mitchell to ask for a swift court test of the law's validity. The Supreme Court, ruling in *Oregon v. Mitchell* only weeks before the law was due to take effect, sustained its application to federal elections but held it unconstitutional in regard to state and local elections.

After the Court ruled, Congress wasted little time in approving and sending to the states a proposed Twenty-sixth Amendment to the Constitution, stating: "The right of citizens of the United States, who are eighteen years of age or older, to vote shall not be denied or abridged by the United States or any State on account of age. The Congress shall have power to enforce this article by appropriate legislation." The proposal received final congressional approval March 23, 1971, and was ratified by the necessary three-fourths of the states by July 1, record time for a constitutional amendment.

More than 25 million Americans became eligible to vote for the first time in the 1972 presidential election. It was the biggest influx of potential voters since women won the right to vote in 1920. But the younger age group has never fulfilled its potential power at the polls; in election after election, younger voters have had the lowest turnout rate of any age category. *(See Table 1-2, p. 6.)*

The Census Bureau, however, reported that young adults in the eighteen- to twenty-four-year-old range showed a substantial increase in both registration and voting between the 2000 and 2004 national elections. Its voter survey showed that between those two elections the registration rate increased 7 percentage points and the voting rate increased 11 percentage points.

REMOVING OBSTACLES TO VOTING

In the late twentieth century the federal government and the states took steps to increase participation in the electoral process. The Voting Rights Act of 1970 helped pave the way in removing residency restrictions on new voters. Another major federal initiative, the "motor-voter" law of 1993, was designed to increase the ease of voter registration. Other measures to increase voter turnout came at the state level, with a number of states experimenting with new voting methods, such as mail-in ballots.

Reducing Residency Requirements

Every state at some time has imposed a minimum period of residence in the state (and some of them a shorter period of residence in a county or voting district) as a qualification for voting. The rationale for this practice has been that individuals cannot vote intelligently, at least on state and local affairs, until they have lived in an area for a given period of time. Until the 1970s most of the states required one year's residence for voting. At one time or another, Alabama, Louisiana, Mississippi, Rhode Island, and South Carolina required residency of as much as two years.

In 1970 thirty-three states imposed residency requirements of one year, fifteen required six months, and two (New York and Pennsylvania) three months. As another condition for voting in 1970, every state except New Hampshire required voters to have lived in the same county or voting district for a stipulated period of time. The most stringent of these requirements were in Maryland and Texas, where six months was required in the county and voting district.

Federal voting rights legislation in 1970 permitted voting in presidential elections after thirty days of residence. This provision, upheld by the Supreme Court, extended the franchise to about 5 million people who might otherwise have been disqualified from voting in the 1972 presidential election. Soon thereafter the Court decided (*Dunn v. Blumstein*) that a state cannot constitutionally restrict the franchise to persons who lived in the state at least one year and in the county at least three months. The 6–1 opinion, rendered March 21, 1972, caused all the states to change their residency requirements. By 1980 nineteen states and the District of Columbia had no minimum residency requirement, and no other state imposed more than a thirty-day residence requirement except Arizona, which required fifty days. Ten years later, Arizona lowered its requirement to twenty-nine days.[14]

Voters Living Abroad

In 1976 President Gerald R. Ford signed legislation establishing uniform voting procedures for American citizens who lived overseas. The law gave Americans abroad the right to vote by absentee ballot in federal elections in the state in which they had their last voting address. The Senate Rules Committee had reported in May 1975 that studies showed that "nearly all of these private citizens outside of the United States in one way or another are strongly discouraged, or are even barred by the rules of the states of their last domicile, from participation in presidential and congressional elections." [15]

In 1978 Congress approved legislation that prevented states from using evidence that an American living overseas voted in a state or federal election as proof of residency for tax purposes. Sponsors said many Americans living abroad did not vote because they feared they might have to pay additional taxes.

New Registration, Voting Efforts

With the exception of North Dakota, all states require a person to register before being allowed to vote. Consequently, numerous organizations including political parties, interest groups, and citizen organizations have increasingly focused on getting individuals on the voting rolls well in advance of election day.

In most Western nations government agencies sign up voters, but the United States places the burden for qualifying for electoral participation on the citizen. Although the procedure is still somewhat cumbersome, a variety of state and federal legislation, capped by the National Voter Registration Act or so-called motor-voter act, and a 2002 law—Help America Vote Act—has made voter registration a higher profile activity and in many ways more convenient.

Signed into law by President Bill Clinton on May 20, 1993, motor-voter required states to provide all eligible citizens the opportunity to register when they applied for or renewed a driver's license. It also required states to allow mail-in registration and to provide voter registration forms at agencies that supplied public assistance, such as welfare checks or help for people with disabilities. Compliance with the federally mandated program was required by 1995. Costs were to be borne by the states.

Partly as a result of the legislation, a record number of new voters, some 10 million, signed up in the first three years following implementation of the act. By the 2004 elections, the Census Bureau reported that 142 million Americans who were eligible to vote were registered.

Congressional Republicans had opposed the legislation on political grounds, namely that it would allow citizens of traditional Democratic constituencies—the urban poor and minorities, among others—easier access to the voting booth. Opponents also argued that easier registration could lead to election fraud.

But motor-voter had neither the negative results that critics feared nor the positive impact that supporters hoped. One year after the law was enacted, Republicans won control of both houses of Congress, which they retained until 2006. Meanwhile, in spite of the increased number of registered voters, election turnout continued to decline until the elections starting in 2000.

For the 2004 election, according to the Census Bureau's survey for that year, 19 percent of registered voters obtained their registration while getting a driver's license or identification card at a motor vehicle department. This was second to registrations done at a county or other government registration office, a quarter of the registered total.

The Help America Vote Act of 2002 was mostly an outgrowth of the controversies that swirled around the contentious 2000 national election—the closest and perhaps the most hotly debated presidential election in modern U.S. history—but also of election problems that had been obvious to voting officials for years. The law covered a wide array of voting issues and sought to help states upgrade their election systems, techniques, and controls. Among its many provisions it authorized funds to help states replace punch-card and lever voting machines, required states by 2006 to create a computerized voter registration database, provided "provisional voting" for persons whose eligibility was in question, required stiffer identification standards when registering (in most cases, a driver's license or Social Security number), and set up a commission to help implement the law. By the turn of the twenty-first century states were also experimenting with various other measures designed to increase voter turnout, including election-day voter registration, easier absentee balloting, and elections by mail.

In the late 1970s President Jimmy Carter proposed federal legislation to allow voters to register at the polls on election day, but it was not enacted. Several states, though, have adopted election-day registration on their own, including Minnesota. In 1998, when Reform Party candidate Jesse Ventura won the Minnesota governorship, more than 330,000 citizens registered to vote on election day (which represented 16 percent of the ballots cast). As of 2006, five states allowed election-day registration. Of the remaining states, most required registration twenty to thirty days before an election, but a small number set the deadline at fifteen or fewer days before the polls opened.

Because many potential voters do not have the time or capability to travel to the polls on a given day absentee voting gained wider acceptance in the first years of the new century, especially in western states. About half the states had an "early voting" option, including "no-fault" absentee voting open to all voters with no need to plead sickness, disability, or any other reason for wanting to vote before election day. A few states, such as Colorado, Texas, and Tennessee, tried opening voting-style booths before election day in stores or other public places.

A couple of states have tested another alternative: dispensing with voting booths altogether and conducting elections by mail to encourage higher participation. Proponents argue that the benefits of voting by mail—including convenience, speed, and lower costs—outweigh the disadvantages, including the possible abuse of the system, and the lost sociability that comes with gathering at the polls.

By the 2004 election, according to the Census Bureau's survey that year, 80 percent of voters reported they voted on election day and 20 percent voted earlier, either in person or by mail. More than 12 percent of those votes were by mail. Oregon led the way to mail voting, starting with using mail-in votes to fill a vacant Senate seat in 1996. The winner was Democrat Ron Wyden, the first senator elected by mail. The new procedure, begun that year, received good reviews. More than three-quarters of those Oregonians polled said they preferred voting by mail over going to the polling places. Women and older voters were strongest in favor of mail voting.

Oregon subsequently became the first state to decide to hold all elections by mail, approving a ballot measure in 1998 requiring vote by mail in biennial primary and general elections. The measure eliminated polling places, but it did not affect existing law allowing absentee ballots or voting at local election offices.

Emerging Issues After 2000

The midterm congressional elections in 2006 were the first held after the 2002 Help America Vote Act was fully in force. The elections were widely considered a success because only one race was challenged over registration or voting irregularities that would have changed the outcome. In Florida's 13th district, the race was decided by 369 votes, with Republican Vern Buchanan declared the winner. He was sworn in at the beginning of the 110th Congress. The loser, Christine Jennings, contested the outcome, charging that it was skewed by electronic voting machine errors. Jennings filed suit in a Florida court. A task force of the House Administration Committee also was looking into the dispute in mid-2007.

But voter activist groups pointed to problems in numerous jurisdictions, including incorrect registration information, voter identification rules involving photo IDs, voting machine problems and insufficient ballots, poorly trained or absent poll workers, and long waiting lines. Nevertheless, the potential voting catastrophe that some observers had predicted, partly from major issues that surfaced during 2006 primaries, did not materialize.

Perhaps the most striking change in the 2006 elections was the continuing movement in states to electronic voting machines. Several types of voting machines were in use in the United States: optical scan systems, in which a machine scans an individual's ballot; direct response electronic voting machines, usually referred to as touch-screen voting; lever machines; punch cards; and paper ballots. Some states use a mix of these types.

For a period it appeared the touch-screen system would sweep away the other voting machine methods. In the 2004 presidential elections just under 30 percent of voters were reported to have used touch-screen machines, compared to 12 percent in 2000. However, continued questions about the machines' accuracy, reliability, and security sent them into a freefall after the 2006 elections. A federal panel charged with advising the Election Assistance Commission set up by the 2004 Help America Vote Act said in December 2006 that electronic voting machines "cannot be made secure," reflecting the view of many computer scientists. The difficulty and in many cases inability of these systems to provide a paper trail of voting was criticized by many voter analysts as an insurmountable obstacle to their use. Then, in February 2007 the newly elected Florida governor, Charlie Crist, a Republican, announced that touch-screen machines would be abandoned in the state and replaced by optical scanners. The Florida decision, which was supported by prominent Democrats, was seen as a near death-blow to the system because Florida had invested heavily in the new technology and was considered a front-runner in its use.

Although voting systems emerged from the 2006 election as the most urgent concern, other issues troubled groups ranging from secretaries of state to activist citizen groups that monitor U.S. elections. Among the issues noted by many were:

- Poll Workers. Better screening and much enhanced training was urged for the persons hired to run the voting booths on election day, especially as registration verification and voting systems became more complex.
- Poll Watchers. These are groups, usually associated with political parties, that are present outside polling places who are sometimes confused by voters as being election officials. Poll watchers historically emerged to challenge potential voter fraud, with individuals from all parties keeping watch on others. But local officials were

increasingly worried that voters might be intimidated by challenges from these groups.

- Voter Registration Groups. Another concern of voting analysts is the role played by organizations formed, or hired, to register voters. While getting more people registered to vote is desirable in principle, there were increasing instances of registration groups innocently or intentionally misusing the registration information they gathered, such as by turning in only names they think support their interests or creating false registrations that election officials have inadequate time to check.

NOTES

1. Max Farrand, ed., *The Records of the Federal Convention of 1787* (New Haven, Conn.: Yale University Press, 1966), vol. 2, 178.
2. Mellman and Scammon are quoted in *President Bush, The Challenge Ahead* (Washington, D.C.: Congressional Quarterly, 1989), 3.
3. United States Elections Project, George Mason University, http://elections.gmu.edu.
4. Rhodes Cook, *The Rhodes Cook Letter* (December 2006): 13.
5. Benjamin Highton and Raymond E. Wolfinger, "The Political Implications of Higher Turnout" (paper presented at the 1998 annual meeting of the American Political Science Association), Boston, September 1998, 10.
6. Richard Winger, *Ballot Access News* 22, no. 9 (January 1, 2007): 10. www.ballot-access.org/2007/010107.html#11.
7. Gunnar Myrdal, *An American Dilemma: The Negro Problem and Modern Democracy* (New York: Harper and Row, 1944), 445.
8. Paul Lewinson, *Race, Class and Party: A History of Negro Suffrage and White Politics in the South* (New York: Oxford University Press, 1932), 194.
9. Frederic D. Ogden, *The Poll Tax in the South* (University: University of Alabama Press, 1958), 2–4.
10. Myrdal, *An American Dilemma*, 485.
11. U.S. Commission on Civil Rights, *Voter Participation* (May 1968), 223. See also U.S. Commission on Civil Rights, *The Voting Rights Act: Ten Years Later* (January 1975), 60.
12. Joan Biskupic and Elder Witt, *Guide to the U.S. Supreme Court* (Washington, D.C.: Congressional Quarterly, 1997), 529.
13. Mary Costello, "Women Voters," *Editorial Research Reports* (Washington, D.C.: Congressional Quarterly, 1972), 776.
14. Information from annual editions of *The Book of the States* (Washington, D.C.: The Council of State Governments), and from the Arizona Secretary of State's Office.
15. Senate Committee on Rules and Administration, "Overseas Citizens Voting Rights Act of 1975," 94th Cong., 1st sess., 1975, S Rept 94–121, 2.

SELECTED BIBLIOGRAPHY

Abramson, Paul R., John H. Aldrich, and David W. Rohde. *Change and Continuity in the 2004 and 2006 Elections.* Washington, D.C.: CQ Press, 2007.

Berelson, Bernard, Paul F. Lazarsfeld, and William A. McPhee. *Voting: A Study of Opinion Formation in a Presidential Campaign.* Chicago: University of Chicago Press, 1954.

Brady, David W., John F. Cogan, and Morris P. Fiorina, eds. *Continuity and Change in House Elections.* Stanford, Calif.: Stanford University Press: Hoover Institution Press, 2000.

Brady, Henry E., and Richard Johnston, eds. *Capturing Campaign Effects.* Ann Arbor: University of Michigan Press, 2006.

Burden, Barry C., and David C. Kimball. *Why Americans Split Their Tickets: Campaigns, Competition, and Divided Government.* Ann Arbor: University of Michigan Press, 2002.

Burton, Michael J., and Daniel M. Shea. *Campaign Mode: Strategic Vision in Congressional Elections.* Lanham, Md.: Rowman and Littlefield, 2003.

Campbell, Angus. *The Voter Decides.* New York: Harper and Row, 1954.

Campbell, Angus, Philip E. Converse, Warren E. Miller, and Donald E. Stokes. *The American Voter.* New York: Wiley, 1960.

Campbell, James E. *The Presidential Pulse of Congressional Elections.* 2nd ed. Lexington: University Press of Kentucky, 1997.

———. "The Revised Theory of Surge and Decline." *American Journal of Political Science* 31 (November 1987): 965–979.

Carroll, Susan J., and Richard L. Fox, eds. *Gender and Elections: Shaping the Future of American Politics.* New York: Cambridge University Press, 2006.

Ceaser, James W., and Andrew E. Busch. *Red over Blue: The 2004 Elections and American Politics.* Lanham, Md.: Rowman & Littlefield, 2005.

Chadwick, Andrew. *Internet Politics: States, Citizens, and New Communication Technologies.* New York: Oxford University Press, 2006.

Conway, M. Margaret. *Political Participation in the United States.* 3rd ed. Washington, D.C.: CQ Press, 2000.

Conway, M. Margaret, Gertrude A. Steuernagel, and David W. Ahern. *Women and Political Participation: Cultural Change in the Political Arena.* 2nd ed. Washington, D.C.: CQ Press, 2005.

Cook, Rhodes. *How Congress Gets Elected.* Washington, D.C.: CQ Press, 2000.

CQ's Politics in America. Washington, D.C.: CQ Press, 1999– .

Cummings, Milton C. *Congressmen and the Electorate: Elections for the U.S. House and the President, 1920–1964.* New York: Free Press, 1966.

Farrand, Max, ed. *The Records of the Federal Convention of 1787.* 4 vols. New Haven, Conn.: Yale University Press, 1966.

Fenno, Richard F. *Congress at the Grassroots: Representational Change in the South, 1970–1998.* Chapel Hill: University of North Carolina Press, 2000.

Fiorina, Morris P. *Retrospective Voting in American National Elections.* New Haven, Conn.: Yale University Press, 1981.

Fiorina, Morris P., Samuel J. Abrams, and Jeremy C. Pope. *Culture War? The Myth of a Polarized America.* 2nd ed. New York: Pearson Longman, 2006.

Flanigan, William H., and Nancy H. Zingale. *Political Behavior in Midterm Elections.* Washington, D.C.: CQ Press, 2003.

———. *Political Behavior of the American Electorate.* 11th ed. Washington, D.C.: CQ Press, 2006.

Glaser, James M. *The Hand of the Past in Contemporary Southern Politics.* New Haven, Conn.: Yale University Press, 2005.

Green, John C. *Faith Factor: How Religion Influences American Elections.* Westport, Conn.: Praeger Publishers, 2007.

Green, John C., Mark J. Rozell, and Clyde Wilcox, eds. *The Values Campaign? The Christian Right and the 2004 Elections.* Washington, D.C.: Georgetown University Press, 2006.

Gronke, Paul. *The Electorate, the Campaign, and the Office: A Unified Approach to Senate and House Elections.* Ann Arbor: University of Michigan Press, 2000.

Guide to U.S. Elections. 5th ed. Washington, D.C.: CQ Press, 2005.

Hamilton, Alexander, James Madison, and John Jay. *The Federalist Papers with Letters of Brutus.* Introduction by Terence Ball. New York: Cambridge University Press, 2003.

Haynes, George H. *The Election of Senators.* New York: Henry Holt, 1906.

Heard, Alexander, and Donald S. Strong. *Southern Primaries and Elections, 1920–1949.* University: University of Alabama Press, 1950. Reprint. Plainview, N.Y.: Books for Libraries Press, 1970.

Herrnson, Paul S. *Congressional Elections: Campaigning at Home and in Washington.* 4th ed. Washington, D.C.: CQ Press, 2004.

Hill, David L. *American Voter Turnout: An Institutional Perspective.* Boulder, Colo.: Westview Press, 2006.

Jacobson, Gary C. *The Politics of Congressional Elections.* 6th ed. New York: Pearson Longman, 2004.

Key, V. O. *The Responsible Electorate.* New York: Vintage Books, 1966.

Lewinson, Paul. *Race, Class and Party: A History of Negro Suffrage and White Politics in the South.* New York: Oxford University Press, 1932.

Magleby, David B., J. Quin Monson, and Kelly Patterson, eds. *Electing Congress: New Rules for an Old Game.* Upper Saddle River, N.J.: Pearson Prentice Hall, 2007.

Mann, Thomas E. *Unsafe at Any Margin: Interpreting Congressional Elections.* Washington, D.C.: American Enterprise Institute, 1978.

Mayer, Robert H., ed. *The Civil Rights Act of 1964.* San Diego: Greenhaven Press, 2004.

Mayhew, David R. *Congress: The Electoral Connection.* 2nd ed. New Haven, Conn.: Yale University Press, 2004.

McGovney, Dudley O. *The American Suffrage Medley.* Chicago: University of Chicago Press, 1949.

Myrdal, Gunnar. *An American Dilemma: The Negro Problem and Modern Democracy.* New York: Harper & Row, 1944.

Nie, Norman H., Sidney Verba, and John R. Petrocik. *The Changing American Voter.* Cambridge, Mass.: Harvard University Press, 1976.

Ogden, Frederic D. *The Poll Tax in the South.* University: University of Alabama Press, 1958.

Pomper, Gerald M., et al. *The Election of 2000: Reports and Interpretations.* Chatham, N.J.: Chatham House, 2001.

Rosenstone, Steven J., and John M. Hansen. *Mobilization, Participation, and Democracy in America.* New York: Macmillan, 1993.

Shea, Daniel M., and John C. Green, eds. *Fountain of Youth: Strategies and Tactics for Mobilizing America's Young Voters.* Lanham, Md.: Rowman & Littlefield, 2007.

Skinner, Richard M. *More Than Money: Interest Group Action in Congressional Elections.* Lanham, Md.: Rowman & Littlefield, 2007.

Sulkin, Tracy. *Issue Politics in Congress.* New York: Cambridge University Press, 2005.

Teixeira, Ruy A. *The Disappearing American Voter.* Washington, D.C.: Brookings Institution, 1992.

Theriault, Sean M. *The Power of the People: Congressional Competition, Public Attention, and Voter Retribution.* Columbus: Ohio State University Press, 2005.

Thurber, James, ed. *The Battle for Congress: Consultants, Candidates, and Voters.* Washington, D.C.: Brookings Institution Press, 2000.

Wattenberg, Martin P. *Is Voting for Young People?* New York: Pearson/Longman, 2007.

———. *Where Have All the Voters Gone?* Cambridge, Mass.: Harvard University Press, 2002.

Wolfinger, Raymond E., and Steven J. Rosenstone. *Who Votes?* New Haven, Conn.: Yale University Press, 1980.

chapter 2

Political Parties and Elections

Political parties are vital elements in the structure and function of Congress and its members. Although not specifically mentioned in the Constitution, political parties have been important in Congress almost since its creation. They help select and elect candidates for Congress through the electoral process and organize and distribute power within the institution. The party that holds a majority of seats in either the Senate or the House of Representatives normally controls all key positions of authority within that chamber.

In the broadest sense, political parties are coalitions of people who join together to try to gain governmental power by winning elections. They seek that power in order to further their social, economic, or ideological goals. Members of a party supposedly share a loosely defined set of common beliefs, although members of the same party often hold different opinions and outlooks. Citizens rely on political parties to define issues, and they support or oppose candidates on the basis of those issues. These citizens then expect the people they elect to carry out the agreed-upon policies when the party is in power.

FUNCTIONS OF PARTIES

Political parties in America serve many functions. Most importantly, parties help elect the president by nominating candidates for the office and then working to get them elected. Political parties also put forward candidates for most state and local offices and help elected leaders mobilize support for their programs.

Since the mid-nineteenth century, most members of Congress have belonged either to the Democratic or the Republican Party. Occasionally, however, some members of other parties—the Progressive Party in the early 1900s, for example—have been elected. *(See Figure 2-1, p. 27.)* Sometimes a member is elected as an independent with no direct affiliation to any political party but gives support primarily to one or the other of the major parties. At the start of the 110th Congress in 2007, the Senate had two independents, Bernard Sanders of Vermont and Joseph I. Lieberman of Connecticut, both of whom aligned themselves informally with Senate Democrats.

The Democrats and Republicans each have been dominant in Congress at different times. For much of the period between the Civil War and the Great Depression of the 1930s, Republicans held majorities in both the House and the Senate. Democrats dominated through much of the rest of the twentieth century, controlling both chambers for fifty-two of the sixty-two years from the election of 1932 until the election of 1994. From 1995 until 2007 the Republicans held the upper hand in the House and for most of the period in the Senate as well. But in the 2006 midterm elections Democrats won back control of both chambers as the Republican Party, burdened with an unpopular president—George W. Bush—and an equally unpopular war in Iraq, suffered significant losses. At these elections Democrats had a net gain of thirty seats in the House and six in the Senate.

Choosing Congressional Candidates

One essential function of the parties is to provide a mechanism for choosing and supporting congressional candidates. Before the emergence of the Jacksonian era, named for Andrew Jackson, who won the presidency in 1828 and reelection in 1832, the legislative caucus was the usual method of nominating candidates for both state and federal office. Caucuses were informal party groupings in Congress. From 1800 to 1824 congressional members of the Democratic-Republican Party even used the caucus to select the party's nominee for the presidency. In 1824 Jackson's followers, realizing their candidate had no chance of winning endorsement in the party caucus, set out to substitute party conventions as a more democratic means of selecting the party's candidate. They aggressively attacked the closed operations of what they called "King Caucus," a label that was still used in modern times to signify an elite and powerful group—often in Congress but in other political settings as well—that excluded rank and file party members from participation.

By 1828 states had begun to abandon use of the caucus for nominating purposes for state and federal offices. In its place arose the convention in which party members outside the congressional ranks could play a role, although the convention as the source of presidential nominations did not emerge until the early 1830s. The first true political nominating convention for the presidency in American history is credited to the Anti-Masonic Party, which selected its presidential candidate in September 1831 in Baltimore. Eight months later, in 1832 Jacksonian Democrats also sent delegates to Baltimore, where they nominated Jackson for president and Martin Van Buren for vice president.

In the early 1900s the Progressives worked to abolish the convention and replace it with the direct primary. Proponents of the primary contended that powerful organizations had seized control of the nominating conventions and frequently had ignored the preferences of the party rank and file. Under the leadership of its governor, Robert M. La Follette Sr., a leading Progressive who later served in Congress, Wisconsin in 1903 enacted the first mandatory primary law. By 1917 the direct primary had been adopted in almost every state, and the convention persisted only for the selection of presidential candidates, candidates for a few state offices, and for Republican Party nominations in the Democratic South.

Bernard Sanders of Vermont was one of two independents in the 110th Senate. He and Joseph I. Lieberman of Connecticut aligned themselves informally with Senate Democrats.

During this same period, the Progressives also succeeded in pushing through Congress a constitutional amendment calling for direct popular election of senators; previously, they had been chosen by their state legislatures. Beginning in 1914 senators were not only elected by popular vote, but also nominated in most states through party primaries.

The direct primary considerably broadened the range of positions that a political party might take. Political scientist V. O. Key Jr. noted in his 1964 book *Politics, Parties, and Pressure Groups* that "rival factions and leaders could now fight out their differences in a campaign directed to the electorate—or a substantial segment of it—rather than be bound by the decision of an assembly of delegates." [1]

Nevertheless, the concept of a primary was to lead, half a century later, to complete dominance of the presidential selection process at the expense of nominating conventions, which became primarily show pieces for television to highlight the candidate selection already decided in primary voting booths. By 2007 the importance of presidential primaries was so overwhelming that states were vying to be among the first to hold their elections. States that held primaries several months into a presidential election year realized that the early-voting states were in a position to effectively decide the presidential nominee. Even though voters in states with later primary dates could still cast ballots for candidates of their preference, and thereby pledge convention delegates to those persons, the influence of these votes was greatly diminished. Only if the early primaries did not establish a clear preference for a single candidate would the later-voting states have a significant impact on the decision. The voters in the states with later primaries believed themselves to be in effect disenfranchised from any meaningful role in the party's decision.

By mid-2007, more than a year before the next national election, the impact of early primaries was becoming more clear as a number of large population states jockeyed to schedule voting dates in early February or even January. Although both the Republican and Democratic parties officially resisted this trend, they had little leverage over the states to prevent it from happening. Although not all primary dates were firm as of August 2007, it appeared that 2008 would have a telescoped primary season beginning early in the year that would force candidates to campaign, at great expense and personal energy, in all the major states with early primaries. Although the early primary phenomenon has less impact on candidates for lower offices, parties must frequently make choices for these positions many months prior to the fall elections, often before many voters are paying attention.

Organizing Congress

Parties also play an essential role in the internal organization of Congress. Formal authority in Congress is arranged according to party. The party that holds the majority in a chamber will select its leaders, such as the Speaker of the House or the majority leader in the Senate. Normally committee and subcommittee chairs are members of the majority party—although occasionally an independent has been given a committee chairmanship—and majority party leaders control the legislative agenda. Within each party a whip system enables leaders to pressure party members to support the party position on key issues.

FIGURE 2-1 **American Political Parties, 1789–2004**

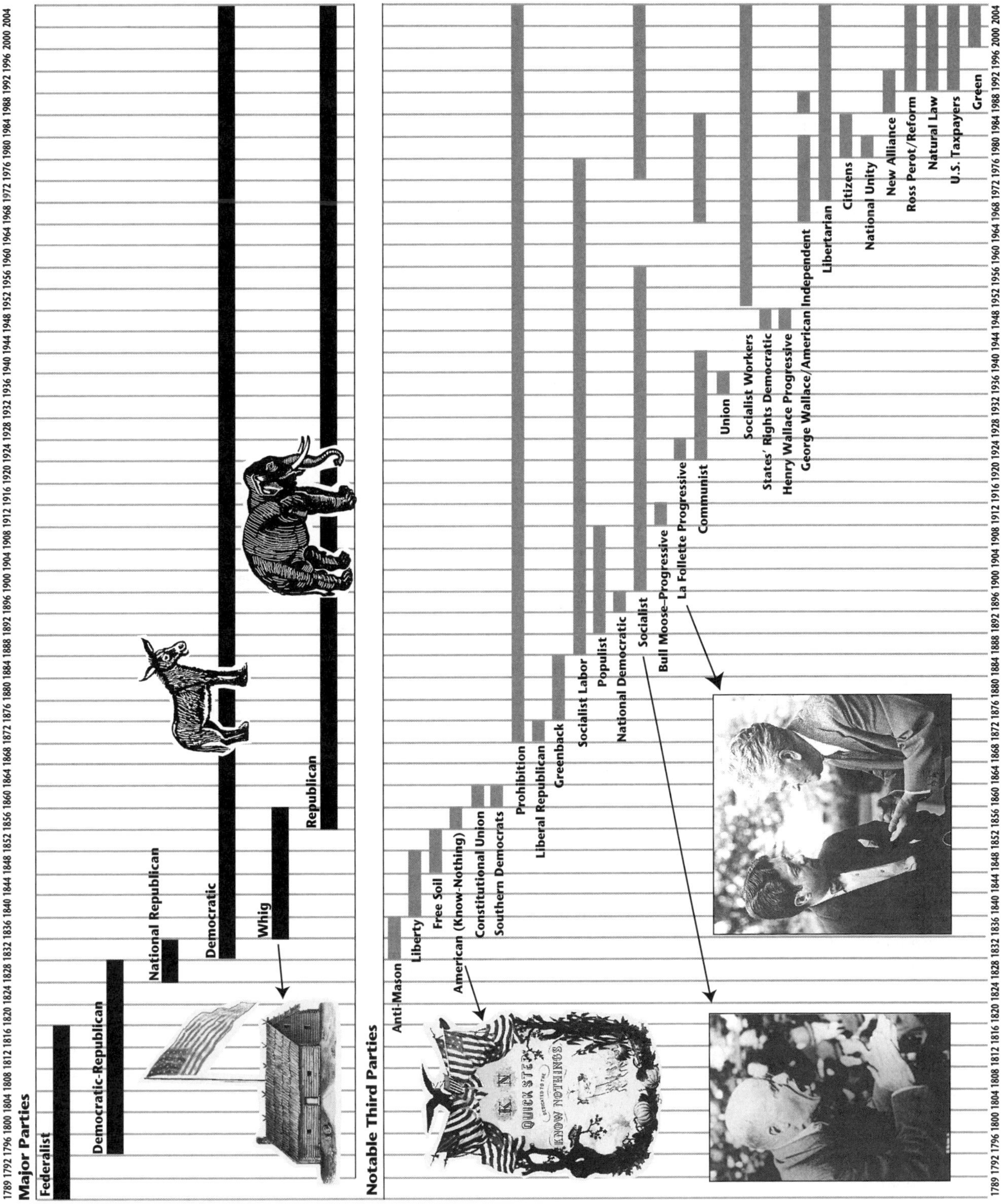

NOTE: Throughout U.S. history there have been more than 1,500 political parties. For this chart Congressional Quarterly editors have selected those parties that achieved national significance during presidential election years. The spaces between the rules on this chart indicate the election year only. For example, the Constitutional Union Party and the Southern Democrats were in existence for the 1860 election only and were gone by 1864. Similarly, the Green Party first fielded a presidential candidate in 1996.

Without parties to unite like-minded members in common action, Congress might find itself in constant chaos as each member fought to advance an individual agenda. A party's members, however, are under no binding obligation to support its positions or obey its leaders. At certain times during Congress's long history, individual legislators have built their constituencies with little reference to party labels.

Seniority had always played a significant role throughout Congress's history but it became increasingly important as members began making service in the House or Senate a life-long career. This pattern was seen increasingly after President Franklin D. Roosevelt, beginning in 1932, solidified a political realignment in the nation that gave Democrats control of Congress for much of the next half century. With longer service, seniority became the key to gaining and holding the most important levers of power in both houses. This allowed Democrats from the South and some city political machines to chair committees with impunity and follow their own agenda, which was often in conflict with the objectives of the national Democratic Party. The seniority system, as it was called, became more entrenched after World War II and lasted until reforms in both houses, starting in the 1970s, broke the iron grip of long-serving members and opened up career opportunities to middle-level and even on occasion newly elected rank and file members.

With the Republican takeover of Congress in 1995, partisanship—reflected in the amount of party-line voting—reached some of its highest levels in the last half of the twentieth century on both sides of Capitol Hill. This partisanship continued until 2007, when the GOP controlled the House continuously. House Republican leaders imposed extraordinarily tight control over the GOP caucus, including the selection of committee chairs. Through its tough enforcement of rewards and punishments for its members, the GOP leadership was able to exercise discipline rarely seen in Congress in modern times. During these years the Democrats also became much more skilled at keeping members of their caucus in lock-step in order to present a unified front against what they considered a GOP steamroller that was excluding them from meaningful participation in the legislative process.

PARTY SYSTEM: UNFORESEEN DEVELOPMENT

The nation's Founders never envisioned the importance that political parties would develop in Congress and on the national political scene. The authors of the Constitution, a largely unified political elite, had little understanding of the functions of political parties. Generally they were hostile to the new party system as it developed in the early years of the Republic, seeing in it the dangers of what they called "factions" in society. "If I could not go to heaven but with a party, I would not go there at all," Thomas Jefferson said in 1789.[2]

The Constitution did not mention parties, either to authorize them or prohibit them. It made possible a permanent role for parties, however, by giving citizens civil liberties and the right to organize. At the same time it erected safeguards against partisan excesses by creating a system of checks and balances within the government. The "great object" of the new government, wrote James Madison in *Federalist* No. 10, was "to secure the public good and private rights against the danger of such a faction [party], and at the same time to preserve the spirit and the form of popular government." [3]

But "popular government" took on different meanings from those embraced by the Founders as the new Constitution and government opened opportunities and increased expectations for the expanding electorate. Inevitably, an expanding voter base gave rise to varying views of government, which took expression in the institutionalization of parties.

Emergence of Parties

The first political parties emerged soon after the adoption of the Constitution. Some of the Founders, led by Alexander Hamilton, George Washington's secretary of the treasury, favored developing a strong central government that they thought was embodied in the Constitution. They were known as Federalists and they dominated the political scene during the 1790s. They were drawn from merchants and bankers in the Northeast and had less support among western farmers and southern planters. Under Hamilton's tutelage they favored assumption of state debts, the chartering of a national bank to facilitate economic growth and international commerce, support of manufacturing interests, and a flexible interpretation of the Constitution. In foreign policy matters they advocated protecting commercial and other ties with Great Britain, even though lingering resentment of the former colonial overseers remained strong among many Americans. Although in principle they were committed to a republican form of government, many Federalists believed that politics was more properly the purview of a "natural aristocracy" of wealthy and talented men.

The Federalists were opposed by a group that later became known as the Democratic-Republican Party. Led by Thomas Jefferson and James Madison, the Democratic-Republicans were largely southern planters and western farmers who opposed a strong central government and were fearful of the increasing commercial and industrial developments in the Northeast. They sought policies to make it easier to borrow money, which Northeastern merchants believed would produce inflation and debase the currency. Democratic-Republicans favored expanded suffrage, states' rights over the national government, and a narrow and literal interpretation of the Constitution. They opposed a national bank and were more favorably disposed to France than to Great Britain.

In the early sessions of Congress, party lines were fluid, with members drifting between one loose coalition and the other. By the mid-1790s, however, the factions had hardened enough for one senator to observe that "the existence of two parties in Congress is apparent." Federalists generally held the upper hand in these early years, controlling the Senate and contending equally for power with the Democratic-Republicans in the House.

Although George Washington identified himself with no political party, John Adams, his successor, was unabashedly Federalist. But by 1800 Jefferson's supporters had gained a majority, and when Jefferson replaced Adams in 1801, Democratic-Republicans occupied the White House and controlled Congress until 1829. The 1816 elections signaled the effective end of the Federalist Party, as its representation in Congress dropped off to a small minority, and even the semblance of a two-party system disappeared.

PARTY NAME CONFUSION

The nomenclature used to define political parties in the early years of the nation has perplexed students ever since because of the reuse of a few common labels. The Democratic-Republican Party developed in the early 1790s as the group opposed to the Federalists and as successor to the Anti-Federalists, a loose coalition of individuals opposed to ratification of the Constitution. This new party, led by Thomas Jefferson, also called its members Republicans, which became the name used in most areas, but they also were called Jeffersonian Republicans, Jeffersonian Democrats, and National Republicans. Historians tend to use Democratic-Republicans to distinguish the Jeffersonians from the modern Republican Party, which emerged in 1854. The Jeffersonian party that dominated in the first two decades of the nineteenth century unraveled by the end of the 1820s, with many of its members moving to form what became known as the Whig Party, which lasted until it too dissolved by the time of the Civil War. Nevertheless, the Democratic-Republican Party is seen as the forerunner of the modern-day Democratic Party, which became a recognizable entity with the election of Andrew Jackson as president in 1828. He defeated incumbent John Quincy Adams, the son of Federalist president John Adams. Jackson is seen as the first president to represent the "Democratic Party," which has maintained that name ever since.

Along with the dominance of the Democratic-Republicans, the first twenty years of the nineteenth century saw growth in the power of the party caucus over Congress's operations. Important decisions were made in private meetings of the Democratic-Republicans, and party members in Congress were pressed to follow the party's position.

The size and power of the Democratic-Republican Party soon led to the development of internal factions as different regional groups struggled for influence within the only national political organization. By the mid-1820s two groups emerged: the National Republicans, a coalition of eastern manufacturers, large southern plantation owners, and westerners who favored internal economic development projects and a protective tariff against foreign goods; and the Democrats, who represented agrarian interests from the South and West and held that the common people, not the rich, should have the dominant voice in government.

The Democrats captured control of Congress in 1826 and the White House in 1828, under Jackson, and remained the dominant party in Congress for the next three decades. To show their disgust with what they considered to be the "mob rule" of the Jacksonians, the National Republicans in 1834 changed their name to Whigs, an English political term signifying antagonism to excessive use of executive power. The Whigs twice won the presidency, in 1840 and 1848, and always held a substantial number of seats in Congress. But the party was able to capture a majority of either body on only a few occasions—the 1840 and 1846 elections in the House and the 1840 and 1842 elections in the Senate.

Republican Party Founded

The Whigs faded rapidly during the 1850s and ceased to exist in 1856. In their place rose the Republican Party of today. Initially, the party was composed of "Free Soil" Democrats, who wanted to keep slavery out of the new Southwest territories, and Whigs. The new Republican Party won control of the House in 1854 but lost it in 1856, even as its first presidential candidate, John Charles Frémont, was winning a third of the popular vote. During the next four years the party broadened its appeal to owners of small farms and businesses by promising a homestead law for western settlement and a protective tariff. In 1858 the party recaptured control of the House. In 1860 it won the Senate and, with the election of Abraham Lincoln, the presidency.

The Republican Party controlled Congress and the presidency for most of the next seventy years. Democrats were occasionally able to win a majority of House seats and a Senate majority. But the Republicans, who soon gained the nickname of "Grand Old Party" (GOP), dominated the era. Backed by eastern business interests, they favored high tariffs and tight controls on the amount of money in the economy. The Democrats were the party of the South and of disaffected agricultural interests from the West. They generally sought low tariffs and liberal credit.

Two-Party Dominance

It was during this period of Republican rule that the role of the parties themselves became much more important in

The Republican convention of 1860 in Chicago nominated Abraham Lincoln for the presidency. Republicans controlled Congress and the presidency for most of the next seventy years. They became known as the "Grand Old Party" (GOP).

Congress. Although the Congress of the pre–Civil War period tended to be dominated by brilliant individuals, the postwar Senate and House were the arenas of powerful party leaders. This trend was particularly apparent in the Senate, where many of the members were "party bosses" who had gained power through political organizations in their own states. These men placed a high value on party loyalty and on the need for party discipline. They were often ready to compromise their ideals to maintain harmony within the party.

The first attempt at developing a strong party structure came in the 1870s, when New York Republican Roscoe Conkling organized a faction that controlled the Senate on procedural matters. Conkling's group had little effect on legislation, however, and the Senate returned to individualistic ways after Conkling left.

The birth of modern party discipline came in the 1890s. Republican senators William B. Allison of Iowa and Nelson W. Aldrich of Rhode Island organized an informal group of senators, who first met only for poker and relaxation. In 1897, after Allison was elected chair of the Senate Republican Caucus, the organization of party members, the group assumed control of the Senate. Allison used his office to solidify his control of the party and the party's control of the Senate.

Allison controlled the Steering Committee, which directed floor proceedings, and the Committee on Committees, which made committee assignments. Although chairs of committees were determined primarily by seniority, Allison had great leeway to appoint committee members who would follow his wishes. Access to positions of influence soon depended on the favor and support of the party leaders.

Republicans used the caucus to work out party positions in private and then to speak in a unified voice on the Senate floor. Although they were not bound to obey the party position, members who ignored it risked losing most of their power in the Senate. The Democrats soon followed the Republicans by organizing their own internal power structure.

On the House side, Republican Speakers Thomas Bracket Reed of Maine in the 1890s and Joseph G. Cannon of Illinois in the first decade of the 1900s imposed a similar degree of party control over their rank and file. Reed's rule firmly established the authority of the majority to prevail over the minority, ending a period in which the minority used obstructionist tactics that frequently brought legislative activity in the House to a standstill.

Attacks on the System

The system of strict party control was not popular among many people outside of Congress, who saw it as violating the principles of representative democracy. There were also critics of the system within Congress, including the Liberal Republicans of the 1870s, the antileadership Republicans of the 1880s, and representatives of third parties.

The most important of these third parties were the Populists, who represented an agrarian reform movement based in the Midwest and West. The Populists won three Senate seats and eleven House seats in 1892. They reached their peak in the crucial election of 1896, when they and their allies won seven Senate seats and thirty House seats. Much of their program, which stressed the loosening of controls on the amount of money circulating in the economy, was adopted by the Democrats, and the Populists soon faded from the scene.

The cause of reform was soon taken up by the progressives. This movement sought both economic changes, such as antitrust legislation and introduction of the income tax, and political measures aimed at opening up the system, such as direct election of senators and laws against corrupt election practices. The progressives were composed of reformist Republicans and members of the separate Progressive Party. The Bull Moose–Progressives, as they were called in honor of their leader, former president Theodore Roosevelt, elected seventeen House members in 1912. The progressives played key roles in the congressional reform movement of the early 1900s, working to reduce the autocratic power of House Speaker Joseph Cannon and pushing for curbs on the filibuster.

Despite these attacks, the system of party control of Congress developed into a formal institution. During the 1910s, Senate Democrats and Republicans elected a single member to serve both as chair of the party caucus and as floor leader. Soon the majority and minority leaders were the acknowledged spokespeople for their parties in the Senate. In the House the revolt against the power of the Speaker led to a great increase in the power of the party caucuses. The Democrats, who controlled the House from 1911 to 1919, worked out most legislative decisions within party meetings, and party rules obliged members to vote for the party position if it was endorsed by a two-thirds majority.

Republicans regained control of both houses of Congress in 1918, and they maintained their power until the early years of the Great Depression. However, the party was torn by deep divisions between regular forces and the progressives, who often cooperated with the Democrats in pushing legislation favorable to the economic interests of western farmers. Progressive Republicans who tried to challenge their party leadership were quickly punished by the loss of seats on important committees.

Democrats as Majority Party

The Republicans lost their exclusive control of Congress in 1930, when Democrats gained a narrow majority in the House. That election proved to be a harbinger of the avalanche that came two years later. The 1932 elections were a watershed in the history of partisan divisions in Congress. Led by presidential candidate Franklin D. Roosevelt, who promised relief from the economic disaster that had befallen the nation, the Democrats swept to commanding majorities in both the House and Senate. By the 1936 elections, the Republicans had been reduced to a small minority. The Democrats held 331 House seats as a result of that election; the Republicans 89. The Democratic majority in the Senate was an overwhelming 76–16.

With a few exceptions, the Democrats then remained in complete control of Congress until the mid-1990s. Between 1930 and 1994, they lost their House majority only twice, in the 1946 and 1952 elections. Those elections also gave Republicans brief control of the Senate, but the Democrats regained control again in 1948 and 1954. The GOP also controlled the Senate during the first six years of Ronald Reagan's presidency, 1981–1987. However, Democrats regained a substantial majority in the 1986 elections, which they maintained into the early 1990s.

In 1992 Democrats won the White House for only the second time in a quarter century. But their control of both ends of Pennsylvania Avenue was short-lived. Redistricting at the beginning of the 1990s provided new opportunities for the GOP by creating House districts favorable to Republicans, particularly in the rapidly growing suburbs around central cities. In addition, the South—historically a Democratic stronghold—moved into the Republican column as old-line Democrats from the region retired and southern voters found themselves more comfortable with the increasingly conservative Republican Party.

Democrats, for their part, suffered nationally from the perception of an arrogance of power, epitomized by a House banking scandal that was a major factor in the defeat of nineteen House incumbents (mainly Democrats) in the 1992 primary season; the number was a postwar record. Nor were the Democrats helped in 1993 and 1994 by the struggling start of the new Clinton administration, which in 1994 lobbied Congress for a complex overhaul of the nation's health care system that died in spite of the Democratic majorities in both the House and Senate.

The confluence of these factors produced an unexpected political swing in the 1994 elections that propelled the Republicans into power in both houses of Congress for the first time in forty years.

DIVIDED GOVERNMENT

The Republican congressional takeover in 1995 returned Washington for the next six years to the divided government that prevailed during most of the second half of the twentieth century. Yet the combination of a Democratic president and a Republican Congress was the reverse of the combination that had existed before. *(See Table 2-1, p. 33.)*

In 1952 and 1956, war hero Gen. Dwight D. Eisenhower carried the Republicans to the White House, even as the GOP in 1954 slumped into its long-running minority status on Capitol Hill. Recurrent economic recessions under President Eisenhower and the vigorous campaign of presidential candidate John F. Kennedy enabled the Democrats to recapture the White House in 1960 and retain it with Lyndon B. Johnson's election in 1964.

But Republicans, led by former vice president Richard M. Nixon, who had lost to Kennedy in 1960, regained the presidency in 1968 from a Democratic Party badly split over the Vietnam War and under attack from third-party candidate George C. Wallace. Nixon, reelected by a huge majority in 1972, tried to create a new party alignment by courting the once solidly Democratic South with conservative domestic programs. But the results were mixed, and the party was badly damaged when the Watergate scandal, involving a Republican-sponsored break-in at Democratic headquarters and a subsequent effort to cover up the action, forced Nixon to resign in 1974. The scandal paved the way for Democrat Jimmy Carter to triumph in 1976.

But in 1980 a conservative tide, economic problems, and the Iranian hostage crisis, in which a group of Americans were held hostage in the U.S. embassy in that country for 144 days, swept Republican Ronald Reagan into the presidency. Eight years later Reagan's vice president, George H. W. Bush, succeeded him, and in his first two years in office scored some of the highest popularity ratings of any modern president, Democrat or Republican.

As the 1990s began, there was considerable conjecture as to why the Democratic Party was able to thrive in congressional and state elections while repeatedly losing the presidency. It had become the "oddest riddle of American politics of recent years," political analyst Alan Ehrenhalt wrote in his book *The United States of Ambition.* Ehrenhalt, executive editor of *Governing* magazine and former political editor of the *Congressional Quarterly Weekly Report,* argued that the best answer was that "Democrats have generated the best supply of talent, energy, and sheer ambition," which over time "enabled them to win an extra 10 percent of the seats in a state legislature, or an extra two or three seats in a congressional delegation. It adds up. . . ."[4]

The era that Ehrenhalt described was interrupted dramatically by the election of 1994, when Republicans not only won both houses of Congress, but also captured a majority of the nation's governorships and made inroads in the state legislatures. In the elections of 1996 and 1998, Democrats inched back toward parity in the House and continued to hold more seats than the Republicans in the state legislatures, still a prime source of congressional candidates. *(See Table 2-2, p. 34.)*

Democratic hopes lasted only until the 2000 elections when Republicans won both the White House, under the candidacy of the elder Bush's son, George W. Bush, and—at least initially—both chambers of Congress, the first time since Clinton in 1992 that one party controlled both branches. As it turned out, the GOP victory was temporary, when six months into the new Congress a disaffected Republican, James Jeffords of Vermont, left the party to become an independent but caucused with the Democrats. The Senate had been divided evenly with fifty Democrats and fifty Republicans, with the GOP vice president holding the tie-breaking vote. But with Jeffords' defection to, in effect, the Democrats, the Republicans lost their majority. Democrats took control of the Senate for the remainder of that Congress; Republicans continued to control the House.

The return to divided government was temporary. In the 2002 and 2004 elections, Republicans won firm control of both chambers, returning the federal government to unified control. But that, too, did not last. Democrats swept back in 2006 to gain thirty seats in the House and six in the Senate, giving them control of both and once again creating divided government in Washington.

Party Affiliation

It is probably no coincidence that the rise in divided government in the latter half of the twentieth century has coincided with the proliferation of independent voters—voters who profess no party choice or call themselves independent Republican or independent Democrat. They accounted for only 16 percent of the electorate in 1937, but 32 percent—nearly one-third—in 1990, and 38 percent in early 1999, according to Gallup surveys. Another long-running examination of voter orientation, the American National Election Studies (ANES), showed similar trends. Its survey in 2004 showed 33 percent of respondents said they were Democrats, 28 percent said they were Republicans, and 39 percent said they were independents, using responses that included the "independent" party designation. In 1952, when the predecessor of ANES first started tracking affiliation, the numbers were 57, 34, and 6 percent. *(See "Growth of Independents," p. 5, Table 1-2, p. 6.)*

Yet the two major parties were still held in relatively high regard by the end of the twentieth century. When independents were asked in the 1999 Gallup survey whether they leaned toward the Republican or Democratic parties, the number that defined themselves as staunchly independent dropped to about 10 percent. The ANES surveys showed a

TABLE 2-1 **Divided Government, 1860–2006**

During the last half of the twentieth century and into the early years of the twenty-first, it was not unusual for one party to occupy the White House and for the other party to dominate Congress. But for almost a century before that, beginning with the election of the first Republican president (Abraham Lincoln) in 1860, one party or the other tended to control both ends of Pennsylvania Avenue. The chart below indicates the party that won control of the House and Senate in each national election since 1860, and notes the president that was either elected then or serving at the time (in the case of midterm elections). Changes in the presidency between elections are indicated by a slash.

		Party winning control					Party winning control		
Election	President	House	Senate	Control of presidency and Congress[a]	Election	President	House	Senate	Control of presidency and Congress[a]
1860	Lincoln (R)	R	R	All Republican	1934	F. Roosevelt (D)	D	D	All Democrat
1862	Lincoln (R)	R	R	All Republican	1936	F. Roosevelt (D)	D	D	All Democrat
1864	Lincoln/A. Johnson (R)	R	R	All Republican[b]	1938	F. Roosevelt (D)	D	D	All Democrat
1866	A. Johnson (R)	R	R	All Republican	1940	F. Roosevelt (D)	D	D	All Democrat
1868	Grant (R)	R	R	All Republican	1942	F. Roosevelt (D)	D	D	All Democrat
1870	Grant (R)	R	R	All Republican	1944	F. Roosevelt/Truman (D)	D	D	All Democrat
1872	Grant (R)	R	R	All Republican	1946	Truman (D)	R	R	Divided
1874	Grant (R)	D	R	Congress Split	1948	Truman (D)	D	D	All Democrat
1876	Hayes (R)	D	R	Congress Split	1950	Truman (D)	D	D	All Democrat
1878	Hayes (R)	D	D	Divided	1952	Eisenhower (R)	R	R	All Republican
1880	Garfield/Arthur (R)	R	R	All Republican	1954	Eisenhower (R)	D	D	Divided
1882	Arthur (R)	D	R	Congress Split	1956	Eisenhower (R)	D	D	Divided
1884	Cleveland (D)	D	R	Congress Split	1958	Eisenhower (R)	D	D	Divided
1886	Cleveland (D)	D	R	Congress Split	1960	Kennedy (D)	D	D	All Democrat
1888	B. Harrison (R)	R	R	All Republican	1962	Kennedy/L. Johnson (D)	D	D	All Democrat
1890	B. Harrison (R)	D	R	Congress Split	1964	L. Johnson (D)	D	D	All Democrat
1892	Cleveland (D)	D	D	All Democrat	1966	L. Johnson (D)	D	D	All Democrat
1894	Cleveland (D)	R	R	Divided	1968	Nixon (R)	D	D	Divided
1896	McKinley (R)	R	R	All Republican	1970	Nixon (R)	D	D	Divided
1898	McKinley (R)	R	R	All Republican	1972	Nixon/Ford (R)	D	D	Divided
1900	McKinley/T. Roosevelt (R)	R	R	All Republican	1974	Ford (R)	D	D	Divided
1902	T. Roosevelt (R)	R	R	All Republican	1976	Carter (D)	D	D	All Democrat
1904	T. Roosevelt (R)	R	R	All Republican	1978	Carter (D)	D	D	All Democrat
1906	T. Roosevelt (R)	R	R	All Republican	1980	Reagan (R)	D	R	Congress Split
1908	Taft (R)	R	R	All Republican	1982	Reagan (R)	D	R	Congress Split
1910	Taft (R)	D	R	Congress Split	1984	Reagan (R)	D	R	Congress Split
1912	Wilson (D)	D	D	All Democrat	1986	Reagan (R)	D	D	Divided
1914	Wilson (D)	D	D	All Democrat	1988	George H. W. Bush (R)	D	D	Divided
1916	Wilson (D)	D	D	All Democrat	1990	George H. W. Bush (R)	D	D	Divided
1918	Wilson (D)	R	R	Divided	1992	Clinton (D)	D	D	All Democrat
1920	Harding (R)	R	R	All Republican	1994	Clinton (D)	R	R	Divided
1922	Harding/Coolidge (R)	R	R	All Republican	1996	Clinton (D)	R	R	Divided
1924	Coolidge (R)	R	R	All Republican	1998	Clinton (D)	R	R	Divided
1926	Coolidge (R)	R	R	All Republican	2000	George W. Bush (R)	R	D[c]	Congress Split
1928	Hoover (R)	R	R	All Republican	2002	George W. Bush (R)	R	R	All Republican
1930	Hoover (R)	D	R	Congress Split	2004	George W. Bush (R)	R	R	All Republican
1932	F. Roosevelt (D)	D	D	All Democrat	2006	George W. Bush (R)	D	D	Divided

NOTES: Key to abbreviations: D—Democrat; R—Republican. a. "All" indicates that one party controlled the White House and both houses of Congress. "Divided" indicates that one party held the presidency while the other party controlled both houses of Congress. "Congress Split" indicates that control of Congress was split, with one party holding the House and the other the Senate. b. The pro-Republican majority in Congress elected in 1864 was designated Unionist. c. At the beginning of the 107th Congress in 2001, Republicans controlled the Senate as a result of the 2000 elections. The chamber was evenly divided between fifty Democrats and fifty Republicans, with the GOP vice president casting a deciding vote in any tie. However, six months into the session, a disaffected Republican—James Jeffords of Vermont—left the party to become an independent and caucus with the Democrats. Jeffords' decision to lend his support to the Democrats gave that party a one-vote majority to organize the chamber. For the remainder of the 107th Congress Democrats controlled the Senate.

similar core independent voter in its 2004 numbers. Still, there was no denying that the last half of the twentieth century saw a rise in ticket-splitting, a willingness of voters of all stripes to go back and forth across the ballot rather than vote a straight-party ticket. *(See Table 2-3, p. 35.)*

Even party regulars sometimes vote for candidates in the opposing party, according to findings reported by political scientists William H. Flanigan and Nancy H. Zingale. "The proportion of strong partisans who report having voted for different parties has increased substantially since 1952," they wrote in a comparison of voting habits in the 1952 and 1988 elections.[5]

Flanigan and Zingale noted that southern whites "have become dramatically less Democratic, while blacks throughout the country have become slightly more Democratic and the most consistently loyal Democratic group." The authors found that Jews "have shifted away from their extremely one-sided Democratic identification" but toward independent, rather than Republican, status. Independents also made inroads among Catholics and white Protestants in the North, at the expense of both parties. Despite these changes, Flanigan and Zingale wrote "there is partisan stability among both Republicans and Democrats, and the shifting of political fortunes is accomplished without intensity or extreme political appeals." [6]

Sen. Joseph I. Lieberman, I-Conn., ran for reelection in 2006 as an independent after he was defeated as a Democrat in the primary. Lieberman won the race and caucused with the Democrats in the 110th Congress.

The Gallup survey of early 1999 and later surveys after 2000 found a continuation of the gender gap, which had been a visible feature of American politics for the previous quarter century. While men were almost evenly divided between the Democrats and Republicans as their party of choice, women preferred the Democrats by a margin of 10 percentage points. By the 2006 election, exit polls showed women preferred Democrats 55 percent to 43 percent, while men voted Democratic 50 percent to 47 percent.

TABLE 2-2 **The House 1994 to 2006: From Democratic to Republican and Back to Democratic**

The House of Representatives went from Democratic to Republican control starting with the GOP's unexpected sweep in the 1994 elections. Control remained in GOP hands until 2006, fueled by the Republican upsurge in the South. The GOP lost seats outside the South for the rest of the 1990s, then made new gains in most areas in the first three elections of the 2000s. The party then suffered significant setbacks in all regions in the 2006 midterm voting.

	South				West			Midwest			East				Total House			
	R	D	I		R	D		R	D		R	D	I		R	D	I	
1994	73	64	0	R	53	40	R	59	46	R	45	54	1	D	230	204	1	R
1996	82	55	0	R	51	42	R	55	50	R	39	60	1	D	227	207	1	R
1998	82	55	0	R	49	44	R	54	51	R	38	61	1	D	223	211	1	R
2000	81	55	1	R	43	50	D	57	48	R	40	59	1	D	221	212	2	R
2002	85	57	0	R	46	52	D	61	39	R	37	57	1	D	229	205	1	R
2004	91	51	0	R	45	53	D	60	40	R	36	58	1	D	232	202	1	R
2006	85	57	0	R	41	57	D	51	49	R	25	70	0	D	202	233	0	D
Net GOP Change[a]		+12				–12			–8				–20				–28	

NOTES: Key to abbreviations: D—Democrat; I—Independent; R—Republican. Traditionally, Congressional Quarterly has defined the four U.S. regions as follows: East—Connecticut, Delaware, Maine, Maryland, Massachusetts, New Hampshire, New Jersey, New York, Pennsylvania, Rhode Island, Vermont, West Virginia; Midwest—Illinois, Indiana, Iowa, Kansas, Michigan, Minnesota, Missouri, Nebraska, North Dakota, Ohio, South Dakota, Wisconsin; South—Alabama, Arkansas, Florida, Georgia, Kentucky, Louisiana, Mississippi, North Carolina, Oklahoma, South Carolina, Tennessee, Texas, Virginia; West—Alaska, Arizona, California, Colorado, Hawaii, Idaho, Montana, Nevada, New Mexico, Oregon, Utah, Washington, Wyoming. a. Change in GOP seats, 1994–2006.

The 1999 survey also indicated that the Democrats were supported by a coalition of the young and elderly. Democrats were preferred by a margin of 11 percentage points over the Republicans among voters age eighteen to twenty-nine (exit polls showed the gap grew to a huge 22 percentage points in the 2006 vote) and by 10 percentage points among those age sixty-five and older (in 2006 that gap had shrunk to an even split).[7]

Party Decline in Congress

During the years after World War II, when Democrats dominated Capitol Hill, party leaders and parties suffered a noticeable decline in their influence on Congress. Members of Congress increasingly functioned as individuals rather than loyal party members, both in their electoral campaigns and in the way they voted in committee and on the floor.

In many respects, the increasing individualism was a natural outgrowth of divided government. While many districts were voting Republican for president, they were electing Democrats to Congress. It created a situation where many members of Congress felt they had to buck their party often in order to stay in favor with their constituents.

The growth of party primaries as a means for selecting congressional candidates also added to the decline of the importance of parties. Originally introduced to reduce the power of corrupt party bosses, by giving the choice of the party nominee to party members as a whole, primaries have had the unintended effect of undermining the parties as institutions. Congressional candidates learned they could bypass the established party leadership in their area and appeal directly to the voters.

Other factors have contributed to the decline of the parties within Congress. In the 1950s and 1960s the conservative coalition of Republicans and southern Democrats effectively controlled both the House and Senate, and for many years it was able to frustrate efforts by the Democratic leadership to push through civil rights and other legislation. In the 1970s the congressional reform movement stripped away much of the power of the old-line party leaders. That has made it possible for members to ignore the position of the party leadership and to vote according to their own interests, without fear of much punishment. And as the century waned, interest groups took an increasingly active role in congressional campaigns, often independent of both the parties and the candidates.

Republicans and Democrats in Congress responded with vigorous efforts to restore some of their influence in electoral politics. Each party has a House and Senate campaign committee, and all four committees play key roles in recruiting, training, organizing, and funding campaigns. In the 2006 election, for example, the Democratic campaign committee in the House was widely credited with a major role in the party's recapture of the chamber through such activities as recruitment of appealing candidates and generous funding of their campaigns. The Republicans in particular developed their campaign committees into wealthy, high-technology centers able to wage a coordinated national campaign for GOP candidates. But in the 2006 election, the Democratic committee in the House ran a vigorous recruitment and support operation that was widely credited with playing a major role in recapturing control of that chamber.

But nothing rejuvenated the parties in Congress as much as the Republican takeover in 1995. Democrats were stunned. Republicans were ebullient and quickly began to push their conservative reform agenda called the Contract with America. By the end of 1995 the proportion of votes in which a majority of one party had voted against the majority of another had reached a forty-year high in both the

TABLE 2-3 **Ticket-Splitting between Presidential and House Candidates, 1900–2004**

		Districts with split results[b]	
Year	Districts[a]	Number	Percentage
1900	295	10	3.4
1904	310	5	1.6
1908	314	21	6.7
1912	333	84	25.2
1916	333	35	10.5
1920	344	11	3.2
1924	356	42	11.8
1928	359	68	18.9
1932	355	50	14.1
1936	361	51	14.1
1940	362	53	14.6
1944	367	41	11.2
1948	422	90	21.3
1952	435	84	19.3
1956	435	130	29.9
1960	437	114	26.1
1964	435	145	33.3
1968	435	139	32.0
1972	435	192	44.1
1976	435	124	28.5
1980	435	143	32.8
1984	435	196	45.0
1988	435	148	34.0
1992	435	100	23.0
1996	435	111	25.5
2000	435	86	19.8
2004	435	59	13.6

NOTES: a. Prior to 1952 complete data are not available on every congressional district. b. Congressional districts carried by a presidential candidate of one party and a House candidate of another party.

SOURCE: Norman J. Ornstein, Thomas E. Mann, and Michael J. Malbin, eds., *Vital Statistics on Congress, 1997–1998* (Washington, D.C.: Congressional Quarterly, 1998), 71. Harold W. Stanley and Richard G. Niemi, *Vital Statistics on American Politics, 2007–2008* (Washington, D.C.: CQ Press, 2008), 50.

House and Senate. The proportion of party-unity votes declined in both 1996 and 1997, but spiked upward again in 1998, a year capped in the House by the highly partisan votes to impeach President Bill Clinton. These trends continued and increased after 2000 when both parties strongly coalesced around party objectives in the increasingly strident partisanship that characterized the years after George W. Bush won the White House. The Republicans successfully kept their troops in line after 1995, but the Democrats became equally effective after 2000.

ELECTION OF MEMBERS: EVOLVING PROCESS

The creation of the U.S. Senate was a result of the "Great Compromise" at the Constitutional Convention in 1787. The small states wanted equal representation in Congress, fearing domination by the large states if representation was determined by population. The larger states, however, naturally wished for a legislature based on population, in which their strength would prevail. In resolving this dispute, delegates simply split the basis of representation between the two chambers—population for the House of Representatives, equal representation by state for the Senate. Each state was entitled to two senators.

Senate Elections

The Founders let state legislatures, instead of the people themselves, elect U.S. senators. The argument was that legislatures were more able than the electorate to give sober and reflective thought to the selection, and by doing so would take a greater supportive interest in the fledgling national government. The legislatures, after all, had chosen the members of the Continental Congress and the delegates to the Constitutional Convention.

Some legislatures looked upon the senators as their ambassadors to the federal government and went so far as to instruct them on how to vote. This raised severe problems of conscience among senators on occasion and resulted in several resignations.

At first, the legislatures made their own arrangements for electing senators. Many states required the two houses of the legislature, sitting separately, to agree on the same candidate. Others required a ballot of the two houses in a joint session. In 1866 Congress decided to exercise its authority. Procedures requiring concurrent majorities in both houses resulted in numerous delays and vacancies. So Congress established procedures for the legislatures to follow in the election of senators, as was authorized by the Constitution.

Article I, Section 4, states in part: "The times, places and manner of holding elections for Senators and Representatives shall be prescribed in each state by the legislature thereof; but the Congress may at any time by law make or alter such regulations, except as to the places of chusing Senators."

The new federal law required the first ballot for senator to be taken by the two houses separately. If no candidate received a majority of the vote in both houses—that is, if a deadlock resulted—then the two houses were to meet and vote jointly until a majority choice emerged. However, the new system did not have the desired effect. The requirement for a majority vote continued to result in voting deadlocks.

A notable instance occurred in Delaware at the turn of the nineteenth century. With the legislators divided between two factions of the Republican Party, and the Democrats in the minority, they could not reach agreement by the time Congress went into session on March 4, 1899. So bitter was the Republican factional dispute that neither side would support a candidate acceptable to the other. Nor would the Democrats play kingmaker by siding with one group or the other. The dispute continued throughout the 56th Congress (1899–1901), leaving the seat unfilled.

Furthermore, the term of Delaware's other Senate seat ended in 1901, necessitating another election. The same pattern prevailed, with the legislature failing to fill either Senate seat, leaving the state unrepresented in the Senate from March 4, 1901, until March 1, 1903, when at last the deadlock was broken by the choice of one faction's Senate candidate to one seat, and the other faction's candidate to the other seat.

The system had other faults besides election deadlocks. The party caucuses in the state legislatures and individual members were subject to intense and unethical lobbying by supporters of various senatorial candidates. Because of the frequency of allegations of illegal methods used in securing elections, the Senate found itself involved in election disputes. The Constitution makes Congress the judge of its own members. Article I, Section 5, states that "Each House shall be the Judge of the Elections, Returns, and Qualifications of its own Members. . . ."

Critics of the legislative election of senators had still another grievance. They contended that elections to the state legislatures often were overshadowed by senatorial contests. Thus when voters went to the polls to choose their state legislators, they would sometimes be urged to disregard state and local issues and vote for a legislator who promised to support a certain candidate for the U.S. Senate. This, the critics said, led to a neglect of state government. Moreover, drawn-out Senate contests tended to hold up the consideration of state business.

The main criticism of legislative elections was that they distorted, or even blocked, the will of the people. Throughout the nineteenth century, a movement for popular elections had in several states taken away from legislatures the right to choose governors and presidential electors. Now attention focused on the Senate.

Toward the turn of the nineteenth century, the House on five occasions approved proposed constitutional amendments for popular Senate elections. But each time the Senate refused to act. Frustrated in Congress, the reformers began implementing various formulas for selecting Senate candidates. In some cases, party conventions endorsed nominees for the Senate, enabling the voters to know which candidates the legislature was likely to support.

Oregon took the lead in instituting nonbinding popular elections. Under a 1901 law, voters expressed their choice for senator in popular ballots. While the results of the vote had no legal force, the law required that the election returns be formally announced to the state legislature. When first tried in 1902, the Oregon legislators ignored the ballot winner. But the reformers increased their pressure, including demands that candidates for the legislature sign a pledge to vote for the winner of the popular vote. By 1908 the plan was working as its authors had hoped, with a Republican legislature electing Democrat George Chamberlain, the winner of the popular contest. Within a few years Colorado, Kansas, Minnesota, Montana, Nevada, and Oklahoma adopted the Oregon method.

It was not until June 12, 1911, that the Senate, infused with a number of Democratic and Republican progressives, approved a constitutional amendment for the popular election of senators by a vote of 64–24. The House concurred on May 13, 1912, by a vote of 238–39. The Seventeenth Amendment was then put before the states for their approval. It was ratified April 8, 1913.

In 1938, Gen. Walter Faulkner of Tennessee, left, lost his bid for a seat in the House. Here he pursues the farm vote.

The amendment did not bring a wholesale changeover in the Senate's membership. In fact, all but two of the twenty-five incumbents who sought election in November 1914 were successful. Seven other senators had retired or died.

House Elections

The House of Representatives was designed by the Founders to be the branch of government closest to the people. Its members, unlike the Senate or the president, were to be chosen directly by the voters. They were given two-year terms, so the people would have a chance to monitor and pass judgment on their activities at brief intervals. In addition, members of the House, the larger of the two legislative bodies, would have relatively small constituencies.

The lower houses of the colonial and state legislatures served as models for the U.S. House. In each state, at least one house was elected by popular vote.

The Constitution left the qualification of voters to the states, with one exception: the qualifications could be no more restrictive than for the most numerous branch of a state's own legislature. At first, property qualifications for voting were common. But a democratic trend early in the nineteenth century swept away most of these, producing practically universal white male suffrage by the 1830s.

Many delegates to the Constitutional Convention preferred annual elections for the House, believing that the body should reflect as closely as possible the wishes of the people. James Madison, however, argued for a three-year term, to let the representatives gain knowledge and experience in national and local affairs. The result was a compromise on a two-year term.

The two-year term has not been universally popular. From time to time, proposals have been made to extend it. President Lyndon B. Johnson advocated a four-year term in his 1966 State of the Union address. That proposal received more applause than any other part of his speech, but it came to nothing.

The size of the original House of Representatives was written into Article I, Section 2, of the Constitution, along with directions to apportion the House according to population, as recorded in the first census in 1790. Until then, the original thirteen states were assigned the following number of members: New Hampshire three, Massachusetts eight, Rhode Island one, Connecticut five, New York six, New Jersey four, Pennsylvania eight, Delaware one, Maryland six, Virginia ten, North Carolina five, South Carolina five, and Georgia three. This apportionment of seats—sixty-five in all—remained in effect during the First and Second Congresses (1789–1793).

Congress in 1792 determined that the House should have one representative for every 33,000 inhabitants, 105 members in all, and fixed the number for each state. This method of dividing the population of the various states by 33,000 was devised by Thomas Jefferson and known as "rejected fractions," for all remainders were disregarded. Congress enacted a new apportionment measure, including the mathematical formula to be used, every ten years (except 1920) until a permanent law became effective in 1929. *(See Chapter 5, Reapportionment and Redistricting.)*

Changing Election Practices

Five New England states at one time or another required a majority vote (50.01 percent) to win election to the House. If no candidate gained a majority, new elections were held until one contender managed to do so. Multiple races were necessary sometimes because none of the candidates could win a majority. In the Fourth District of Massachusetts in 1848–1849, for example, twelve successive elections were held to try to choose a representative. None was successful, and the district remained unrepresented in the House during the 31st Congress (1849–1851). However all of the states had phased out the requirement by the end of the nineteenth century.

Prior to ratification of the Twentieth Amendment in 1933, regular sessions of Congress began in December of odd-numbered years. There was, therefore, a long period between elections in November of even-numbered years until the beginning of the regular congressional session. As a consequence, several states moved congressional elections to odd-numbered years—a practice that continued until late in the nineteenth century.

Practices in the South

Many of the anomalies in the election of U.S. representatives have occurred in the South, where slavery, the Civil War, Reconstruction, and racial antagonisms have on occasion created special problems for the regular electoral process.

Article I, Section 2, of the Constitution contained a formula for counting slaves for apportionment purposes: every five slaves would be counted as three persons. Thus, the total population of a state to be used in determining its congressional representation would be the free population plus three-fifths of the slave population.

After the Civil War and the emancipation of the slaves, blacks were fully counted for the purposes of apportionment. The Fourteenth Amendment, ratified in 1868, required that apportionment be based on "the whole number of persons in each State. . . ." On this basis, several southern states tried to claim immediate additional representation on their readmission to the Union. Tennessee, for example, chose an extra U.S. representative, electing him at large in 1868. Virginia took similar action in 1869 and 1870, and South Carolina in 1868 and 1870. But the House declined to seat the additional representatives, ruling that the states would have to await reapportionment after the 1870 census for any changes in their representation.

Another provision of the Fourteenth Amendment provided for reducing the House representation of any state that denied the voting franchise to any male citizen over twenty-one. This effort to prevent the southern states from denying the vote to newly freed slaves was never applied. Congress instead frequently considered election challenges filed against members-elect from the South. Between 1881 and 1897, eighteen Democrats from the former Confederate states were unseated by the House, often on charges that black voting rights were abused in their districts.

Contested Elections

Decentralization of control over elections in the United States may have strengthened participatory democracy, but it has led frequently to controversy over election results. Losing candidates and their supporters believe in many cases that more voters were on their side than the official count showed. Floyd M. Riddick wrote in *The United States Congress: Organization and Procedure:* "Seldom if ever has a Congress organized without some losing candidate for a seat in either the Senate or House contesting the right of the member-elect to be senator or representative, as the case might be, as a result of the election in which the losing candidate participated." [8]

To avert partisanship, a 1798 law established procedures to settle contested House elections. After the law expired in 1804, a new law was passed in 1851 and amended in 1873 and 1875. These laws sought to give a judicial rather than partisan character to contested election proceedings, but party loyalty usually governed the outcomes.

The Federal Contested Election Act of 1969 superseded the earlier legislation. The new law, which also applied only to House contests, prescribed procedures for instituting a challenge and presenting testimony but did not establish criteria to govern decisions. It was more restrictive than earlier laws because it allowed only candidates on the ballot or bona fide write-in candidates to contest election results. Previously, anyone having an interest in a congressional election could initiate proceedings.

Senators were chosen by state legislatures until the adoption in 1913 of the Seventeenth Amendment, which provided for direct popular elections. Before then, contested senatorial elections often involved accusations of corruption in the legislatures. As of the early twenty-first century, Congress had never passed a law on contested Senate elections comparable to that for the House.

The number of contested congressional elections since 1789 probably is in the hundreds, most experts agree. But an exact number has never been determined because students of the subject disagree on what constitutes a contested election. Four contested senate elections in the twentieth century illustrate the complexity of such proceedings.

Senate Cases

Lorimer. William Lorimer, R-Ill., was elected a senator by the Illinois Legislature and took his seat on June 18, 1909. In May 1910 he requested that the Committee on Privileges and Elections examine press reports of bribery and corruption in the election. The Senate on March 1, 1911, rejected a resolution declaring that Lorimer had not been "duly and legally elected." The vote was 40–46.[9]

The case was reopened in the next Congress and the decision reversed after a specially appointed committee heard more testimony. While the committee majority favored dropping the charges, the minority pressed to overturn Lorimer's election. On June 13, 1912, the Senate adopted a resolution by a vote of 55–28 that declared the election invalid. Throughout the proceedings on Lorimer, his Republican Party held almost a 2-to-1 majority in the Senate.

Vare. Corruption also was the central issue in the case of Republican William S. Vare of Pennsylvania. During the primaries in 1926, newspapers reported illegal activities by Vare supporters to aid their candidate. Vare won the primary and the November election.

The Senate meanwhile, on May 19, 1926, had appointed a committee to investigate Pennsylvania's senatorial primaries and the fall election. Vare's Democratic rival, former secretary of labor William B. Wilson, charged that Vare's victory was won illegally. When Congress met, Vare was asked to stand aside while other senators-elect were sworn in.

Proceedings dragged on for two years. The Senate received a series of reports on the case, including one from a special committee, February 22, 1929, that said Vare, because of excessive use of money to get nominated and elected, was not entitled to a seat. On December 5, the Senate Committee on Privileges and Elections reported that Vare had received a plurality of the legal votes cast in the election. But the Senate the following day voted 58–22 to deny Vare a seat and 66–15 that Wilson had not been elected. The Pennsylvania governor later appointed Republican Joseph R. Grundy to the vacant Senate seat. Republicans controlled the Senate throughout the proceedings on Vare.

Wyman-Durkin Contest. The closest Senate election since popular voting for the chamber was instituted in 1913 occurred November 5, 1974, in New Hampshire, where Republican Louis C. Wyman led Democrat John A. Durkin by only two votes after the ballots were counted and recounted. The election spawned a long, bitter, and embarrassing dispute in the Senate covering seven months and forty-one roll-call votes. It ended when the Senate for the first time declared a vacancy because of its inability to decide an election contest.[10]

The dispute began when final unofficial returns gave Wyman a 355-vote margin over Durkin. A recount then found Durkin the winner by ten votes. The state ballot commission examined the recount and found Wyman the winner by two votes.

Wyman actually served for a short period. His predecessor, Republican senator Norris Cotton, who was retiring, resigned late in December 1974 to take advantage of a special early-retirement pension bonus. The New Hampshire governor appointed Wyman to fill the remaining sixty hours of Cotton's term, until noon January 3, 1975. Had Wyman been seated, the few extra hours would have helped establish seniority rights over other newly elected senators.

Durkin filed a petition of contest with the Senate December 27, 1974, challenging Wyman's right to the seat and defending the validity of his own recount victory. On January 5, 1975, Wyman filed a petition in the Senate urging that Durkin's petition be dismissed. He also asked that the seat be declared vacant to open the way for a new election in New Hampshire. Wyman and his supporters feared Durkin would win if the Senate, with its 61–38 Democratic majority, reviewed the ballot commission findings as the Democratic candidate requested.

The first skirmish occurred soon after the Senate convened. On January 28, the Senate turned aside Republican attempts to seat Wyman temporarily and to declare the seat vacant and voted, 58–34, to send the dispute to the Senate Rules and Administration Committee. This move had been argued for by Senate majority leader Mike Mansfield, D-Mont., and rules chair Howard W. Cannon, D-Nev., who cited the constitutional provision that each house of

Congress should be the judge of its own elections and said the Rules Committee should at least try to determine who won before calling for a new election.

Democrats also said that the conflicting rulings of the New Hampshire authorities precluded seating either of the contestants, even though Wyman had the most recent certification. Republicans claimed that precedent dictated the temporary seating of Wyman without prejudice to Durkin's challenge. But the motion to temporarily seat Wyman failed on a 34–58 vote, while a motion to declare the seat vacant lost 39–53.

The Rules Committee agreed to examine and recount the ballots in dispute. By April 25 nearly one thousand ballots had been examined, but the committee failed to agree on twenty-seven of them, splitting on 4–4 tie votes. Tie votes also occurred on eight legal and procedural issues. The eight issues and twenty-seven ballots were sent to the Senate floor to be resolved.

Floor consideration of the disputed election began June 12 with a second attempt by the Republicans to declare the seat vacant. The motion was defeated, 43–55, and a filibuster by Republicans and several southern Democrats supporting the Republican position began. An unprecedented six attempts were made to invoke cloture (close debate), but they all failed to obtain the required sixty votes. An attempt to settle one of the eight disputed issues in Wyman's favor July 15 was defeated on a 44–49 vote. After this loss, the Republicans charged that a Democratic "steamroller" was in operation and refused to allow a vote on any other issue.

The Senate began to spend less time each day on the New Hampshire dispute and returned to debate on substantive legislation. But neither side appeared ready to compromise. In the absence of any definitive Senate action, public pressure mounted for a vacancy to be declared and a new election held. Finally, Durkin relented and asked for a new election. Durkin's change of mind was a surprise to the Senate Democratic leadership, but there was a feeling of relief that the impasse had been broken. The Senate on June 30 voted 71–21 to declare the seat vacant as of August 8.

Durkin won the special September 16 election with a plurality of 27,771 votes (taking 53.6 percent of the vote) and was sworn in September 18, 1975.

Landrieu-Jenkins Contest. The last contested Senate election of the twentieth century was a throwback to those at the beginning of the century, when corruption was cited as the main issue.

At issue was a 1996 open-seat election in Louisiana that Democrat Mary L. Landrieu narrowly won over Republican state representative Louis "Woody" Jenkins by 5,788 votes out of 1.7 million cast. Republican governor Mike Foster certified Landrieu as the winner barely two weeks after the election. But Jenkins, who had the strong backing of conservatives and the Republican right, alleged that skullduggery endemic to Louisiana's Democratic Party cost him the election and propelled Landrieu to victory. He leveled no specific charges at Landrieu but alleged that systematic illegality marred the contest. Jenkins's charges included vote buying, multiple voting, fraudulent voter registration, campaign finance violations, voting machine malfunctions, election commissioner wrongdoing, and the illegal transporting of voters to the polls.

Jenkins initially pursued a challenge of the election results in the Louisiana courts, but he abandoned that effort for lack of time. Since the Senate is the final arbiter of its membership, Jenkins petitioned that body to unseat Landrieu and order a new election. The Senate Rules and Administration Committee hired two outside counsels to investigate the charges and then, under pressure from conservatives who turned the case into a cause célèbre, rejected its independent lawyers' recommendations for a limited probe. On a party-line vote April 17, the panel chose to pursue an aggressive inquiry.

Over a six-month period, the investigation was marked by partisan fits and starts. Democrats delayed the investigation until ground rules were firmly established on the use of federal investigators and on the authority to issue subpoenas. John W. Warner, R-Va., chair of the committee, directed that election-law attorneys from one of his home state's top law firms spearhead the investigation.

In June, a few weeks after the second phase of the probe had begun, Democrats withdrew from the inquiry, saying investigators had found that a political operative for Jenkins had paid witnesses to invent stories of voter fraud. The committee's minority referred incidents of alleged election tampering to the Justice Department's criminal division.

In July, over the strong objections of the panel's Democrats, Republicans decided to widen their open-ended investigation and granted Warner unprecedented subpoena power. The next month, the chair was a one-man show in New Orleans, questioning Democratic officials and representatives from the gambling industry, which had placed a gambling initiative on the ballot and had spent liberally during the 1996 campaign.

On October 1, the committee concluded there were isolated incidents of fraud, election irregularities, and lax record-keeping, but nothing on the scale of Jenkins's allegations of widespread, organized wrongdoing. The committee voted 16–0 to end its investigation, saying "the evidence collected to date does not meet the applicable burden to justify further consideration" of Jenkins's petition.

In a final action, the committee decided against reimbursing either Landrieu or Jenkins for their legal fees, as lawmakers were leery of encouraging a losing candidate to challenge an election knowing that the taxpayers would eventually foot the bill.

House Cases

William F. Willoughby stated in *Principles of Legislative Organization and Administration* in 1934: "The whole history of the handling of election contests by the House has constituted one of the major scandals of our political system." [11] He also noted that after enactment of the 1851 law on procedures for adjudicating elections, "for many years the House made little or no pretense of settling election contests on any basis of equity, political considerations in practically all cases determining the decision reached."

In 1955 John T. Dempsey, a doctoral candidate at the University of Michigan, made a case-by-case examination of the 546 contested election cases he had counted in the House. He found that only on forty-seven occasions, less than 10 percent of the total, did the controlling party award a contested seat to a member of the minority party.

Mississippi Dispute. Perhaps the most dramatic election dispute settled by the House in recent years was that of the Mississippi Five in 1965. The governor of Mississippi certified the election to the House in 1964 of four Democrats and one Republican. The Democrats were Thomas G. Abernethy, William M. Colmer, Jamie L. Whitten, and John Bell Williams; the Republican was Prentiss Walker.

Their right to be seated was contested by a biracial group, the Mississippi Freedom Democratic Party, formed originally to challenge the seating of an all-white delegation from the state to the 1964 Democratic National Convention. This group, when unsuccessful in getting its candidates on the 1964 congressional election ballot, conducted a rump election in which Annie Devine, Virginia Gray, and Fannie L. Hamer were the winners.[12]

The three women were barred when they sought entrance to the House floor. However, Speaker John W. McCormack, D-Mass., asked the regular Mississippi representatives-elect to stand aside while the other members of the House were sworn in. William F. Ryan, D-N.Y., sponsor of the challenge, contended that the regular congressional election in Mississippi was invalid because blacks had been systematically prevented from voting. A resolution to seat the regular Mississippi delegation was adopted on January 4, 1965, by a voice vote.

Later that year Congress enacted the Voting Rights Act of 1965, which contained strict sanctions against states that practiced discrimination against minority voters.

McCloskey-McIntyre Contest. Three 1984 House races were so close that the losers contested the results. One race, in Indiana, led to four months of acrimony between Democrats and Republicans over what appeared to be the closest House contest in the twentieth century. Debate on the race took up far more time than almost any other issue the House considered in 1985.

After the November 6 election, incumbent Democrat Frank McCloskey appeared to have won reelection to his Indiana Eighth District seat by seventy-two votes. But correction of an arithmetical error (ballots in two precincts were counted twice) gave Republican challenger Richard D. McIntyre an apparent thirty-four-vote victory. On that basis, the Indiana secretary of state December 14 certified McIntyre the winner.

But when Congress convened January 3, 1985, the Democratic-controlled House refused to seat McIntyre, voting instead to declare the seat vacant pending an investigation of alleged irregularities in the election. Three times after that—in February, March, and April—Republicans pushed the seating of McIntyre to a vote, losing each time while picking up no more than a handful of votes from the Democrats.

A recount completed January 22 showed McIntyre's lead had increased to 418 votes, after more than 4,800 ballots were thrown out for technical reasons. But a House Administration Committee task force, with auditors from the General Accounting Office, conducted its own recount and, on a 2–1 partisan split, found McCloskey the winner by four votes. Republicans then tried to get a new election by declaring the seat vacant. Their attempt lost, 200–229, although nineteen Democrats joined 181 Republicans in voting for a new election.

The next day, before the House Administration Committee's recommendation to seat McCloskey came to a vote, Republicans moved to send the issue back to the panel with orders to count thirty-two controversial absentee ballots that the task force had decided, on a 2–1 vote, not to count. That motion was rejected by a 183–246 vote.

The House then approved the resolution to seat McCloskey 236–190, with ten Democrats joining the Republicans in voting against it. GOP members walked out of the House chamber in protest, accusing Democrats of stealing the election.

On February 7, a federal district court in Indiana dismissed a suit filed by McIntyre challenging recount procedures in two of the district's counties and ruled that the House alone was responsible for determining the validity of contested ballots.

A U.S. district court judge in Washington, D.C., dismissing a separate suit brought by McIntyre against House Democrats and House officers, ruled March 1 that the House had the constitutional right to judge its own membership.

The Supreme Court May 28 refused to get involved in the dispute. Without a dissenting vote, it denied Indiana permission to sue the House in the Supreme Court.

Ultimately, McIntyre challenged McCloskey to a rematch in 1986, but he lost by more than 13,000 votes.

Other 1984 Contested Elections. Results in two other close House races also were contested, but those challenges, in Guam and Idaho, were unsuccessful. On July 24, the

House agreed by voice vote to a resolution dismissing a challenge by Democrat Antonio Borja Won Pat, the former nonvoting delegate from Guam, against Republican Ben Blaz. Won Pat, who had represented Guam in Congress since 1973, had lost the November 1984 election by about 350 votes. Won Pat had protested, among other things, that Blaz had not won an absolute majority of the votes cast, as required by law.

On October 2, the House threw out a challenge by former representative George Hansen, R-Idaho, against Democrat Richard H. Stallings. Hansen, who was convicted in 1984 of filing false financial disclosure forms, charged, among other things, vote fraud in his 170-vote loss to Stallings. The House dismissed the challenge by a 247–4 vote, with 169 members, mostly Republicans, voting "present."

Sanchez-Dornan Contest. Thirteen months of acrimonious debate with ethnic overtones ended in February 1998 when the Republican-led House refused to overturn the election of California Democrat Loretta Sanchez. Republican Robert K. Dornan claimed that Sanchez had unseated him by 984 votes in 1996 because of a rash of illegal voting by noncitizens in his demographically changing Orange County district. Sanchez, who was Hispanic, contended Dornan's charges were racially motivated.

A three-member task force within the House Oversight Committee conducted the investigation. It focused particularly on Hermandad Mexicana Nacional, a group that helped register Hispanic voters in California in 1996. The task force found evidence of 748 illegal votes cast by noncitizens, a total that fell short of Sanchez's margin of victory. But Republicans said the results showed that Dornan's challenge was not frivolous and that the GOP was not unfairly targeting Hispanics.

As the House probe proceeded through the fall of 1997, Dornan began using his privileges as a former member to visit the House floor. After a verbal altercation with Robert Menendez, D-N.J., about the probe, Dornan's floor access was denied. More than one hundred Republicans joined a nearly unanimous bloc of Democrats to adopt a resolution that barred Dornan from the House floor or surrounding areas until the contested election was resolved.

Meanwhile, Democrats were raising a ruckus on the House floor, introducing a slew of privileged resolutions to stop the probe, charging that it targeted Hispanic voters. While none of the resolutions succeeded, Democrats did bring action on the floor to a halt several times. Minority Leader Richard A. Gephardt, D-Mo., in October offered a privileged resolution calling for an end to the probe. The House rejected the proposal, 204–222.

Throughout the following months Republicans and Democrats conducted behind-the-scenes talks to find a face-saving way to end the probe. Finally in February 1998 the House ended the investigation by agreeing there had been vote fraud in Sanchez's election but not enough to justify continuation of Dornan's challenge. The House first defeated, 194–215, a Democratic motion to return the resolution to the House Oversight Committee and strip most of its findings of election fraud. Then the House voted 378–33 for a resolution to drop the inquiry into Dornan's challenge. All thirty-three votes against the resolution were cast by Republicans.

Dornan subsequently sought to regain his seat in the 1998 general election, but he lost to Sanchez by nearly 15,000 votes.

NOTES

1. V. O. Key Jr., *Politics, Parties, and Pressure Groups,* 5th ed. (New York: Crowell, 1964), 378.
2. Letter to Francis Hopkinson, March 3, 1789. Quoted in Elizabeth Frost, ed., *The Bully Pulpit: Quotations from America's Presidents* (New York: Facts on File, 1988), 149.
3. *The Federalist Papers,* with an introduction by Clinton Rossiter (New York: New American Library, 1961), 80.
4. Alan Ehrenhalt, *The United States of Ambition: Politicians, Power, and the Pursuit of Office* (New York: Times Books, 1991), 23.
5. William H. Flanigan and Nancy H. Zingale, *Political Behavior of the American Electorate* (Washington, D.C.: CQ Press, 1991), 43–44.
6. Ibid., 68, 83.
7. Lydia Saad, "Independents Rank as Largest U.S. Political Group" (Gallup News Service, April 9, 1999), 1–3. Exit polls, CNN.com/Election/2006.
8. Floyd M. Riddick, *The United States Congress: Organization and Procedure* (Washington, D.C.: National Capitol Publishers, 1949), 12.
9. George H. Haynes, *The Senate of the United States* (Boston, Mass.: Houghton-Mifflin, 1938), 131.
10. For more background, see *Congressional Quarterly Almanac 1975,* 699.
11. William F. Willoughby, *Principles of Legislative Organization and Administration* (Washington, D.C.: Brookings Institution, 1934), 277.
12. For more background, see *Congressional Quarterly Almanac 1965,* 609.

SELECTED BIBLIOGRAPHY

Abramson, Paul R., John H. Aldrich, and David W. Rohde. *Change and Continuity in the 2004 and 2006 Elections.* Washington, D.C.: CQ Press, 2007.

Bibby, John F., and Brian F. Shaffner. *Politics, Parties, and Elections in America.* 6th ed. Boston, Mass.: Thomson-Wadsworth, 2007.

Bibby, John F., and L. Sandy Maisel. *Two Parties, or More? The American Party System.* 2nd ed. Boulder, Colo.: Westview Press, 2003.

Brady, David W., and Craig Volden. *Revolving Gridlock: Politics and Policy from Carter to George W. Bush.* 2nd ed. Boulder, Colo.: Westview Press, 2005.

Burden, Barry C., and David C. Kimball. *Why Americans Split Their Tickets: Campaigns, Competition, and Divided Government.* Ann Arbor: University of Michigan Press, 2002.

Ceaser, James W., and Andrew E. Busch. *Red over Blue: The 2004 Elections and American Politics.* Lanham, Md.: Rowman & Littlefield Publishers, 2005.

Cohen, Jeffrey E., Richard Fleisher, and Paul Kantor. *American Political Parties: Decline or Resurgence?* Washington, D.C.: CQ Press, 2001.

Cox, Gary W. *The Politics of Divided Government.* Edited by Samuel Kernell. Boulder, Colo.: Westview Press, 1991.

Ehrenhalt, Alan. *The United States of Ambition: Politicians, Power, and the Pursuit of Office.* New York: Times Books, 1991.

Eilperin, Juliet. *Fight Club Politics: How Partisanship Is Poisoning the House of Representatives.* Lanham, Md.: Rowman & Littlefield, 2006.

Flanigan, William H., and Nancy H. Zingale. *Political Behavior of the American Electorate.* 11th ed. Washington, D.C.: CQ Press, 2006.

Fiorina, Morris P. *Divided Government.* 2nd ed. Boston, Mass.: Allyn and Bacon, 1996.

Glaser, James M. *The Hand of the Past in Contemporary Southern Politics.* New Haven, Conn.: Yale University Press, 2005.

Green, John C., and Daniel J. Coffey. *The State of the Parties: The Changing Role of Contemporary American Parties.* 5th ed. Lanham, Md.: Rowan and Littlefield, 2007.

Herrnson, Paul S., Colton C. Campbell, Marni Ezra, and Stephen K. Medvic. *Guide to Political Campaigns in America.* Washington, D.C.: CQ Press, 2005.

Hetherington, Marc J., and William J. Keefe. *Parties, Politics, and Public Policy in America.* 10th ed. Washington, D.C.: CQ Press, 2007.

Jacobson, Gary C. *The Politics of Congressional Elections.* 6th ed. New York: Pearson Longman, 2004.

Kahn, Kim F., and Patrick J. Kenney. *No Holds Barred: Negativity in U.S. Senate Campaigns.* Upper Saddle River, N.J.: Pearson/Prentice Hall, 2004.

Ladd, Everett Carll, and Charles D. Hadley. *Transformation of the American Party System.* 2nd ed. New York: Norton, 1978.

Maisel, L. Sandy, ed. *The Parties Respond: Changes in American Parties and Campaigns.* 4th ed. Boulder, Colo.: Westview Press, 2002.

Mayhew, David R. *Electoral Realignments: A Critique of an American Genre.* New Haven, Conn.: Yale University Press, 2002.

McDonald, Michael D., and Ian Budge. *Elections, Parties, Democracy: Conferring the Median Mandate.* New York: Oxford University Press, 2005.

Nelson, Michael. *The Elections of 2004.* Washington, D.C.: CQ Press, 2005.

Nichols, Roy F. *The Invention of the American Political Parties.* New York: Macmillan, 1967.

Norris, Pippa. *Democratic Phoenix: Reinventing Political Activism.* New York: Cambridge University Press, 2002.

Paulson, Arthur C. *Electoral Realignment and the Outlook for American Democracy.* Boston, Mass.: Northeastern University Press, 2007.

Reichley, James. *The Life of the Parties: A History of American Political Parties.* New York: Free Press, 2000.

Sabato, Larry, and Bruce A. Larson. *The Party's Just Begun: Shaping Political Parties for America's Future.* 2nd ed. New York: Longman, 2001.

Schattschneider, E. E. *Party Government.* New York: Holt, Rinehart and Winston, 1942.

———. *The Semisovereign People: A Realist's View of Democracy in America.* New York: Holt, Rinehart and Winston, 1960.

Schlesinger, Arthur M., Jr., ed. *History of U.S. Political Parties.* 4 vols. New York: Bowker, 1981.

Schlesinger, Joseph A. *Political Parties and the Winning of Office.* Ann Arbor: University of Michigan Press, 1991.

Schofield, Norman, and Itai Sened. *Multiparty Democracy: Elections and Legislative Politics.* New York: Cambridge University Press, 2006.

Shea, Daniel M., and Michael J. Burton. *Campaign Craft: The Strategies, Tactics, and Art of Political Campaign Management.* 3rd ed. Westport, Conn.: Praeger Publishers, 2006.

Shea, Daniel M., and John C. Green. *The State of the Parties: The Changing Role of Contemporary American Parties.* 2nd ed. Lanham, Md.: Rowan and Littlefield, 1996.

Stonecash, Jeffrey M. *Political Parties Matter: Realignment and the Return of Partisan Voting.* Boulder, Colo.: Lynne Rienner Publishers, 2006.

Sundquist, James L. *Dynamics of the Party System: Alignment and Realignment of Political Parties in the United States.* Rev. ed. Washington, D.C.: Brookings Institution, 1983.

Tarrance, V. Lance, Jr., Walter De Vries, and Donna L. Mosher. *Checked and Balanced: How Ticket-Splitters Are Shaping the New Balance of Power in American Politics.* Grand Rapids, Mich.: Eerdmans, 1998.

Theriault, Sean M. *The Power of the People: Congressional Competition, Public Attention, and Voter Retribution.* Columbus: Ohio State University Press, 2005.

Ware, Alan. *The American Direct Primary: Party Institutionalization and Transformation in the North.* New York: Cambridge University Press, 2002.

Wattenberg, Martin P. *The Decline of American Political Parties: 1952–1996.* Cambridge, Mass.: Harvard University Press, 1998.

Wayne, Stephen J. *Is This Any Way to Run a Democratic Election? Debating American Electoral Politics.* Boston, Mass.: Houghton Mifflin, 2001.

chapter 3

Who Gets Elected

Americans elect a new Congress on the first Tuesday after the first Monday in November of even-numbered years. Early the following January the elected representatives and senators begin their first session of the new two-year Congress. Those elected November 7, 2006, for instance, were sworn in January 4, 2007, on the opening day of the 110th Congress. They included many new faces—ten new senators (nine Democrats and one Republican) and fifty-five new representatives (forty-two Democrats and thirteen Republicans)—as occurs in each Congress, along with the seasoned hands and those with tenure that fell in between.

As an institution, Congress has suffered public criticism almost since the nation's beginnings. Alexis de Tocqueville, the astute French visitor of the late 1820s, observed the "vulgar demeanor" of the House of Representatives, where often he could not detect even one "distinguished man." In contrast, as he wrote in his classic *Democracy in America,* the Senate was "composed of eloquent advocates, distinguished generals, wise magistrates, and statesmen of note, whose arguments would do honor to the most remarkable parliamentary debates of Europe."[1]

Subsequent views of the entire Congress often have been no more charitable than de Tocqueville's opinion of the House. Gallup polls measuring American's trust and confidence in governmental institutions show Congress ranking poorly compared with the presidency and the U.S. Supreme Court. In a June 2006 Gallup poll, 19 percent of respondents said they had "a great deal" or "quite a lot" of confidence in Congress as an institution. For the presidency the corresponding response was 33 percent; for the Supreme Court, 40 percent. Thirty-two percent said they had "very little" confidence in Congress, compared with 25 percent for the presidency and 15 percent for the Court.

Moreover, of the fifteen categories Gallup presented to respondents, Congress rated higher than only big business and health maintenance organizations in the combined categories of "a great deal" and "quite a lot" of confidence. A related Gallup question, in early 2007, asking respondents if they approved of the job Congress was doing, showed that only 35 percent approved while 55 percent disapproved.[2]

These polls, although revealing volatility in public attitudes, have shown over many years a consistent skepticism about Congress. Paradoxically, voters generally return incumbents to office, indicating a more generous attitude among voters toward their own representatives and senators than the institution as a whole. Only in years when a broad-based national concern arises about specific issues, such as war, the economy, or congressional performance, have many incumbents been threatened with losing their jobs. This occurred in 1994, when Republicans swept Democrats out of control of Congress, and in 2006, when Democrats did the same to the GOP.

In the modern era the power of incumbency has remained strong with the turnover rate from deaths, resignations, and election defeats averaging about 10 percent or less, historically an exceptionally low level. In the 2006 elections, for example, 94 percent of House incumbents who ran were reelected. In the Senate, the reelection rate was 78.6 percent. Even so, the turnover record was high by recent standards. In the House the number of incumbents who lost was the highest since 1994. In the Senate in 2006 the six incumbents who lost represented the largest number in a general election since 1980, when nine were defeated.

An incumbent's appeal rests on more than the person's record in Congress and is significantly influenced by the public image projected through television, direct mail, telephone banks, the Internet, and other devices used in election campaigns. But projecting that image, particularly through television advertising, is extremely expensive, requiring any candidate to raise substantial campaign funds. Incumbents are particularly well placed to raise money from special interest groups, whether business, labor, or ideological, as a result of their service in Congress and participation in important decisions that may affect the donors' organizations. This incumbency advantage generally tilts voter recognition toward the member and away from a challenger who often will have more difficulty raising money from the interest groups.

Incumbency during the 1990s, however, provided less protection, particularly in the House. In the 1992 and 1994 congressional elections more than eighty incumbents lost reelection bids. Voters were increasingly wary of long-service incumbents, labeled "career politicians" by their critics. Many challengers ran antigovernment campaigns presenting the absence of having held elected office as a reason to be elected. Some challengers vowed to serve only a limited number of terms to avoid becoming out of touch with the voters, although some winners by the end of their pledged terms found reasons to run again.

As congressional scholars Roger H. Davidson and Walter J. Oleszek have written: "During the early 1990s political unrest, Capitol Hill scandals, an economic recession (in 1992), and voter anger at those in charge (the Democrats and President Bill Clinton in 1994) and further partisan shifts conspired to produce the largest turnover in two generations." Davidson and Oleszek also noted that "the anti-incumbent atmosphere emboldened many strategically minded nonincumbents to try for House or Senate seats. Even so, turnover resulted less from electoral defeats than from retirements (some of them involuntary, to be sure). In those years of upheaval (1990 to 1994) 194 members retired and 112 were defeated for reelection." [3]

The anti-incumbent mood of the 1990s was clearly evident when the 107th Congress convened in January 2001. Almost two-thirds of the members of the House, 65 percent, were first elected in 1992 or later. Two out of every three representatives had not held congressional office during any of the most momentous events of the post–World War II years. They had never experienced an economic recession, had not been part of the long twilight struggle of the cold war, did not have to take positions or vote on the vast changes brought by the 1960s civil rights movement, were not in office when the Soviet Union broke up, and did not have to vote on waging war against Iraq in the Persian Gulf. Almost half of the House in 2001—48 percent—had never served in a Congress that was not Republican-controlled. Turnover in the Senate was less dramatic but significant nevertheless. As the 107th Congress began, forty-five senators had been in the chamber for six years or less, a figure not matched since 1981.

In 1994 a landmark election swept Republicans to power in both chambers. Democrats had controlled either the House or Senate, and usually both, since 1955. Since 1933, when the Great Depression realigned political power, Republicans had managed to control both houses only twice—in the 80th Congress (1947–1949) and the 83rd Congress (1953–1955). Republicans also held a Senate majority from 1981 to 1987.

In congressional elections after 1994, the power of incumbency was seen again as sitting members won reelection at rates in the high 90 percent range. But like 1994, incumbency was less a shield in 2006 when voters expressed their displeasure with—more than any other issue—the continuing and seemingly intractable war in Iraq. The poll ratings of the party's president, George W. Bush, who had launched the war in 2003, were at an all-time low. Even so, the GOP held on to many seats that were thought to be toss-ups. Moreover, some losses were expected because historically most parties that hold the White House experience losses—sometimes large losses—in the midterm elections six years into the president's term. In that light, some scholars thought the Republican Party managed relatively well in 2006.

CHARACTERISTICS OF MEMBERS

Whether the turnover is large or small, a certain uniformity pervades Congress. Congress has been dominated since its inception by middle-aged white men with backgrounds in law or business. Their levels of income and education have consistently been above the national average. But for many of the lawmakers in the first decade of the twenty-first century, business occupations were less prominent than in many previous Congresses. Ethics rules increasingly limited the amount and type of income that can be earned outside of Congress. Moreover, serving in Congress had become a full-time job. Since at least the 1970s Congress attracted career politicians, whose primary earnings came from government service.

Ever so slowly, other changes crept into the makeup of Congress. The numbers of women, African American, and Hispanic American members increased in the latter decades of the twentieth century, although still not in proportion to their share of the total population. Of the 535 members at the beginning of the 110th Congress in 2007, eighty-seven were women, forty-one were black, twenty-six were Hispanic, six were of Asian or Pacific Island descent, and one was of Native American heritage. The election of Sen. Barack Obama, D-Ill., made him the third African American popularly elected to the Senate in U.S. history. In addition, of the five nonvoting delegates sent to the House, three were women, two were black, one was Hispanic, and one was of Pacific Island descent.

Average Age

The average age of members of Congress went up substantially between the post–Civil War period and the 1950s, but it remained fairly constant until the mid-1970s. In the 41st Congress (1869–1871), the average was 44.6 years; by the 85th Congress (1957-1959), it was 53.8. During the next eighteen years, the average fluctuated only slightly. But when the 94th Congress met in January 1975, the average age was 50.9 years. The difference was made in the House, where ninety-two freshmen members reduced the average age of representatives to 49.8 years, the first time since World War II that the average in either chamber had fallen below 50.0.

TABLE 3-1 **Age Structure of Congress, 1949–2007**

Year	House	Senate	Congress
1949	51.0	58.5	53.8
1951	52.0	56.6	53.0
1953	52.0	56.6	53.0
1955	51.4	57.2	52.2
1957	52.9	57.9	53.8
1959	51.7	57.1	52.7
1961	52.2	57.0	53.2
1963	51.7	56.8	52.7
1965	50.5	57.7	51.9
1967	50.8	57.7	52.1
1969	52.2	56.6	53.0
1971	51.9	56.4	52.7
1973	51.1	55.3	52.0
1975	49.8	55.5	50.9
1977	49.3	54.7	50.3
1979	48.8	52.7	49.5
1981	48.4	52.5	49.2
1983	45.5	53.4	47.0
1985	49.7	54.2	50.5
1987	50.7	54.4	52.5
1989	52.1	55.6	52.8
1991	52.8	57.2	53.6
1993	51.7	58.0	52.9
1995	50.9	58.4	52.2
1997	51.6	57.5	52.7
1999	52.6	58.3	53.7
2001	55.4	59.8	54.4
2003	54.0	59.7	55.5
2005	55.0	60.4	56.0
2007	56.0	61.2	57.1

NOTE: House and Senate totals reflect the average ages of members at the beginning of each Congress.

SOURCE: Congressional Quarterly.

The 96th Congress (1979–1981) was the youngest since 1949; the overall average age for both chambers had slipped to 49.5 years. It dropped again in January 1981, when the House had eight members under thirty, the most since World War II. The younger trend bottomed out in 1983 when the average hit 47.0 years.

During the next twenty years the average age climbed gradually, reaching a record high 57.1 years at the start of 110th Congress. *(See Table 3-1, p. 47.)*

That aging trend was partly attributable to the nation's population as a whole. But low turnover in Congress was also a big factor. The youngest Congress of the 1990s was the 104th when the Republicans took control. The average age in January 1995 was 52.2, with House members averaging 50.9 years. By January 2007 the average age had risen to 56.0 in the House and 61.2 in the Senate—both were record highs.

Occupations

The legal profession was long the dominant occupational background of members of Congress since its beginning. In the First Congress, more than one-third of the House members had legal training. The proportion of members with a legal background crested at 70 percent in 1840 but remained high. From 1950 to the mid-1970s it was in the 55–60 percent range. *(See Table 3-2, p. 48.)*

The first significant decline in members with a law background began with the 96th Congress. Although sixty-five of the one hundred senators were lawyers in 1979, lawyers in the House made up less than a majority for the first time in at least thirty years. The situation continued through the 1990s. When the 109th Congress convened in January 2005, 178 representatives and 64 senators were lawyers, or about 45 percent of both chambers. In 2005, for the first time, business or banking, which had long been the second most listed category by members, overtook law. In the 109th Congress, 205 representatives and 40 senators claimed a business or banking background, or nearly 46 percent. Two years later, at the start of the 110th Congress, the rankings reversed again. In January 2007, 162 House members and 59 senators listed law as a profession, a little over 41 percent of the membership. Meanwhile, 166 House members and 27 senators put themselves in the business and banking category, dropping the overall ratio to 36 percent of all members.

However, another category topped both law and business in 2005 and highlighted the trend toward career politicians. (Note that some members have had more than one occupation.) In the 109th Congress, 254 members, or 47 percent, listed backgrounds in public service or politics. By 2007, that number had dropped markedly to 206 members, or 38.5 percent. This change reflected the composition of the large freshman Democratic class. Roughly half, nineteen of forty-two Democrats sworn in for the first time in January 2007, had never before held political office, indicating to many observers the voters' displeasure with status quo politics in Congress. Many new members stood out for their different backgrounds. The group included a social worker, a wind-turbine executive, an allergist, two college professors, a publisher of an alternative newspaper, and a former professional football quarterback. But there were hardly any political neophytes among Republican freshmen.

David T. Canon, a political scientist who studies Congress, said the preponderance of Democrats without a political background and Republicans with those credentials is consistent with historical patterns. If an election goes strongly for one party, as it did for Democrats in 2006, persons elected for the first time often have included many political amateurs. He noted that the Republican freshman class of 1994, when the GOP was swept into control of the House, also had a large contingent of such amateurs.

But even with the occasional large class of members with little political background, the long-term trend of a new breed of legislator that emerged in the 1970s remained true:

TABLE 3-2 **Members' Occupations, 110th Congress**

	House			Senate			Congress
Occupation	Dem.	Rep.	Total	Dem.	Rep.	Total	Total
Actor/entertainer	3	0	3	1	0	1	4
Aeronautics	0	2	2	0	0	0	2
Agriculture	8	15	23	2	4	6	29
Arts/creative	0	1	1	2	0	2	3
Business/banking	70	96	166	9	18	27	193
Clergy	1	2	3	0	0	0	3
Education	55[a]	33	88	8[a]	6	14	102
Engineering	2	1	3	0	1	1	4
Health care	6	3	9	0	0	0	9
Journalism	3	4	7	4	4	8	15
Labor/blue collar	7	6	13	2	1	3	16
Law	94	68	162	32	27	59	221
Law enforcement	7	3	10	0	0	0	10
Medicine	3	10	13	0	3	3	16
Military	2	2	4	0	1	1	5
Professional sports	1	0	1	0	1	1	2
Public service/politics	106	68	174	19	13	32	206
Real estate	4	32	36	1	2	3	39
Technical/skilled labor	1	1	2	0	0	0	2
Miscellaneous	2	0	2	0	0	0	2

NOTES: Because some members have more than one occupation, totals are larger than the number of members. a. Includes the Senate's two Independents, Bernard Sanders of Vermont and Joseph I. Lieberman of Connecticut. Both caucus with the Democrats.

SOURCE: Congressional Quarterly.

the career politician whose primary earnings had always come from political office at the local, state, or federal level. This trend became possible because states and localities had begun to think of political positions as full-time jobs and had raised salaries accordingly. In addition, the demands of modern political campaigns left less time for the pursuit of other careers. This trend continued through the following decades. In the 109th Congress 72 percent of new House members and 88 percent of new senators had held prior office. The Senate class included several experienced former House members. A few years earlier, in the 107th Congress, only 64 percent of new senators had held previous office. Even in the 110th Congress, the amateur group was confined to the House. All ten of the freshman senators held other political offices, including three who had served in the House.

The number of members with military experience declined dramatically into the twenty-first century, in part a reflection of the advent of an all-volunteer army in 1973. At the start of the 91st Congress in 1969, 73 percent of members were military veterans. By 1991 the percentage of veterans in Congress dropped to 52 percent. At the start of the 109th Congress in 2005, only 140, or 26 percent, cited military service.

In 2007, at the start of the 110th Congress, only 24 percent of the members of Congress were veterans: 101 in the House and 29 in the Senate. Still, there were two notable freshmen: Democratic representatives Joe Sestak, a retired Navy vice admiral who was the highest-ranking military officer ever to serve in Congress, and Patrick J. Murphy, of Pennsylvania. Murphy was the only member of Congress who was a veteran of the Iraq war that began in 2003.

Other fields represented by members of the 110th Congress included real estate (thirty-nine), agriculture (twenty-nine), medicine or physician (sixteen), and journalism (fifteen). Members of the clergy continue to be underrepresented in Congress. Only a handful of Protestant ministers have served in Congress, and no Catholic priest had done so until 1971, when Rep. Robert F. Drinan, D-Mass., a Jesuit, took a House seat. (Father Gabriel Richard was the nonvoting delegate of the Territory of Michigan from 1823 to 1825.) Drinan did not seek a sixth term in 1980 after Pope John Paul II that year ordered priests not to hold public office. The pope's directive also prompted Robert J. Cornell, a Catholic priest and former House member, to halt his political comeback bid in Wisconsin. Cornell, a Democrat elected in 1974, served two terms before he was defeated in 1978. Only three members of the House listed their occupation as clergy in the 110th Congress.

Religious Affiliations

Among religious groups, Protestants have made up nearly three-fourths of the membership of both houses in recent

Rep. Patrick Murphy, D-Pa., here with House Speaker Nancy Pelosi, in 2006 became the first Iraq war veteran elected to Congress.

In 2006 Rep. Keith Ellison, D-Minn., became the first Muslim elected to Congress. He was also the first African American from Minnesota to be elected to the House.

years. However, Roman Catholics form the biggest single religious group—a distinction they have held since taking the lead from Methodists in 1965. In the 110th Congress Roman Catholics made up the largest religious congregation in both chambers with a total of 153.

Among Protestant denominations, Baptists were most numerous (sixty-seven), followed by Methodists (sixty-three), Presbyterians (forty-four), Episcopalians (thirty-eight), and Lutherans (nineteen). There were forty-three Jewish members. In all, members listed affiliations with some twenty religious groups. Forty-seven simply listed "Protestant," and only six did not specify a religious preference.[4]

WOMEN IN CONGRESS

A total of 239 women had been elected or appointed to Congress by the beginning of 2007. Of these, 236 served (two women were never sworn in and one resigned her seat the day after she was sworn in)—203 in the House only, 26 in the Senate only, and 7 in both chambers. All but one of those seven—Margaret Chase Smith of Maine—were in the Senate at the beginning of the 110th Congress. The climb in women's membership had been long and slow, but it continued to accelerate as the twenty-first century got under way. Significantly, women were enjoying more positions of influence in both chambers as their seniority pushed them toward high-ranking committee positions, including chairs.

Rep. Debbie Wasserman-Schultz, D-Fla., shown here with Rep. John Murtha, D-Pa., is one of a handful of mothers raising young children while serving in the House or Senate.

But the crowning achievement came in 2007 when Nancy Pelosi, a California Democrat, became the first female Speaker of the House.

The first woman to be a member of Congress was Rep. Jeannette Rankin, R-Mont., elected in 1916. Her state gave women the right to vote before the Nineteenth Amendment to the Constitution enfranchising women was ratified in 1920. Rankin's election was not followed by a surge of women members, even after women received the vote. The first notable increase came in the 71st Congress (1929–1931), when nine women served in the House. The number had scarcely more than doubled by the 87th Congress (1961–1963), when twenty women—two senators and eighteen representatives—were members.

Women's membership declined slightly after that and did not reach twenty again until the 95th Congress (1977–1979). The total went down to seventeen in the next Congress but was up to twenty-three in the 97th Congress (1981–1983). Since then, the number has increased in all but two Congresses, and in those two the total remained the same as in the previous Congress. *(See Table 3-3, p. 51.)*

The elections of 1992 saw a large jump in the number of women running for and being elected to Congress. The 103rd Congress, which opened in 1993, included forty-eight women in the House, an increase of nineteen, and seven in the Senate, an increase of four.

Several factors contributed to the success of these candidates. Many capitalized on an unusually large number of retirements to run in open seats. They also benefited from reapportionment, which created dozens of opportunities for newcomers in the South and West. Another factor was public dissatisfaction with Congress, which allowed women to portray themselves positively as outsiders. The Senate's questioning of law professor Anita F. Hill's accusations of sexual harassment in the 1991 confirmation hearings of Supreme Court associate justice nominee Clarence Thomas also had an impact. The televised image of an all-male Senate Judiciary panel sharply questioning Hill brought home dramatically to many women their lack of representation in Congress.

The 109th Congress opened in 2005 with an all-time high of seventy-nine women (sixty-five in the House—excluding nonvoting delegates—and fourteen in the Senate). Later special House elections added three more women. Two years later in the 110th Congress there were eighty-seven women in office: sixteen in the Senate and seventy-one in the House. More than two-thirds were Democrats.

Several women have served out unexpired terms of less than one year. Rebecca L. Felton, the first woman to serve in the Senate, did so for only one day. Felton, a Georgia Democrat, was appointed October 1, 1922, to fill the Senate vacancy created by the death of Thomas E. Watson. She was not sworn in until November 21, and the next day yielded her seat to Walter F. George, who had meanwhile been elected to fill the vacancy.

TABLE 3-3 **Women in Congress, 1947–2007**

Congress	Senate	House
80th (1947–1949)	1	7
81st (1949–1951)	1	9
82nd (1951–1953)	1	10
83rd (1953–1955)	1	12
84th (1955–1957)	1	17
85th (1957–1959)	1	15
86th (1959–1961)	1	17
87th (1961–1963)	2	18
88th (1963–1965)	2	12
89th (1965–1967)	2	11
90th (1967–1969)	1	10
91st (1969–1971)	1	10
92nd (1971–1973)	1	13
93rd (1973–1975)	1	16
94th (1975–1977)	0	17
95th (1977–1979)	2	18
96th (1979–1981)	1	16
97th (1981–1983)	2	19
98th (1983–1985)	2	22
99th (1985–1987)	2	22
100th (1987–1989)	2	23
101st (1989–1991)	2	28
102nd (1991–1993)	3	29
103rd (1993–1995)	7	48
104th (1995–1997)	8	48
105th (1997–1999)	9	51
106th (1999–2001)	9	56
107th (2001–2003)	13	61
108th (2003–2005)	14	60
109th (2005–2007)	14	67
110th (2007–2009)	16	71

NOTE: House totals reflect the number of women members at the start of each Congress and exclude nonvoting delegates.

Gladys Pyle, a South Dakota Republican, was elected November 9, 1938, to fill the unexpired term of Rep. Peter Norbeck, who died in office. But his term ended the following January 3 before Congress convened and thus Pyle apparently never took the oath of office.

Former first lady Hillary Rodham Clinton captured a Senate seat in 2000, representing the State of New York, as her husband was completing his second term as president. She was the first first lady to serve in Congress. In 2006 she won reelection handily and in 2007 began pursuing the Democratic nomination for president.

The "Widow's Mandate"

In many jurisdictions it became customary for the officeholder's party to run his widow for the seat in the hope of tapping a sympathy vote. Sometimes she filled the office by brief appointment until the governor or party leaders could agree on a candidate.

The "widow's mandate" marked the beginning of political careers for some women. Edith Nourse Rogers, a Massachusetts Republican, entered the House after her husband died in 1925 and remained there until her death in 1960. Margaret Chase Smith filled her late husband's House seat in 1940 and went on to serve four terms in the Senate (1949–1973). Hattie W. Caraway, an Arkansas Democrat, who was appointed to the Senate seat of her late husband in 1931, and was reelected in 1932 and 1938.

Rep. Charlotte T. Reid, R-Ill., and Rep. Marilyn Lloyd, D-Tenn., became their parties' nominees when their husbands died between the primary and general elections (in 1962 and 1974, respectively). As women have become more active in politics at all levels, the congressional tradition of the widow's mandate has weakened.

In the 110th Congress, four women held the House seats of their late husbands. Jo Ann Emerson, R-Mo., first won a special election in 1996 to fill out the term of her husband, Bill Emerson. Two years later, Republican Mary Bono won the California seat that had been held by her husband, former pop singer and businessman Sonny Bono, who was killed in a skiing accident. Lois Capps, D-Calif., in 1998 won the Santa Barbara district of her husband, Walter Capps, who died in 1997. Rep. Doris Matsui, D-Calif., entered Congress in 2005 after the death of her husband, Rep. Robert T. Matsui.

Perhaps the most unusual case was that of Democrat Jean Carnahan of Missouri, who was appointed to a Senate seat in 2001 that was won on November 7, 2000, by her husband, Missouri Gov. Mel Carnahan, who died three weeks earlier in a plane crash. She later lost the 2002 special election to fill the remaining four years of the term.

Marriages have also linked members of Congress. Rep. Emily Taft Douglas, D-Ill., was elected to Congress in 1944, four years before her husband, Sen. Paul H. Douglas, D-Ill. Another woman, Rep. Martha Keys, D-Kan., married Rep. Andrew Jacobs, D-Ind., in 1976. This marriage between colleagues was the first of its kind in congressional history. Rep. Olympia J. Snowe, R-Maine, in 1989 married Maine Gov. John R. McKernan Jr., a former U.S. representative. Rep. Marjorie Margolies-Mezvinsky, D-Pa., was the wife of former Iowa Rep. Edward M. Mezvinsky when she was elected to Congress in 1992. Reps. Susan Molinari, R-N.Y., and Bill Paxon, R-N.Y., were married in 1994. Nancy Landon Kassebaum, after she left office in 1997, married former Sen. Howard H. Baker Jr., R-Tenn. Beginning her first term in 2003, Sen. Elizabeth Dole, R-N.C., was the wife of former Senate Majority Leader Bob Dole, R-Kan. On September 7, 2007, Reps. Connie Mack, R-Fla., and Mary Bono announced their engagement.

Molinari earned another distinction as one of the few women in Congress who were daughters of representatives. She won the Staten Island seat of her father, Rep. Guy Molinari, who left the House to become Staten Island borough president. California Democrat Lucille Roybal-Allard also shared that distinction by winning the House seat of her father, Edward R. Roybal, whose congressional career lasted thirty years. The new House Speaker, California Democrat Nancy Pelosi, who entered the House in 1987, was the daughter of Thomas J. D'Alesandro Jr., a House member from 1939 to 1947 and then mayor of Baltimore.

Progress in the Senate

From 1922 to 1992, only sixteen women served in the Senate, and all but four claimed their seats by means of the widow's mandate. The four elected to full Senate terms were Maurine B. Neuberger, D-Ore. (1960), Nancy Landon Kassebaum, R-Kan. (1978, 1984, 1990), Paula Hawkins, R-Fla. (1980), and Barbara A. Mikulski, D-Md. (1986). Kassebaum was the first woman ever elected to the Senate without being preceded in Congress by her husband.

In 1992 six women were elected to full Senate terms, and the number of women senators continued to increase after that. By 2007 all sixteen women serving in the Senate were elected to full terms. Two states—California and Maine—were represented in the Senate solely by women: Democrats Barbara Boxer and Dianne Feinstein from California and Republicans Olympia J. Snowe and Susan Collins from Maine.

In 1992 the first African American woman was elected to the Senate, Democrat Carol Moseley-Braun of Illinois. She served in the state legislature from 1979 to 1988, where she rose to become the first woman assistant majority leader. The outrage over the Senate's handling of the Thomas confirmation hearings propelled Moseley-Braun into the 1992 Illinois Senate race. She lost her bid for reelection in 1998.

Leadership Positions

Even after women began entering Congress in record numbers at the end of the twentieth century, they still were finding it difficult to move to the top of the committee and party leadership ladders. A major breakthrough came in 2003, when Democrats elected Nancy Pelosi as their party leader, making her the first woman elected leader by either party. Pelosi was elected leader after Rep. Richard A. Gephardt, D-Mo., stepped down as minority leader after the 2002 elections. She defeated Rep. Harold E. Ford Jr., 177–29. Pelosi had set up her victory with another decisive win, in 2002, when she defeated Rep. Steny Hoyer, D-Md., in a race for House Democratic whip. Then, in 2007, Pelosi became the first female House Speaker in history when the Democrats recaptured control of the House from the GOP.

In 1995 Nancy Landon Kassebaum became the first woman to chair a major Senate committee—Labor and Human Resources. A fellow Kansas Republican, Jan Meyers, chaired the House Small Business Committee. Before Meyers, no woman had chaired a full House committee since 1977, when Merchant Marine Committee Chair Leonor K. Sullivan, D-Mo., left Congress. Mae Ella Nolan, a California Republican who served from 1923 to 1925, was the first woman to chair a congressional committee. She headed the House Committee on Expenditures in the Post Office Department.

In 1989 Barbara Mikulski became the first woman to chair a Senate Appropriations subcommittee—the VA, HUD, and Related Agencies panel. She became its ranking minority member when the GOP took control of the Senate in 1995. After the Senate switched to Democratic control in June 2001 when James M. Jeffords of Vermont left the Republican Party, Mikulski became the chair again. Three other Democratic women were also elevated to chairs of Senate Appropriations subcommittees after the 2001 changeover: Dianne Feinstein of California, Mary Landrieu of Louisiana, and Patty Murray of Washington.

On the House Appropriations Committee, Barbara Vucanovich, R-Nev., chaired the Military Construction Subcommittee in the 104th Congress. In the 107th Congress, Ohio's Marcy Kaptur served as the ranking member of the Appropriations Agriculture subcommittee and Pelosi was the ranking member of that panel's Foreign Operations subcommittee.

By the beginning of the 110th Congress in 2007, women had gained even more committee authority, chairing four panels in the House and two in the Senate. In the House the chairs were Juanita Millender-McDonald (Administration), who died in April 2007; Louise M. Slaughter (Rules); Nydia M. Velázquez (Small Business); and Stephanie Tubbs Jones (Standards of Official Conduct). In addition, women chaired a number of subcommittees including three panels on the powerful Appropriations Committee. In the Senate the chairs were Barbara Boxer (Environment and Public Works) and Dianne Feinstein (Rules and Administration). As in the House, women chaired a number of subcommittees including four on the Appropriations panel.

Congress has been an important starting point for women seeking national office. Shirley Chisholm, a Democratic representative from New York, ran for president in 1972. Geraldine A. Ferraro, another New York Democrat who served in the House, was her party's vice presidential nominee in 1984, another first. Former Illinois Sen. Carol Moseley-Braun was among the crowd seeking the Democratic nomination for president in 2004.

BLACKS IN CONGRESS

In 137 years, from 1870 to 2007 with the swearing-in of the 110th Congress, 115 black Americans served in Congress—5 in the Senate and 110 in the House. *(See Table 3-4, p. 53.)*

John W. Menard holds the distinction of being the first black person elected to Congress. But his 1868 election in Louisiana was disputed and the House denied him a seat in the 40th Congress. Hiram R. Revels of Mississippi, who filled an unexpired Senate term from February 1870 to March 1871, thus became the first black person to serve in Congress. The first black person to serve in the House was Joseph H. Rainey of South Carolina, from December 1870 to March 1879.

Menard, Revels, and Rainey were elected during the post–Civil War Reconstruction era (1865–1877), when many white voters were disenfranchised and Confederate veterans were barred from holding office. During that period sixteen black men were sent to Congress from Alabama, Georgia, Florida, Louisiana, Mississippi, North Carolina, and South Carolina. But from the end of Reconstruction until the end of the nineteenth century, only seven black men were elected to Congress, all from the Carolinas and Virginia. They, as with their predecessors, were Republicans.

As federal controls were lifted in the South, literacy tests, poll taxes, and sometimes violence eroded black voting rights. From the time Blanche K. Bruce of Mississippi left the Senate in 1881, no other black person served in that body until Edward W. Brooke, R-Mass., did from 1967 to 1979. In 1992 Illinois Democrat Carol Moseley-Braun was elected to the Senate, becoming the first black woman to gain a Senate seat. She served one term, losing her reelection bid in 1998. In 2005 Democrat Barack Obama was elected to the Senate from Illinois. The son of a black Kenyan father and a white mother from Kansas, Obama had served in the state senate. But because of his national prominence brought on by his rousing keynote speech at the 2004 Democratic National Convention in Boston, he was a major fund-raising figure for Democrats even before he began serving his term in 2005. In 2007 he announced that he was running for president and became a leading candidate for the 2008 Democratic nomination.

The last black person elected to the House in the nineteenth century was Republican George Henry White of North Carolina. He was elected in 1896 and 1898 but did not seek renomination in 1900. For nearly three decades there were no black members of Congress—not until Oscar De Priest, R-Ill., entered the House in 1929 and served three terms. During the next quarter century only three other blacks were elected to Congress: Arthur W. Mitchell in 1934, William L. Dawson in 1942, and Adam Clayton Powell Jr. in 1944. All three represented big-city black constituencies, in Chicago (Mitchell and Dawson) and New York (Powell).

Moreover, all three were Democrats, reflecting a switch in black voting habits. President Franklin D. Roosevelt had pulled a majority of black voters away from the party of Abraham Lincoln into a coalition of Depression-era urban laborers, farmers, and intellectuals. Mitchell, the first black Democrat elected to the House, was brought in by the Democratic sweep in the 1934 election.

That election also removed the Republican, De Priest, and marked the beginning of a fifty-six-year absence of black representation among House Republicans. That drought was broken in November 1990 when Connecticut elected Gary Franks, a black Republican real estate investor from Waterbury who had once captained Yale's basketball team. Franks was defeated for reelection in 1996.

House Democrats, in contrast, steadily gained black members. Only two were added in the 1950s—Charles C. Diggs Jr., D-Mich., and Robert N. C. Nix, D-Pa.—but after that the pace quickened. Five more were elected in the 1960s, and fourteen each in the 1970s and 1980s. The number of black Americans elected to Congress more than doubled during the 1990s—thirty-six were elected to the House (all but two Democrats) and one (Mosley-Braun) to the Senate.

The Supreme Court's one-person, one-vote rulings in the early 1960s, ratification of the Twenty-fourth Amendment in 1964, and congressional passage of the 1965 Voting Rights Act are credited with opening up the polls to black voters as never before. The Voting Rights Act provided for federal oversight in jurisdictions where black registration and voting was exceptionally low; the Twenty-fourth

TABLE 3-4 **Blacks in Congress, 1947–2007**

Congress	Senate	House
80th (1947–1949)	0	2
81st (1949–1951)	0	2
82nd (1951–1953)	0	2
83rd (1953–1955)	0	2
84th (1955–1957)	0	3
85th (1957–1959)	0	4
86th (1959–1961)	0	4
87th (1961–1963)	0	4
88th (1963–1965)	0	5
89th (1965–1967)	0	6
90th (1967–1969)	1	5
91st (1969–1971)	1	9
92nd (1971–1973)	1	12
93rd (1973–1975)	1	15
94th (1975–1977)	1	16
95th (1977–1979)	1	16
96th (1979–1981)	0	16
97th (1981–1983)	0	17
98th (1983–1985)	0	20
99th (1985–1987)	0	20
100th (1987–1989)	0	22
101st (1989–1991)	0	24
102nd (1991–1993)	0	26
103rd (1993–1995)	1	39
104th (1995–1997)	1	38
105th (1997–1999)	1	37
106th (1999–2001)	0	37
107th (2001–2003)	0	36
108th (2003–2005)	0	39
109th (2005–2007)	1	40
110th (2007–2009)	1	40

NOTE: House totals reflect the number of black members at the start of each Congress and exclude nonvoting delegates.

Amendment outlawed poll taxes and similar restrictions on voting; and the courts eventually ended a southern practice of diluting black voting power by gerrymandering voting districts. As black voter turnouts increased, so did black representation in Congress.

In 1968 Rep. Shirley Chisholm, D-N.Y., became the first black woman to be elected to Congress. She was joined in the House by Yvonne Brathwaite Burke, D-Calif., and Barbara C. Jordan, D-Texas, who both served from 1973 until 1979. In a 1973 special election, Cardiss Collins won the House seat previously held by her late husband, George W. Collins. Next came Katie Hall, D-Ind., the winner of a special election in November 1982, followed by two victors in the November 1990 general election, Maxine Waters, D-Calif., and Barbara-Rose Collins, D-Mich.

Jordan and Andrew Young, D-Ga., both elected in 1972, were the first blacks in the twentieth century to go to Congress from states of the Old Confederacy. Both Georgia and Texas later sent other black representatives, who were joined by black House members from Tennessee (Harold E. Ford), Mississippi (Mike Espy), and Louisiana (William J. Jefferson).

The 103rd Congress (1993–1995) had included several firsts for black Americans. In addition to Moseley-Braun becoming the first black woman ever elected to the Senate, for the first time since the Reconstruction era, the House delegations from Alabama, Florida, North Carolina, South Carolina, and Virginia included black members. Georgia elected its first black woman representative, Cynthia A. McKinney. The dramatic gains for African Americans in the 1992 elections was in large measure a result of redistricting aimed at increasing minority strength in Congress—a legacy of the civil rights era. This effort to draw so-called minority-majority districts, however, came under attack as the 1990s wore on. By the end of the decade, the Supreme Court in several decisions set new standards that limited this method of increasing black representation in Congress.

The new generation of African Americans elected to Congress in the 1990s reflected the changes begun during the civil rights era. Many came to Congress with considerable experience in state legislatures and other local government positions. Bobby L. Rush of Illinois, a leader of the militant Black Panther movement during the 1960s, had served for a decade on the Chicago city council. Earl F. Hilliard, Alabama's first black representative since Reconstruction, was an eighteen-year veteran of his state's legislature. Cynthia McKinney had been a member of the Georgia Legislature, and Corrine Brown had served in the Florida Legislature. In a 1995 special election, Jesse L. Jackson Jr., whose father, the Rev. Jesse Jackson Sr., was a civil rights crusader and two-time Democratic presidential contender, was elected from Illinois. He was thirty-one years old when he was sent to Congress. In 1996 Julia Carson of Indiana won the seat of her former boss, Democrat Andrew Jacobs Jr., and became the first black to represent Indianapolis in the House. She had served in both the Indiana House and Senate. Another African American woman, Carolyn Cheeks Kilpatrick, won her House seat after serving seventeen years in the Michigan House. In 1998 the Cleveland district seat of retiring black Rep. Louis Stokes was won by African American Democrat Stephanie Tubbs Jones, a judge and prosecutor in Cuyahoga County.

As the number of black Americans continued to increase in the House, those elected earlier gained seniority and, in some instances, committee chairmanships. Dawson served as chair of the Committee on Expenditures in the Executive Departments (later renamed the Government Operations Committee) from 1949 until his death in 1970 (except for 1953–1955 when the Republicans controlled the House). Other notable black chairs included Powell (Education and Labor Committee, 1961–1967); William H. Gray III, D-Pa. (Budget Committee, 1985–1989); Augustus F. Hawkins, D-Calif. (Education and Labor, 1984–1991); and Louis Stokes, D-Ohio (Permanent Select Committee on Intelligence, 1987–1989, and Standards of Official Conduct, 1981–1985, 1991–1993).

In 1989 Democrats elected Gray as majority whip, the third-highest ranking job in the House. Gray held the post until 1991 when he resigned from Congress to become president of the United Negro College Fund. In 1991 Rep. John Lewis, D-Ga., a veteran of the civil rights movement, moved up into the House Democratic leadership as a chief deputy whip.

By the end of the twentieth century, a few black members of Congress had served in the House for more than twenty-five years. California Democrat Ronald V. Dellums, who retired from the House in the 105th Congress after fourteen terms, served as chair of the Armed Services Committee in the 103rd Congress. In the 106th Congress, William L. Clay of Missouri, a former chair of the Post Office and Civil Service Committee, served as the ranking member on the Education and Workforce Committee. He retired at the end of that Congress.

In 2007, at the beginning of the 110th Congress, all forty-one black members of Congress (forty House members plus Obama in the Senate) were Democrats, the same total as in the 109th Congress. In addition, Democrats Eleanor Holmes Norton of the District of Columbia and Donna M. C. Christensen of the Virgin Islands were elected as nonvoting delegates.

However, the 110th Congress was back in the control of Democrats following the 2006 elections in which Republicans lost many seats in both chambers. This meant that by virtue of their seniority, five blacks in the House claimed committee chairmanships: Charles B. Rangel of New York, Ways and Means; John Conyers Jr. of Michigan,

Judiciary; Bennie Thompson of Mississippi, Homeland Security; Juanita Millender-McDonald of California, Administration; and Stephanie Tubbs Jones of Ohio, Standards of Official Conduct. Moreover, James E. Clyburn, who was elected in 1992 as South Carolina's first black representative in a century, became the majority whip. (One of these members, Millender-McDonald, died of cancer a few months into the new Congress. She was replaced by a white male next in line by seniority.)

Despite the steady gains of blacks being elected to Congress and the growing power of senior black members, African Americans remained numerically underrepresented in Congress. In 2007 they made up about 13 percent of the population but just 9 percent of the House and 1 percent of the Senate.

Redistricting Battles

Following the 1990 census, many states redrew congressional district lines under the provisions of the 1965 Voting Rights Act, which required that interests of minority voters be protected. Districts in which minorities made up a majority of the voting-age population were known as majority-minority districts. As state mapmakers pulled districts this way and that to pick up minority voters, many old boundaries were tugged out of shape. In some states, oddly shaped majority-minority districts emerged.

Congressional remapping that went to extreme lengths to elect minorities quickly came under scrutiny by the Supreme Court. In 1993 in *Shaw v. Reno,* the Court ruled against North Carolina's bizarrely shaped majority-minority districts, inviting a new round of lawsuits challenging the constitutionality of districts drawn to ensure the election of minorities. Two years later in *Miller v. Johnson,* the Court struck down a Georgia redistricting plan that created three black-majority districts. The Court cast heavy doubt on any district lines for which race was the "predominant factor." In 1995 a panel of three federal judges imposed a new plan that reduced the black population share to about one-third in two of the districts.

Even though the black-majority Eleventh District in Georgia was invalidated by the Supreme Court decision, Cynthia A. McKinney, the district's black representative, scored a comfortable victory in 1996 in the newly drawn white-majority Fourth District. Only one-third of the new district's voting-age population was black, compared with 64 percent in her old district. In fact, all three of Georgia's black Democrats in the House were reelected to redrawn districts in 1996. Moreover, McKinney won again in 1998 and the following three elections in the redrawn district but was defeated in a primary contest in 2006 by Hank Johnson, a black man, who went on to win in the fall election.

The thrust of the Court's opinions threatened those who defended majority-minority districts as a way to empower minority voters. But the justices did not make sweeping determinations affecting all such districts. They seemed inclined to carve out new limits in a sequence of slightly different cases. After the 2000 census the majority-minority district issue became less contentious as the focus switched to partisan redistricting. *(See Chapter 5, Reapportionment and Redistricting.)*

Most blacks in the 110th Congress, twenty-three in total, represented districts in which the majority population is African American. But a number of other districts, primarily in the South, have populations that are a third black and who voted heavily Democratic. In these cases, however, their votes are swamped by the overwhelming Republican vote of the white majority. A number of scholars who followed election trends doubted that blacks could significantly increase their numbers in the House in light of judicial decisions limiting majority-minority districts in combination with as of 2007, the largely Republican white vote in the South.

HISPANICS IN CONGRESS

The rapidly expanding Hispanic American population was expected to become a powerful voting bloc in Congress, but by 2007 the group remained significantly underrepresented. At the start of the 110th Congress, twenty-six members and one nonvoting delegate from Puerto Rico identified themselves as Hispanics—people of Spanish ancestry. *(See Table 3-5, p. 56.)*

However, the 2000 census showed the nation's Hispanic population continuing to grow rapidly, to 12.5 percent of the population—35.3 million persons—up from 9 percent a decade earlier. If Hispanics were represented proportionally in Congress, they would hold sixty-seven seats. By 2007, Hispanics were estimated to be 14 percent of the population, but their members in Congress were only 5 percent of the total. Hispanic voter turnouts traditionally have fallen well below the national average, which group activists attribute to poverty, lack of education, language barriers, alienation resulting from discrimination, large numbers of young people, immigration status, and often a continuing attachment to their homelands. As a result, by 2007 there were as many majority-Hispanic districts as majority-black districts—twenty-four of each—yet there were nearly twice as many black members.

As of January 2007, a total of forty-eight Hispanics had served in Congress—six in the Senate in total including three who served only as senators, and forty-five in the House including forty-two who served only in that chamber. Three Hispanics served in both houses. Several other Hispanics represented territories as nonvoting delegates or resident commissioners. The 110th Congress included Luis Fortuno, the resident commissioner of Puerto Rico.

TABLE 3-5 **Hispanics in Congress, 1947–2007**

Congress	Senate	House
80th (1947–1949)	1	1
81st (1949–1951)	1	1
82nd (1951–1953)	1	1
83rd (1953–1955)	1	1
84th (1955–1957)	1	1
85th (1957–1959)	2	0
86th (1959–1961)	2	0
87th (1961–1963)	2	1
88th (1963–1965)	1	3
89th (1965–1967)	1	4
90th (1967–1969)	1	4
91st (1969–1971)	1	5
92nd (1971–1973)	1	6
93rd (1973–1975)	1	6
94th (1975–1977)	1	6
95th (1977–1979)	0	5
96th (1979–1981)	0	6
97th (1981–1983)	0	7
98th (1983–1985)	0	10
99th (1985–1987)	0	11
100th (1987–1989)	0	11
101st (1989–1991)	0	11
102nd (1991–1993)	0	11
103rd (1993–1995)	0	17
104th (1995–1997)	0	17
105th (1997–1999)	0	18
106th (1999–2001)	0	18
107th (2001–2003)	0	19
108th (1993–2005)	0	24
109th (2005–2007)	2	23
110th (2007–2009)	3	23

NOTE: House totals reflect the number of Hispanic members at the start of each Congress and exclude nonvoting delegates.

The growth of Hispanic representation in the House was in large part the result of judicial interpretations of the Voting Rights Act requiring that minorities be given maximum opportunity to elect members of their own group to Congress. After the 1990 census, congressional district maps in states with significant Hispanic populations were redrawn with the aim of sending more Hispanics to Congress, a goal accomplished by the 1992 elections. Before the 1992 elections, there were only thirteen Hispanic members of Congress.

Between 1977 and 2005 no Hispanic candidate served in the Senate after Joseph Montoya completed his second and last term. Dennis Chavez, his fellow Democrat from New Mexico, was the first Hispanic to serve in the Senate (1935–1962) for an extended period. (For about three months from late 1928 until early 1929, Octaviano Larrazolo, a Republican, served as a senator from New Mexico.)

But in 2005 and 2006 three more Hispanics joined the Senate. In the 2004 elections, Mel Martinez, R-Fla., and Ken Salazar, D-Colo., were elected to six-year terms starting in 2005. Next was Robert Menendez, a Democratic representative from New Jersey, who was appointed in late 2005 to the Senate seat vacated by Jon S. Corzine, who became New Jersey's governor. Menendez was sworn in January 18, 2006, and won reelection to a full term the following fall.

Salazar's brother, John Salazar, D-Colo., also began serving in the House in 2005, making the brothers one of three pairs serving in Congress. A second Hispanic pair of brothers was Lincoln Diaz-Balart, R-Fla., and Mario Diaz-Balart, R-Fla. Two other Hispanic siblings, Linda T. Sanchez, D-Calif., and Loretta Sanchez, D-Calif., made history in 2003 when they became the first sisters ever to serve in Congress.

Rep. Romualdo Pacheco, R-Calif., was the only Hispanic to serve in Congress during the nineteenth century. Mexican-born, with an English stepfather and an English education, Pacheco helped to bridge the cultural gap between the Spanish-speaking settlers of California and the newly arrived Americans. After California was taken from Mexico and given statehood, Pacheco moved upward in a succession of political offices to the governorship in 1875, filling out the term of his predecessor who resigned to become a U.S. senator.

The next year Pacheco ran for Congress and was certified the victor in a disputed election and took his seat early in 1877. But the House subsequently decided that his opponent was the rightful winner. Pacheco returned home and ran again—successfully—twice more. After leaving Congress he became ambassador to Honduras and then Guatemala. No other Hispanic American was elected to Congress until 1912. After that, Congress was without any Hispanic American members only for short periods in the 1920s and early 1940s.

TURNOVER IN MEMBERSHIP

Congress experienced high turnover rates in the nineteenth and early twentieth centuries, principally in the House. The Senate experienced more stability because its members were selected for six-year terms and because state legislatures tended to send the same men to the Senate time after time. The Senate's turnover rate began to increase only after the popular election of senators was instituted by the Seventeenth Amendment in 1913. In the middle decades of the twentieth century, congressional turnover held steady at a relatively low rate. For a quarter century after World War II each Congress had an average of about seventy-eight new members. An increase began in the 1970s. More than one hundred new members entered Congress in 1975. Turnover remained fairly high through the early 1980s and then came a spell of strong incumbency and relatively low turnover that lasted through the 1990 election.

The 1988 election brought only thirty-three new faces to the House and ten to the Senate, the smallest turnover in history, both numerically and as a share (8 percent) of total membership. Another small turnover followed in 1990. The combined turnover for both chambers, including retirement, amounted to just 10 percent. The 1990 Senate incumbent reelection rate of 96.9 percent was the highest since direct elections began in 1914.

Several factors contributed to the turnover rates in the 1970s and early 1980s. The elections of 1972 and 1974 were affected by redistricting that followed the 1970 census. Many House veterans retired to avoid facing strong new opposition. Those two elections also were the first in which eighteen-year-olds could vote. Probably the chief reason for change in 1974 was the Watergate scandal, which put an end to the Nixon administration and badly damaged the Republican Party. Democrats gained forty-three seats in the House that year, and the following January seventy-five of the ninety-two freshman representatives in the 94th Congress were Democrats.

Most of those Democrats managed to hold their seats in the 1976 elections. The upheavals in that year's voting were in Senate races. Eighteen new senators took their oath of office in January 1977, marking the Senate's largest turnover since 1959.

An even larger Senate turnover came in the 1978 elections. It resulted in a 1979 freshman class of twenty senators, the biggest since the twenty-three-member class of 1947. In 1978, ten incumbent senators retired, more than in any year since World War II. Three other incumbents were beaten in primaries, the most in a decade. Seven more were defeated for reelection, the second-highest number in twenty years. In the House a record fifty-eight seats were opened by retirement, death, primary defeat, and other causes. Moreover, nineteen incumbents fell in the general election, giving the House seventy-seven freshmen when the 96th Congress opened in January 1979.

Mel Martinez, a Republican from Florida, was one of three Hispanics to be elected to the Senate in 2004 and 2006.

In 1980, when Republican Ronald Reagan won the White House, the GOP took control of the Senate for the first time since 1957, ending the longest one-party dominance in that body in its history. They also netted thirty-three House seats, the biggest Republican gain since 1966. But the Democrats made a comeback in the 1982 midterm elections: of the eighty-one new representatives, fifty-seven were Democrats. Republicans lost twenty-six seats in the House, half of them held by freshmen.

As in the early 1970s, redistricting was an important factor in the 1982 election. The 1980 census shifted seventeen seats from the Northeast and Midwest to the Sun Belt states of the South and West. Democrats took ten of these seats despite the Sun Belt's propensity to vote for Republican presidential candidates.

In 1984, a presidential election year, Republicans gained fourteen House seats and Democrats two Senate seats in an election that resulted in little turnover. Forty-three new representatives and seven new senators entered the 99th Congress. On only four previous occasions since 1914 had there been fewer than ten Senate newcomers. In 1986 Democrats regained control of the Senate, with eleven of the thirteen freshmen senators.

The 1986 House elections were extraordinarily good for incumbents of both parties. Only six House members lost in the general election; two others had been defeated in the primaries. But enough seats were open from retirement and death to yield a freshman House class of fifty members—twenty-three Republicans and twenty-seven Democrats.

In 1988 George H. W. Bush became the first Republican in sixty years to hold the White House for his party for a third consecutive term. But he also became the first candidate since John F. Kennedy in 1960 to win the presidential election while his party lost seats (three) in the House. Again in 1990, for the third straight election, Democrats gained House seats (nine). That feat had not been accomplished since the string of Democratic victories in 1954, 1956, and 1958.

In the presidential election year of 1992, voters opted to give the Democrats a chance to run both Congress and the White House by electing Democrat Bill Clinton, the former governor of Arkansas, as president. Clinton was elected with only 43 percent of the popular vote over Bush and independent candidate H. Ross Perot. Not since Democrat Jimmy Carter had relinquished the White House to Republican Reagan in 1981 had Congress been controlled by the president's party.

Heading into the 1992 campaign, some observers thought that the American political system had lost its capacity for renewal. Low turnover in the 1980s fostered a perception of Congress as an incumbency club, fueled by special interest cash that nearly always defeated any challengers. But 1992 redistricting as a result of the 1990 census dramatically reshaped many districts, prodding some members into retirement and forcing others to run in unfamiliar constituencies. Reports of lax management and overdrawn checks at the House Bank also contributed to a high congressional turnover.

All this tumult resulted in 110 new members entering the House in January 1993, an influx of freshmen exceeding anything Washington had seen in more than forty years. In

LIMITING TERMS

Although a push for term limits for elected officials became popular in the early 1990s, both the House and Senate in the 104th Congress (1995–1997) failed to pass a constitutional amendment limiting the terms of members of Congress. When another try in the House failed in the 105th Congress, the momentum for this change in the elections system failed.

Many members who campaigned on term limits had their enthusiasm cool for the idea once in office. Rep. George Nethercutt, R-Wash., who toppled Speaker Thomas S. Foley, D-Wash., in 1994 while promising to limit his own service to three terms, reneged on his term limits pledge, saying, "I've changed my mind." He continued, when seeking reelection in 2000: "I made a mistake when I chose to set a limit on my service. The work I've done will not be finished by the end of this term." Nethercutt left the House two terms later in 2005. Rep. Jeff Flake, R-Ariz., also broke his term limits promise and ran for and won a third term in 2006. "It was naive and stupid for me to make such a pledge," Flake said of his 2000 promise to limit himself to three terms.

The term limits movement was kicked off in 1990 when Colorado became the first state to seek to limit the number of terms that members of Congress could serve. A referendum approved by more than two-thirds of Colorado voters limited House members to six two-year terms and senators to two six-year terms. The measure also set term limits on state legislators and statewide elected offices.

By 1995 backers of term limits had won ballot initiatives or laws in at least twenty-three states. In 1995 the U.S. Supreme Court ruled in *U.S. Term Limits v. Thornton* and *Bryant v. Hill* that states could not impose limits on congressional terms. These rulings left term limits supporters only one solution: a constitutional amendment. But constitutional amendments are difficult to pass: they must receive a two-thirds majority vote from both chambers of Congress and then be ratified by three-fourths (thirty-eight) of the states.

Supporters of term limits argued that mandatory retirement after twelve years was necessary to bring new people and viewpoints into Congress, to reduce the constant pressure to get reelected, and to control federal spending, which they said resulted from career politicians getting too close to special interest groups seeking federal funds. Opponents countered that term limits would strip Congress of experienced legislators, diminish the political power of less-populated states that were helped by their members gaining seniority, and merely speed up, not solve, the problem of legislators getting too friendly with special interest groups. Depriving voters of the right to vote for an incumbent would be undemocratic, opponents added.

In the House the term limits constitutional amendment ran into trouble from the start. The House Judiciary Committee agreed on February 28, 1995, to send its version of the measure to the floor without recommendation. Committee chair Henry J. Hyde, R-Ill., staunchly opposed term limits, calling the concept "a terrible mistake, a kick in the stomach of democracy." He even filed a brief outlining his opposition when the Supreme Court took up the issue in its 1994–1995 term. Hyde, elected in 1974, retired in 2007.

On March 29, 1995, the House rejected a term limits constitutional amendment that proposed a twelve-year lifetime limit on members of each chamber. The 227–204 vote fell sixty-one votes short of a two-thirds majority. Forty Republicans voted against the measure, of which thirty of them chaired a committee or subcommittee.

In the Senate, a term limits constitutional amendment restricting senators to two six-year terms and representatives to six two-year terms stalled on the floor in April 1996. A vote to shut off debate on the measure failed, 58–42, two short of the sixty votes needed. All fifty-three Senate Republicans voted for cloture, even though some opposed limiting congressional terms, leaving the Democrats to take the heat for blocking the Senate from moving to an up-or-down vote.

Term limits supporters again tried to get a constitutional amendment through the House in 1997. In February members voted on eleven versions of a term limits amendment based on different initiatives begun in nine states. The underlying broad measure—restricting House members to six years and senators to twelve—received a simple majority of 217–211. The tally was sixty-nine votes short of the necessary two-thirds majority needed for passage. The House then considered ten proposals beyond the underlying measure. Some would have made the limits retroactive, giving the states the authority to adopt stricter limits, or restricted House members to six or eight years. All were soundly defeated.

the postwar era, only one House freshman class was larger—the 118 newcomers to the 81st Congress in 1949. No other freshman class had so many women (twenty-five) and minorities, including sixteen African Americans, eight Hispanics, and one Korean American.

The Senate freshman class of the 103rd Congress was the largest since 1981, with nine men and five woman, including the chamber's first black woman (Democrat Carol Moseley-Braun of Illinois) and its first Native American (Democrat Ben Nighthorse Campbell of Colorado) since Charles Curtis, a Republican from Kansas who stepped down in 1929 to become vice president under Herbert Hoover.

The midterm elections of 1994 brought even more upheaval as the Republicans gained control of both the House and Senate for the first time since 1955. The Democratic loss was truly national in scope. Republicans won thirty-seven million votes in 1994—nearly nine million more than the party had won in the 1990 midterm elections. It was the first time since 1946 that Republican House candidates received a majority (52.3 percent) of the total House vote. Democrats in 1994 drew almost one million fewer votes than in 1990, continuing a general downward slide in their congressional voting strength that had begun in the mid-1980s.

The GOP tide of 1994 was caused by large surges in voter support for the Republicans and voter apathy for the Democrats. The election marked the middle of Democrat Clinton's first term, and the president's party had difficulty motivating its core constituency. Although Clinton had some successes during his first two years in office, most notably deficit reduction and the North American Free Trade Agreement, his failure in getting Congress to agree to comprehensive health care reform seemed to stall his administration's programs. In addition, Republican candidates reaped the gains they had anticipated from redistricting after the 1990 census. The remapping was largely favorable to the GOP.

Money also made the difference for some Republican challengers. According to the Federal Election Commission, Republican candidates had an easier time raising money from political action committees and other sources than in previous years. Conservative groups—from the National Rifle Association to term limit advocates—played active roles in several congressional races. Several GOP freshmen were elected with the prominent support of conservative Christian activists.

In 1994 Republicans gained fifty-two House seats, increasing their number from 178 to 230. The Democrats dropped from 256 to 204 seats. For the Republicans, seventy-three freshmen were elected, 157 incumbents were reelected, and thirty-four incumbents were defeated.

At the start of the 104th Congress, Georgia Rep. Newt Gingrich became the first Republican Speaker of the House from the South. His ascendancy accompanied the long-anticipated realignment of the South away from Democratic dominance to a Republican majority. For the first time since the end of Reconstruction in the 1870s, Republicans won a majority of southern congressional districts.

Republicans also swept the Senate in 1994, after eight years in the minority. The Republicans captured all nine open seats and ousted two Democratic incumbents, gaining control by a margin of 52–48 seats. The day after the general election, Sen. Richard C. Shelby, D-Ala., announced that he was switching parties. The incoming Senate freshman class had eleven Republicans and no Democrats. Since 1914, when the popular election of senators began, there had never been an all-GOP Senate freshman class.

The 1996 elections also ended up in the record books. Never before had voters reelected a Democratic president and at the same time entrusted both the House and the Senate to the Republican Party. Clinton, who was almost written off after the 1994 midterm elections, scored a political comeback by winning handily in November 1996. The Republicans also won their first back-to-back majority in the House since the 1920s. The Democrats managed, however, to cut into the GOP's numbers. Democrats gained a net of nine seats, leaving a party breakdown in the House of 227 Republicans and 207 Democrats, and Bernard Sanders of Vermont as the lone Independent.

In 1996 a total of twenty incumbents were defeated; all but three were Republicans. The heaviest toll in 1996 was among the mainly conservative and contentious GOP freshman class—eleven freshmen Republicans were defeated. The GOP held on to its majority in the House by its performance in the open seats. Of fifty-three open seats, Republicans won twenty-nine, ten of them given up by Democratic incumbents. Democrats won twenty-four, only four of which had been held by Republicans.

In the Senate, the Republicans built on their gains in the 1994 election. For the 105th Congress, the GOP had a solid 55–45 majority over the Democrats. That was the Republicans' highest total in the Senate following any election since 1928.

By 1998 the turnover in the House and Senate seemed to have settled down. All but seven of the 401 House members seeking reelection were returned to office. The Democrats also regrouped in 1998—Clinton's second midterm election—and managed to close the partisan gap even further in the House. The Democrats picked up five House seats, giving the 106th Congress 223 Republicans, 211 Democrats, and one Independent. This twelve-seat majority was the slimmest majority in the House since 1955.

The Senate's partisan breakdown remained the same in 1999 with fifty-five Republicans and forty-five Democrats. Just three of the thirty-four senators up for reelection in 1998 were defeated. Eight Senate freshmen joined the 106th Congress—four Democrats and four Republicans.

The pattern continued in the 2000 elections. Although the GOP maintained control in both chambers, its margin was reduced to nine votes in the House. In the Senate, a tie resulted: fifty Democrats and fifty Republicans. However, the Republicans retained control because their party won back the White House, which allowed Dick Cheney, the new vice president and presiding Senate officer, to vote to break a tie. This rare arrangement was short-lived, however, as moderate Republican James M. Jeffords of Vermont left the GOP to become an Independent in June 2001, giving majority control of the Senate to the Democrats for the first time since 1994.

The Republicans regained control of both houses in the 2002 elections. For only the third time in a century, and the first time since 1934, the party in control of the White House won seats in a midterm election. The GOP regained the Senate by winning two seats and expanded its majority in the House by picking up six seats. Only sixteen of the 398 incumbents seeking reelection to the House were defeated, giving House incumbents a success rate of 96 percent. Incumbents in the Senate had an 85.7 percent success rate as four incumbents out of the twenty-eight seeking reelection lost.

In 2004 the Republicans held onto the White House while picking up seats in both houses of Congress. In the Senate the GOP gained four seats to widen their majority to fifty-five versus forty-four Democrats and one Independent. In the House the GOP added three seats to increase their majority to 232 versus 202 Democrats and one Independent. Incumbents continued to be returned to Congress at a high rate. In the House 97.8 percent of those incumbents seeking reelection won. Only one incumbent in the Senate lost reelection while twenty-five won—a 96.2 percent success rate. The 109th Congress began with nine new senators and forty-one new representatives.

Then, in the 2006 elections, the Republican ascendancy stalled. In a national sweep that resembled the Republican takeover of Congress in 1994, Democrats regained control of both chambers by picking up a net of thirty seats in the House and six in the Senate. The Democrats gained seats in each of the four national regions including eleven House seats—the largest number—in the Northeast. Only one Republican survived in that part of the country, making the once rock-solid GOP region more like a Demo-

DELEGATES IN CONGRESS

In the U.S. House, in addition to the 435 members representing districts in the fifty states, four delegates and a resident commissioner represent the District of Columbia and the four U.S. territories—American Samoa, Guam, Puerto Rico, and the U.S. Virgin Islands. These members are elected to office and serve two-year terms, except for the resident commissioner from Puerto Rico, who serves a four-year term. The four delegates and the resident commissioner may vote in committee, give floor speeches, and even hold chairmanships. Over the years, their right to vote on the House floor, under certain conditions, has been alternately granted and taken away. All four overseas members serve on the House Resources Committee, which has jurisdiction over U.S. territorial affairs.

Legislation introduced in the 110th Congress (2007–2009) would change the status of the District of Columbia. The proposal would grant the District full voting rights in the House, raising its status to the same as the other 435 districts. In addition, Utah would receive another seat. The District likely would elect a Democrat and Utah a Republican, negating any partisan advantage. The House would be permanently increased in size to 437 members. However, in early March 2007 the White House said it opposed the legislation—without initially threatening a presidential vote—because of concern, a spokesman said, that the District was not a state as defined in the U.S. Constitution. The Constitution, however, does not actually define the District. In Article I, Section 8, it simply says Congress has the power to "exercise exclusive Legislation in all Cases whatsoever, over such District" as may become the seat of the new government. The language presumed that states would cede and Congress would accept land up to ten square miles for that purpose. Opponents point to other sections of the Constitution that specifically address the formation, powers, and representation in Congress of states and argue that none of those provisions support the contention that the District is equivalent to a state.

DISTRICT OF COLUMBIA

In 1871 Congress established a territorial form of government over the entire District of Columbia. The new city administration included an elected nonvoting delegate to the House of Representatives—Republican Norton P. Chipman—as well as an appointed governor; a territorial assembly, with one elected and one appointed chamber; and a new board of public works. Gross financial mismanagement by Alexander Shepherd, board member and later District governor, led Congress to replace the District territorial government with three commissioners appointed by the president. The territorial assembly and the position of House delegate were abolished. Chipman's term expired in 1875.

Although permanent suppression of representative government for the District clearly was not intended, the changes made were incorporated in the 1878 act that established the capital city's government. For the next century Congress acted as the city's governing council while the president chose its administrators.

In 1970 Congress cleared legislation providing for the first nonvoting delegate from the District of Columbia since 1875. Democrat Walter E. Fauntroy, a black Baptist minister, was elected to the U.S. House on March 23, 1971. The D.C. delegate was given all House privileges except that of voting on the floor. (The delegate could vote in committee.) The legislation also amended city election laws to provide for primary and general elections for the post.

The measure had been briefly detained in the Senate, as Edward M. Kennedy, D-Mass., requested that action be held up until senators considered his proposal to give the District voting representation in both the House and Senate. In a subsequent meeting with city officials, Kennedy agreed to release the bill, saying that the delay had highlighted his view that the nonvoting delegate is important but the position should be created only as an interim measure.

cratic bastion. In the Midwest, Democrats picked up nine House seats, reducing the Republican majority there to a near dead heat, 51–49. Even in the South, which by the first decade of the new century had become the core of Republican strength, the Democrats picked up six House seats, although they still trailed the GOP by a substantial margin, 57–85.

President Bush's declining popularity, reflected most significantly in widespread disapproval of the war in Iraq, was seen in Democratic gains in districts carried by Bush in the 2004 presidential elections: two-thirds of Democratic gains came in states or districts that favored Bush just two years earlier.

The defeat of GOP incumbents accounted for all the Senate Republican losses. In the House, Democrats picked up twenty-two Republican seats in which an incumbent was running in the general election. The other eight Democratic wins were in open-seat contests. Not a single Democratic incumbent lost.

Nevertheless, incumbency remained an important bulwark for both parties. All Democratic incumbents won, and all open seats previously held by a Democrat were retained by the party. On the Republican side only one in ten GOP incumbents running lost in the general election. Overall 94 percent of House incumbents won; in Senate races the figure was almost 79 percent.

Election analysts noted that most defeated Republican House candidates did not have close races in 2004 and were veteran members with at least eight years in the chamber. All of these seats were expected to be vigorously contested in the last two elections of the decade before another round of redistricting would take place after the 2010 census.

Elections expert Rhodes Cook said Democrats made House gains

> largely because they were able to expand the playing field, which had shrunk dramatically in recent elections. When Republicans won control of Congress in 1994, there were nearly 100 competitive House races (as measured by a winning percentage of less than 55 percent of the total vote). In 2002, that number was less than fifty, and two years ago [2004] the total of such competitive House contests fell to just thirty-two. But [in 2006] the number of sub-55 per-

The D.C. delegate still has limited voting rights, causing some city residents to complain of taxation without full representation. (D.C. residents pay federal income taxes.) At the start of the 110th Congress, Democrat Eleanor Holmes Norton, first elected in 1990, was the D.C. delegate.

TERRITORIES

A U.S. possession since 1898, Puerto Rico became a commonwealth in 1952. The first resident commissioner from Puerto Rico, Federico Degetau, was sent to the House in 1900. With a population of more than three million, Puerto Rico is the largest U.S. territory. Luis G. Fortuno, a Republican, first elected in 2004, was the resident commissioner in the 110th Congress.

The United States acquired Guam from Spain in the Treaty of Paris after the Spanish-American War of 1898. The United States bought the Virgin Islands from Denmark in 1917. Under acts passed by Congress, both territories are governed by locally elected legislatures. Proposals for representation of the two territories were considered by every Congress since the mid-1950s. In 1972 Congress authorized one nonvoting House delegate each from Guam and the Virgin Islands. In the 110th Congress, Democrat Madeleine Z. Bordallo, first elected in 2002, represented Guam, and Donna M. C. Christensen, first elected in 1996, was the delegate from the Virgin Islands.

The United States gained the islands of American Samoa from the United Kingdom and Germany under the 1899 Treaty of Berlin. These South Pacific islands are administered by the Department of the Interior. American Samoa sent its first delegate to the House in 1979. In 2007 Democrat Eni F. H. Faleomavaega, first elected in 1988, was the delegate.

VOTING RIGHTS

In December 1992, while organizing for the 103rd Congress, Democrats approved a proposal to give the nonvoting members the right to vote on the floor when the House considered legislation in the Committee of the Whole—a parliamentary framework under which House members meet to debate and amend legislation. The full House accepted the proposal as part of a package of rule changes in January 1993.

D.C. delegate Eleanor Holmes Norton persuaded her fellow Democrats that no legal distinction existed between voting in committee, which the delegates had the right to do, and voting on the floor in the Committee of the Whole. Some Democrats had reservations about giving the delegates the right to floor votes and the caucus eventually approved a compromise measure. The compromise required that whenever a question was decided on the strength of delegate votes, regardless of whether it was approved or rejected, the committee would dissolve and the House would immediately vote on the issue again without the delegates. Of the 404 times that the five delegates were eligible to vote during the 103rd Congress, only three times did their votes prove decisive, thus triggering an automatic revote.

Republicans were not happy with the rules change—at the time all five delegates were Democrats. On January 7, 1993, House minority leader Robert H. Michel, R-Ill., a dozen GOP members, and three citizens filed suit in U.S. District Court challenging the delegates' new voting rights. District judge Harold H. Greene ruled that the delegate voting procedure was constitutional because "the votes . . . are meaningless." Greene went on to say that, without the provision for a second vote in close calls, the rule plainly would have been unconstitutional. Not surprisingly, the delegates' limited floor-voting privileges were stripped away at the beginning of the 104th Congress, when the Republicans gained the House majority. That was again reversed when Democrats took back control of the House in 2007.

TABLE 3-6 **Longest Service in Congress**

Member	Years of service	Total years[a]
Carl T. Hayden, D-Ariz.	1912–1927 (H), 1927–1969 (S)	57
Robert C. Byrd, D-W.Va.	1953–1959 (H), 1959– (S)	54
Jamie L. Whitten, D-Miss.	1941–1995 (H)	53
John D. Dingell, D-Mich.	1955– (H)	52
Carl Vinson, D-Ga.	1914–1965 (H)	50
Emanuel Celler, D-N.Y.	1923–1973 (H)	50
Sam Rayburn, D-Texas	1913–1961 (H)	49
Daniel K. Inouye, D-Hawaii	1959–1963 (H), 1963– (S)	48
Strom Thurmond, R-S.C.	1955–1956 (S), 1957–2003 (S)	48
Wright Patman, D-Texas	1929–1976 (H)	47
Joseph G. Cannon, R-Ill.	1873–1891 (H), 1893–1913 (H), 1915–1923 (H)	46
Adolph J. Sabath, D-Ill.	1907–1952 (H)	46
Lister Hill, D-Ala.	1923–1938 (H), 1938–1969 (S)	45
Edward M. Kennedy, D-Mass.	1962– (S)	45
George H. Mahon, D-Texas.	1935–1979 (H)	44
Warren G. Magnuson, D-Wash.	1937–1944 (H), 1944–1981 (S)	44
Justin S. Morrill, R-Vt.	1855–1867 (H), 1867–1898 (S)	44
Melvin Price, D-Ill.	1945–1988 (H)	44
William B. Allison, R-Iowa	1863–1871 (H), 1873–1908 (S)	43
Henry M. Jackson, D-Wash.	1941–1953 (H), 1953–1983 (S)	43
John Conyers Jr., D-Mich.	1965– (H)	42
John C. Stennis, D-Miss.	1947–1989 (S)	41

NOTES: H = House; S = Senate. a. Years of service are as of January 2007. Totals, based on exact dates of service, are rounded to nearest year. Minor differences in days or months of service determine rankings of members with the same total of years. Inouye was reelected in 2004 for a six-year term, Byrd and Kennedy were reelected in 2006 for six-year terms, and Dingell and Conyers were reelected in 2006 for two-year terms.

SOURCES: Congressional Research Service; Congressional Quarterly.

cent winners jumped to sixty-eight, the highest total in a decade. Going into the elections, the bulk of these seats were [*sic*] held by Republicans. But Democrats won many of them Nov. 7, with the result that a number of marginal House seats are now held either by Democratic challengers who won narrowly or Republican incumbents who barely escaped defeat. Altogether, thirty-five Republicans won in 2006 with less than fifty-five percent of the vote, compared to thirty-three Democrats.[5]

SHIFTS BETWEEN CHAMBERS

From the early days of Congress, members have sometimes shifted from one chamber to the other. Far fewer former senators have gone to the House than vice versa. In the 1790s, nineteen former representatives became senators and three former senators moved to the House. The same pattern continued through the nineteenth century and into the twentieth. By the end of the twentieth century, it was common to find House members running for the Senate, but senators rarely, if ever, returned to the House. Former senators were more likely to return home to pursue a race for governor, run as their party's vice presidential candidate, or seek the office of president. *(See Table 3-6, p. 62.)*

Although both chambers are equal under the law, the Senate's six-year terms offer the officeholder greater stability. That body also has larger staffs and more generous perquisites. A senator's opportunity to make his mark is undoubtedly better in a chamber of one hundred members than in the 435-member House. The Senate's role in foreign affairs may add to its luster, and senators enjoy the prestige of statewide constituencies.

Perhaps the most notable shift from the Senate to the House was Henry Clay's journey in 1811. Giving up a Senate seat from Kentucky, he entered the House and was promptly elected Speaker, a position he used to prod the country to go to war with Britain in 1812. After five terms in the House, Clay returned to the Senate in 1823. Another prominent transfer was that of John Quincy Adams of Massachusetts. He served in the Senate (1803–1808), as secretary of state (1817–1825), as president (1825–1829), and finally in the House (1831–1848).

Only one other former president, Andrew Johnson, returned to Congress in later years. He had served in both houses of Congress (from Tennessee) before he entered the White House. As vice president in 1865, Johnson was elevated to the presidency when Abraham Lincoln was assassinated. Johnson left office in 1869 a bitter man, having survived impeachment charges instigated by his Republican Party. The Tennessee Legislature sent him back to the U.S. Senate in 1875, where he served the last five months of his life.

NOTES

1. Alexis de Tocqueville, *Democracy in America* (New York: Vintage Books, 1971), vol. 1, 231.

2. Gallup Poll, "Confidence in Institutions," June 1-4, 2006, and "Congress and the Public," February 1–4, 2007, available at www.galluppoll.com/topics/.

3. Roger H. Davidson and Walter J. Oleszek, *Congress and Its Members,* 10th ed. (Washington D.C.: CQ Press, 2006), 61–62.

4. Greg Giroux, "An Old Boys' Club with New Twists," *CQ Weekly,* February 26, 2007, 604.

5. Rhodes Cook, *The Rhodes Cook Letter,* December 2006, 13; summary available at rhodescook.com.

SELECTED BIBLIOGRAPHY

American Political Leaders: 1789–2005. Washington, D.C.: CQ Press, 2005.

Berg, John C. *Unequal Struggle: Class, Gender, Race, and Power in the U.S. Congress.* Boulder, Colo.: Westview Press, 1994.

Brady, David W., John F. Cogan, and Morris P. Fiorina, eds. *Continuity and Change in House Elections.* Stanford, Calif.: Stanford University Press, 2000.

Canon, David T. *Actors, Athletes, and Astronauts: Political Amateurs in the United States Congress.* Chicago: University of Chicago Press, 1990.

CQ's Politics in America. Washington, D.C.: CQ Press, 1999– .

Davidson, Roger H., and Walter J. Oleszek. *Congress and Its Members.* 10th ed. Washington, D.C.: CQ Press, 2006.

Doron, Gideon, and Michael Harris. *Term Limits.* Lanham, Md.: Lexington Books, 2001.

Ehrenhalt, Alan. *United States of Ambition: Politicians, Power, and the Pursuit of Office.* New York: Times Books, 1991.

Fenno, Richard F. *Going Home: Black Representatives and Their Constituents.* Chicago: University of Chicago Press, 2003.

———. *Home Style: House Members and Their Districts.* New York: Longman, 2003.

———. *Senators on the Campaign Trail: The Politics of Representation.* Norman: University of Oklahoma Press, 1996.

Fowler, Linda, and Robert D. McClure. *Political Ambition: Who Decides to Run for Congress.* New Haven, Conn.: Yale University Press, 1989.

Freedman, Eric, and Stephen A. Jones. *African Americans in Congress: A Documentary History.* Washington, D.C.: CQ Press, 2007.

Gertzog, Irwin N. *Congressional Women: Their Recruitment, Integration, and Behavior.* 2nd ed. Westport, Conn.: Praeger, 1995.

———. *Women and Power on Capitol Hill: Reconstructing the Congressional Women's Caucus.* Boulder, Colo.: Lynne Rienner Publishers, 2004.

Gordon, Ann, and Jerry Miller. *When Stereotypes Collide: Race/Ethnicity, Gender, and Videostyle in Congressional Campaigns.* New York: Peter Lang, 2005.

Hibbing, John R. *Congressional Careers: Contours of Life in the U.S. House of Representatives.* Chapel Hill: University of North Carolina Press, 1991.

Jacobson, Gary C. *The Politics of Congressional Elections.* 6th ed. New York: Pearson Longman, 2004.

Jones Evans, Jocelyn. *Women, Partisanship, and the Congress.* New York: Palgrave Macmillan, 2005.

Kaptur, Marcy. *Women of Congress: A Twentieth-Century Odyssey.* Washington, D.C.: CQ Press, 1996.

Kura, N. O., ed. *Congressional Leadership.* New York: Nova Science Publishers, 2004.

Maisel, L. Sandy. *From Obscurity to Oblivion: Running in the Congressional Primary.* Rev. ed. Knoxville: University of Tennessee Press, 1986.

Mayhew, David R. *America's Congress: Actions in the Public Sphere, James Madison Through Newt Gingrich.* New Haven, Conn.: Yale University Press, 2000.

Merriner, James L., and Thomas P. Senter. *Against Long Odds: Citizens Who Challenge Congressional Incumbents.* Westport, Conn.: Praeger, 1999.

O'Connor, Karen, ed. *Women and Congress: Running, Winning, and Ruling.* New York: Haworth Press, 2001.

Price, David E. *The Congressional Experience.* 3rd ed. Boulder, Colo.: Westview Press, 2004.

Ragsdale, Bruce A., and Joel D. Treese. *Black Americans in Congress, 1870–1989.* U.S. House of Representatives, Office of the Historian. Washington, D.C.: Government Printing Office, 1990.

Reeher, Grant. *First Person Political: Legislative Life and the Meaning of Public Service.* New York: New York University Press, 2006.

Rosenthal, Cindy S., ed. *Women Transforming Congress.* Norman: University of Oklahoma Press, 2002.

Sabato, Larry, ed. *The Sixth Year Itch: The Rise and Fall of the George W. Bush Presidency.* New York: Pearson/Longman, 2007.

Schickler, Eric. *Disjointed Pluralism: Institutional Innovation and the Development of the U.S. Congress.* Princeton, N.J.: Princeton University Press, 2001.

Sidlow, Edward I. *Freshman Orientation: House Style and Home Style.* Washington, D.C.: CQ Press, 2006.

Smythe, April N., ed. *Women in Congress 1917–2005 with Biographies.* New York: Nova Science, 2005.

Swain, Carol M. *Black Faces, Black Interests: The Representation of African Americans in Congress.* Enl. ed. Lanham, Md.: University Press of America, 2006.

Tate, Katherine. *Black Faces in the Mirror: African Americans and Their Representatives in the U.S. Congress.* Princeton, N.J.: Princeton University Press, 2003.

Wawro, Gregory J. *Legislative Entrepreneurship in the U.S. House of Representatives.* Ann Arbor: University of Michigan Press, 2001.

chapter 4

Campaign Financing

Congress passed the first significant campaign finance law in 1907. Other landmark laws followed. Yet a century later members were still at work trying to limit the influence of money in politics.

Although campaign finance changed dramatically over the years—from a freewheeling to a heavily regulated system—the issues remained much the same: how to curb the ability of special interests and wealthy individuals to dominate the flow of campaign money, and how to establish level playing fields for challengers as well as incumbents, for politicians of modest means as well as wealthier campaigners.

The costs of elections spiraled upward by the early twenty-first century. Congressional candidates spent $1.4 billion in the 2006 elections.[1] Members found themselves under relentless pressure to raise funds for their campaigns—a time-consuming task that critics said took its toll not only on the members personally but on Congress as an institution. When members announced their retirement from Congress, more often than not the demands of campaign fund-raising were among the reasons for their decision.

Still, for those willing to stay in the game, it was a system that paid off more often than not. Even in 2006, when there was more turnover than had been seen in recent elections, 94 percent of House incumbents and 79 percent of Senate incumbents who sought reelection were returned to office. Odds like those left members with the challenge of figuring out how much they wanted to change in a system that returned the vast majority of them to the halls of Congress election after election. As reform advocate Sen. Robert C. Byrd, D-W.Va., once explained: "We are afraid to let go of the slick ads and the high-priced consultants, afraid to let go of the PAC [political action committee] money and the polls, unsure that we want to change the rules of the game that we all understand and know so well." [2]

Beyond this apparent love-hate relationship with the system was the very real question of what effective campaign finance reform might entail. Even critics of election finance knew there were no easy answers or quick fixes. For starters, there was no consensus on what was wrong with the system, let alone what would make it right. Issues came and went, and views spanned the spectrum from those who wanted to remove all restrictions other than disclosure to those who thought financing elections with public money was the only real solution.

Additionally, no one was certain how various proposals would ultimately affect the system. The history of campaign finance has notable examples of unintended consequences resulting from changes in the system. A small change in one area might lead to a dramatic change in another, or the closing of one loophole might open another.

UNCERTAINTIES, CONTROVERSIES SURROUND SYSTEM

Reformers of the campaign finance system faced the enormous task of proposing legislation that would bridge the differences between Democrats and Republicans, representatives and senators, incumbents and challengers. Members of Congress were afraid of the unknowns that surrounded change—how their own party would adapt to it and whether it might give the opposing party an advantage.

Their caution was well-founded. It was, indeed, difficult to calculate all the ramifications of the reform proposals. As Frank J. Sorauf described it: "Available money seeks an outlet, and if some outlets are narrowed or closed off, money flows with increased pressure to the outlets still open. It is the law that systems of campaign finance share with hydraulic systems." [3] Members feared that those outlets might benefit their opponents more than themselves.

Congressional attempts to curtail the influence of the wealthy "fat cat" donors in the wake of the 1970s Watergate scandal resulted in more stringent limits on individual contributions than on those from political committees. This made contributions through PACs much more attractive to some donors and in turn led to a rise in the number of PACs.

The dramatic growth of "soft money" was another example of a development many had not anticipated. Soft money referred to the unlimited, largely unregulated money contributed primarily to political parties for activities and expenses not directly related to federal elections. It was called "soft" to distinguish it from the "hard money" that was used for federal election campaigns and regulated by the Federal Election Campaign Act (FECA)—money that was "hard" to raise because of the FECA's limits and restrictions. Corporations and labor unions had been prohibited from participating directly in federal elections for a good part of the twentieth century, and in the 1970s an aggregate contribution limit was placed on individual donors. But there was no limit at that point on the amount of soft money they could contribute to the parties or spend on nonfederal election activities.

In the 1970s the Federal Election Commission (FEC), the independent agency charged with overseeing compliance with the federal election laws, relaxed some of the rules covering the separation of federal campaign funds from state and local parties' nonfederal money. The FEC allowed the state and local parties for the first time to use nonfederal soft money to pay for a portion of their administrative expenses,

CAMPAIGN FINANCING GLOSSARY

Following is a glossary of some commonly used terms in the campaign finance field. It was drawn from documents produced by the Federal Election Commission, (FEC), Center for Responsive Politics, Congressional Research Service of the Library of Congress, and Congressional Quarterly. The definitions reflect the laws and regulations in force as of May 2007.

Bundling. The practice of aggregating separate contributions from various individuals for delivery to a candidate, thereby generating clout for the individual or organization that collected and delivered the contributions. The bundler could focus on employees of a particular business, members of a particular profession, or activists committed to a particular policy. Because the bundler merely forwarded batches of checks made out by individuals to a candidate, the contributions did not count against the bundler's own contribution limits.

Electioneering Communication. Term used in the 2002 Bipartisan Campaign Reform Act (BCRA) to describe any broadcast, cable, or satellite communication that referred to a clearly identified federal candidate, was publicly distributed within sixty days of a general election or thirty days of a primary, and was targeted to the relevant electorate, which in the case of House and Senate elections was defined as something that could be received by 50,000 or more people in a state or district.

Hard Money. Money raised and spent for federal election campaigns under the limitations and prohibitions of the Federal Election Campaign Act (FECA).

Independent Expenditures. Money spent for communications (such as broadcast advertisements or direct mail) that expressly advocated the election or defeat of a candidate. Such spending was deemed "independent" so long as the entity making the expenditure did not coordinate, cooperate, or consult in any way with the candidate's campaign.

These expenditures were regulated by federal election laws. Thus, while individuals, groups, or political parties could spend unlimited amounts of money on independent campaign efforts, they had to report these expenditures to the FEC once they reached a certain level. In addition, the entity sponsoring the independent advertising campaign had to identify itself in its ads and note that the ad was not authorized by the candidate's committee.

Issue Advocacy Advertising. Advertisements advocating a particular position on an issue. Such advertising often implicitly supported the candidates of one political party by advocating the same position they held on an issue. The BCRA placed restrictions on ads that met the definition of "electioneering communication."

Political Action Committee (PAC). Organizations created to raise and spend money for candidates for federal office. They were typically begun by corporations, industries, trade associations, labor unions, ideology groups, or others with shared policy interests.

A "leadership PAC" was such a committee run by one or more congressional leaders, or other members who might aspire to leadership positions or other offices, or might be trying to win support for certain policies or legislation. When members outside the leadership structure started creating PACs, the term "personal PAC" also came into use. Contributions to this type of PAC were considered separate from contributions to the campaign committee of the individual member who sponsored the PAC. A contributor who had given the maximum amount allowed to the House Speaker's campaign committee, for example, still could give to the Speaker's leadership PAC. These PACs were subject to the same constraints as other PACs.

Section 527 Organizations. Tax-exempt "political organizations" organized under Section 527 of the Internal Revenue Code and involved in federal, state, and local elections, as well as nonelectoral activities. Those that were engaged primarily in federal election activities and subject to federal campaign finance laws included party committees, candidate committees, and PACs. But usually the term "527" or "527 organization" referred to a type of 527 that did not expressly advocate the election or defeat of candidates but instead focused on election-related activities such as issue advocacy and voter mobilization that were financed largely by soft money. The previously secretive groups were required in 2000 to disclose their existence and file reports on their receipts and expenditures with the Internal Revenue Service. As of early 2007, however, they remained outside the limits of federal campaign finance laws and continued to be major outlets for soft money.

Soft Money. Money raised and spent outside the limitations and prohibitions of the Federal Election Campaign Act and, therefore, not to be used for activities directly related to federal election campaigns. Prior to enactment of BCRA, this money was raised primarily by the national, state, and local Republican and Democratic parties for get-out-the-vote efforts, administrative costs, generic party advertising, and to help state and local candidates. Activities that benefited federal, state, and local candidates had to be funded in part by hard money. There was no limit on the amount of money that a donor (an individual, corporation, labor union, or PAC) could give to a party's soft money account, but the party had to disclose the source of contributions in excess of $200. The BCRA banned the national parties and federal candidates from accepting or spending soft money. The 2002 law allowed state and local political parties to spend soft money on voter registration and mobilization in federal elections only under certain conditions. In the wake of the BCRA, a new type of soft money channeled through Section 527 organizations gained prominence.

as well as voter drives and generic party activities, even if they had an indirect effect on federal campaigns. Congress then passed legislation to encourage greater participation of these parties in presidential election campaigns, allowing them to spend unlimited amounts of hard money on voter drives, campaign materials, and the like.

The combination of these actions by the FEC and Congress triggered a surge in soft money. Once the national parties determined that they, too, could use soft money for certain expenses, they began raising millions of dollars for their nonfederal accounts. Soon the money was being spent not only for get-out-the-vote drives but for major advertising campaigns said to promote party issues, not candidates. Being able to use soft money for certain party expenses had the added advantage of freeing up more hard dollars for direct aid to federal candidates, further fueling the upward spiral of campaign spending. The aggressive pursuit of soft money during the 1996 election campaign by the parties and the Clinton White House, along with a variety of illegal campaign contributions, helped produce the most significant campaign finance scandal since Watergate and renewed calls for reforms. *(See "1996 Scandal," p. 100.)*

A law enacted in 2002 banned the national parties from using soft money and placed restrictions on issue ads. But unregulated money had already started moving through another outlet—tax-exempt political organizations known as "527s" after the section of the Internal Revenue Code under which they were organized. When the new law went into effect, millions of dollars shifted to Section 527 groups.

Public Opinion

Americans have found much to criticize in the way campaigns are financed, according to public opinion surveys. In the wake of the 1996 scandal, a public opinion survey in 1997 found that a majority (57 percent) of Americans was dissatisfied with the state of the political system, and the role of money was one of the main sources of that discontent. About two-thirds of those polled cited as major problems the excessive influence of political contributions on elections and government policy and the conflict of interest created when elected officials solicited or took contributions while making policy decisions. A majority also said that elected officials spent too much time fund-raising and that the high cost of campaigns discouraged good people from running for office.

A 2002 survey of public attitudes toward party soft money found that nearly 71 percent of the American public thought that members of Congress sometimes decided how they would vote on an issue based on what big contributors to their political party wanted, even if it was not what most of their constituents wanted or what they thought was best for the country. An even larger majority—84 percent—thought members would be more likely to listen to contributors who gave to their political party in response to their solicitation for large donations. The survey also found that 71 percent of Americans agreed that members spent so much time raising funds for their political parties that it interfered with their ability to do their jobs properly. The principal investigators for the survey—Democratic pollster Mark Mellman and Republican pollster Richard Wirthlin—said it was uncommon to have 70 percent or more of the public see an issue the same way. Their poll was submitted as evidence in support of the 2002 Bipartisan Campaign Reform Act (BCRA) in the court case challenging the new law.

Polls have continued to show that a majority of Americans have problems with the system. For example, a 2004 survey found that 76 percent of Americans were bothered by the amount of money politicians spent on campaigns—and of those, 59 percent were "very much" bothered.

In a 2007 Harris poll on which groups had the most power in influencing government policy, politicians, and policymakers in Washington, participants put "political action committees, which give money to political candidates" at the top of the list—over big companies, political lobbyists, and the news media, among other groups. When asked whether specific groups had too much or too little power and influence in Washington, 85 percent agreed that PACs had too much influence and 84 percent said the same about big companies, 79 percent about lobbyists, and 71 percent about the media.[4]

Search for Solutions

Attempts to reform the campaign finance system were nothing new. Campaign finance reformers over the years have sought to curb campaign spending by limiting and regulating campaign expenditures and donations made to candidates, as well as by informing voters of the amounts and sources of the donations, and the amounts, purposes, and recipients of the expenditures. Disclosure was intended to reveal which candidates, if any, were unduly indebted to interest groups in time to forewarn the voters.

Congress had argued the issues of campaign finance since the first law regulating campaigns was enacted during the administration of Theodore Roosevelt in 1907. Over the next century, major new laws, however, came only after the scandals of Teapot Dome in the 1920s, Watergate in the 1970s, and the 1996 election.

Reform never comes easily. "There are no fights like campaign finance fights because they are battles about the essence of politics and power," as then–Common Cause president Fred Wertheimer once put it.[5]

In 1925 the Teapot Dome scandal yielded the Federal Corrupt Practices Act, an extensive statute governing the conduct of federal campaigns. That act codified earlier laws limiting campaign expenditures, but the limits were so unrealistically low and the law so riddled with loopholes that it was ineffectual.

From left: Sens. John Glenn, D-Ohio, Dennis DeConcini, D-Ariz., and John McCain, R-Ariz., were three of the Keating Five senators accused of aiding savings and loan association head Charles Keating when he was under investigation for his banking practices. The five senators had all received substantial campaign contributions from Keating. McCain went on to make campaign finance reform a key legislative goal.

Watergate, however, changed all that. The June 1972 break-in at Democratic national headquarters in Washington, D.C.'s Watergate office building touched off a scandal that became the 1970s' code word for governmental corruption. Although the scandal had many aspects, money in politics was at its roots. Included in Watergate's catalog of misdeeds were specific violations of campaign spending laws such as corporate contributions, violations of other criminal laws facilitated by the availability of virtually unlimited campaign contributions, and instances of probable influence peddling.

Congress had begun to move on campaign finance even before Watergate. Less than six months before the break-in, Congress had adopted two pieces of legislation containing some of the ground rules under which elections were still being conducted in the 2000s. First, Congress approved legislation allowing a one-dollar tax checkoff to finance presidential campaigns. (The amount was increased to three dollars by 1993 legislation.) Congress also passed the Federal Election Campaign Act (FECA), requiring comprehensive disclosure of campaign contributions and expenditures by candidates for federal office and placing a limit on the amount of money candidates could spend on media advertising. (The media spending limits were repealed in 1974.) However, the 1971 FECA ultimately had a limited impact on controlling campaign spending.

But Watergate focused public attention on campaign spending at all levels of government. In the aftermath came the most significant overhaul in campaign finance legislation in the nation's history. Major legislation was enacted in 1974 (the House passed its version on the day Richard Nixon announced he would resign the presidency) and 1976. Coming on the heels of the 1971 legislation, these laws radically altered the system of financing federal elections.

The FECA Amendments of 1974 set limits on contributions and expenditures for congressional and presidential elections, established the FEC, and created the framework for providing presidential candidates with public financing.

Before the sweeping 1974 act received its first real test, it was extensively pruned by the Supreme Court. The Court in its 1976 decision in *Buckley v. Valeo* upheld the FECA's disclosure requirements, contribution limitations, and system for the public financing of presidential elections. But it struck down spending limits for congressional and presidential races, including restraints on the use of a candidate's personal assets, except for presidential candidates who accepted public financing. It also struck down limits on independent expenditures—expenditures made in support of, or in opposition to, a candidate but without the knowledge or cooperation of the candidate.

The justices weighed First Amendment rights against the 1974 act's underlying purpose: prevention of the abuses that surfaced during Watergate. In the case of contributions, the Court concluded that First Amendment considerations were outweighed because "the quantity of communication by the contributor does not increase perceptibly with the size of his contribution." But it found limiting expenditures to be a "substantial" restraint on free speech that could preclude "significant use of the most effective modes of communication."

Many subsequent congressional efforts to change the campaign finance system were driven by the desire to find a way to limit congressional campaign spending without violating the mandates of the Court decision. With the ceilings on expenditures removed, campaign costs grew apace and candidates became increasingly dependent on raising money in the easiest and most cost-effective way—from PACs.

In striking down restraints on independent expenditures, the Supreme Court opened the door for individuals and PACs to spend millions of dollars; such spenders were generally derided by candidates and party leaders as unwelcome "loose cannons" in the political process. Sharply negative ads underwritten by the independent expenditures of nonconnected, or ideological, PACs especially gained the enmity of both parties.

In 1979 Congress amended the FECA, in part to encourage more grassroots and political party activity in federal campaigns. Included in the package of amendments was the section allowing state and local parties to underwrite voter drives on behalf of presidential tickets without regard to financial limits.

After the 1970s Congress proved less amenable to further major changes in campaign financing. Proposals were debated but it would be a decade before either chamber passed a major campaign finance bill. Once again it would be scandals that provided the impetus.

In 1989 allegations of ethical violations and questionable financial dealings involving Speaker Jim Wright, D-Texas, intensified pressures on House Democrats to act on campaign finance legislation. Wright, facing charges that would lead to his resignation from Congress, embraced campaign finance reform and created a bipartisan task force to develop a reform plan.

Further pressure for change came the following year in the form of the Keating Five scandal, so named for five senators suspected of doing favors for a wealthy campaign contributor, Charles H. Keating Jr. The controversy, an offshoot of the savings and loan scandal, added fuel to a fire that Common Cause, a public interest lobby, had lit under Congress to revise the campaign system.

At the heart of the Keating Five scandal was $1.5 million in contributions made or solicited by Keating, the powerful owner of a thrift and real estate empire, for the campaigns or other political causes of the five senators. More than half of the money—$850,000—was paid out of corporate funds to nonprofit voter registration organizations with which one of the senators, Alan Cranston, D-Calif., was affiliated. Keating also employed a technique called "bundling," through which he raised many individual contributions from family members, associates, and employees of his companies and handed them over in a lump sum designed to impress the recipient politicians. Televised hearings and news stories revealing Keating's use of his fund-raising skills to assemble clout in Washington proved far more effective at raising questions about the relationship between elected officials and major contributors than the flood of statistics about PACs that were issued by government watchdog groups. But repeated attempts to enact new legislation in the early 1990s proved fruitless.

Many expected that the scandal surrounding the 1996 election would renew fervor for reform. At the root of the scandal were allegations that foreign money had made it into the campaign in violation of federal law, and that the Democrats' pursuit and use of soft money might have crossed the line into illegal activity. President Bill Clinton and Vice President Al Gore were embarrassed by revelations of what could only be described as fund-raising excesses, the Democratic National Committee returned nearly $3 million in illegal or suspect contributions, and some contributors to the Democrats were convicted of campaign finance law violations. *(See "1996 Scandal," p. 100.)*

Although it took several attempts, Congress did pass legislation in 2002 to ban party use of soft money and to restrict issue ads.

CONGRESSIONAL CANDIDATES' CONTRIBUTIONS AND EXPENDITURES

The modern congressional election is a complex financial affair. Fund-raisers, accountants, lawyers, webmasters, and a variety of consultants play crucial roles in today's campaigns. Decisions on how to raise money and how to marshal a campaign's resources can be key to electoral success.

Money pours in from a vast array of sources—not all of them controlled by the candidate—including individuals, PACs, party committees, candidates themselves and their families, and independent organizations seeking to influence the outcome. Money flows out for rent, computers, salaries, polls, consulting fees, printing, postage, and radio, television, and newspaper advertising.

Much of the money that at one time moved in the shadows of campaigns is now a matter of public record, thanks to the stringent disclosure provisions of the FECA. All candidates for federal office, once they cross a certain threshold, periodically must submit to the FEC itemized accounts of contributions and expenditures in excess of $200 and debts and obligations owed to or by the candidate or committee. These detailed reports, which are made public by the FEC online and in the agency's Public Records office, provide a window on the modern political campaign.

Political Contributions

FEC figures indicated that congressional candidates raised more than $1.4 billion during the 2005–2006 election cycle. House and Senate incumbents together raised about $792 million; challengers raised $375 million. Almost $254 million was raised by candidates for open seats.

When broken down by chamber, the figures showed that Senate candidates raised a total of nearly $565 million, with incumbents attracting more than $278 million, challengers almost $187 million, and open-seat candidates almost $100 million.

House candidates took in more than $875 million. The incumbents' share was almost $533 million, while challengers raised about $189 million and open-seat candidates $154 million.

Much of this money came from two principal sources: individual contributions and PACs. Candidates' personal money—either in the form of loans or direct contributions—was also an important source of funding. Lesser amounts came from the political parties.

Individual Contributions

Political campaigns have traditionally been financed by the contributions of individual donors. The biggest difference today is that many more contributors are now involved in the process. The pre-Watergate contributors of unlimited amounts of money to federal candidates—the so-called "fat cats"—have been largely replaced by smaller donors who either give directly or contribute through a political party committee or PAC. The big donors, of course, have not disappeared. After coming up against statutory limits on direct contributions to federal campaigns, they found other outlets. These might include members' "leadership PACs" or groups outside the scope of federal campaign finance law, such as Section 527 political organizations. *(See "Political Action Committees," p. 70 and "Section 527 Groups," p. 82.)*

The BCRA of 2002 raised limits on individual contributions and indexed them for inflation. Under the new law individuals could contribute $2,000—double the previous limit—per candidate per election (primary elections, general elections, and special elections are considered separate elections with separate limits). The aggregate limit for an individual's contributions during a two-year cycle was set at $95,000—$37,500 to candidates and $57,500 to parties and PACs. To give that two-year contribution maximum, an individual had to contribute at least $20,000 to the national parties. By 2007, the inflation-adjusted limit on contributions to candidates had climbed to $2,300 and the aggregate limit to $108,200. *(See Table 4-1, p. 93.)*

Individual donors' reasons for giving are varied, as political scientist Paul Herrnson pointed out in a study of House races. People may give simply because they want to see a change in Congress. They may want access to influential incumbent members or enjoy hobnobbing with political elites. They may want to support those with whom they share a common ethnic, racial, or religious bond.[6]

Whatever the motive, individual contributions to congressional candidates in 2005–2006 amounted to $862 million, or about 60 percent of candidates' total receipts of $1.4 billion. When broken down by chamber, individual contributions accounted for about 68 percent ($383 million) of Senate candidates' receipts and about 55 percent ($479 million) of House candidates'.

Although scarcely used by individuals in congressional elections, an "independent expenditure" is another avenue for affecting elections. This is an expenditure for communications advocating the election or defeat of a candidate that is made without the knowledge or cooperation of the candidate or the candidate's campaign organization. Congress had placed a limit on such expenditures in the 1974 FECA amendments but this, along with most other limits, was thrown out by the Supreme Court in 1976 as a violation of First Amendment rights. PACs and, more recently, political parties have used independent expenditures on a far larger scale than individual donors have. Independent expenditures must be reported to the FEC when they exceed $250 per year.

Political Action Committees (PACs)

Labor unions, corporations, and incorporated trade and membership organizations are prohibited by law from using their general treasury funds to make contributions or expenditures in federal elections. They therefore participate indirectly in the electoral process through separate segregated funds. These separate segregated funds, along with the political committees of other organizations (such as ideological and issue groups) that raise money for candidates, are known as political action committees (PACs). Most PACs are permitted to contribute $5,000 per candidate per election, with no overall limit. They also may give $15,000 per year to a national party committee.

PACs have been around for many years. The Congress of Industrial Organizations (CIO) founded the first modern PAC in 1943 when labor unions were barred from contributing to campaigns directly. According to the FEC, the number of registered PACs at the end of 1974 was 608. By mid-2007 there were 4,168 PACs registered.

The more telling statistics on PAC growth are those on PAC contributions. In the 1977–1978 election cycle, PACs contributed $34 million to congressional candidates. By 2005–2006 the total had reached nearly $349 million. PAC contributions in the 2006 cycle constituted 32 percent of House candidates' receipts and 12 percent of contributions to Senate candidates.

Why the explosive growth in PAC numbers and dollars? The answer can be found in part in the reform legislation of the 1970s. In 1971 Congress sanctioned the use of regular corporate and union funds to pay the overhead costs of PACs. Legislation in 1974 placed more stringent limits on individual contributions than on those from PACs. Most PACs at that time could give five times more than an individual contributor to a candidate—$5,000 versus $1,000. (The 2002 reform law raised the individual contribution limit to $2,000 and indexed it for inflation.) That same year Congress also lifted restrictions on the formation of PACs by government contractors.

PACs also tended to fill a void left by weakened political parties in the 1970s. "As citizen loyalties to political parties waned, as the party organizations weakened, and as the parties lost control of campaigns to the media and candidates, interest groups became the political organization of choice for many Americans concerned about specific (and even narrow) interests and issues," explained Frank Sorauf.[7]

Further impetus for growth came in 1975 when the FEC ruled that the Sun Oil Co. could establish a PAC and solicit contributions to SunPAC from stockholders and employees; the ruling eliminated the last barrier that had prevented corporations from forming PACs. FEC figures show that the number of corporate PACs jumped from 139 at the time of the SunPAC ruling in November 1975 to 433 by the end of 1976. PACs also reaped benefits from the Supreme Court's 1976 decision striking down restrictions on independent spending. *(See "1976 Amendments," p. 96.)*

Reaction to the rapid growth of PAC numbers and influence varied dramatically. Some saw it as a manifestation of democracy at work in a pluralist society, while others perceived it as a threat by special interests to the integrity of the electoral system and governmental process. *(See "PAC Phenomenon," p. 79.)*

But certain facts about PACs have been beyond dispute. One is that PACs have been overwhelmingly oriented toward incumbents. FEC figures showed that of the nearly $349 million that candidates reported receiving from PACs during the 2006 campaign, about $280 million went to incumbents, while only about $34 million went to challengers and about $32 million to open-seat candidates.

While some critics contend that PACs are out to buy votes with their contributions, many observers believe that their aim is to get access to members in positions to help—or hinder—their cause. An example of this could be seen in the jump in contributions business PACs made to Democratic incumbents in the House during the 1980s. This increase was attributed to the persuasive powers of California Rep. Tony Coelho, chair of the Democratic Congressional Campaign Committee in the early 1980s, who was said to have convinced traditionally conservative PACs of the logic of having access to a sitting member of the House instead of wasting money on a challenger who was likely to lose.

Thus, pragmatism won out over ideology, as corporate PAC contributions to Democrats edged up to more than 50 percent. That same pragmatism could be seen after the Republicans took control of Congress in 1995 and again when the Democrats returned to power in 2007. A *Wall Street Journal* analysis of data for the first quarter of 2007 described the shift in corporate PAC contributions from the Republicans to the Democrats in the House as "swift and stark" and said Senate contributions showed a similar trend. Congressional Quarterly's *PoliticalMoneyLine* reported that 62 percent of all PAC contributions to federal candidates in that first quarter went to Democrats and 38 percent to Republicans. In the 2005–2006 election cycle 45 percent had gone to Democrats and 55 percent to Republicans.[8]

Labor PACs, however, showed none of the corporate PACs' pragmatism. They were in the Democratic camp when the Democrats controlled Congress; they were in the Democratic camp when the GOP was in control.

Independent Expenditures. In addition to direct contributions to candidates, PACs also can make independent expenditures. PACs reported independent expenditures of $22 million for congressional candidates in the 2005–2006 election cycle, and nearly $15 million against candidates. Those figures represented a substantial jump over the $7.5 million spent for candidates and the $1.5 million against in the previous congressional election.

Still, the numbers were small compared to overall PAC spending. Independent spending has not become a major PAC tactic because, as Sorauf pointed out, independent expenditures can earn more enmity than gratitude from candidates and do not produce the close political relationship with candidates that PACs are seeking.[9]

Leadership PACs. Although PACs are usually associated with interest groups outside Congress, a small but influential group of PACs called leadership PACs—also known as personal PACs, member PACs, or politicians' PACs—exists within Congress. These are separate PACs formed by members of Congress or other political leaders independent of their own campaign committees. They often are the PACs of presidential hopefuls, congressional leaders, or would-be leaders. "In almost all cases—and this is central to their role as brokers—sponsoring individuals are raising and giving money at least in part to support their own political careers, positions, or goals," Sorauf wrote.[10]

Members initially used such PACS primarily to contribute to other candidates, but they increasingly have used them to pay for their own travel or other officeholder expenses supposedly not connected with their own campaigns. Because a member's leadership PAC is considered to be separate from the member's campaign committee, contributors can give to both up to the statutory limits. More than 350 leadership PACs reported receipts and usually disbursements in the 2006 election cycle.[11]

Political Parties

Political parties traditionally have provided direct assistance to candidates in two ways: through contributions, and through payments to vendors on a candidate's behalf. The latter, known as coordinated expenditures, fund any number of campaign services such as polling, research, direct mailings, advertising, or buying TV time.

Party committees also persuade others to contribute. Convincing PACs, individuals, and incumbents to support a party's most competitive challengers and open-seat candidates has been one of the major tasks of the congressional campaign committees.[12] These congressional, or Hill, committees are the Democratic Senatorial Campaign Committee, National Republican Senatorial Committee, Democratic Congressional Campaign Committee, and the National Republican Congressional Committee.

Parties have other ways to aid candidates, such as making independent expenditures in support of a party's candidates. For a time parties used soft money donations for get-out-the-vote drives and issue advertising, but the 2002 reform act put parties out of the soft money business.

Direct Contributions. National committees, which include the parties' national committees as well as the House and Senate campaign committees, are each permitted to make contributions of $5,000 per candidate per election. That amounts to a total of $20,000 in party money for candidates' primary and general election races for the House. For Senate candidates the 2002 law set a limit of $35,000 to be indexed for inflation. As of 2007, the Senate limit was $39,900. State, district, and local party committees may give a combined total of $5,000 per election.

Coordinated expenditures are made only in general elections, and the amount the parties may spend on behalf of a candidate is set by formula. For House candidates in states with more than one member, the national party expenditure limit is set at $10,000, adjusted for inflation, which translated into a $39,600 limit for the 2006 election. For House candidates in states with only one member, the national parties could spend up to the limit for Senate candidates in those states, which in 2006 was $79,200. For Senate candidates, the party could spend the greater of either $20,000, adjusted for inflation—$79,200 in 2006—or two cents for every person of voting age, again adjusted for inflation. According to this formula, coordinated expenditures for Senate candidates in 2006 ranged from the base figure of $79,200 in the less populous states to a high of $2.1 million in California.

State party committees are also allowed to make coordinated expenditures in the same amounts as the national party. State parties, however, often do not have that kind of money, so the national party is permitted to use its money to make the expenditures on behalf of the state, in effect doubling its expenditure limit for a particular state or district.

The Republican Party has proven itself over the years to be the more successful fund-raiser of the two parties. GOP fund-raising prowess certainly could be expected when it was the majority party in Congress, but Herrnson wrote that some aspects of their advantage were more permanent, including a superior direct-mail fund-raising list and a wealthier constituency.[13]

The bulk of the money political parties raise goes for party-building, electoral, and fund-raising activities. In the 2005–2006 election cycle, for example, national, state, and local Republican Party committees reported federal receipts of more than $602 million and expenditures of more than $608 million. Of this, they contributed only $1.4 million directly to congressional candidates and made coordinated expenditures of not quite $14 million. Democrats raised a total of $483 million and spent more than $472 million. They contributed $1.3 million to congressional candidates and spent more than $18 million on their behalf. Direct contributions and expenditures by the parties constitute a comparatively small percentage of the overall receipts of candidates. Parties, however, help candidates in other ways.

Independent Expenditures. A new avenue for parties' use of hard dollars was opened in 1996 when the Supreme Court threw out restrictions on independent expenditures by political parties (*Colorado Republican Federal Campaign Committee v. Federal Election Commission*). The ruling meant that the parties could spend unlimited amounts on such things as advertising that called for the election—or defeat—of specific candidates, as long as they did not coordinate those expenditures with the campaigns of their candidates.

The 2002 law included a provision requiring parties to choose between making coordinated expenditures or independent expenditures for a candidate. That provision, however, was struck down by the Supreme Court in its 2003 ruling in *McConnell v. Federal Election Commission.*

Party independent expenditures grew dramatically after that, becoming a particularly potent tool for the congressional campaign committees. In the 2006 election the Republican Party committees spent almost $116 million on independent expenditures, as compared to $88 million in the 2004 election, and about $2 million in the 2002 midterm election. The Democratic Party committees spent $108 million in 2006, more than $176 million in 2004, and $1.7 million in 2002.

Independent expenditures allowed the parties to shift at will significant amounts of money into competitive races. In the 2006 Senate race in Missouri, for example, the Democratic Party's independent expenditures against Republican Sen. Jim Talent totaled nearly $8 million, while the party's independent expenditures for its candidate, Claire McCaskill, amounted to about $1.8 million. The Republican Party's independent expenditures against McCaskill totaled almost $10 million. The two parties' direct, coordinated, and independent spending in the Missouri Senate race added up to a combined total of more than $21 million.

Other Assistance. Political parties like to act as conduits, passing contributions through their committees to candidates. Thanks to sophisticated computers and mass mailings, a party can target those who might be interested in a race and encourage them to contribute. Through a practice called earmarking, a contributor can direct money to a candidate or committee through an intermediary, such as the party. The money counts against the donor's contribution limits.

Computers and such techniques as electronic bank drafts have also facilitated the practice of bundling, in which checks from a number of contributors are grouped together and presented as a package to a candidate. For bundling to be legal, however, the original donors must retain control over designation of the eventual recipient.

Soft Money. The BCRA put an end to the national parties' raising of unlimited amounts of soft money from unions, corporations, trade associations, and individuals. The parties had spent the money on issue ads as well as grassroots activities—such as voter registration, education, and turnout—that were supposedly to benefit party candidates at all levels. The 2002 reform law, however, did allow state and local parties to spend soft money on voter registration and mobilization under certain conditions and limits. Such activities would benefit all candidates, including federal. (These limited funds were referred to as "Levin funds," after Sen. Carl Levin, D-Mich., who authored the exception in the 2002 law.)

Candidate's Own Money

Another source of money for campaigns is the candidate's own bank account. Candidates can reach as deeply into their own pockets as they want because there are no limits on how much candidates may contribute or loan to their own campaigns. But opponents of self-financed candidates are now allowed to compensate for that advantage by fund-raising above the standard limits.

In 1974 Congress attempted to set limits on how much House and Senate candidates could contribute to their own campaigns, but before the limits could take effect they were ruled unconstitutional by the Supreme Court in the 1976 *Buckley* decision. The Court ruled that "the candidate, no less than any other person, has a First Amendment right to engage in the discussion of public issues and vigorously and tirelessly to advocate his own election."

In keeping with the law's intent to clean up campaign finance activities, the justices also wrote that "the use of personal funds reduces the candidate's dependence on outside contributions and thereby counteracts the coercive pressure and attendant risks of abuse to which the act's contribution limitations are directed."

Most political observers agreed that the Court had given wealthy contenders a tremendous advantage. Simply having access to money and a willingness to pour a lot of it into a campaign did not guarantee election victory. But wealthy candidates were able to afford expensive, professional consultants and plan their strategy with greater assurance than candidates without a personal fortune.

And money enabled the wealthy, but unknown, candidate to make the first splash in a crowded field of relatively obscure contenders for an open seat in Congress. While dozens of potential candidates might jockey for position, the one who could begin a campaign with an early television blitz was likely to start several lengths ahead.

Television stations require campaigns to pay their bills before any material is aired. For this reason, candidates with the ability to loan or contribute a sizable sum could purchase expensive television advertising whenever they wanted, while those less well-off financially were forced to wait until money came in before beginning their media buy.

With these advantages in mind, Congress included in the 2002 law a section that became known as the "millionaire's amendment." Although House and Senate candidates had different formulas, the amendment basically allowed candidates facing self-financed opponents to accept contributions from individuals above the standard limit once their opponents crossed a certain personal spending threshold. The amendment also allowed for increased coordinated expenditures by national and state party committees.

As a campaign progresses, especially after the primary, the advantage of personal wealth diminishes. Candidates without a personal fortune then have greater access to other sources of money, particularly from party coffers; the field is smaller, making it easier for voters to draw clear distinctions between the candidates; and more free publicity is available as the general election draws nearer. There are many cases where a rich candidate was able to clear out the primary field but then lost in the general election.

While being able to bankroll a large portion of one's own campaign has many advantages, it also has several clear disadvantages. The most obvious and frequently encountered is that it opens self-financed candidates to charges that they are trying to "buy" the election. Sometimes the opposition levels the charge; often the media raises it.

Another disadvantage is that outside money can be harder to raise. Potential contributors often assume the rich candidates do not need their money. In some cases that may be true. But from a political standpoint a healthy list of contributors can give a campaign more credibility by indicating that the candidate, besides having a fat war chest, has a broad base of support.

FEC figures for the 2005–2006 election cycle showed that congressional candidates loaned themselves $103 million—about $47 million in the Senate and $56 million in the House. Candidates contributed more than $52 million to their campaigns—almost $38 million in the Senate and nearly $15 million in the House.

The largest user of personal money in the 2006 election was Democrat Ned Lamont of Connecticut, who spent nearly $17 million of his own money ($3 million of which was in loans) in an unsuccessful attempt to unseat incumbent Sen. Joseph I. Lieberman, who ran as an independent after losing to Lamont in the Democratic primary. But Lamont's use of his personal fortune still fell short of the more than $28 million ($12 million of which was in loans) that first-term Republican Rep. Michael Huffington put into his unsuccessful 1994 campaign to unseat Democratic Sen. Dianne Feinstein of California.

Candidates usually opt to loan rather than give money to their campaigns in the hope that, if they win, they might get some of it back from fund-raising after the election.

Campaign Expenditures

Congressional candidates spent approximately $1.4 billion in the 2005–2006 election cycle, as compared to not quite $1.2 billion in the previous one. House and Senate incumbents together spent more than $776 million, while challengers spent nearly $373 million and open-seat candidates almost $252 million. Incumbents ended the campaign with a cash surplus of almost $207 million—proof that they had plenty of firepower to summon had they felt the need.

Figures for Senate candidates showed total expenditures of $563 million. Incumbents spent just over $274 million; challengers, $187 million; and open-seat candidates, more than $101 million. House candidates spent $855 million, with incumbents spending $519 million; challengers, almost $186 million; and open-seat candidates, $150 million.

How money is spent varies from one campaign to another. The needs of a House candidate are different from those of a Senate candidate. The needs of a challenger are different from those of an incumbent. A Senate candidate in a large state runs a different campaign than a candidate in a small state. Representatives of urban, suburban, and rural congressional districts run vastly different campaigns. Costs skyrocket in hotly contested races and are negligible in races with little or no opposition.

But some generalizations may be made. Campaigns have to pay for staff and rent. They hire consultants, media experts, and polling firms. They send out computerized mailings. They buy postage, campaign buttons, bumper stickers, billboards, newspaper ads, radio spots, and television time—lots of television time.

Television Costs

Television advertising plays a significant role in campaigns. Airtime—or the lack thereof—can decide elections. "The hard fact of life for a candidate is that if you are not on TV, you are not truly in the race," Sen. Ernest F. Hollings, D-S.C., told a congressional committee in 1990.[14]

And it is costly. "You simply transfer money from contributors to television stations," as Sen. Bill Bradley, D-N.J., said in 1991.[15] Sen. Barbara Boxer, D-Calif., shared Bradley's exasperation. During a 2001 floor debate, she talked about her 1998 race: "To say the costs are unreasonable is an understatement. They are confiscatory. They are taking 80 percent or 90 percent of our budget after we pay our overhead. . . . I raised $20 million and huge sums went to television."[16]

The Congressional Research Service (CRS), in a 1997 report on proposals to give candidates free or reduced-rate television time, found electronic media advertising to be the single largest category of aggregate Senate and House campaign expenditures. (This category included radio and TV airtime, production costs, and consultant fees.) Studies of the 1990, 1992, and 1994 elections cited by CRS found these costs consumed about 27 percent of campaign budgets in House races and about 40–45 percent in Senate races. The percentages went up for more competitive races and in Senate races in larger states, as well as for challengers and open-seat contenders.[17]

Although television has been an important tool in House campaigns, it has not been consistently so. For example, Sara Fritz and Dwight Morris, in a *Los Angeles Times* study, found that in the 1990 campaign more than one-fourth of House incumbents reported spending no money on broadcast advertising.[18] In urban centers such as Los Angeles, New York, and Chicago, it had not been cost effective, as an assistant to Rep. Howard L. Berman, D-Calif., who represented the San Fernando Valley suburbs of Los Angeles, explained:

> You spend thousands for one thirty-second spot on one TV station, in a city where cable is rampant and there are a zillion channels. There are sixteen to seventeen congressional districts in L.A., so the vast majority of those who see it are not your constituents and can't vote for you anyway.[19]

A study by the Brennan Center for Justice found in the 2000 election that more than $176 million was spent on TV ads in the general election campaigns for thirty-four U.S. Senate seats. Candidates accounted for 72 percent of that spending. One candidate in particular helped drive up those numbers—New Jersey Democrat Jon Corzine's campaign spent nearly $33 million on television in his successful race for the Senate.

In House general election races in 2000, more than $147 million was spent on TV ads, with candidates accounting for about 54 percent of that spending. But television's use and practicality in House races varied widely. As the Brennan Center report noted, TV ads were "often too expensive for House candidates, and compact districts often make television advertising inefficient." Nearly three-quarters of the advertising aired within forty-five races considered competitive—about 10 percent of all House races.[20]

Other Costs

Congressional candidates face a variety of other costs in their pursuit of a seat in the House or Senate. As with media costs, there are many variables. Incumbents, challengers, and open-seat candidates will allocate funds differently, depending on the competitiveness of the race, the size of their constituency, and, of course, their resources.

In a study of the 1992 races, Dwight Morris and Murielle E. Gamache found that House incumbents on average spent about 25 percent of their money on overhead, which included such items as rent, office furniture, telephones, computers, salaries, taxes, travel, and food. About 15 percent was spent on fund-raising efforts like events, direct mail, and telemarketing; 4 percent on polling; 27 percent on electronic and other advertising; 20 percent on other campaign activity (voter contact mail, actual campaigning, and food, gifts, etc., for staff and volunteers); 5 percent on donations to other candidates, political parties, and civic organizations; and 4 percent on miscellaneous gifts and expenses.

Senate incumbents reported about 25 percent on overhead, 21 percent on fund-raising, 3 percent on polling, 41 percent on advertising, 8 percent on other campaign activity, 1 percent on donations, and 2 percent on miscellaneous items.[21]

CAMPAIGN FINANCE ISSUES AND CONTROVERSIES

The debates on campaign finance proposals after the 1970s highlighted the vastly different views members of Congress held on the system and what, if anything, needed fixing. Democrats and Republicans took opposing views on issue after issue, with many votes routinely dividing along partisan lines. The chamber they belonged to was also a factor in their views.

From left to right: Reps. Christopher Shays of Connecticut and Martin T. Meehan of Massachusetts, and Sens. John McCain of Arizona and Russell Feingold of Wisconsin have submitted campaign finance reform measures in their respective chambers.

For many, there were certain basic problems in the campaign finance system. One was the high cost of running for office. That in turn led to another problem: the incessant search for contributions to pay the bills, a problem that had both personal and institutional ramifications.

The relentless search for money then spawned other controversies. For a time, PACs were seen by many reformers as the villains. Others saw the fund-raising advantage of incumbents as a nearly insurmountable obstacle for challengers. Some proposed public financing of campaigns as a solution.

Then new campaign finance controversies erupted and the targets for reform changed. Soft money contributions and issue advocacy ads emerged in the 1990s as major loopholes in the system. After passage of the 2002 reform act restricting those practices, tax-exempt political organizations—Section 527 groups—became the focus of attention. Many thought political spending by 501(c) groups would follow Section 527 groups as the next controversy.

Also troubling to some reformers were independent expenditures, especially those of the political parties, and the practice of bundling political contributions to a member from a number of donors. Campaigning on the Internet generated controversy as well.

Campaigns' High Costs

"Politics has got so expensive that it takes lots of money to even get beat with," humorist Will Rogers remarked in 1931.[22] If it was true then, it became much more so by the early twenty-first century. The $1.4 billion congressional candidates spent during the 2005–2006 election cycle was a great deal more than the $765 million spent just a decade earlier in 1995–1996. *(See Figure 4-1, p. 76.)*

For some that cost is too high. These people see "[t]he high cost of elections and the perception that they are 'bought and sold' . . . as contributing to public cynicism about the political process," observed CRS analyst Joseph E. Cantor. Others have raised concerns that the cost of running for office has given wealthy candidates the advantage over others of more modest means and that it may have fueled reliance on more sophisticated—often negative—media advertising. But on the other side of the issue, Cantor pointed out, are those who say that the expenditures are not too high—maybe not even high enough—when compared to overall government spending or commercial advertising. For example, noted Cantor, "the nation's two leading commercial advertisers in 1996, Proctor & Gamble and General Motors, spent more to promote their products that year ($5 billion) than was spent on all U.S. elections."[23]

Senate Costs. A study by Cantor found that average Senate campaign costs went from $595,000 to $3.3 million between 1976 and 1996. (When adjusted for inflation, the average rose by 102 percent.) Ten years later, in the 2006 election, the average was still $3.3 million, according to the Center for Responsive Politics.[24]

There certainly were exceptions. The most expensive Senate race on record through the 2006 election was the 2000 New York race between Democrat Hillary Rodham Clinton and Republican Rick A. Lazio. Together they spent about $82 million in the 1999–2000 election cycle. Moreover, Republican Rudy Giuliani had spent more than $20 million before he dropped out and Lazio entered the race.[25]

FIGURE 4-1 **Congressional Candidates' Campaign Spending by Election Year, 1980–2006**

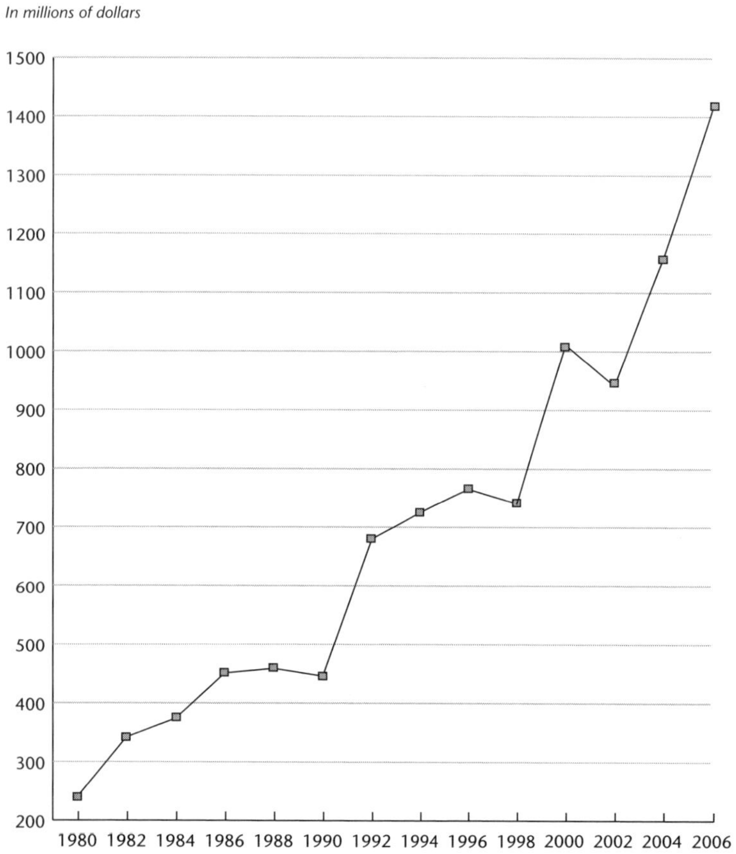

SOURCE: Federal Election Commission.

House Costs. Cantor's study for CRS found average spending by House candidates rose from $73,000 in 1976 to $493,000 in 1996. (When adjusted for inflation the average rose by 143 percent.) By 2006, according to the Center for Responsive Politics, the average was $646,500.[26]

The most expensive House race on record through 2006 was the 2000 race in California's twenty-seventh district. Republican James E. Rogan and Democrat Adam Schiff spent a combined $11.5 million.[27]

Why So Costly? Several factors account for the spiraling costs of congressional campaigns. The most obvious cause has been inflation. As the costs of other goods and services in the economy inflated, so too did those of campaigns.

But even when inflation is accounted for, the cost of campaigns has increased dramatically. A key reason has been the rise in the cost of fund-raising and of educating the electorate.

Since the 1960s congressional campaigns have undergone tremendous change. Most have been transformed from a volunteers-stuffing-envelopes-and-canvassing-voters type of system to highly technical, mechanized processes that are likely to use computerized mass mailings to solicit contributions and thirty-second TV ads to get their message across to voters. Candidates hire political consultants to direct their campaigns and polling companies to tell them how they are doing. All of the high-tech trappings of modern campaigns cost money—big money.

Population growth affects campaigns. As the electorate expands, so too does the cost of reaching voters. The costs of individual campaigns are also affected by the demographics of districts. Candidates in urban, suburban, or rural districts run very different campaigns with very different price tags. TV ads may not be cost-effective in an urban district, but they may be the only way a rural candidate can reach far-flung constituents.

The proliferation of media outlets has increased the cost as well. People are listening to or watching many more stations than they used to, so to reach them, campaigns have to spread their ads around.

The level of competition in a campaign also drives up its price. Costs stay down if an incumbent has little or no opposition, but they rise sharply if an electoral threat appears. This is also true of contests for an open seat, which frequently are the most competitive races. In open-seat races, according to political scientist Gary Jacobson, "neither candidate enjoys the benefits of incumbency, both parties normally field strong candidates, and the election is usually close." Senate races also tend to attract money, according to Jacobson, because incumbent senators are often perceived as vulnerable, most of their challengers are well-known public figures, and elections to the 100-member Senate have a greater political impact than do those to the 435-member House.[28]

Some observers believe that so much money is raised in campaigns because so much money is available. But incumbents have reasons to raise as much money as they can. One of these is deterrence. They want to use their campaign war chests to scare off potential opponents. Incumbents also feel more secure with sizable reserves in the bank. They want to be ready in case a wealthy opponent decides to run against them or they need to counter negative issue ads or independent expenditures. House members may anticipate a tough challenge because of an upcoming redistricting. Others stockpile money in case they decide to run for higher office, such as a House member running for the Senate or a senator running for the presidency.

Quest for Money

By many accounts, one of the most onerous tasks a legislator faces is fund-raising. It "takes a toll of the time, energy, and attention of legislators," according to Sorauf. "It is a task that tires even the most enthusiastic fund-raisers, and it depresses those incumbents who find it distasteful." [29]

Facing reelection contests every two years, members of the House are essentially campaigning and fund-raising all the time. One election campaign runs into the next. And even in the Senate, where the six-year term was once considered a luxury, members are beginning their campaigns earlier and earlier. Multimillion dollar price tags on races require increasing attention to fund-raising.

More than a few find the task demeaning as well. At one Democratic Party training session, candidates were offered the following advice: "Learn how to beg, and do it in a way that leaves you some dignity." [30] That may be easier said than done, as Sen. Tom Daschle, D-S.D., found during his successful 1986 campaign to unseat an incumbent senator: "You're with people you have nothing in common with. You have a cosmetic conversation. You paint the best face you can on their issues and feel uncomfortable through the whole thing. You sheepishly accept their check and leave feeling not very good." [31]

At least he left with the check, which is more than can be said for many challengers. Attempting to unseat a sitting member of Congress is an enormously difficult task for a number of reasons, not the least of which is the obstacle of having to bankroll a campaign. Rep. David E. Price, D-N.C., a political scientist who ran successfully against an incumbent in 1986, said that he had undertaken few ventures as difficult and discouraging as raising money for his primary campaign. He held small fund-raisers, sent mail appeals to party activists, and approached potential large contributors, with mixed success. He and his wife contacted people on their old Christmas card lists, as well as professional colleagues and family members. They took out a second mortgage on their home. Price won the primary but still found fund-raising for the general election a continuing struggle. He later reflected on his campaign:

> I will . . . never forget how difficult it was to raise the first dollars. I understand quite well why many potentially strong challengers and potentially able representatives simply cannot or will not do what it takes to establish financial "viability" and why so many who do reach that point can do so only on the basis of personal wealth. The modus operandi of most large contributors, PACs, and even party committees often makes their calculations of an incumbent's "safety" a self-fulfilling prophecy.[32]

The difficulties that surround fund-raising can have institutional, as well as personal, consequences. For one thing, the time members spend raising money is time away from the business of legislating. Sen. Robert Byrd, D-W.Va., said that one of his biggest problems when he served as Senate majority leader was accommodating the senators' need for time away from the floor to raise money for their campaigns. "They have to go raise the money and they don't want any roll-call votes," Byrd lamented. "Now how can a majority leader run the Senate under such circumstances?" To Byrd the culprit was clear: "Mad, seemingly limitless escalation of campaign costs." [33] Byrd ended up revamping the Senate's work schedule in 1988 to give members time off to campaign and attend fund-raisers.

As Rep. Price indicated, there is another institutional consequence: the high cost of elections discourages people from running for Congress. "Potential challengers or candidates for open seats realize that unless they can raise a lot of money, they have little chance of winning," wrote David Magleby and Candice Nelson. As a result, party committees have found "it is increasingly hard to convince people to run, given the low probability of success and the high investment of time and money necessary to even hope to be competitive." [34]

The problem is alleviated somewhat when the parties manage to find millionaires willing to run—and assist their own campaigns.

Public Funding of Campaigns

Some advocates of reform thought public funding might be the answer to the mounting cost of campaigns. A system to publicly finance the campaigns of presidential candidates who agreed to abide by spending limits was adopted as part of the post-Watergate campaign finance reforms. Attempts were also made to extend public financing to congressional campaigns, but none had been successful as of 2007.

Bills to provide public funding for congressional campaigns had been introduced in almost every Congress since 1956, according to a 2007 CRS report, and were prominently debated in the mid-1970s and the late 1980s through early 1990s.[35] Only one bill cleared Congress—one that would have provided partial public funding—and it was vetoed by President George H. W. Bush in 1992.

Backers of the idea argued that public funding of congressional campaigns would slow the rising costs of modern campaigns. Since the Supreme Court had ruled in *Buckley v. Valeo* that mandatory limits on campaign spending were unconstitutional, public funding with voluntary limits was seen as a way around that decision. Supporters said public funding would limit the influence—real or perceived—of special interests and wealthy contributors and reduce the pressure on politicians to trade legislative favors for campaign contributions, as happened in the Jack Abramoff lobbying scandal in the 2000s. Finally, it was seen as a way of increasing the competitiveness of campaigns, by lowering the price of entry. *(See Buckley v. Valeo, p. 94.)*

But public funding of campaigns had plenty of critics, in and outside Congress. For starters, some dismissed the contention that too much money was being spent in political campaigns. They also said that it coerced money from taxpayers to support candidates they might not approve of, and some derided public funding as "welfare" for politicians. Moreover, they said such a system would be almost impossible to administer, given the vast differences in members' districts and states and their campaigns.

Others cited the presidential system as reason enough not to extend public funding to congressional elections. By 2007 fewer than one taxpayer in ten was checking off the box on the 1040 income tax form directing $3 to the presidential campaign fund, and more presidential candidates seemed to be opting out of the voluntary system because of spending limitations.

Incumbent Advantage

There was much talk of turnover in the 2006 midterm election, but in the end voters reelected 94 percent of House incumbents who ran and 79 percent of Senate incumbents.

This very decided advantage of incumbents at the polls has produced much study and speculation. According to Roger H. Davidson and Walter J. Oleszek, political scientists have launched "a veritable cottage industry" to answer the question of why incumbents are so formidable.[36]

Several reasons can be cited. Incumbents have name recognition. They have a public record to run on, which can be especially helpful if they can demonstrate they have voted to protect the interests of their constituents and have brought home federal grants and projects. Incumbents are highly visible because of easy and regular access to the media.

Incumbents enjoy a number of perquisites, the most important being large staffs on Capitol Hill and in state or district offices ready to respond to the needs and inquiries of constituents. Thanks to the franking privilege, most letters and newsletters to constituents can be mailed free of charge, although there are restrictions aimed at curtailing blatant use of the privilege for political purposes. Members also benefit from allowances for phone calls and for travel back to their home district or state. Previously, members had the advantage of a regular salary during a campaign, something many challengers had to forego. However, in its rules implementing the BCRA, the FEC permitted the use of campaign funds for a nonincumbent candidate's salary.

Incumbents also hold a distinct advantage in raising money for their reelection campaigns. FEC figures showed that House incumbents had a fund-raising advantage over challengers of about three to one in 2005–2006. Incumbents raised about $533 million, compared with about $189 million raised by challengers. And incumbents clearly had more to spend—altogether, they had a surplus of almost $162 million.

The advantage of Senate incumbents during the 2005–2006 election cycle was not as great. They raised more than $278 million, while challengers raised almost $187 million. Incumbents finished the campaign with a combined reserve of more than $47 million.

FIGURE 4-2 **Incumbency Advantage in Reelection, 1946–2006**

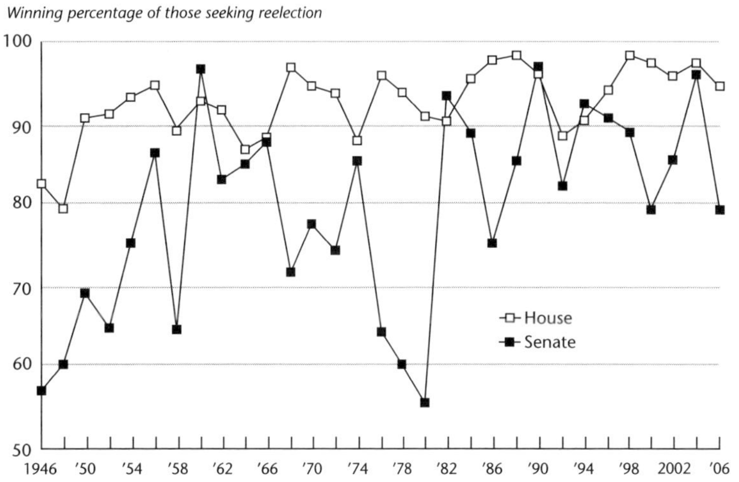

SOURCE: Harold W. Stanley and Richard G. Niemi, *Vital Statistics on American Politics 2007–2008* (Washington, D.C.: CQ Press, 2008), 55–56.

Both individual donors and PACs favored incumbents. About 53 percent of all individual contributions went to incumbents. The percentage was much higher for PAC contributions—80 percent went to incumbents.

Over the years the implications of the tilt toward incumbents have preoccupied members, reformers, and observers of Congress alike. Some warned of a trend toward a "permanent Congress" with little turnover, and they deplored PACs "buying" access to members of Congress. But others dismissed the notion and framed these contributions in a more positive light—contributors wanted to go with a winner, and most incumbents were seen as sure bets.

Fears of incumbents' advantage were allayed somewhat after the 1994 midterm election when the Republicans took control of both houses of Congress for the first time in forty years. The return to Democratic control twelve years later again demonstrated that despite incumbents' distinct advantages, change was still possible.

PAC Phenomenon

The rapid growth in the 1970s and 1980s of PAC money and influence in the electoral process generated much controversy for a time. Defenders of PACs insisted they were an outgrowth of a democratic society. "PACs are both natural and inevitable in a free, pluralist democracy," political scientist Larry J. Sabato wrote. "In fact, the vibrancy and health of a democracy depend in good part on the flourishing of interest groups and associations among its citizenry." [37]

But critics branded PACs as a source of tainted money because their giving often was tied to specific legislation, to a leadership position, to membership on a certain committee, or to the mere fact of incumbency. Fred Wertheimer voiced Common Cause's view before the Senate Rules Committee in 1989: "It is increasingly clear that PAC participation represents a threat to the public trust in the integrity of our electoral and congressional decision-making processes." [38]

As PACs became a dominant issue in campaign finance debates, the question of what, if anything, to do about them divided the parties and the chambers. Democrats were more dependent on PAC contributions than were Republicans, and House members relied on them more than senators. Those who wanted to curb PAC influence put forward proposals ranging from banning them completely to limiting either how much PACs could give or how much candidates could receive from them.

However, the urgency to do something about PACs diminished as their numbers leveled off and other issues began to overshadow them. "The PAC issue was largely supplanted by more fundamental issues of election regulation, with one-time critics finding new appreciation for the limited, disclosed nature of PAC funds," explained Cantor.[39]

Soft Money

The controversy surrounding PACs paled in comparison to the uproar in the 1990s over the hundreds of millions of unregulated money flowing into the coffers of the national parties. Congress put an end to it with passage of the 2002 Bipartisan Campaign Reform Act.

Campaign finance law bars corporations and unions from contributing to federal campaigns and sets limits on contributions by individuals. For a time, however, they were

FIGURE 4-3 **National Party Soft Money Receipts, 1993–2002**

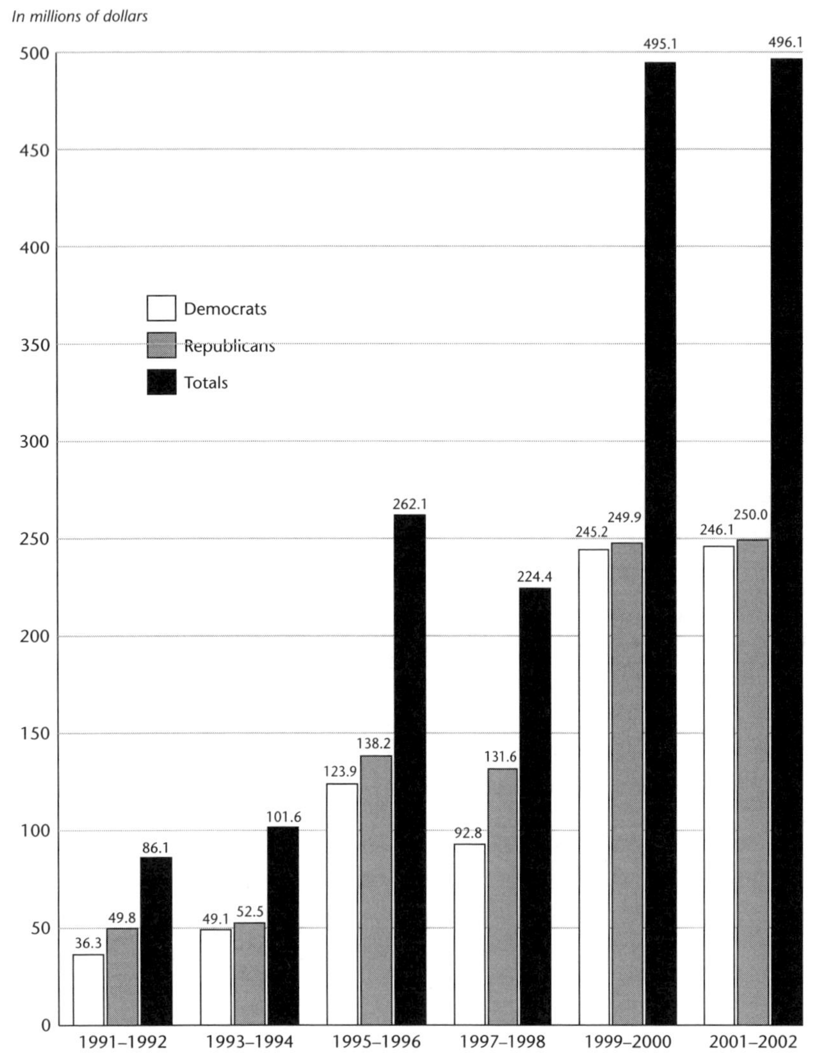

SOURCE: Federal Election Commission.

permitted to give soft money—unlimited and largely unregulated contributions—to political party committees for activities ostensibly unrelated to federal candidates. It was called "soft" to distinguish it from the tightly regulated "hard" dollars (money that is "hard" to raise within the limitations) that can go straight to parties, PACs, and candidates for direct use in federal campaigns.

Soft money donations skyrocketed in the 1990s and early 2000s, as did the controversy surrounding them. For some, soft money represented a return to the Watergate era when fat cat contributors won special access to politicians with six-figure donations. But party officials lauded the contributions, saying they kept party organizations relevant and strong.

Soft money was an outgrowth of the tough post-Watergate reforms that sought to clamp down on flagrant campaign finance abuses. The FECA in 1974 set limits on contributions and introduced some public financing of presidential elections. But the new law was so strict that candidates, party committees, and even academics protested after the 1976 election cycle that the new rules were stifling volunteer and grassroots party activity. For example, bumper stickers, lawn signs, and the like were considered in-kind contributions to the candidates. Also, public financing of presidential campaigns had brought with it restrictions on spending and tight limits on additional fund-raising by parties and campaign committees. The campaigns opted to spend their resources on advertising rather than local party activities. Party leaders complained that the new law had almost completely eliminated state and local party organizations from presidential campaigns.

Responding to those complaints, the FEC issued a controversial ruling in 1978 allowing a state party to use money that was not permitted under federal campaign finance law—in this case, corporate and labor contributions—to pay for a portion of grassroots and generic party activities, even if those activities indirectly aided federal candidates. Previously, the FEC had allowed the use of nonfederal money to pay a portion of a party's overhead and administrative costs but had barred the use of such money to pay for any portion of get-out-the-vote or voter registration activities because of their indirect effect on federal races.

FEC commissioner Thomas E. Harris issued a sharp dissent to the agency's 1978 ruling, arguing that it would allow the use of corporate and union money to pay most of the costs of voter drives because there usually were more state and local elections than federal races in a state. "His point was not lost on party leaders, who quickly began to adapt their financial strategies to take advantage of the new opportunities inherent in the FEC's decision," political scientist Anthony Corrado observed. Because the national parties also were involved in state and local election activities, it was assumed that they too could use money not permitted under the FECA for certain expenses as long as they kept this nonfederal money in a separate account.[40]

And then in 1979 Congress approved amendments to the FECA allowing state and local parties to spend as much as they wanted on campaign materials for volunteer activities to promote any federal candidate. Such items included buttons, bumper stickers, handbills, brochures, posters, and yard signs. Also, those party organizations were allowed to conduct, without financial limit, certain kinds of voter registration and get-out-the-vote drives on behalf of presidential tickets.

The 1978 FEC ruling and the 1979 amendments gave rise to the soft money phenomenon. The ruling had sanctioned the use of both federal and nonfederal money for election activities as long as it was kept in separate accounts, and the 1979 law allowed state parties to spend unlimited amounts of hard dollars for activities that would aid their entire slate of candidates, including federal candidates.

With traditional funding sources restricted by the FECA contribution limits, there was a strong incentive for parties to find other sources of money so they could take advantage of the new avenues opened to them. Republicans were faster to seize on soft money's possibilities in the 1980 presidential campaign, but Democrats quickly caught up and resisted early calls to abolish the practice. The rapid growth of soft money led Common Cause to sue the FEC to force it to tighten its regulations. In a partial victory, a federal judge ordered the agency to amend its rules; one of the effects of the new rules, which went into effect in 1991, was to require that most soft money be reported.

In the 1992 election cycle, the first in which soft money had to be reported, the national party committees reported soft money receipts of $86 million. About $50 million went to the Republicans and $36 million to the Democrats. By the 1996 cycle, the parties were aggressively seeking soft money and managed to raise $262 million, $138 million of which went to the GOP and $124 million to the Democrats. Moreover, they had found an important new use for it: television issue advocacy advertising. "To a certain extent, there was only so much money you could spend on get-out-the-vote," explained Corrado. "But once you started moving to advertising, the demand for soft money rose dramatically." [41]

The parties' pursuit of soft money played a key role in the scandal that erupted in the 1996 presidential election, the most significant campaign finance scandal since Watergate. *(See "1996 Scandal," p. 100.)*

Despite the scandal and resulting embarrassment, the parties' appetite for soft money continued unabated. In fact, soft money, which previously had been largely a phenomenon of presidential politics, became a major factor in congressional politics as well. One study found the growth in party soft money activity, including party issue advocacy, to be "the most important money and politics development in the 1998 congressional elections." [42]

FEC figures showed the four congressional campaign committees posted record gains in soft money receipts in the 1998 election cycle compared with 1994. The Democratic Senate and House campaign committees raised $42.7 million in 1998 in contrast with $5.5 million in 1994; the Republican congressional committees raised $64.8 million in 1998 and $13 million in 1994. Soft money contributions to the national parties climbed to almost $500 million in the 2001–2002 election cycle, with the four congressional campaign committees taking in nearly $288 million of that.

Before Congress banned it in 2002, the booming soft money business on Capitol Hill had some wondering why, if soft money was to be used for generic party-building activities and for state and local elections, were the congressional campaign committees raising so much of it? Most of the committees claimed to be taking on broader party functions and therefore were giving to state and local candidates. Soft money also became an attractive option for congressional fund-raisers who believed that the two national committees were so focused on presidential contests that they had neglected voter turnout in competitive House and Senate races. But a big reason for their aggressive pursuit of soft money was the purchase of issue ads.[43]

Issue Advocacy Ads

The 2002 campaign finance law also restricted issue advocacy advertising, a type of communication that was supposed to promote certain ideas or issues, as opposed to express advocacy ads that called for the election or defeat of particular candidates. In reality, however, issue ads were often thinly veiled campaign ads bankrolled by soft money. The ads usually pointed out a particular candidate's position on a given issue, painting either a dark or glowing picture of the candidate based on that one issue, such as abortion or the environment. But, most importantly, the ads stopped just short of specifically asking for a vote for or against a candidate.

The Supreme Court in its 1976 *Buckley* decision ruled that limits on campaign contributions applied only to "communications that in express terms advocate the election or defeat of a clearly identified candidate for federal office." A footnote in the ruling defined express terms as including such phrases as "vote for," "elect," or "support." As a result, many took the position that if issue ads did not include such terms—which came to be known as the "magic words test"—they were not subject to any reporting requirements or spending limits.

The use of issue ads by the parties and outside groups grew dramatically in the 1990s. Studies by the University of Pennsylvania's Annenberg Public Policy Center estimated that seventy-seven groups and committees spent between $275 million and $340 million on issue ads during the 1997–1998 election cycle, compared with the $135 million to $150 million spent in 1995–1996. Cantor reported that the total rose to $509 million in 2000 but he pointed out that such figures did not distinguish between campaign-related and noncampaign-related communications.[44] Soft money was used for the first time in a big way to pay for such ads in the 1996 election. Their potency was vividly illustrated, when the AFL-CIO spent $35 million on an issue ad campaign that focused on such issues as Medicare, minimum wage, education, and pensions, and ran heavily in vulnerable Republican districts. A coalition of business groups formed to counter labor's effort spent $5 million on issue ads. Federal regulations barred the national parties from using soft money for more than 40 percent of the costs of such ads, while limits on state parties varied depending on the ratio of federal to nonfederal candidates. Interest groups and individuals, however, had no restrictions on how much unregulated money they could spend on the ads.

Supporters insisted that the ads educated the public and helped create a better-informed electorate. Furthermore, they argued that any limits on issue advocacy would impede the constitutional right to free speech. But opponents saw the ads as nothing more than pitches for or against individual candidates, representing a giant loophole in campaign spending law that should be closed.

Restrictions on issue ads were a key component of the BCRA. The law barred labor unions, corporations, and nonprofits from funding broadcast advertising if the ad referred to a federal candidate, reached at least 50,000 people within the candidate's electorate, and ran within sixty days of a general election or thirty days before a primary. They could fund such ads—now called "electioneering communications"—only through a PAC with regulated hard money contributions.

In its 2003 *McConnell v. Federal Election Commission* decision, the Supreme Court held that the advertising provision was not unconstitutional on its face. However, in 2007 the Court—with two new justices—examined the provision "as applied" to a specific set of ads. In *Federal Election Commission v. Wisconsin Right to Life, Inc.*, the Court majority agreed with Wisconsin Right to Life, Inc., a nonprofit corporation, that three of its issue ads constituted "grassroots lobbying advertisements" and therefore the law's restrictions as applied to those ads were unconstitutional.

Section 527 Groups

After Congress barred national parties and candidates from accepting soft money, large amounts of unregulated money soon found another outlet: tax-exempt political organizations called "527s" for the section of the Internal Revenue Code under which they were organized.

Section 527 was written in 1975 after the Watergate scandal to set tax rules for political groups. But these groups did not gain national prominence until 2000 when one of them targeted Sen. John McCain, R-Ariz., who was seen by many as Congress's leading advocate of campaign finance overhaul. A Section 527 group called Republicans for Clean Air ran TV ads attacking McCain during his race against Texas Gov. George W. Bush for the GOP presidential nomination. It was later learned that wealthy Texas backers of Bush were behind the ads.

Although the Texas group grabbed the headlines, it was far from alone. The Section 527 groups spanned the political and ideological spectrum, but little was known about them because at that time such groups did not fall under campaign finance law. Individuals, corporations, and labor unions could donate unlimited amounts of money to these organizations, and the groups did not have to disclose any information to the FEC as long as they did not expressly advocate the election or defeat of specific candidates. The groups generally were involved in issue advocacy.

After McCain's experience during the March 2000 primaries, he and his allies moved quickly to shine some light on Section 527 activity. Legislation was signed into law in July of that year to require Section 527 groups to disclose information about their organization and file reports on their finances with the Internal Revenue Service.

It soon became apparent that Section 527 groups had become the vehicle of choice for moving six- and seven-figure donations in the wake of the BCRA's restrictions on soft money. Key groups involved in federal elections in the 2000 election cycle reported spending $88.6 million and taking in $61.3 million. By the 2004 election cycle, those numbers had jumped to $431.5 million in receipts and $435 million in expenditures. Of the $431.5 million, Democratic-oriented groups reported receiving $264 million and Republican-oriented groups took in almost $166 million.[45]

With both the White House and Congress at stake in 2004, Democrats relied heavily on funding from Section 527 groups for voter registration and mobilization activities and broadcast advertising, according to David Magleby.[46] Their fund-raising advantage was not lost on Republicans, who began to push hard for legislation to rein in the groups. The Republican-led House in 2006 approved a bill to bring the groups under the same campaign finance requirements that applied to political parties and PACs. Republicans also managed to attach their proposal to lobbying and ethics reform legislation. Although an unfolding scandal involving Washington lobbyist Jack Abramoff and his connections with lawmakers had spurred renewed interest in possible changes to lobbying and campaign finance rules, the Senate refused to take up the separate Section 527 bill or include its provisions in the ethics bill.

Totals for Section 527 money dropped in the 2006 election cycle, which was no surprise in a midterm election. Key groups reported receipts of nearly $224 million and expenditures of $252 million. Democratic-oriented groups reported receipts of almost $113 million and Republican-oriented groups just over $107 million.

Even if Section 527 groups were brought under campaign law restrictions, experts predicted that big money would find another outlet and that it most likely would be tax-exempt civic and social welfare organizations, labor unions, and business associations organized under Section 501(c) of the Internal Revenue Code. As long as a 501(c) group was not created for the primary purpose of partisan political activity, it could legally advance an electoral agenda and even endorse a candidate. As of early 2007, such groups did not have to disclose their donors' identities to the public or submit detailed reports of their expenditures; they merely had to file an annual tax return. In a report on soft money in the 2006 election, the Campaign Finance Institute said it knew of about $90 million in expenditures by 501(c) groups on federal election activities in the 2006 election, but because there was no official disclosure the report said that figure was "clearly an underestimate." [47]

Independent Expenditures

The Supreme Court in the *Buckley* decision ruled that the 1974 FECA's $1,000 ceiling on independent expenditures was a clear violation of the First Amendment right of free expression. Independent expenditures are defined as communications that expressly advocate the election or defeat of a candidate but are made without consultation or coordination with the candidate.

Although there no longer is a limit on the amount that can be spent, independent expenditures are subject to FECA disclosure requirements and must be paid for with funds legally permitted in a federal election campaign. In other words, an independent expenditure could not be financed by labor or most corporate money (certain small, ideologically based nonprofit corporations are exempt), nor by a contribution from a foreign national.

Independent expenditures have been controversial for several reasons. Some question whether such expenditures are truly independent. Others criticize the clout it gives a wealthy individual or an organization to influence the outcome of an election. Still others point out that candidates themselves sometimes resent this outside interference even when the communication favors their campaigns. The debate over independent expenditures intensified when the Supreme Court issued its 1996 ruling that political parties could make them. In the *Colorado Republican Federal Campaign Committee v. Federal Election Commission* decision, the Court held that state and national parties were free to make unlimited expenditures in a congressional campaign as long as the party and the candidate were not working together. The Court thus rejected the prevailing assumption that a party was uniquely connected to its candidates—especially given the coordinated expenditures it made on their behalf—and could not act independently of them.

The 2002 reform law barred parties from making both coordinated and independent expenditures on behalf of the same candidate, but the Supreme Court overturned the provision.

Reformers were not happy with the parties' dual role. As political scientist Thomas E. Mann put it, "Many scholars and practitioners consider party independent expenditures an oxymoron at best, a perversion of the whole purpose of political parties at worst." Mann said one possible solution would be to remove the limits on coordinated spending, thereby eliminating the need for independent expenditures. But Cantor noted in a CRS report that opponents thought parties were already playing a significant role and such a move would send the wrong message to a cynical electorate.[48]

Candidates are not always happy with their party's independent expenditures either. The themes and tone of the party message are determined by strategists who usually are from outside the candidates' districts or states—and sometimes can conflict with or overshadow their own message. Moreover, candidates risk losing control of their campaigns when the national parties flood the airwaves. Most members of the voting public don't really distinguish between party-sponsored and candidate-sponsored ads.

Campaigning on the Internet

As with so many aspects of modern life, the Internet became an increasingly important factor in electoral politics in the 2000s, impacting everything from campaign fund-raising to political advertising to the expression of views by bloggers. And as with so many aspects of campaign finance, it generated controversy.

Because the Internet offered a quick, cheap way to raise funds, it quickly became a potent tool, especially for political parties. As David Magleby explained, ". . . it's beneficial to the parties because the cost of fundraising is so much lower than prospecting through the mail or on the phone, and the cash is in your hand immediately. So, the turnaround is instantaneous, and for political operations in a tight cycle, that's a huge advantage." Although largely a "party phenomena" in the 2004 elections, Thomas Mann predicted explosive growth in its use by presidential candidates in the 2008 race.[49] How extensive a role it would have in congressional campaigns remained to be seen.

While there was no question that contributions over the Internet would be subject to federal campaign finance law restrictions, initially there was no such clarity about other uses of the medium.

The 2002 campaign finance law had barred state and local party committees from using soft money for certain types of "federal election activity," including "public communications" that referred to a clearly identified candidate for federal office and either promoted, supported, attacked, or opposed that candidate, regardless of whether the communication expressly called for a vote for or against the candidate. But when the Federal Election Commission (FEC) promulgated regulations implementing the law, it exempted communications over the Internet.

The House sponsors of the 2002 law—Reps. Martin T. Meehan, D-Mass., and Christopher Shays, R-Conn.—sued in federal court, arguing that the FEC had been too lax in enforcing the law. The judge in the case agreed, ruling in September 2004 that the FEC could not completely exempt the Internet from the statute. In March 2006 the commission issued new rules that included paid advertising placed on third-party Web sites in its definition of "public communications." The commission did exempt individual online political speech, including blogs, from regulation to avoid choking off grassroots democratic activity on the Web.[50]

Bundling of Contributions

Bundling refers to an intermediary pulling together contributions to a certain candidate from a number of individual donors and passing those checks on in a "bundle" to the candidate. (The checks could also be sent separately but it still would be obvious who had instigated the flow.) The intermediary earns the gratitude of the candidate without having the money count against its own contribution limits. Bundling can be done by an individual, PAC, or political party committee.

Critics argue that, because there are no limits on the overall amount a conduit group may collect and pass on to a candidate, bundling essentially allows the group to circumvent election law. But bundlers say they are simply matching donors with like-minded candidates.

The Council for a Livable World, a nuclear arms control lobbying group, first bundled checks in 1962, sending contributions to a then-obscure Democratic Senate candidate from South Dakota named George McGovern. But it was EMILY's List, a group backing Democratic women candidates who favored abortion rights, that perfected the practice. In addition to its regular PAC contributions, EMILY's List required its members to contribute a minimum of $100 to at least two candidates endorsed by the group.

EMILY's List was something of an exception. In most cases, according to Sorauf, bundlers and the interests they represented were not publicly known. In a discussion of PAC bundling, Sorauf wrote: "Virtually all the important information that PACs must and do disclose to the FEC is lost if organized giving is simply bundled instead." [51]

Under legislation proposed in 2007, congressional and presidential candidates would be required to report when lobbyists arranged donations and delivered them as bundled contributions if the bundles reached $15,000 during a six-month period.

FINANCING CAMPAIGNS: HISTORICAL DEVELOPMENT

In early American politics the source of money to finance a political campaign was never a question. Politics was a gentleman's pursuit and the gentleman was to pay. But, as political scientist Robert Mutch points out, the expenses were small and campaigns in the modern sense were few. "Candidates were supposed to attract support by virtue of their reputations, not by actually mingling with voters," Mutch wrote.[52] Candidates' expenses might have included the costs of printing and distributing campaign literature or perhaps providing food and drink for the voters on Election Day.

George Washington, for example, during his campaign for the House of Burgesses in Virginia in 1757, dispensed twenty-eight gallons of rum, fifty gallons of rum punch, thirty-four gallons of wine, forty-six gallons of beer, and two gallons of cider royal. "Even in those days this was considered a large campaign expenditure," writer George Thayer observed, "because there were only 391 voters in his district, for an average outlay of more than a quart and a half per person." [53]

By the early nineteenth century politics no longer was the exclusive domain of the wealthy merchant or the gentleman farmer. The professional politician had emerged. Lacking personal wealth, the new breed was dependent on others for campaign support and on salaries for their livelihood. Modern political parties also began to emerge, and with them came the spoils system. When a new president came in, government jobs were transferred to his supporters. It was not long before the new appointees had to pay for the privilege of a government job, with the political

Links between money and politics were a target for editorial cartoonists even before Thomas Nast drew this illustration in 1871.

parties exacting percentages from the salaries of federal employees.

The first known cases of assessments on government workers were levied by the Democratic Party on U.S. customs employees in New York City during the 1830s. But attempts to legislate against the practice went nowhere because, as Mutch noted, "few politicians were willing to eliminate such a valuable source of party funds, and the system of assessments continued to grow." [54]

The first provision of federal law relating to campaign finance was incorporated into an act of March 2, 1867, making naval appropriations for fiscal year 1868. The final section of the act read:

> And be it further enacted, That no officer or employee of the government shall require or request any workingman in any navy yard to contribute or pay any money for political purposes, nor shall any workingman be removed or discharged for political opinion; and any officer or employee of the government who shall offend against the provisions of this section shall be dismissed from the service of the United States.

Reports circulated the following year that at least 75 percent of the money raised by the Republican Congressional Committee came from federal officeholders. Continuing agitation on this and other aspects of the spoils system in federal employment—tragically highlighted by the assassination in 1881 of President James A. Garfield by a disappointed office seeker—led to the adoption of the 1883 Civil Service Reform Act. The act, also known as the Pendleton Act, authorized the establishment of personnel rules, one of which stated, "That no person in the public service is for that reason under any obligation to contribute to any political fund . . . and that he will not be removed or otherwise prejudiced for refusing to do so." The law made it a crime for any federal employee to solicit campaign funds from another federal employee.

But shrewd campaign managers found money elsewhere. Business money had become increasingly important in the post–Civil War period and was dominant by the close of the century. In the legendary 1896 campaign between Republican William McKinley and Democrat-Populist William Jennings Bryan, McKinley's successful effort was managed by Marcus A. (Mark) Hanna, a wealthy Ohio financier and industrialist who turned the art of political fundraising into a system for assessing campaign contributions from banks and corporations.

As these political contributions grew, so too did public concern over the role of corporate money in politics. "The concern among the electorates of the industrialized nineteenth century was that their elected representatives might not be the real policymakers, that government might still be controlled by those who provided campaign funds," Mutch wrote.[55] In the late 1800s several states enacted campaign finance laws, some requiring disclosure of information on the sources and uses of campaign contributions and others actually prohibiting corporate contributions. The push was on for action on the national level.

Early Legislation

Reacting to the increasingly lavish corporate involvement in political campaigns, the hearty band of reformers known as the "muckrakers" pressed for the nation's first extensive campaign finance legislation. During the first decade of the twentieth century, they worked to expose big business's influence on government through unrestrained spending on behalf of favored candidates.

Corporate Contribution Ban

Revelations during congressional hearings that several corporations had secretly financed Theodore Roosevelt's 1904 presidential campaign provided impetus for change. The establishment of the National Publicity Law Organization, headed by former Rep. Perry Belmont, D-N.Y., focused further attention on the issue. President Roosevelt, in his annual message to Congress, proposed on December 5, 1905, that "all contributions by corporations to any political committee or for any political purpose should be forbidden by law." Roosevelt repeated the proposal the following December, suggesting that it be the first item of congressional business.

Congress in 1907 passed the first federal campaign finance law, the Tillman Act, which made it unlawful for a corporation or a national bank to make "a money contribution in connection with any election" of candidates for federal office. Although Roosevelt is generally regarded as having initiated the series of actions leading to the 1907 law, Mutch points out that the bill passed by Congress had actually been written and introduced five years earlier.[56]

In his December 1907 annual message, Roosevelt joined those calling for the "very radical measure" of public funding of party organizations. But no action was taken.

Disclosure Mandated

Three years later the first Federal Corrupt Practices Act (also known as the Publicity Act of 1910) was passed, establishing disclosure requirements for U.S. House candidates. Specifically, the law required every political committee "which shall in two or more states influence the result or attempt to influence the result of an election at which Representatives in Congress are to be elected" to file with the clerk of the House of Representatives, within thirty days after the election, the name and address of each contributor of $100 or more, the name and address of each recipient of $10 or more from the committee, and the total amounts that the committee received and disbursed. Individuals who engaged in similar activities outside the framework of committees also were required to submit such reports.

The following year legislation was passed extending the filing requirements to committees influencing Senate elections and requiring candidates for House and Senate seats to file financial reports. (Popular election of senators, in place of election by state legislatures, was mandated by the Seventeenth Amendment, approved by Congress in 1912, and ratified in 1913.) Both pre- and postelection reports were required. The most important innovation of the 1911 act was the limit that was placed on the amount a candidate could spend campaigning for his nomination and election: a candidate for the Senate could spend no more than $10,000 or the maximum amount permitted in his state, whichever was less; a candidate for the House, no more than $5,000 or the maximum amount permitted in his state, whichever was less.

1925 Corrupt Practices Act

No further changes in federal campaign law were made for more than a decade. But then the system was overhauled with passage of the Federal Corrupt Practices Act of 1925, which served as the basic campaign finance law until the early 1970s.

The Teapot Dome scandal gave Congress the push it needed to pass reform legislation. During a congressional investigation of alleged improprieties in the Harding administration's leasing of naval oil reserves to private operators, it had been discovered that an official of the company that had leased the Teapot Dome reserve in Wyoming had not only bribed the official in charge of the leasing but had also contributed generously to the Republican Party to help retire its 1920 campaign debt. The contribution had been made in a nonelection year and therefore did not have to be reported under existing law—a loophole that was closed by the 1925 act's requirement that contributions of $100 or more be reported, whether made in an election year or not.

The 1925 act regulated campaign spending and disclosure of receipts and expenditures by House and Senate candidates, as well as disclosure by national political committees and their subsidiaries and by other committees seeking to influence elections in more than one state. The 1925 act limited its restrictions to general election campaigns because the Supreme Court in 1921 had ruled that Congress did not have jurisdiction over primaries. *(See "Restrictions on Primaries," p. 87.)*

The act revised the amounts that candidates could legally spend. Unless a state law prescribed a smaller amount, the act set the ceilings at $10,000 for a Senate candidate and $2,500 for a House candidate; or an amount equal to three cents for each vote cast in the last preceding election for the office sought, but not more than $25,000 for the Senate and $5,000 for the House.

The 1925 act incorporated the existing prohibition against campaign contributions by corporations and national banks, the ban on solicitation of political contributions from federal employees by candidates or other federal employees, and the requirement that reports on campaign finances be filed. It prohibited giving or offering money to anyone in exchange for his or her vote. In amending the provisions of the 1907 act on contributions, the new law substituted for the word "money" the phrase "a gift, subscription, loan, advance, or deposit of money, or anything of value."

The Corrupt Practices Act, however, was riddled with loopholes and contained no provisions for enforcement. It did not mandate publication of the reports or review of the reports for errors and omissions. It did not require reports of contributions and expenditures in either presidential or congressional primary campaigns, nor in connection with a party's presidential nomination. It did not require reports by political committees so long as they confined their activities to a single state and were not actual subsidiaries of a national political committee. Frequently, congressional candidates reported they had received and spent nothing on their campaigns, maintaining that the campaign committees established to elect them to office had been working without their "knowledge or consent."

Candidates were able to evade the spending limitations by channeling most of their campaign expenditures through separate committees that were not required to report federally, thus making the federal ceilings, from a practical standpoint, meaningless.

No candidate for the House or the Senate ever was prosecuted under the 1925 act, although it was widely known that most candidates spent more than the act allowed and did not report it all. Only two persons elected to Congress—Republicans William S. Vare of Pennsylvania and Frank L. Smith of Illinois, both elected to the Senate in 1926—ever were excluded from office for spending in excess of the act's limits.

The 1925 act's requirement that political committees seeking to influence the election of presidential electors in two or more states file contribution and spending reports was challenged in the courts as an unconstitutional infringement on states' rights. The Supreme Court in 1934, in *Burroughs and Cannon v. United States*, upheld the act's applicability to the election of presidential electors and implicitly sanctioned federal regulation of campaign financing in congressional elections.

On the topic of disclosure, the Court stated: "Congress reached the conclusion that public disclosure of political contributions, together with the names of contributors and other details, would tend to prevent the corrupt use of money to affect elections. The verity of this conclusion reasonably cannot be denied."

Hatch Act and Labor Restrictions

During the period between the early efforts to regulate spending and the broad reforms of the 1970s, some laws related to campaign financing were enacted, although they had less direct effects than the corrupt practices laws.

A 1939 law, commonly called the Hatch Act but also known as the Clean Politics Act, barred federal employees from active participation in national politics and prohibited collection of political contributions from persons receiving relief funds provided by the federal government.

A 1940 amendment to the Hatch Act made several significant additions to campaign finance law. It placed a ceiling of $3 million in a calendar year on expenditures by a political committee operating in two or more states. (In practice, however, the parties easily evaded this stipulation.) The amendment forbade federal contractors, whether individuals or companies, to contribute to any political committee or candidate. It also asserted Congress's right to regulate primary elections for the nomination of candidates for federal office and made it unlawful for anyone to contribute more than $5,000 to a federal candidate or political committee in a single year. But Congress opened a big loophole when it specifically exempted from this limitation "contributions made to or by a state or local committee."

Three years later Congress passed the War Labor Disputes Act (Smith-Connally Act), temporarily extending the 1907 prohibition on political contributions by national banks and corporations to include labor unions. This prohibition was made permanent by the Labor-Management Relations Act of 1947 (Taft-Hartley Act).

Restrictions on Primaries

Legislative and judicial decisions in the first half of the twentieth century repeatedly redefined the relationship of campaign finance laws to primary elections. The 1911 act limiting campaign expenditures in congressional elections covered primaries as well as general elections. In 1921, however, the Supreme Court in the case of *Newberry v. United States* struck down the law's application to primaries on the ground that the power the Constitution gave Congress to regulate the "manner of holding election" did not extend to party primaries and conventions. The Corrupt Practices Act of 1925 exempted primaries from its coverage.

The Hatch Act amendments of 1940 made primaries again subject to federal restrictions on campaign contributions despite the *Newberry* decision. This legislation was upheld in 1941, when the Supreme Court in *United States v. Classic* reversed its *Newberry* decision by ruling that Congress had the power to regulate primary elections when the primary was an integral part of the process of selecting candidates for federal office. The *Classic* decision was reaffirmed by the Court in 1944 in *Smith v. Allwright*. When the Taft-Hartley Act was adopted in 1947, its prohibition of political contributions by corporations, national banks, and labor organizations was phrased to cover primaries as well as general elections.

Loopholes Abound

Even with the revisions of the 1930s and 1940s, the campaign system was filled with loopholes. In a 1967 message to Congress proposing election reforms, President Lyndon B. Johnson said of the Corrupt Practices and Hatch acts: "Inadequate in their scope when enacted, they are now obsolete. More loophole than law, they invite evasion and circumvention."

Contributors' Loopholes

The Corrupt Practices Act required the treasurer of a political committee active in two or more states to report at specified times the name and address of every donor of $100 or more to a campaign. To evade being reported, a donor could give less than $100 to each of numerous committees supporting the candidate of his choice. A Senate subcommittee in 1956 checked the contributions of sums between $50 and $99.99 to one committee. It found that of ninety-seven contributions in that range, eighty-eight were over $99, including fifty-seven that were exactly $99.99.

Technically, an individual could not contribute more than $5,000 to any national committee or federal candidate. However, he or she could contribute unlimited funds to state, county, and local groups that passed along the money in the organization's name.

Members of the same family could legally contribute up to $5,000 each. A wealthy donor wanting to give more than $5,000 to a candidate or a political committee could privately subsidize gifts by relatives. Each such subsidized gift could amount to $5,000. According to data from the Survey Research Center at the University of Michigan, only about 8 percent of the population contributed in 1968. Both parties relied on big contributors. In every presidential election in the 1950s and 1960s, with one exception, the Democratic National Committee relied on contributors of more than $500 for more than 60 percent of its funds. For the same period, again with the exception of one election year, the Republican National Committee received more than 50 percent of its contributions from donations of more than $500.

Each party could count on support from certain wealthy contributors. Among the Republicans were the Mellons, Rockefellers, and Whitneys. Among the Democrats were the Laskers, Kennedys, and Harrimans. Large contributions also came from foreigners.

Corporations. Corporations could skirt the prohibition of contributions to a political campaign by giving bonuses or salary increases to executives in the expectation that as individuals they would make corresponding political contributions to candidates favored by the corporation.

Political campaign managers learned to watch for contribution checks drawn directly on corporate funds and to return them to avoid direct violation of the law. Often this money made its way back to the political managers in some other form.

Corporations were allowed to place advertisements in political journals, even though there was no apparent benefit to the corporations from the ads, and they could lend billboards, office furniture, equipment, mailing lists, and airplanes to candidates or political committees. If a loan of this kind was deemed a violation of the letter of the law, the corporation could rent these items to a candidate or committee, instead of lending them, and then write off the rental fee as uncollectible.

Unions. Labor unions could contribute to a candidate or political committee funds collected from members apart from dues. Money could be taken directly from union treasuries and used for technically "nonpartisan" purposes, such as promoting voter registration, encouraging members to vote, or publishing the voting records of members of Congress or state legislators.

Organized labor's registration and get-out-the-vote drives overwhelmingly supported Democratic candidates, being keyed to areas where regular Democratic efforts were considered deficient or where an overwhelming Democratic vote was traditionally necessary to overcome a Republican plurality in some other section of the district, state, or country.

Public service activities, such as union newspapers or radio programs, could be financed directly from regular union treasuries. As with corporate newspapers and radio programs, a sharply partisan viewpoint could be, and often was, expressed.

Candidates' Loopholes

Federal or state limitations on the amount of money a candidate might knowingly receive or spend were easily evaded. A loophole in the law enabled numerous candidates to report that they received and spent not one cent on their campaigns because any financial activity was conducted without their "knowledge or consent." In 1964 four senators reported that their campaign books showed zero receipts and zero expenditures—Vance Hartke, D-Ind.; Roman L. Hruska, R-Neb.; Edmund S. Muskie, D-Maine; and John C. Stennis, D-Miss.

Four years later, when Sen. George McGovern, D-S.D., reported no receipts or expenditures, one of his staff explained that they were careful to make sure that McGovern never saw the campaign receipts. Two senators elected in 1968—William B. Saxbe, R-Ohio, and Richard S. Schweiker, R-Pa.—reported general election expenditures of $769,614 and $664,614, respectively, to their state authorities, but expenditures of only $20,962 and $5,736, respectively, to the secretary of the Senate.

Another measure of the recorded figures' incompleteness was the contrast between the reported total political spending in 1960—$28,326,322—and the $175 million spending estimate by political experts. In 1962, a total of $18,404,115, was reported spent in congressional races, but Congressional Quarterly estimated the actual total at almost $100 million.

The credibility gap fostered by the "knowledge or consent" loophole was widened further because the Federal Corrupt Practices Act applied only to political committees operating in two or more states. If a committee operated in one state only and was not a subdivision of a national committee, the law did not apply. If a committee operated in the District of Columbia only, receiving funds there and mailing checks to candidates in a single state, the law did not cover it.

Limits on the expenditures that a political committee might make were evaded by establishing more than one committee and apportioning receipts and expenditures among them, so that no one committee exceeded the limit. Because the law limited annual spending by a political committee operating in two or more states to $3 million, the major parties formed committees under various names, each of which was free to spend up to $3 million.

Although the Corrupt Practices Act provided criminal penalties for false reporting or failure to report, successive administrations ignored them, even though news reporters repeatedly uncovered violations. Eisenhower administration Attorney General Herbert Brownell stated in 1954 the Justice Department's position that the initiative in such cases rested with the secretary of the Senate and the clerk of the House, and that policy was continued.

Secretaries of the Senate and clerks of the House for many years winked at violations of the filing requirements. The situation changed after Rep. W. Pat Jennings, D-Va., became House Clerk in 1967. During his tenure he sent lists of violations to the Justice Department for prosecution, but the department refused to act.

Attempts at Reform

Attempts to rewrite the 1925 act were made regularly during the late 1950s and the 1960s but with little success.

In April 1962 the President's Commission on Campaign Costs issued a report recommending proposals to encourage greater citizen participation in financing presidential campaigns. The commission had been named in October 1961 by President John F. Kennedy. Alexander Heard, then-dean of the University of North Carolina Graduate School, was the chair and Herbert Alexander, then-director of the Citizens' Research Foundation, was the executive director. Among the commission's recommendations were that:

- Tax credits or deductions be given for certain levels of individuals' political contributions.
- The existing limits on expenditures of interstate political committees and individual contributions to those committees be repealed, leaving no limit.
- All candidates for president and vice president and committees spending at least $2,500 a year be required to report expenditures made in both primary and general election campaigns.
- A Registry of Election Finance be established to help enforce political financing regulations.
- The government pay the transition costs of a president-elect during the period between election and inauguration.

In May 1962 President John F. Kennedy submitted to Congress five draft bills encompassing proposals identical or similar to the commission's. But the only bill reported was one to finance transition costs, and it died on the House floor.

Tax Checkoff Attempt. Congress did not act again in the area of campaign finance until the mid-1960s, when it passed a tax checkoff plan to provide government subsidies to presidential election campaigns. An act approved in 1966 authorized any individual paying federal income tax to direct that one dollar of the tax due in any year be paid into a Presidential Election Campaign Fund. The fund, to be set up in the U.S. Treasury, was to disburse its receipts proportionately among political parties whose presidential candidates had received five million or more votes in the preceding presidential election. Congress, however, failed to adopt the required guidelines for distribution of the funds, so the 1966 act was in effect voided in 1967.

Skyrocketing Costs. But the mood in Washington was beginning to change. In addition to growing irritation with the toothlessness of the disclosure laws, uneasiness was increasing over campaign costs.

Rising campaign costs were evident soon after World War II. Heard wrote in 1960:

> Radio and television broadcasting eat up millions. Thousands go to pay for rent, electricity, telephone, telegraph, auto hire, airplanes, airplane tickets, registration drives, hillbilly bands, public relations counsel, the Social Security tax on payrolls. Money pays for writers and for printing what they write, for advertising in many blatant forms, and for the boodle in many subtle guises. All these expenditures are interlarded with outlays for the hire of donkeys and elephants, for comic books, poll taxes and sample ballots, for gifts to the United Negro College Fund and the Police Relief Association, for a $5.25 traffic ticket in Maryland and $66.30 worth of "convention liquor" in St. Louis.[57]

Radio and television ads came to occupy a greater and greater portion of campaign budgets, as broadcasting emerged as the dominant political medium in the 1960s. "Overall, political broadcasting increased from 17.3 percent of the estimated total of all political spending ($200 million) in 1964 to 19.6 percent (of $300 million) in 1968, ensuring its position as the largest single cost in political campaigns," according to Herbert Alexander.[58]

Congressional incumbents feared that limits on media costs were needed to prevent them from draining campaign treasuries and making candidates increasingly dependent on wealthy contributors and powerful lobbying groups. Many Democrats saw a limit on TV outlays as a way to overcome what they viewed as the Republicans' lopsided advantage in raising money.

In addition, incumbents of both parties feared that rich challengers could use TV "blitzes" to overpower them, a fear that had been fanned in 1970 by the high-cost campaigns of two relative unknowns—Rep. Richard L. Ottinger of New York and Ohio parking-lot magnate Howard M. Metzenbaum—who succeeded in winning Democratic primary races for the U.S. Senate, although they lost in the general election.

Against this backdrop of skyrocketing campaign costs, the administration of Richard Nixon tightened enforcement of the Federal Corrupt Practices Act, successfully pressing charges in 1969 against corporations (mostly in California) that had contributed money the previous year.

MAJOR REFORM LAWS ENACTED IN THE 1970S

By the 1970s all sides acknowledged the need for new campaign finance legislation. Between 1971 and 1976 Congress passed four major laws that changed the way political campaigns for national office were financed and conducted. Stunned by the campaign abuses that came to light during the Watergate scandal, state governments and the courts also moved to alter the methods of campaign financing.

1971 Reform Laws

In 1971 Congress passed two separate pieces of legislation: the FECA, which for the first time set a ceiling on the amount federal candidates could spend on media advertising and required full disclosure of campaign contributions and expenditures; and the Revenue Act, which included a tax checkoff section to allow taxpayers to contribute to a general public campaign fund for eligible presidential candidates.

FECA: Limits and Disclosure

The 1971 act was the first major piece of campaign finance legislation passed since 1925. It combined two sharply different approaches to reform. One section clamped limits on how much a federal candidate could spend on all forms of communications media. The second part provided, for the first time, for relatively complete and timely public reports by candidates on who was financing their campaigns and how much they were spending. Meaningful disclosure would reduce the likelihood of corruption and unfair advantage, it was theorized.

Media Limits. The bill went into effect April 7, 1972, sixty days after President Richard Nixon signed it. The heart of the new law was the section placing ceilings on media costs, which was applicable separately to the primary campaign and to the general election. For a House candidate, the limit was set at either $50,000 or ten cents for each voting-age person in the congressional district, whichever was greater. For a Senate candidate, the limit was $50,000 or ten cents for each voting-age person in the state.

The ceiling, which was to rise automatically with the cost of living, applied to spending for television, radio, newspaper, magazine, billboard, and automated telephone advertising. The centerpiece of this section was the restriction that no more than 60 percent of the overall media total could go for radio and television advertising. In practice, this meant in the 1972 elections that a candidate for the House could spend no more than $52,150 for *all* media outlays in the primary campaign and no more than $52,150 in the general election campaign. (The cost-of-living factor had raised these figures from the initial $50,000.) In each case, only $31,290 of the overall media total could go for radio and television.

Because of population differences between states, the figures for Senate races ranged from an overall media limit of $52,150 in thinly populated states such as Alaska and Montana (of which only $31,290 could be for radio and TV) to as much as $1.4 million in California (of which about $840,000 could be for radio and TV).

Presidential limits also were computed on the basis of ten cents per voting-age person. For each presidential candidate, the overall media limit was $14.3 million, of which less than $8.6 million could be used for radio and TV.

Disclosure Requirements. The 1971 FECA required that any candidate or political committee in a federal campaign file quarterly spending and receipts reports that itemized receipts or expenditures of $100 or more by listing the name, address, occupation, and place of business of the contributor or recipient. During election years, added reports were required to be filed fifteen and five days before an election, and any contribution of $5,000 or more had to be reported within forty-eight hours if received after the last pre-election report.

Closing numerous loopholes in previous law, the statute applied the reporting requirements to primaries, conventions, and runoffs as well as to the general election. Every political committee had to report, even if it operated in only one state, provided it spent or received in excess of $1,000 a year. This meant, in effect, that the loophole of presidential candidates avoiding reports by having separate political accounts in each state was eliminated and members of Congress with political accounts operating only in their home states henceforth had to report their receipts and expenditures.

The reports were to be filed with the House Clerk for House candidates, Secretary of the Senate for Senate candidates, and General Accounting Office (GAO) for presidential candidates. They would be made available for public inspection within forty-eight hours of being received and periodically published; reports also were required to be filed with the secretary of State of each state and made available for public inspection by the end of the day on which received.

On the theory that disclosure alone would eliminate corruption, all the ineffective spending and contribution limits were repealed, except for provisions barring contributions directly from corporate funds and directly from union funds raised from dues money. (However, *voluntary* funds raised from union members and administered by a union unit were permitted.)

Proponents of reform, cognizant of partisan considerations that could threaten any revision of campaign laws, worked to avoid writing a law that would favor any political party or candidate. Republicans, aware of the relatively healthy financial condition of their party in 1971, were eager to protect their coffers; Democrats did not want to jeopardize their large contributions from organized labor.

The reform movement also included various groups outside Congress, such as the National Committee for an Effective Congress, the chief pressure group; Common Cause; labor unions; and some media organizations.

Income Tax Checkoff

The Revenue Act of 1971 containing the income tax checkoff cleared Congress on December 9 after a bitter partisan debate dominated by the approaching 1972 presidential election. President Nixon reluctantly signed the bill but forced a change in the effective date of the fund from the 1972 election to 1976 as the price of his acquiescence.

The plan gave each taxpayer the option beginning in 1973 of designating one dollar of his or her annual federal income tax payment for a general campaign fund to be divided among eligible presidential candidates. Those filing joint returns could designate two dollars.

Democrats, whose party was $9 million in debt following the 1968 presidential election, said the voluntary tax checkoff was needed to free presidential candidates from obligations to their wealthy campaign contributors. Republicans, whose party treasury was well stocked, charged that the plan was a device to rescue the Democratic Party from financial difficulty.

The Watergate Election

Both 1971 laws were campaign finance milestones, but they left intact the existing system of private financing for the 1972 presidential campaign. While the FECA drew high marks for improving campaign disclosure and received some credit for reducing media costs, its successes were overshadowed by the massive misuse of campaign funds that characterized Watergate, one of the nation's worst political scandals.

The predominant theory at the time of passage was that merely by writing a good, tight campaign finance law emphasizing disclosure, Congress could reduce excessive contributions from any one source to any one candidate. Candidates, according to this theory, would want to avoid the appearance of being dominated by a few large donors. Good disclosure would allow the public to identify the political activities of special interest groups and take necessary corrective action at the polls.

But it did not work that way. Huge individual and corporate donations were near the center of the Watergate scandal as largely unreported private contributions financed the activities of the 1972 Nixon reelection campaign. Of the $63 million collected by the Nixon camp, nearly $20 million was in contributions from 153 donors giving $50,000 or more. More than $11 million was raised during the month before the FECA disclosure rules took effect on April 7, 1972, including $2.3 million on April 5 and $3 million on April 6.[59]

The Finance Committee for the Reelection of the President kept its pre–April 7 lists confidential until a Common Cause lawsuit sought disclosure under provisions of the old Federal Corrupt Practices Act and forced them into the open in 1973. Such reticence was partly explained by the existence of questionable contributions to the Nixon campaign: $200,000 in financier Robert Vesco's attaché case; a $100,000 secret donation from millionaire industrialist Howard Hughes, which Nixon confidant Bebe Rebozo purportedly kept locked in a safe deposit box; and $2 million pledged to Nixon by the dairy industry.

Illegal corporate gifts also motivated secrecy. In a report issued in July 1974, the Senate Select Committee on Presidential Campaign Activities (known as the Senate Watergate Committee) charged that "during the 1972 presidential campaign, it appears that at least thirteen corporations made contributions totaling over $780,000 in corporate funds. . . . Of these, twelve gave approximately $749,000 to the president's reelection campaign, which constituted the bulk of the illegal corporate contributions."

The primary sources of such corporate money, according to the Senate committee, were "foreign subsidiaries." Other sources included corporate reserves and expense accounts. The committee added that "although the bulk of the contributions preceded April 7, 1972, there was no disclosure of any of the contributions until July 6, 1973—or fifteen months after almost all of them were made."

Presidential lawyer Herbert Kalmbach, who headed the corporate gifts campaign, in June 1974 was sentenced to six to eighteen months in jail and fined $10,000 after pleading guilty to illegal campaign operations. Kalmbach collected more than $10 million from U.S. corporations, the bulk of it prior to April 7, 1972.

According to staff reports of the Senate Watergate Committee, Kalmbach and other fund-raisers sought donations on an industry-by-industry basis, using an influential corporate executive to raise money among other executives in his industry.

The leading individual giver in the 1972 campaign was Chicago insurance executive W. Clement Stone, chair of the Combined Insurance Co. of America. In the April 7–December 31, 1972, reporting period monitored by the GAO, Stone was listed as giving $73,054 to reelect Nixon. But even before the revelations forced by Common Cause, Stone had admitted to pre-April giving of $2 million. The second highest giver was Richard Scaife, heir to the Mellon banking and oil fortune, who contributed $1 million to Nixon's reelection before April 7.

John Gardner, then the head of Common Cause, said in April 1973:

> Watergate is not primarily a story of political espionage, nor even of White House intrigue. It is a particularly malodorous chapter in the annals of campaign financing. The money paid to the Watergate conspirators before the break-in—and the money passed to them later—was money from campaign gifts.[60]

Gardner's charge was dramatically confirmed by President Nixon's August 5, 1974, release of a June 23, 1972, tape recording of conversations between himself and his chief of staff, H. R. Haldeman. The tape revealed that Nixon was told at that time of the use of campaign funds in the June 17, 1972, Watergate break-in and agreed to help cover up that fact. Nixon's resignation August 9, 1974, followed the August 5 disclosure.

Disclosure Provisions

The campaign disclosure provisions of the 1971 FECA proved extremely useful, enabling scholars and the relevant committees of Congress to get a clear picture for the first time of patterns of contributions and spending. Emerging from the reports were data on enormous contributions by the milk industry, corporate contributions, formerly concealed large contributions by individuals, and "laundered money"—information that played a key role in uncovering misconduct in the Watergate scandal.

Although thousands of reports were late or faulty, overall compliance with the disclosure law probably was fairly good. Nevertheless, a great many problems remained. The reports, especially those made in the last few days before the election, were extremely difficult for a reporter or a rival political camp to collate and decipher. Multiple contributions by a wealthy individual made to one candidate through a system of dummy organizations with cryptic names were difficult to track rapidly. Investigating an industry-wide campaign of financial support to a candidate or a group of candidates proved to be an extremely tedious task.

State finance committees and other committees—with titles such as Democrats for Nixon or Writers for McGovern—were created to prevent big contributors from being inhibited by high gift taxes. An individual could give up to $3,000, tax-free, to an independent campaign committee. Records showed that the Nixon campaign benefited from 220 of these finance committees. McGovern had 785 such committees, according to his national campaign treasurer, Marian Pearlman, "created for Stewart Mott." General Motors heir Mott, who donated about $400,000 to McGovern, even declared himself a campaign committee.

The Internal Revenue Service interpreted campaign committees as being independent if one out of three officers was different from officers for other committees, if the candidates supported by the committees were different, or if the committees' purposes were different. As a result, campaign finance committees proliferated in 1972, and contributors were hardly deterred from giving large sums to one candidate.

More important, the crucial element in effectiveness of the law was enforcement. The Justice Department was given sole power to prosecute violations, despite its forty-six-year record of somnolence in enforcing previous regulations. It was traditionally understood that Justice Department bureaucrats feared to undertake vigorous enforcement lest they endanger the party in power and be fired.

The question became: Would the department make a powerful, massive effort not only to round up serious violators but to require that reports be on time and complete? Without such action from the department, the practice of filing sloppy, incomplete, or even misleading reports, and filing them late, would clearly vitiate much of the effect of the law and render it null in practice.

Although thousands of violations—some serious but most technical (late or incomplete reports)—were referred to the Justice Department in 1972 and 1973 by the House, Senate, and GAO, only a handful of prosecutions resulted. During the 1972 campaign the department reportedly had only one full-time attorney supervising enforcement of the act.

Another provision in the law requiring periodic reporting of contributions and expenditures further impeded enforcement. According to many members of Congress, the frequent filing of these reports during primary and general election campaigns created monumental bookkeeping chores for the candidates. Correspondingly, the mammoth number of reports filed with the House Clerk, the Senate Secretary, and the comptroller general made closer scrutiny practically impossible.

To remedy the latter problem, Common Cause, at a cost of more than $250,000 and thousands of hours from volunteer workers, organized teams of people in 1972 to collect and collate information on reports, which it then distributed to the press in time for use before Election Day.

Fred Wertheimer, who was then the legislative director of Common Cause, said the aim was to make the law work and to give it a good start. But it was clear that depending on private organizations alone probably would be inadequate. Unless some permanent way was found, perhaps at government expense, to speed up collation and distribution of the materials—particularly late in the campaign—the objectives of disclosure would be undermined.

Media Expenditures

The 1972 election was more expensive than any that preceded it. About $425 million was spent in all races, with the Senate Watergate Committee estimating that the presidential race cost about $100 million, more than double the $44.2 million spent in the 1968 presidential election. During the 1972 campaign, presidential and Senate outlays for radio and television campaign advertising dropped sharply compared with 1968 and 1970, but whether this decline resulted from the FECA's media advertising limits was unclear.

In the presidential race, part of the drop was due to the strength of the incumbent, who had loads of free airtime available to him when he chose to address the nation in "nonpolitical" speeches as president.

The drop in Senate spending was less easily explained, but many senators said one factor was the realization that electronic media, while enormously effective, did not provide the quantum leap in campaigning techniques that had been expected. The notion that television could "do it all," which was virtually an article of faith in the late 1960s and in 1970, had begun to fade, and more resources were put into other forms of advertising and into traditional organizational and legwork efforts. Broadcast spending totals also were reduced by the requirement in the 1971 law that TV stations charge politicians the lowest unit rate for any time slot.

Also, many senators learned in 1972 that TV station coverage was not well designed for campaign purposes in many areas. In some states, such as Kentucky, it was impossible to cover the whole state with stations broadcasting only within that state. To cover border areas, it was necessary to buy time on stations located in other states, only a portion of whose viewers were in Kentucky. To send a message to one corner of the state a candidate had to pay for coverage outside the state as well, a wasteful and costly practice.

The same was true in some large central metropolitan areas located between two or three states. For northern New

Jersey, a candidate had to pay rates for other states too, since many of the stations in that area broadcast simultaneously to New York City and Connecticut as well as the target area of northern New Jersey.

Some senators found it cheaper under these conditions to use other ways of reaching the voters. Federal Communications Commission (FCC) reports showed that while a handful of senators went slightly over their campaign limits, the TV limits as a whole were observed. Because of the TV "targeting" problems, many in Congress began to argue that a flat spending limit for TV was too inflexible. They said an overall spending limit for all campaign costs—similar to that repealed in 1971, but with real scope and enforcement teeth—would be better. Such a proposal, they argued, would still limit any massive use of TV because a candidate would not be able to exceed his total campaign spending limit. But it would allow greater flexibility as to which portion of overall costs went to TV and which to other items.

The media limits were repealed in 1974.

1974 Reform Law

Almost two and a half years after it passed the FECA of 1971, Congress, reacting to presidential campaign abuses and public opinion favoring reform, enacted another landmark campaign reform bill that substantially overhauled the existing system of financing election campaigns. Technically, the 1974 law was a set of amendments to the 1971 legislation, but in fact it was the most comprehensive campaign finance bill Congress had ever passed.

TABLE 4-1 **Contribution Limits for 2007–2008**

	Recipients				
Donors	Candidate committee	PAC[a]	State, district, and local party committee[b]	National party committee[c]	Special limits
Individual	$2,300* per election[d]	$5,000 per year	$10,000 per year combined limit	$28,500* per year	Biennial limit of $108,200* ($42,700 to all candidates and $65,000[e] to all PACs and parties)
State, district, and local party committee	$5,000 per election combined limit	$5,000 per year combined limit	Unlimited transfers to other party committees		
National party committee	$5,000 per election	$5,000 per year	Unlimited transfers to other party committees		$39,900* to Senate candidate per campaign[f]
PAC multicandidate[g]	$5,000 per election	$5,000 per year	$5,000 per year combined limit	$15,000 per year	
PAC not multicandidate	$2,300* per election[h]	$5,000 per year	$10,000 per year combined limit	$28,500* per year	

*These limits are indexed for inflation in odd-numbered years.

NOTES: a. These limits apply both to separate segregated funds (SSFs) and political action committees (PACs). Affiliated committees share the same set of limits on contributions made and received. b. A state party committee shares its limits with local and district party committees in that state unless a local or district committee's independence can be demonstrated. These limits apply to multicandidate committees only. c. A party's national committee, Senate campaign committee, and House campaign committee are each considered national party committees and each have separate limits except with respect to Senate candidates. See Special limits column. d. Each of the following is considered a separate election with a separate limit: primary election, caucus or convention with the authority to nominate, general election, runoff election, and special election. e. No more than $42,700 of this amount may be contributed to state and local parties and PACs. f. This limit is shared by the national committee and the Senate campaign committee. g. A multicandidate committee is a political committee that has been registered for at least six months, has received contributions from more than fifty contributors and, with the exception of a state party committee, has made contributions to at least five federal candidates. h. A federal candidate's authorized committee(s) may contribute no more than $2,000 per election to another federal candidate's authorized committee(s). 2 U.S.C. Section 432(e)(3)(B) and 11CFR 102.12(c)(2).

SOURCE: Federal Election Commission.

The new measure, which President Gerald R. Ford signed into law October 15, repealed some provisions of the 1971 law, expanded others, and broke new ground in such areas as public financing and contribution and expenditure limitations.

The Federal Election Campaign Act Amendments of 1974:

- Established a Federal Election Commission consisting of six voting members—two appointed by the president and four designated by congressional leaders—as well as two nonvoting members, the House Clerk and Secretary of the Senate. All six voting members had to be confirmed by both the House and Senate.
- Instituted numerous contribution limitations, including: for individuals, a limit of $1,000 per candidate per primary, runoff, or general election, not to exceed $25,000 to all federal candidates annually; for political committees, a limit of $5,000 per candidate per election, with no aggregate limit; and for presidential and vice presidential candidates and their families, a limit of $50,000 to their own campaigns. A limit of $1,000 was established for independent expenditures on behalf of a candidate. Cash contributions of more than $100 were prohibited, as were foreign contributions in any amount.
- Set limits on spending by federal candidates and the national parties, including: a total of $10 million per candidate for all presidential primaries, $20 million per candidate in the presidential general election, and $2 million for each major political party's nominating convention and lesser amounts for minor parties' conventions; $100,000 or eight cents per voting-age person in their state, whichever was greater, for Senate primary candidates and $150,000 or twelve cents per voting-age person, whichever was greater, for Senate general election candidates; and $70,000 for House primary candidates and $70,000 for House general election candidates. National party spending was limited to $10,000 per candidate in House general elections; $20,000 or two cents per the voting-age population in the state, whichever was greater, for each candidate in Senate general elections; and two cents for every voting-age person in presidential general elections. (The party expenditures were above the candidates' individual spending limits.) Senate spending limits were applied to House candidates who represented a whole state. The act exempted certain expenditures from the limits and provided that the limits would increase with inflation. The act repealed the media spending limits adopted in 1971.
- Extended public funding for presidential campaigns to include not only general election campaigns but also prenomination campaigns and national nominating conventions. Eligible candidates seeking presidential nomination would receive public funds matching their privately raised money within prescribed limits. Eligible candidates in a general election would each receive $20 million in U.S. Treasury grants (to be adjusted for inflation) to finance their campaigns. Eligible political parties would receive grants of $2 million (to be adjusted for inflation) to conduct their nominating conventions. The amendments stipulated that if the level of money in the tax checkoff fund established by the 1971 Revenue Act was insufficient to finance all three stages of the electoral process, the funds would be disbursed for the general election, the conventions, and the primaries, in that order.
- Created a number of disclosure and reporting procedures requiring: establishment by each candidate of one central campaign committee through which all contributions and expenditures on behalf of that candidate would be reported; the reporting of names and addresses, as well as occupation and place of business, of those contributing more than $100; and the filing of full reports of contributions and expenditures with the FEC ten days before and thirty days after each election, and within ten days of the close of each quarter. Presidential candidates were not required, however, to file more than twelve reports in any one year.

The final bill did not contain Senate-passed provisions for partial public financing of congressional campaigns. Senate conferees dropped the fight for some form of public financing for House and Senate races in return for higher spending limits for congressional campaigns and a stronger independent election commission to enforce the law.

Buckley v. Valeo

As soon as the 1974 law took effect, it was challenged in court by a diverse array of plaintiffs, including Sen. James L. Buckley, C-N.Y.; former Sen. Eugene J. McCarthy, D-Minn.; the New York Civil Liberties Union; and *Human Events,* a conservative publication. They filed suit on January 2, 1975.

Their basic arguments were that the law's new limits on campaign contributions and expenditures curbed the freedom of contributors and candidates to express themselves in the political marketplace, and that the public financing provisions discriminated against minor parties and lesser-known candidates.

The U.S. Court of Appeals for the District of Columbia on August 14, 1975, upheld all of the law's major provisions, thus setting the stage for Supreme Court action. The Supreme Court handed down its ruling, *Buckley v. Valeo,* on January 30, 1976, in an unsigned 137-page opinion. In five separate, signed opinions, several justices concurred with and dissented from separate issues in the case.

In its decision, the Court upheld the provisions that:

- Set limits on how much individuals and political committees could contribute to candidates.

- Provided for the public financing of presidential primary and general election campaigns.
- Required the disclosure of campaign contributions of more than $100 and campaign expenditures of more than $100.

But the Court overturned other features of the law, ruling that the campaign spending limits were unconstitutional violations of the First Amendment guarantee of free expression. For presidential candidates who accepted federal matching funds, however, the ceiling on the expenditures remained intact. The Court also struck down the method for selecting members of the FEC.

Spending Limits Overturned

The Court stated: "A restriction on the amount of money a person or group can spend on political communication during a campaign necessarily reduces the quantity of expression by restricting the number of issues discussed, the depth of their exploration and the size of the audience reached. This is because virtually every means of communicating ideas in today's mass society requires the expenditure of money."

Only Justice Byron R. White dissented on this point; he would have upheld the limitations. Rejecting the argument that money is speech, White wrote that there are "many expensive campaign activities that are not themselves communicative or remotely related to speech."

Although the Court acknowledged that contribution and spending limits had First Amendment implications, it distinguished between the two by saying that the act's "expenditure ceilings impose significantly more severe restrictions on protected freedom of political expression and association than do its limitations on financial contributions."

The Court removed all the limits imposed on political spending and, by so doing, weakened the effect of the contribution ceilings. The law had placed spending limits on House, Senate, and presidential campaigns and on party nominating conventions. To plug a loophole in the contribution limits, the bill also had placed a $1,000 annual limit on how much an individual could spend independently on behalf of a candidate.

The independent expenditure ceiling, the opinion said, was a clear violation of the First Amendment. The Court wrote:

> While the . . . ceiling thus fails to serve any substantial governmental interest in stemming the reality or appearance of corruption in the electoral process, it heavily burdens core First Amendment expression. . . . Advocacy of the election or defeat of candidates for federal office is no less entitled to protection under the First Amendment than the discussion of political policy generally or advocacy of the passage or defeat of legislation.

Sen. James L. Buckley, C-N.Y., was the lead plaintiff in the lawsuit that prompted the Supreme Court to overturn several provisions of the 1974 campaign finance law.

The Court also struck down the limits on how much of their own money candidates could spend on their campaigns. The law had set a $25,000 limit on House candidates, $35,000 on Senate candidates, and $50,000 on presidential candidates. "The candidate, no less than any other person, has a First Amendment right to engage in the discussion of public issues and vigorously and tirelessly to advocate his own election and the election of other candidates," the opinion said.

The ruling made it possible for wealthy candidates to finance their own campaigns and thus to avoid the limits on how much others could give them. The Court wrote that "the use of personal funds reduces the candidate's dependence on outside contributions and thereby counteracts the coercive pressures and attendant risks of abuse to which the act's contribution limitations are directed."

Justice Thurgood Marshall rejected the Court's reasoning in striking down the limit on how much candidates may spend on their campaigns. "It would appear to follow," he said, "that the candidate with a substantial personal fortune at his disposal is off to a significant 'head start.'" Moreover, he added, keeping the limitations on contributions but not on spending "put[s] a premium on a candidate's personal wealth."

FEC Makeup Faulted

The Court held unanimously that the FEC was unconstitutional. The Court said the method for appointing commissioners violated the Constitution's separation-of-powers and appointments clauses because some members were named by congressional officials but exercised executive powers. The justices refused to accept the argument that the commission, because it oversaw congressional as well as presidential elections, could have congressionally appointed members. The Court wrote:

> We see no reason to believe that the authority of Congress over federal election practices is of such a wholly different nature from the other grants of authority to Congress that it may be employed in such a manner as to offend well established constitutional restrictions stemming from the separation of powers.

According to the decision, the commission could exercise only those powers Congress was allowed to delegate to congressional committees—investigating and information gathering. The Court ruled that only if the commission's members were appointed by the president, as required under the Constitution's appointments clause, could the commission carry out the administrative and enforcement responsibilities the law originally gave it.

The last action put Congress on the spot, because the justices stayed their ruling for thirty days, until February 29, 1976, to give the House and Senate time to "reconstitute the commission by law or adopt other valid enforcement mechanisms." But Congress took much longer than thirty days to act, and instead of merely reconstituting the commission, it passed a whole new campaign finance law.

1976 Amendments

The Court decision forced Congress to return to campaign finance legislation once again. The 1976 election campaign was already under way, but the Court said that the FEC

FEDERAL ELECTION COMMISSION

Given all the controversy that has surrounded the campaign finance system, it is no surprise that the agency established to monitor that system has been steeped in controversy as well.

FEC MANDATE

The Federal Election Commission (FEC) was created by Congress in 1974 to administer and enforce the Federal Election Campaign Act (FECA) of 1971 and its amendments. The FEC's duties include receiving and making public the campaign finance reports mandated by the FECA. These reports are available for examination at the FEC, as well as at the FEC Web site: *http://www.fec.gov.*

FEC staff members review the reports for omissions and may request additional information. If the FEC finds an apparent law violation, it has the authority to seek a conciliation agreement, sometimes with a civil penalty. If a conciliation agreement cannot be reached, the FEC may sue for enforcement in U.S. District Court. The commission may refer possible criminal violations to the Justice Department for prosecution.

The FEC also administers the Presidential Election Campaign Fund, which makes possible the public funding of presidential primaries, national party conventions, and presidential general elections.

FEC MEMBERS

The 1974 amendments established the FEC as a six-member commission, with the Clerk of the House and Secretary of the Senate serving as nonvoting ex officio members. No more than three of the six commissioners were to be from the same political party.

The 1974 law stipulated that four of the six members would be selected by Congress, a provision the Supreme Court soon found, among others, to be unconstitutional. In its 1976 *Buckley v. Valeo* decision, the Court declared the method violated the Constitution's separation of powers clauses because the four commissioners were appointed by congressional officials but exercised executive powers.

Amendments passed in 1976 reconstituted the FEC as a six-member commission appointed by the president and confirmed by the Senate. However, Congress in effect continued to control four of the appointments by providing the White House with a list of acceptable nominees for these slots.

The makeup of the FEC was again called into question when the D.C. Circuit Court of Appeals in 1993 ruled that the commission had violated the constitutional separation of powers by including the two nonvoting congressional staff members in its deliberations. The FEC reconstituted itself without the Clerk of the House and the Secretary of the Senate but asked the Supreme Court to review the decision. The Court in 1994 rejected the appeal on technical grounds, ruling that the agency lacked authority to appeal the matter to the Supreme Court (*Federal Election Commission v. NRA Political Victory Fund*). The Court held that the FECA gave only the solicitor general the authority to make such appeals.

In other action affecting the makeup of the commission, Congress in 1997 limited future nominees for FEC commissioner slots to one six-year term, beginning in 1998. An attempt to place term limits on the FEC's general counsel and staff director failed in 1998.

AGENCY CRITICS

Criticism of the FEC spanned the spectrum. At one end were those who thought the agency had been too independent and aggressive in its actions and wanted to see it, along with campaign finance regulation in general, weakened. Political scientist Thomas E. Mann noted that at times some members of Congress had accused the agency of "overly zealous and partisan enforcement of the law," could not continue to disburse public funds to presidential candidates so long as some commission members were congressional appointees.

President Ford had wanted only a simple reconstitution of the commission, but Congress insisted on going much further. The new law, arrived at after much maneuvering and arguing between Democrats and Republicans, closed old loopholes and opened new ones, depending on the point of view of the observer.

In its basic provision, the law signed by the president May 11, 1976, reconstituted the FEC as a six-member panel appointed by the president and confirmed by the Senate. Commission members were not allowed to engage in outside business activities. The commission was given exclusive authority to prosecute civil violations of the campaign finance law and was vested with jurisdiction over violations formerly covered only in the criminal code, thus strengthening its enforcement power. But the bill also required an affirmative vote of four members for the commission to issue regulations and advisory opinions or initiate civil actions and investigations. The commission was limited to issuing advisory opinions only for specific fact situations. And Congress was given the power to disapprove proposed regulations.

A major controversy that delayed enactment stemmed from organized labor's insistence that corporate fund-raising activity through PACs be curtailed. Labor was angered by the FEC's SunPAC decision in November 1975 that encouraged the growth of corporate PACs.

In the wake of Watergate many corporations had been skittish about what they were permitted to do. Not until the FEC released its landmark ruling in the case involving the Sun Oil Co.'s political action committee, SunPAC, did many businesses feel comfortable in establishing PACs. The FEC decision was in response to Sun Oil's request to use general funds to create, administer, and solicit voluntary contributions to its PAC. Besides approving the request, the decision allowed business PACs to solicit all employees and stockholders for contributions. Labor PACs had been restricted to soliciting only their members.

although an independent audit in 1998–1999 by PricewaterhouseCoopers in response to such criticism found that the agency was operating in "a fair, impartial manner."

Many more critics were at the other end of the spectrum, insisting that the commission had not been aggressive enough and should be either strengthened or replaced. They put much of the blame for FEC shortcomings on Congress. Mann wrote that ". . . Congress had no interest in an independent, powerful FEC . . . lawmakers designed the agency carefully to ensure that they would be able to keep it on a tight leash."

For starters, Mann pointed out, Congress gave itself the authority to appoint four of the six commissioners and supply two of its officers as ex officio members. The requirement that no more than three commissioners could be from the same party resulted in a three Democrat–three Republican commission. After the commission was reconstituted with presidential appointees, Congress tightened its hold by requiring an affirmative vote by four members for the commission in order to issue regulations and advisory opinions and initiate civil actions and investigations. The FEC was given no authority to impose sanctions other than fines and had to depend instead on the federal court and the Justice Department to pursue violators. Congress even had veto power over FEC rules and regulations until the Supreme Court declared all legislative vetoes unconstitutional in 1983.

Moreover, according to Mann, Congress took other steps "to ensure that delay and timidity would become the watchwords of the agency." These included denying the FEC the multiyear budgeting authority enjoyed by other independent agencies, skeptically reviewing FEC requests for budget increases despite the agency's expanding workload, banning random audits of candidates, insisting on time-consuming procedures, and keeping up "a barrage of criticism that weakened the FEC's legitimacy and reinforced the contempt with which political operatives came to view the commission."[1]

Critics who wanted to see a tough enforcement agency were particularly vocal in the wake of the 1996 campaign finance scandal because the FEC failed to take much action in the face of numerous allegations of campaign funding irregularities. The agency had indirectly exposed some of the 1996 irregularities through its required disclosure reports. An FEC staff audit charged that both the Democratic and Republican presidential campaigns had illegally coordinated with their national party committees to spend millions of dollars in soft money on issue ads that benefited their candidates, which amounted to spending in excess of the federal grants. FEC commissioners, however, unanimously rejected the staff recommendations that the campaigns be required to return that excess money to the federal Treasury. Donald Simon of Common Cause accused the agency of "protecting the two parties who have joined hands to run roughshod over the law" instead of the public interest. *(See "1996 Scandal," p. 100.)*

Sponsors of the 2002 Bipartisan Campaign Reform Act—Sens. John McCain, R-Ariz., and Russ Feingold, D-Wis., and Reps. Christopher Shays, R-Conn., and Martin T. Meehan, D-Mass.—were so outraged by some of the regulations the FEC promulgated to implement the new law that they filed suit in federal court to have them overturned. The court for the most part agreed.

McCain, Feingold, Shays, Meehan, and others in the reform community have proposed abolishing the FEC and replacing it with a new agency that, in McCain's words "would serve as an independent body to enforce federal campaign laws—something the FEC has been unable, and often unwilling, to do."[2]

1. Thomas E. Mann, "The FEC: Administering and Enforcing Campaign Finance Law," in *The New Campaign Finance Sourcebook,* ed. Anthony Corrado et al. (Washington, D.C.: Brookings Institution, 2005), 232–241.

2. "Statement of Senator John McCain on the Introduction of the Federal Election Administration Act of 2007," February 1, 2007, press release.

Eventually a compromise was reached between the Democrats, who did not hesitate to use their overwhelming numerical strength to make changes that would have severely restricted the ability of business to raise political money, and the Republicans, who lacked the strength to fend off the antibusiness amendments but had the votes to sustain a filibuster and a veto.

Labor succeeded in reaching some but not all of its goal. The final law permitted company committees to seek contributions only from stockholders and executive and administrative personnel and their families. It continued to restrict union PACs to soliciting contributions from union members and their families. Twice a year, however, union and corporate PACs were permitted to seek campaign contributions, by mail only, from all employees. Contributions would have to remain anonymous and would be received by an independent third party that would keep records but pass the money on to the PACs.

The final bill contained another provision prompted by the Supreme Court decision. Besides finding the FEC's makeup unconstitutional, the Court had thrown out the 1974 law's limitations on independent political expenditures as a clear violation of the First Amendment. To plug the potential loophole, Congress required political committees and individuals making independent political expenditures of more than $100 to swear that the expenditures were not made in collusion with the candidate.

The 1976 legislation also set some new contribution limits: An individual could give no more than $5,000 a year to a PAC and $20,000 to the national committee of a political party (the 1974 law had set a $1,000 per election limit on individual contributions to a candidate and an aggregate contribution limit for individuals of $25,000 a year; no specific limits, except the aggregate limit, applied to contributions to political committees). A PAC could give no more than $15,000 a year to the national committee of a political party (the 1974 law had set only a limit of $5,000 per election per candidate). The Democratic and Republican senatorial campaign committees could give up to $17,500 a year to a candidate (the 1974 law had set a $5,000 per election limit).

Hill Public Funding Defeated

Following the 1976 election, the spotlight in campaign finance quickly focused on extending public financing to House and Senate races. Prospects for passage seemed far better than they had been in 1974, the last time the proposal had been considered. At that time, leading officials from the White House on down had been either opposed or seemingly indifferent to its passage.

But in 1977 Jimmy Carter, a strong advocate of public funding, was in the White House. Key congressional leaders favored the proposal. And the Democrats had an overwhelming advantage in the House, far larger than during the 93rd Congress (1973–1975), when the House rejected congressional public financing after it had been approved by the Senate.

Despite the high hopes of public financing supporters, legislation to extend the concept to congressional races was blocked in 1977 by a filibuster in the Senate and opposition in the House Administration Committee. Renewed attempts to push the legislation in 1978 and 1979 also went nowhere.

1979 FECA Amendments

In a rare demonstration of harmony on a campaign finance measure, Congress in late 1979 passed legislation to eliminate much of the red tape created by the FECA and to encourage political party activity. Agreement was not difficult because the drafters concentrated on solving the FECA's noncontroversial problems.

The amendments, signed into law January 8, 1980, reduced the FECA's paperwork requirements in several ways. First, the act decreased the maximum number of reports a federal candidate had to file with the FEC during a two-year election cycle from twenty-four to nine. For Senate candidates, the number of reports mandated over the six-year election cycle was reduced from twenty-eight to seventeen. Second, candidates who raised or spent less than $5,000 in their campaigns did not have to file reports at all. In 1978 about seventy House candidates, including five winners, fell below the $5,000 threshold. Previously, all candidates were required to report their finances regardless of the amount. Also, candidates were allowed to report in less detail. The legislation raised the threshold for itemizing both contributions and expenditures to $200 from $100. The threshold for reporting independent expenditures was also increased, from $100 to $250.

In 1976 political party leaders had complained that the FECA almost completely precluded state and local party organizations from helping with the presidential campaign. Because they had only limited federal funds to spend, both the Democratic and Republican presidential campaigns focused on media advertising. At the same time, they cut back expenditures on items such as buttons and bumper stickers that traditionally were used in promoting grassroots activity.

The 1979 bill permitted state and local party groups to purchase, without limit, campaign materials for volunteer activities to promote any federal candidate. Those items included buttons, bumper stickers, handbills, brochures, posters, and yard signs. Also, those party organizations were allowed to conduct, without financial limit, certain kinds of voter registration and get-out-the-vote drives on behalf of presidential tickets.

The incidental mention of a presidential candidate on the campaign literature of local candidates was no longer counted as a campaign contribution. Previously, such references had been counted, which created paperwork problems in reporting those costs to the FEC. Local party groups would be required to report their finances only if annual spending for volunteer activities exceeded $5,000 or if costs for nonvolunteer projects were more than $1,000. Before, such groups had to file campaign reports if total spending exceeded $1,000 a year.

Volunteer political activity by individuals was encouraged by raising to $1,000, from $500, the amount of money a person could spend in providing his home, food, or personal travel on behalf of a candidate without reporting it to the FEC as a contribution. If the volunteer activity was on behalf of a political party, the person could spend up to $2,000 before the amount was treated as a contribution.

The 1979 act prohibited members from converting leftover campaign funds to personal use. However, those in Congress at the time of the law's enactment were exempted. Because Senate rules flatly prohibited personal use of such funds by former members as well as incumbents, the bill's exemption was of benefit only to sitting House members. The loophole became a target for reformers and caused resentment among senators and younger House members who could not take advantage of it. In 1989 Congress moved to close it by including a provision in an ethics-and-pay law that forced the grandfathered House members to either leave Congress before the beginning of the 103rd Congress in 1993 or lose their right to take the money. The funds that could be converted were frozen at no more than what they had on hand when the 1989 ethics law was enacted.

OVERHAUL AFTER DECADES OF STALEMATES

Congress repeatedly visited the issue of campaign finance reform for over more than two decades before major reform legislation was enacted in 2002.

Repeated Impasses

PACs came to the forefront of the campaign finance debate in the 1980s. The rise in the number of PACs and their influence in political campaigns put lawmakers on the defensive against a public perception that special interest groups had undue influence on politicians.

The House in 1979 passed a bill to reduce PAC contributions, but the bill died in the Senate the following year under threat of a filibuster. Although the bill applied only to House races, opponents in the Senate feared that its passage could renew interest in public financing or could lead to PAC spending ceilings in Senate races.

Several years passed before the issue was debated again. This time, in 1986, the Senate went on record twice in favor of strict new controls on PACs. But the legislation got caught in partisan maneuvering over who should get the credit—or blame—for reforming campaign finance guidelines, and which party would suffer the most under the proposed restrictions. A final vote was never taken.

In the next Congress, the Senate debated the most comprehensive campaign finance bill to come before Congress since 1974. But the legislation—which included spending limits, financial incentives for abiding by the limits, and an aggregate limit on PAC contributions—ultimately was shelved after a record-setting eight cloture votes in 1987–1988 failed to cut off a Republican filibuster. The protracted debate over the bill was marked by extraordinary partisanship and elaborate parliamentary maneuvering. Majority leader Robert C. Byrd, D-W.Va., attempted to break the GOP filibuster by keeping the Senate in session around the clock. During one of two all-night sessions, Republicans responded in kind, by repeatedly moving for quorum calls and then boycotting the floor. That forced Democrats to keep enough members present to maintain the quorum needed for the Senate to remain in session. Byrd then decided to resort to a little-known power of the Senate, last used in 1942, to have absent members arrested and brought to the floor. This led to the spectacle of Oregon Republican Bob Packwood being arrested and physically carried onto the Senate floor in the wee hours of February 24, 1988.

A truce was eventually reached, the final unsuccessful cloture vote taken, and the bill was pulled from the floor. A later attempt to adopt a constitutional amendment to overcome the *Buckley v. Valeo* decision forbidding mandatory campaign spending limits suffered a similar fate, as it would in subsequent Congresses.

The movement in the next Congress (1989–1991) to rewrite campaign finance laws ended where it began, mired in disagreement. The House and Senate passed separate bills—both generally backed by Democrats and strongly opposed by Republicans—containing voluntary spending limits and reducing the influence of PACs. But given that the two chambers' proposals differed substantially, it was late in the session, and President George H. W. Bush was threatening to veto any bill with campaign spending limits, conferees on the two bills never met.

Bush in 1989 had proposed what he called a "sweeping system of reform" that sought to eliminate most PACs, enhance the role of political parties, and grind down the electoral advantages enjoyed by incumbents (including one of the major weapons in an incumbent's arsenal, the frank, by banning "unsolicited mass mailings" from congressional offices). Democrats had assailed the Bush plan as baldly partisan. Even within the GOP, there was no consensus on major items such as curbing the frank and eliminating certain PACs.

Scandals in the next Congress (1991–1993) heightened pressure on both chambers to enact some type of reform measure. The Senate was rocked by the Keating Five savings and loan investigation of 1990–1991, which Common Cause characterized as "the smoking gun" that proved the corruption of the election finance system. On the House side, scandals at the House bank and post office reignited the campaign finance issue in 1992, as House Democratic leaders grasped for reform measures large and small.

Both chambers passed vastly different bills in 1991 to limit spending and subsidize campaigns with public dollars. With the impetus of the ethics scandals, conferees came up with a compromise bill, in part by letting each chamber live by its own rules on public financing. The Senate backed off from its ban on PACs and the House went along with the Senate's more restrictive language on soft money. But in the end what they produced was a Democratic bill and, without bipartisan support, it was doomed. President Bush—objecting to its spending limits, public funding, and creation of separate systems for House and Senate campaigns—vetoed the bill.

Given the strong backing from Democrats in the previous Congress and incoming President Bill Clinton's vow to overhaul the system, the 103rd Congress (1993–1995) opened with high expectations for enactment of a new campaign finance law. Both chambers did pass bills in 1993, but again they were radically different. The Senate bill banned PACs, while the House bill set an aggregate cap on PAC contributions to a campaign. Both measures contained spending limits but offered vastly different incentives to encourage candidates to comply. House and Senate Democrats worked out a compromise but the bill died late in the 1994 session when a GOP-led filibuster blocked the Senate from sending its bill to conference.

Failure to enact the bill in 1994 was a major defeat for Clinton and Democratic congressional leaders. Democrats, however, had set the stage for defeat by waiting until the eleventh hour to come up with a compromise version. Indeed, the long history of the legislation was rich with evidence that many Democrats in both chambers shared GOP objections to establishing a system that would provide congressional candidates with federal subsidies. Other Democrats, particularly in the House, were deeply, if privately, opposed to an overhaul of the system that had protected their seats and majority status for years. In the end, it was the inability of Democrats to iron out their internal differences that delayed the bill so long that it became vulnerable to procedural snags. Some supporters of the legislation blamed Clinton, who had campaigned on the issue but brought little to bear on it in 1994.

The Republican takeover in the next Congress (1995–1997) had little effect on campaign finance legislation. Despite promises to overhaul the system, Republicans had no more success than their Democratic predecessors. A bipartisan effort to revise campaign finance laws was stopped once again by a filibuster in the Senate. The bill called for voluntary spending limits in return for certain incentives and would have banned PAC and soft money contributions. In the House, a GOP bill that would have set new contribution limits for individuals and PACs was defeated, in part because of a provision that would have required labor unions to get signed agreements from workers before using their dues for political contributions. A House Democratic alternative was defeated as well.

1996 Scandal

A major campaign finance scandal erupted during the 1996 election over alleged illegal foreign contributions and the national parties' frenzied quest for soft money to buy issue ads. Advocates of a campaign finance overhaul hoped revelations of campaign abuses would outrage the public sufficiently to put pressure on Congress to move legislation, but with most of the allegations centered on the Democrats, Republican leaders focused instead on investigations.

As the scandal unfolded, it was revealed that the Democratic National Committee (DNC) had accepted nearly $3 million in illegal or suspect contributions, money it said it would return. The fund-raising tactics of President Bill Clinton and Vice President Al Gore were also central to the scandal. The news media provided colorful accounts of the Clintons entertaining large donors at private White House coffees and inviting some contributors for overnight stays in the Lincoln bedroom or to go along on government foreign trade missions, and of Gore making fund-raising calls from his office and accepting donations from Buddhist nuns at a temple in California.

The GOP-led Congress launched investigations in both chambers, which seemed to do little more than embarrass the Democrats for their fund-raising excesses. Senate Governmental Affairs Committee investigators in 1997 came up with no proof to allegations that the Chinese government had conspired to influence U.S. elections through large campaign contributions, that the White House had knowingly accepted illegal foreign contributions, or that the Clinton administration ever changed policy in exchange for campaign contributions. And along the way, Democrats managed to reveal that a Republican National Committee (RNC) think tank, the National Policy Forum, had also accepted foreign money that may have been passed on to the RNC.

Various requests were made for the appointment of an independent counsel to look into alleged Democratic fund-raising abuses, but Attorney General Janet Reno concluded that the allegations did not meet the standard for such an appointment. Reno declined to get into the area of soft money because it did not fall under the provisions of the Federal Election Campaign Act. The attorney general looked at fund-raising calls made by Clinton from the White House and Gore from his office but determined that they were to solicit soft money and therefore did not violate the ban on soliciting hard money contributions on federal property. Moreover, according to Reno, Clinton's calls were from the White House residence, which was not covered by the solicitation ban.

The attorney general also examined the question of whether the Clinton-Gore campaign committees had been illegally involved in the political issue ad campaign financed by the DNC. A preliminary investigation by FEC auditors had concluded that both the DNC and the RNC had coordinated millions of dollars worth of issue ads with their respective presidential candidates' campaign committees, making the ads an in-kind contribution in violation of federal spending limits for presidential candidates who accepted public funding. But Reno found no criminal intent to violate the law by Clinton and Gore, based on the fact that they had been advised by counsel that the advertising campaign complied with the law. The FEC commissioners—three Democrats and three Republicans—subsequently rejected the auditors' findings. *(See box, "Federal Election Commission" p. 96.)*

While rejecting calls for an independent counsel, Reno emphasized that the Justice Department's Campaign Financing Task Force was conducting an ongoing investigation into allegations of wrongdoing in the 1996 election cycle. Ultimately several corporations and more than twenty-five individuals were charged with campaign finance violations that included making illegal foreign or corporate contributions and channeling donations through conduit or "straw" contributors who were later reimbursed, a violation of federal law.

New Issues Refocus Debate

Advocates of a campaign finance overhaul failed again in the 105th Congress (1997–1999). The House passed a sweeping measure known as the Shays-Meehan bill named after sponsors Christopher Shays, R-Conn., and Martin T. Meehan, D-Mass. GOP leaders had attempted to block House consideration of the bill, but they relented in the face of a growing number of signatures on a discharge petition to bring Shays-Meehan to the floor without committee action, a procedural move that would have cost the leadership control of the floor and allowed backers to debate a variety of campaign finance bills on their own terms. A Senate bill—known as McCain-Feingold, after sponsors John McCain, D-Ariz., and Russell D. Feingold, D-Wis.—succumbed once again to a filibuster.

But what was interesting this time around was how much the focus of the campaign finance debate had changed. PAC contributions, spending limits, and public funding were no longer the dominant themes. In fact, the House-passed bill included no provisions in those areas. And on the Senate side, sponsors of campaign finance legislation dropped those provisions in an attempt to broaden GOP support for their bill. The House and Senate bills focused instead on regulating soft money and issue advocacy advertising, reflecting the dramatic growth of both in the 1990s and the enormous controversy surrounding them.

Political scientist Anthony Corrado described the changed environment: "The most important factor in 1996 . . . was the advent of candidate-specific issue advocacy advertisements." Those ads in turn drove the demand for soft money because as long as the ads did not specifically endorse or oppose candidates, soft money could be used to cover most of their costs. "Suddenly, the federal campaign finance system seemed to be awash in undisclosed money from sources that were supposed to be banned by FECA," Corrado said.[61]

Backers of the legislation renewed their efforts in the 106th Congress (1999–2001). The House in 1999 passed an amended campaign finance overhaul bill that was substantively the same as the legislation it had approved the previous year.

The fate of the legislation once again was in the Senate's hands. Senate sponsors quickly unveiled a new strategy aimed at avoiding yet another death by filibuster. They put aside—at least for the time being—their proposal to more closely regulate issue ads and opted instead for a narrow bill that focused on banning soft money. They hoped this move would neutralize GOP opponents' argument that the bill was a violation of free speech rights. But the new strategy failed to attract enough votes to cut off a filibuster and the legislation died when Congress adjourned.

Still, the 106th Congress did not disappoint reform advocates entirely. Legislation was enacted in 2000 to require the secretive, tax-exempt Section 527 groups to disclose information about their organization and finances. One of its sponsors, Senator McCain, had a personal interest in cracking down on Section 527 groups after he became the target of one during his unsuccessful race for the 2000 GOP presidential nomination. *(See "Section 527 Groups," p. 104.)*

Under the new law, a Section 527 group that raised at least $25,000 had to notify the Internal Revenue Service (IRS) of its existence and disclose the group's name, address, e-mail address, purpose, and the names and addresses of its officers and top employees. A list of 527s was to be posted on the Internet and made available through the IRS.

The new law also required a Section 527 group to file periodic reports listing the names, addresses, occupations, and employers of those who contributed more than $200 a year, along with the date and amount of the contributions. In addition, a Section 527 group had to report annual expenditures of more than $500 to any individual. The report was to include the person's name, address, occupation, and employer, as well as the date, amount, and purpose of the expenditure. The IRS had to make the reports public, and in 2002 it was required to post them on the Internet as well. (The Internet-posting requirement was included in a 2002 law exempting certain state and local committees from the filing and reporting requirements.)

Soft Money, Issue Ads Reform

Congress in 2002 finally cleared a major campaign finance bill. The legislation—ushered through the Senate by McCain and Feingold and by Shays and Meehan in the House—barred the national political parties and federal candidates from accepting or spending soft money. It also restricted election-related issue ads broadcast just prior to elections. Issue ads had been largely paid for with soft money.

After years of debate and failed attempts, the pieces of a successful strategy began coming together. Senator McCain had made campaign finance reform the foundation of his 2000 presidential bid, boosting himself and the cause to national prominence. Turnover in the Senate, where legislation had been blocked for years by filibusters, also shifted the balance in favor of an overhaul. The breakthrough came in 2001 when Republican Thad Cochran of Mississippi announced that he would support the bill, giving McCain and Feingold the sixty votes they needed to make their bill filibuster-proof.

After the McCain-Feingold bill finally passed the Senate, the Shays-Meehan companion bill stalled in the House in a standoff with Republican leaders over the rules for floor debate. But the collapse of Enron Corp. in December 2001 triggered a remarkable reversal of fortune for the bill's supporters in the House. The massive bankruptcy exposed the energy trader's network of political giving and influence and triggered a panic among both Democrats and Republicans who had benefited from the company's largess. Many lawmakers faced uncomfortable questions about their campaign fund-raising and were looking to distance themselves from the Enron debacle.

The bill passed the House and cleared Congress in the early months of the next session. To win votes and align their measure with the Senate version, Shays and Meehan had to make some significant changes on the floor—for example, raising the limit on hard money campaign contributions by individuals from $1,000 to $2,000. House Republican leaders did their best to sink the bill on the floor or change it enough to force a conference with the Senate, but the existing system had grown impossible to defend and the measure's momentum proved unstoppable.

President George W. Bush signed the bill into law March 20, 2002, although he described it as "flawed" and pointedly avoided the traditional signing ceremony that would have brought the bill's sponsors, including his former rival McCain, to the White House.

Known formally as the Bipartisan Campaign Reform Act (BCRA)—and more popularly as McCain-Feingold—the 2002 law prohibited national party committees and federal candidates or officials from accepting or spending soft money.

State and local party committees could spend some soft money on voter registration and mobilization in federal elections, but only under certain conditions, including not mentioning a federal candidate and not accepting more than $10,000 per year from a donor. Such money came to be known as "Levin funds" because Sen. Carl Levin, D-Mich., had sponsored the amendment allowing the exception. The Levin amendment had represented a key compromise, particularly for Democrats who were concerned that the ban on soft money would put them at a disadvantage.

Under the new law, labor unions, for-profit corporations, and nonprofits could not fund election-related issue ads—now called "electioneering communication"—if the ad referred to a federal candidate, was broadcast on radio or television within sixty days of a general election or thirty days before a primary, and reached at least 50,000 people within the candidate's electorate. Such ads could be paid for through a PAC with regulated hard money contributions.

The law required that expenditures for electioneering communications totaling $10,000 or more be disclosed to the FEC. The report was to include, among other things, the name of the person making the disbursement and the name(s) of anyone exercising direction or control over the activities of that person.

Republicans, who typically had the advantage in raising hard money, won an important victory when a provision increasing the limits on hard money contributions was included in the bill. The limit on individual contributions to House and Senate candidates was raised to $2,000 per election, double the old limit, and the limit on individual contributions to national party committees was raised to $25,000 per year (from $20,000). The aggregate contribution limit for individuals was raised to $95,000 for a two-year election cycle (from $25,000 per year)—$37,500 to candidates and $57,500 to parties and PACs. All of these limits were indexed to grow with inflation.

The limit for individual contributions to state, district, and local party committees was raised to a combined total of $10,000 per year (from $5,000) but was not indexed for inflation.

The law raised the limit on national party committees' contributions to Senate candidates over a six-year election cycle to a total of $35,000 (from $17,500) and indexed it for inflation.

In what came to be known as the "millionaires' amendment," the law raised the limits on hard money contributions to House and Senate candidates who faced wealthy, self-financed opponents once they exceeded a certain threshold for use of personal funds. It also increased the limits on what political parties could spend in concert with those candidates with self-financing opponents.

The law set more stringent reporting requirements for independent expenditures made on a candidate's behalf.

When spending to help a candidate, political parties were required to choose between making coordinated expenditures (which were limited) and independent expenditures (which were not limited). The law said they could not do both in the same election. This provision was later declared unconstitutional. *(See McConnell v. Federal Election Commission, below.)*

The FEC was directed to issue new regulations on coordinated communications paid for by persons other than candidates, authorized committees of candidates, or party committees. The law specified that the new regulations should not require evidence of formal coordination or agreements between outside people or groups and candidates or parties in order to establish that election activity was "coordinated." The regulations were to address such issues as payments to a common vendor, payments for communications directed by a former employee of a candidate or political party, and payments made by someone who had substantial discussion about the communications with a candidate or party.

Other provisions strengthened existing bans on contributions by foreign nationals and solicitation in government buildings. A provision barring contributions by minors seventeen and younger—which was intended to keep donors from funneling money through their children to circumvent limits on individual contributions—was later declared unconstitutional.

BCRA Court Decisions

Immediately after the bill became law, longtime opponent Sen. Mitch McConnell, R-Ky., and a diverse coalition of groups that included the American Civil Liberties Union, the National Rifle Association, and the AFL-CIO sued to overturn it, saying it trampled on the rights of Americans to speak out and participate freely in the political process. A provision calling for "expedited judicial review" put the measure on a fast track to the Supreme Court.

The fight's first round took place before a special three-judge panel, which issued a fractured and confusing ruling in May 2003. But the judges agreed to set their ruling aside, leaving the law in place until the Supreme Court ruled.

On December 10, 2003, the Supreme Court ruled 5–4 in *McConnell v. Federal Election Commission* to uphold the major provisions of the 2002 law, including its ban on soft money and its restrictions on issue advertising by outside groups.

Opponents of the law had argued, in part, that the soft money ban and the restrictions on ads were an unprecedented infringement on the First Amendment right to political speech. Supporters of the law said that it was simply meant to refine campaign finance regulations to end "massive circumvention" of rules that the Court had long upheld. They said the political parties, candidates, and outside groups had made a mockery of the previous law when they flooded the system with soft money.

The majority opinion in *McConnell*, written by Justices John Paul Stevens and Sandra Day O'Connor, spoke of the need to show "proper deference to Congress' ability to weigh competing constitutional interests in an area in which it enjoys particular experience" and to provide Congress "sufficient room to anticipate and respond to concerns about circumvention of regulations designed to protect the political process's integrity." The majority also strongly said Congress did not need to show a risk of direct quid pro quo corruption to regulate money in politics. The integrity of the process—and the public's faith in democratic institutions—could be undermined by donations meant to curry favor with lawmakers indirectly, such as soft money to political parties, the Court said. Dissenting justices called the decision a clear defeat for the First Amendment.

The Court struck down the law's provisions barring political parties from making both independent and coordinated expenditures on behalf of a candidate and prohibiting contributions from anyone younger than eighteen.

After the Court held in *McConnell* that the act's issue ad provision was not on its face overbroad and unconstitutional, a lawsuit challenging the restrictions "as applied" to a specific set of ads was brought. By the time the Court heard oral arguments in the case, Justice O'Connor had retired and there was much speculation about what effect her departure would have on the Court's decision.

On June 25, 2007, the Court ruled 5–4 in *Federal Election Commission v. Wisconsin Right to Life, Inc.* that Wisconsin Right to Life, Inc., a nonprofit corporation, should have been allowed to run ads in the period just before the 2004 election urging Wisconsin voters to contact Democratic Sens. Feingold and Herb Kohl to ask them to oppose filibusters of President George W. Bush's judicial nominees. Feingold was up for reelection that year. Chief Justice Roberts wrote: ". . . .the First Amendment requires us to err on the side of protecting political speech rather than suppressing it. We conclude that the speech at issue in this as-applied challenge is not the 'functional equivalent' of express campaign speech."

Sen. McConnell said the decision corrected an obstacle to free speech. "This decision is a victory for free speech and confirmation that grass-roots advocacy organizations have the same free speech rights as all Americans," he said.

But Sen. Olympia J. Snowe, R-Maine, who had drafted the advertising provision, called the decision a disservice to the deep-seated problem of sham ads. "The court has regrettably taken a giant step backward by opening a significant loophole for those who wish to blur the lines between issue advocacy and campaigning," she said.

Section 527 Groups

The controversy over unregulated money flowing through the political system was far from over. Congress soon turned its attention to Section 527 political organizations, after the groups spent more than $400 million in the 2004 elections.

The 2000 law requiring disclosure of information about the groups and their finances had placed no restrictions on their activities. Unlike national party committees, political campaigns, or PACs, the Section 527 groups were able to accept—and spend—unlimited contributions from wealthy individuals, unions, and corporations. Groups such as Moveon.org and Swift Boat Veterans for Truth made headlines, fueling the controversy.

Some 527 groups financed GOP attack ads, but Democrats were seen as the main beneficiaries of Section 527 fund-raising. As a result, the effort to revise campaign rules to rein in the groups was driven mainly by Republicans. Some Republicans, however, were interested less in writing new rules for Section 527s than in relaxing existing campaign finance restrictions.

The House in 2006 passed a bill—sponsored again by Shays and Meehan—that would have required Section 527 groups to register as political committees with the FEC and comply with federal campaign finance laws. But Senate leaders refused to take up a companion bill sponsored by McCain, Feingold, and Trent Lott, R-Miss., chair of the Rules and Administration Committee. The House also attached its bill to its version of lobbying and ethics reform legislation, but final agreement on the ethics bill was never reached, largely because Senate Republicans refused to include the language on 527s and House Republicans would not budge without it. The bills died at the end of the 109th Congress, but early in the next Congress in 2007 Shays, Meehan, McCain, and Feingold renewed their efforts to regulate Section 527 groups.

NOTES

1. Unless otherwise noted, the figures in this chapter on campaign receipts and expenditures in the 2006 elections were from the Federal Election Commission and include money that moved during the 2005–2006 election cycle in all congressional races, including those of primary losers. Figures have been rounded.

2. Quoted in Chuck Alston, "Image Problems Propel Congress Back to Campaign Finance Bills," *Congressional Quarterly Weekly Report,* February 2, 1991, 281.

3. Frank J. Sorauf, *Money in American Elections* (Glenview, Ill.: Scott, Foresman, 1988), 73–74.

4. 1997 survey: Center for Responsive Politics and Princeton Survey Research Associates, "Money and Politics: A National Survey of the Public's Views on How Money Impacts Our Political System" (Washington, D.C.: Center for Responsive Politics, April–May 1997). 2002 survey: Conducted September 2002. See Anthony Corrado, Thomas E. Mann, and Trevor Potter, eds., *Inside the Campaign Finance Battle: Court Testimony on the New Reforms* (Washington, D.C.: Brookings Institution Press, 2003), 266–269. 2004 survey: Conducted February 11–16, 2004, by Princeton Survey Research Associates and sponsored by Pew Research Center, available online at www.publicagenda.org. 2007 survey: Conducted February 6–12, 2007, and published March 7, 2007, by The Harris Poll, available online at www.harrisinteractive.com.

5. Quoted in Larry J. Sabato, *PAC Power: Inside the World of Political Action Committees* (New York: Norton, 1984), 171.

6. Paul S. Herrnson, "Money and Motives: Spending in House Elections," in *Congress Reconsidered,* 6th ed., ed. Lawrence C. Dodd and Bruce I. Oppenheimer (Washington, D.C.: CQ Press, 1997), 114.

7. Frank J. Sorauf, "Political Action Committees," in *Campaign Finance Reform: A Sourcebook,* ed. Anthony Corrado et al. (Washington, D.C.: Brookings Institution, 1997), 123.

8. Brody Mullins and Dean Treftz, "Companies Shift More Donations to Democrats," *The Wall Street Journal,* April 30, 2007, A1. Congressional Quarterly's www.politicalmoneyline.com, news item of May 8, 2007.

9. Sorauf, "Political Action Committees," 126.

10. Sorauf, *Money in American Elections,* 174.

11. Congressional Quarterly's www.politicalmoneyline.com, as of May 11, 2007.

12. Herrnson, "Money and Motives," 107–108.

13. Ibid., 105.

14. Senate Committee on the Judiciary, Subcommittee on the Constitution, "Hearing on Campaign Finance Reform," 100th Cong., 2nd sess., February 28, 1990, 7.

15. Quoted in Chuck Alston, "Forcing Down Cost of TV Ads Appeals to Both Parties," *Congressional Quarterly Weekly Report,* March 16, 1991, 647.

16. U.S. Congress, *Congressional Record,* March 21, 2001, S2615.

17. Joseph E. Cantor, Denis Steven Rutkus, and Kevin B. Greely, "Free and Reduced-Rate Television Time for Political Candidates," Library of Congress, Congressional Research Service, Rept. 97-680 GOV, July 7, 1997, iii, 3–4.

18. Sara Fritz and Dwight Morris, *Gold-Plated Politics: Running for Congress in the 1990s* (Washington, D.C.: CQ Press, 1992), 128.

19. Quoted in Alston, "Forcing Down Cost of TV Ads Appeals to Both Parties," 648.

20. Craig B. Holman and Luke P. McLoughlin, *Buying Time, 2000* (New York: Brennan Center for Justice, New York University School of Law, 2001), executive summary, 12; report, 48–49.

21. Dwight Morris and Murielle E. Gamache, *Handbook of Campaign Spending: Money in the 1992 Congressional Races* (Washington D.C.: Congressional Quarterly, 1994), 8–12.

22. Quoted in Larry J. Sabato, *Paying for Elections: The Campaign Finance Thicket* (New York: Twentieth Century Fund/Priority Press, 1989), 11.

23. Joseph E. Cantor, "Campaign Finance: An Overview," Library of Congress, Congressional Research Service, RL33580, March 29, 2007, 3. Available online at www.politicalmoneyline.com.

24. Joseph E. Cantor, "Congressional Campaign Spending: 1976–1996," Library of Congress, Congressional Research Service,

Rept. 97-793 GOV, August 19, 1997, 3–4. Center for Responsive Politics, "2006 Election Overview: Stats at a Glance," available online at www.opensecrets.org.

25. Figures from Congressional Quarterly's www.politicalmoneyline.com.

26. Cantor, "Congressional Campaign Spending: 1976–1996," 3–4. Center for Responsive Politics, "2006 Election Overview: Stats at a Glance," available online at www.opensecrets.org.

27. Figures from Congressional Quarterly's www.politicalmoneyline.com.

28. Gary C. Jacobson, "Money in the 1980 and 1982 Congressional Elections," in *Money and Politics in the United States: Financing Elections in the 1980s,* ed. Michael J. Malbin (Washington, D.C.: American Enterprise Institute, 1984), 58.

29. Sorauf, *Money in American Elections,* 333.

30. Diane Granat, "Parties' Schools for Politicians Grooming Troops for Elections," *Congressional Quarterly Weekly Report,* May 5, 1984, 1036.

31. Quoted in Andy Plattner, "The High Cost of Holdling—and Keeping—Public Office," *U.S. News & World Report,* June 22, 1987, 30.

32. David E. Price, "The House of Representatives: A Report from the Field," in *Congress Reconsidered,* 4th ed., ed. Lawrence C. Dodd and Bruce I. Oppenheimer (Washington, D.C.: CQ Press, 1989), 417–418.

33. Senate Committee on Rules and Administration, *Hearings on Senate Campaign Finance Proposals,* 100th Cong., 1st sess., March 5 and 18, April 22 and 23, 1987, 7–8.

34. Magleby and Nelson, *The Money Chase,* 44.

35. Joseph E. Cantor and R. Sam Garrett, "Public Financing of Congressional Elections: Background and Analysis," Library of Congress, Congressional Research Service, RL33814, January 22, 2007, iii. Available online at www.politicalmoneyline.com.

36. Roger H. Davidson and Walter J. Oleszek, *Congress and Its Members,* 9th ed. (Washington, D.C.: CQ Press, 2004), 61.

37. Sabato, *Paying for Elections,* 4.

38. Senate Committee on Rules and Administration, Hearings on Campaign Finance Reform, 101st Cong., 1st sess., Fred Wertheimer testimony, April 20, 1989, committee handout, 30.

39. Cantor, "Campaign Finance: An Overview," 2.

40. Anthony Corrado, "Party Soft Money," in *Campaign Finance Reform: A Sourcebook,* 172.

41. Quoted in Alan Greenblatt, "Soft Money: The Root of All Evil or a Party-Building Necessity?" *Congressional Quarterly Weekly Report,* September 6, 1997, 2065.

42. David B. Magleby and Marianne Holt, eds., *Outside Money: Soft Money & Issue Ads in Competitive 1998 Congressional Elections* (Provo, Utah: Brigham Young University, 1999), 12.

43. Jackie Koszczuk, "'Soft Money' Speaks Loudly on Capitol Hill This Season," *CQ Weekly,* June 27, 1998, 1738; Cantor, "Campaign Finance: An Overview," 5.

44. Deborah Beck et al., "Issue Advocacy Advertising during the 1996 Campaign: A Catalog" (Philadelphia: University of Pennsylvania, Annenberg Public Policy Center, 1997), 3.

45. Figures taken from Congressional Quarterly's political-moneyline.com website on May 3, 2007. Figures for all the election cycles are subject to change as new reports are filed. PoliticalMoneyLine identified as "key 527 groups" those organizations within the Internal Revenue Service's database that were clearly involved in national election activities.

46. "Financing the 2006 Midterm Elections," transcript of panel discussion at The Brookings Institution, Washington, D.C., September 12, 2006. Available at www.brookings.edu.

47. Stephen R. Weissman and Kara D. Ryan, "Soft Money in the 2006 Election and the Outlook for 2008: The Changing Nonprofits Landscape" (Washington, D.C.: Campaign Finance Institute, 2007), 7. Available online at www.cfinst.org.

48. Thomas E. Mann, "Reform Agenda," in *The New Campaign Finance Sourcebook,* edited by Anthony Corrado et al. (Washington, D.C.: The Brookings Institution, 2005), 270. Cantor, "Campaign Finance: An Overview," 13.

49. "Financing the 2006 Midterm Elections," transcript of panel discussion at The Brookings Institution, 60.

50. L. Paige Whitaker and Joseph E. Cantor, "Campaign Finance Reform: Regulating Political Communications on the Internet," Library of Congress, Congressional Research Service, RS 22272, March 8, 2007, 1-6. Available online at www.politicalmoneyline.com.

51. Sorauf, "Political Action Committees," 128.

52. Robert E. Mutch, *Campaigns, Congress, and Courts: The Making of Federal Campaign Finance Law* (New York: Praeger, 1988), xv.

53. George Thayer, *Who Shakes the Money Tree? American Campaign Financing Practices from 1789 to the Present* (New York: Simon and Schuster, 1973), 25.

54. Mutch, *Campaigns, Congress, and Courts,* xvi.

55. Ibid., xvii.

56. Ibid., 4.

57. Alexander Heard, *The Costs of Democracy* (Chapel Hill: University of North Carolina Press, 1960), 388.

58. Herbert E. Alexander, *Financing the 1968 Election* (Lexington, Mass.: D. C. Heath, 1971), 93.

59. Herbert E. Alexander, *Financing the 1972 Election* (Lexington, Mass.: D. C. Heath, 1976), 7.

60. *Facts on File,* April 29–May 5, 1973, 357.

61. Anthony Corrado, "The Legislative Odyssey of BCRA," in *Life After Reform: When the Bipartisan Campaign Reform Act Meets Politics,* ed. Michael J. Malbin (New York: Rowman & Littlefield, 2003), 28.

SELECTED BIBLIOGRAPHY

Alexander, Herbert E. *Financing Politics: Money, Elections, and Political Reform.* 4th ed. Washington, D.C.: CQ Press, 1992.

Alexander, Herbert E., and Anthony Corrado. *Financing the 1992 Election.* Armonk, N.Y.: M. E. Sharpe, 1995.

Anschutz, August V., ed. *Campaign Financing in the United States: Issues and Laws.* New York: Nova Science, 2002.

Biersack, Robert, Paul S. Herrnson, and Clyde Wilcox. *After the Revolution: PACs, Lobbies, and the Republican Congress.* Boston: Allyn and Bacon, 1999.

Cantor, Joseph E. *Campaign Financing.* Washington, D.C.: Congressional Research Service, Library of Congress, 2001.

———. "Congressional Campaign Spending: 1976–1996." Rept. No. 97793 GOV. Washington, D.C.: Library of Congress, Congressional Research Service, 1997.

———. "Political Action Committees: Their Role in Financing Congressional Elections." Rept. No. 98255 GOV. Washington, D.C.: Library of Congress, Congressional Research Service, 1998.

Cantor, Joseph E., Denis S. Rutkus, and Kevin B. Greely. "Free and Reduced-Rate Television Time for Political Candidates." Rept. No. 97680 GOV. Washington, D.C.: Library of Congress, Congressional Research Service, 1997.

Corrado, Anthony, Thomas E. Mann, and Trevor Potter, eds. *Inside the Campaign Finance Battle: Court Testimony on the New Reforms.* Washington, D.C.: Brookings Institution Press, 2003.

Corrado, Anthony, et al. *The New Campaign Finance Sourcebook.* Washington, D.C.: Brookings Institution Press, 2005.

Dodd, Lawrence C., and Bruce I. Oppenheimer. *Congress Reconsidered.* 8th ed. Washington, D.C.: CQ Press, 2005.

Drew, Elizabeth. *The Corruption of American Politics: What Went Wrong and Why.* New York: Birch Lane Press, 1999.

Dwyre, Diana, and Victoria A. Farrar-Myers. *Legislative Labyrinth: Congress and Campaign Finance Reform.* Washington, D.C.: CQ Press, 2001.

Eismeier, Theodore J., and Philip H. Pollock III. *Business, Money and the Rise of Corporate PACs in American Elections.* New York: Quorum Books, 1988.

Francia, Peter L., et al. *The Financiers of Congressional Elections: Investors, Ideologues, and Intimates.* New York: Columbia University Press, 2003.

Fritz, Sara, and Dwight Morris. *Gold-Plated Politics: Running for Congress in the 1990s.* Washington, D.C.: CQ Press, 1992.

Gierzynski, Anthony. *Money Rules: Financing Elections in America.* Boulder, Colo.: Westview Press, 2000.

Goidel, Robert K., Donald A. Gross, and Todd G. Shields. *Money Matters: Consequences of Campaign Finance Reform in U.S. House Elections.* Lanham, Md.: Rowan and Littlefield, 1999.

Grant, J. Tobin, and Thomas J. Rudolph. *Expression vs. Equality: The Politics of Campaign Finance Reform.* Columbus: Ohio State University Press, 2004.

Green, John, Paul Herrnson, Lynda Powell, and Clyde Wilcox. "Individual Congressional Campaign Contributors: Wealthy, Conservative and Reform-Minded." Washington, D.C.: Center for Responsive Politics, 1998.

Gronke, Paul. *The Electorate, the Campaign, and the Office: A Unified Approach to Senate and House Elections.* Ann Arbor: University of Michigan Press, 2000.

Heard, Alexander. *The Costs of Democracy.* Chapel Hill: University of North Carolina Press, 1960.

Henderson, Harry. *Campaign and Election Reform.* New York: Facts on File, 2004.

Herrnson, Paul S. *Congressional Elections: Campaigning at Home and in Washington.* 4th ed. Washington, D.C.: CQ Press, 2004.

Herrnson, Paul S., Ronald G. Shaiko, and Clyde Wilcox. *The Interest Group Connection: Electioneering, Lobbying, and Policymaking in Washington.* 2nd ed. Washington, D.C.: CQ Press, 2005.

Jackson, Brooks. *Broken Promise: Why the Federal Election Commission Failed.* New York: Priority Press, 1990.

———. *Honest Graft: Big Money and the American Political Process.* Rev. ed. Washington, D.C.: Farragut, 1990.

Jacobson, Gary C. *The Politics of Congressional Elections.* 6th ed. New York: Pearson Longman, 2004.

Krasno, Jonathan S. *Challengers, Competition, and Reelection: Comparing Senate and House Elections.* New Haven, Conn.: Yale University Press, 1994.

Kubiak, Greg D. *The Gilded Dome: The U.S. Senate and Campaign Finance Reform.* Norman: University of Oklahoma Press, 1994.

Lubenow, Gerald C., ed. *A User's Guide to Campaign Finance Reform.* Lanham, Md.: Rowman & Littlefield, 2001.

Magleby, David B., ed. *The Other Campaign: Soft Money and Issue Advocacy in the 2000 Congressional Elections.* Lanham, Md.: Rowman & Littlefield, 2003.

Magleby, David B., Anthony J. Corrado, and Kelly D. Patterson, eds. *Financing the 2004 Election.* Washington D.C.: Brookings Institution Press, 2006.

Magleby, David B., and Marianne Holt, eds. *Outside Money: Soft Money & Issue Ads in Competitive 1998 Congressional Elections.* Lanham, Md.: Rowman & Littlefield, 2000.

Magleby, David B., J. Quin Monson, and Kelly Patterson, eds. *Electing Congress: New Rules for an Old Game.* Upper Saddle River, N.J.: Pearson Prentice Hall, 2007.

Magleby, David B., and Candice J. Nelson. *The Money Chase: Congressional Campaign Finance Reform.* Washington, D.C.: Brookings Institution, 1990.

Makinson, Larry, and Joshua F. Goldstein. *The Cash Constituents of Congress.* 2nd ed. Washington, D.C.: CQ Press, 1994.

———. *Open Secrets: The Encyclopedia of Congressional Money and Politics.* 4th ed. Washington, D.C.: Congressional Quarterly, 1996.

Malbin, Michael J. *The Election after Reform: Money, Politics, and the Bipartisan Campaign Reform Act.* Lanham, Md.: Rowman & Littlefield, 2006.

Mutch, Robert E. *Campaigns, Congress, and Courts: The Making of Federal Campaign Finance Law.* New York: Praeger, 1988.

Nugent, Margaret L., and John R. Johannes, eds. *Money, Elections, and Democracy: Reforming Congressional Campaign Finance.* Boulder, Colo.: Westview Press, 1990.

Ornstein, Norman J. *Campaign Finance: An Illustrated Guide.* Washington, D.C.: American Enterprise Institute, 1997.

Pantesh, Collin V., ed. *Campaign Financing and America's Evolving Election System.* New York: Nova Science Publishers, 2006.

Sabato, Larry J. *PAC Power: Inside the World of Political Action Committees.* New York: Norton, 1984.

———. *Paying for Elections: The Campaign Finance Thicket.* New York: Priority Press/Twentieth Century Fund, 1989.

Samples, John C. *The Fallacy of Campaign Finance Reform.* Chicago: University of Chicago Press, 2006.

———, ed. *Welfare for Politicians? Taxpayer Financing of Campaigns.* Washington, D.C.: Cato Institute, 2005.

Schneider, Jerrold E. *Campaign Finance Reform and the Future of the Democratic Party.* New York: Routledge, 2002.

Skinner, Richard M. *More Than Money: Interest Group Action in Congressional Elections.* Lanham, Md.: Rowman & Littlefield, 2007.

Smith, Bradley A. *Unfree Speech: The Folly of Campaign Finance Reform.* Princeton, N.J.: Princeton University Press, 2001.

Smith, Rodney A. *Money, Power & Elections: How Campaign Finance Reform Subverts American Democracy.* Baton Rouge: Louisiana State University Press, 2006.

Sorauf, Frank J. *Inside Campaign Finance: Myths and Realities.* New Haven, Conn.: Yale University Press, 1994.

———. *Money in American Elections.* Glenview, Ill.: Scott, Foresman/Little, Brown, 1988.

Steen, Jennifer A. *Self-Financed Candidates in Congressional Elections.* Ann Arbor: University of Michigan Press, 2006.

Tedford, Thomas L., and Dale A. Herbeck. *Freedom of Speech in the United States.* 5th ed. State College, Pa.: Strata Pub., 2001.

Thayer, George. *Who Shakes the Money Tree? American Campaign Financing from 1789 to the Present.* New York: Simon and Schuster, 1973.

U.S. Federal Election Commission. *Annual Report.* Washington, D.C.: U.S. Government Printing Office, 1975– .

———. *FEC Reports on Financial Activities.* Washington, D.C.: U.S. Government Printing Office, 1977– .

———. *Twenty Year Report.* Washington, D.C.: U.S. Government Printing Office, 1995.

Vital Statistics on Congress. Washington, D.C.: American Enterprise Institute for Public Policy Research, 1980– .

chapter 5

Reapportionment and Redistricting

Reapportionment, the redistribution of the 435 seats in the House of Representatives among the states to reflect shifts in population, and redistricting, the redrawing of congressional district boundaries for the House within the states, are among the most important and contentious processes in the U.S. political system. They help to determine whether Democrats or Republicans, or liberals or conservatives, will dominate the House and whether districts will be drawn to favor the election of candidates from particular racial or ethnic groups.

Reapportionment and redistricting occur every ten years on the basis of the decennial population census required by Article I, Section 2, of the U.S. Constitution. States where populations grew quickly during the previous ten years typically gain congressional seats, while those that lost population or grew much more slowly than the national average stand to lose seats. The number of House members for the rest of the states remains the same.

The states that gain or lose seats usually must make extensive changes in their congressional maps. Even those states with stable delegations must make modifications to take into account population shifts within their boundaries, in accordance with U.S. Supreme Court one-person, one-vote rulings.

In most states, the state legislatures are responsible for drafting and enacting the new congressional district map. Thus, the majority party in each state legislature is often in a position to draw a district map that enhances the fortunes of its incumbents and candidates at the expense of the opposing party. As political reporter Ron Elving wrote in 1991: "Some members may find their old district no longer recognizable, or their home located in someone else's district. Others will find the music has stopped and they are, quite literally, without a seat. Or they will find themselves thrown together in a single district with another incumbent—often from the same party." Elving said the "scramble to prevent or minimize such political problems involves some of the most brutal combat in American politics, for the power to draw district lines is the power not only to end one politician's career but often to enfranchise or disenfranchise a neighborhood, a city, a party, a social or economic group or even a race by concentrating or diluting their votes within a given district." [1]

Among the many unique features to emerge in the nation-creating endeavor of 1787 was a national legislative body (the House of Representatives) whose membership was to be elected by the people and apportioned on the basis of population. In keeping with the nature of the Constitution, however, only fundamental rules and regulations were provided. The interpretation and implementation of the instructions contained in the document were left to future generations.

Within this flexible framework many questions soon arose. How large was the House of Representatives to be? What mathematical formula was to be used in calculating the distribution of seats among the various states? Were the representatives to be elected at large or by districts? If by districts, what standards should be used in fixing their boundaries? Congress and the courts have been wrestling with these questions for more than two hundred years.

Until the mid-twentieth century such questions generally remained in the hands of the legislators. But with the population increasingly concentrated in urban areas, variations in populations among rural and urban districts in a single state grew more and more pronounced. Efforts to persuade Congress and state legislatures to address the issue of heavily populated but underrepresented areas proved unsuccessful. Legislators from rural areas were so intent on preventing power from slipping through their hands that they managed to block reapportionment of the House for a whole decade after the 1920 census.

Not long afterward, litigants began trying to persuade the Supreme Court to order the states to revise congressional district boundaries to reflect population shifts. For years they found the Court unreceptive. There was incremental progress, and then a breakthrough finally occurred in 1964 in the case of *Wesberry v. Sanders*. In that case, the Court declared that the Constitution required that "as nearly as practicable, one man's vote in a congressional election is to be worth as much as another's."

In the years that followed, the Court repeatedly reaffirmed its one-person, one-vote requirement. Following the 1980 census, several states adopted new maps with districts of nearly equal population that were designed to benefit one party at the expense of the other. These partisan gerrymanders disregarded other traditional tenets of map-drawing, such as making districts compact and respecting the integrity of county and city lines. But as long as the districts in such maps were drawn to be equal in population, these gerrymanders seemed unassailable in the courts.

In 1986, in *Davis v. Bandemer,* a slim majority of the Supreme Court held that partisan gerrymanders were subject to constitutional review by federal courts. But the Court's decision offered little guidance about an impermissible partisan gerrymander. The justices said that successful challengers to a map on partisan grounds had to "prove both intentional discrimination against an identifiable political group and an actual discriminatory effect on that group." Many redistricting experts thought this set such a high standard that proving the discrimination would be all but impossible. As a result, maps drawn with a clear partisan slant continued to appear rounds of redistricting in the 1990s and 2000s.[2]

The Court revisited this issue in 2004 in a case that arose from charges by Pennsylvania Democrats that Republicans had drawn impermissibly partisan districts. The Court rejected the claim, saying that the case had not been proven to the standard set out in *Bandemer,* but the justices did not—as strongly advocated by four of the most conservative members—overturn the 1986 decision on the grounds that a meaningful standard never could be enunciated. That meant that litigation on partisan gerrymandering could still be brought in the future. Moreover, the Court that same year sent back to a Texas trial court a related case about partisan redistricting in that state. The justices said the lower court should reconsider its earlier action on that case in light of the Pennsylvania decision *Vieth v. Jubelirer,* but the Court gave little guidance about its expectations. *(See "Pennsylvania," p. 137.)* The Texas case returned to the Court in 2006, and it overturned a small portion of the redrawn Texas district map on grounds that boundary lines for one district violated provisions of the Voting Rights Act but upheld the mid-decade partisan gerrymander at large because the Texas Democrats failed to offer a workable standard for constitutional review. The question of justiciability, and thus the rulings in *Bandemer* and *Vieth v. Jubelirer,* were not revisited. *(See "Texas," p. 137.)*

Starting in the mid-1980s and continuing through the 1990s, the focus of much redistricting controversy and litigation shifted to the practice of racial gerrymandering—designing constituencies to favor the election of candidates from racial or ethnic groups whose numbers in Congress are lower than their proportion in the general population. Although this issue remained contentious, its importance was diminished for redistricting after the 2000 census following a series of Supreme Court rulings that questioned or prohibited the practice.

In a landmark 1986 ruling (*Thornburg v. Gingles*), the Supreme Court not only said that gerrymandering that deliberately diluted minority voting strength was illegal but also imposed a requirement that mapmakers do all they can to maximize minority voting strength. The expansion of minority rights sparked by *Gingles* changed redistricting dramatically. After the 1990 census, redistricting in many states was done with an eye toward creating constituencies designed to elect minority candidates. Those new maps resulted in record numbers of blacks and Hispanics winning House seats in 1992.

As if taken aback by the pace of change wrought by *Gingles,* the Supreme Court issued a series of rulings in the 1990s that discouraged states from going to extremes to draw districts for minorities. As a result, mapmakers in the twenty-first century found themselves caught between legal and political pressures to enhance election opportunities for minority group members and to adhere to court decisions that posed a rigorous examination of the standards and methods to carry out this obligation.

EARLY HISTORY OF REAPPORTIONMENT

Modern legislative bodies are descended from the councils of feudal lords and gentry that medieval kings summoned for the purpose of raising revenues and armies. The councils represented only certain groups of people, such as the nobility, the clergy, the landed gentry, and town merchants. The notion of equal representation for equal numbers of people or even for all groups of people had not yet begun to develop.

Beginning as little more than administrative and advisory arms of the throne, royal councils in time developed into lawmaking bodies and acquired powers that eventually eclipsed those of the monarchs they served. In England the king's council became Parliament, with the higher nobility and clergy making up the House of Lords and representatives of the gentry and merchants making up the House of Commons. The power struggle between king and council climaxed in the mid-1600s, when the king was executed and a benevolent dictatorship was set up under Oliver Cromwell. Although the monarchy was soon restored, by 1800 Parliament was clearly the more powerful branch of government.

The growth of the powers of Parliament, as well as the development of English ideas of representation during the seventeenth and eighteenth centuries, had a profound effect on the colonists in America. Representative assemblies were unifying forces behind the breakaway of the colonies from England and the establishment of the newly independent nation.

Colonists in America generally modeled their legislatures after England's, using both population and land units as bases for apportionment. Patterns of early representation varied. "Nowhere did representation bear any uniform relation to the number of electors. Here and there the factor of size had been crudely recognized," Robert Luce noted in his book *Legislative Principles*.[3]

The Continental Congress, with representation from every colony, proclaimed in the Declaration of Independence in 1776 that governments derive "their just powers from the consent of the governed" and that "the right of representation in the legislature" is an "inestimable right" of the people. The Constitutional Convention of 1787 included representatives from all the states. However, in neither of these bodies were the state delegations or voting powers proportional to population.

In New England the town was usually the basis for representation. In the Middle Atlantic region the county frequently was used. Virginia used the county with additional representation for specified cities. In many areas, towns and counties were fairly equal in population, and territorial representation afforded roughly equal representation for equal numbers of people. Delaware's three counties, for example, were of almost equal population and had the same representation in the legislature. But in Virginia the disparity was enormous (from 951 people in one county to 22,015 in another). Thomas Jefferson criticized the state's constitution on the ground that "among those who share the representation, the shares are unequal." [4]

The Framers' Intentions

What, then, did the Framers of the Constitution have in mind about who would be represented in the House of Representatives and how? The Constitution declares only that each state is to be allotted a certain number of representatives. It does not state specifically that congressional districts must be equal or nearly equal in population. It also explicitly does not require that a state create districts at all. However, it seems clear that the first clause of Article I, Section 2, providing that House members should be chosen "by the People of the several States," indicates that the House of Representatives, in contrast to the Senate, was to represent people instead of states. *(See box, Constitutional Provisions, p. 109.)*

The third clause of Article I, Section 2, provided that congressional apportionment among the states must be according to population. "There is little point in giving the states congressmen 'according to their respective numbers' if the states do not redistribute the members of their delegations on the same principle," Andrew Hacker argued in his book *Congressional Districting*. "For representatives are not the property of the states, as are the senators, but rather belong to the people who happen to reside within the boundaries of those states. Thus, each citizen has a claim to be regarded as a political unit equal in value to his neighbors." [5]

Hacker also examined the Constitutional Convention, *The Federalist Papers* (essays written by Alexander Hamilton, John Jay, and James Madison in defense of the Constitution), and the state conventions ratifying the Constitution for evidence of the Framers' intentions with regard to representation. He found that the issue of unequal representation arose only once during debate in the Constitutional

CONSTITUTIONAL PROVISIONS

ARTICLE I, SECTION 2

The House of Representatives shall be composed of Members chosen every second Year by the People of the several States, and the Electors in each State shall have the Qualifications requisite for Electors of the most numerous Branch of the State Legislature. . . .

Representatives and direct Taxes shall be apportioned among the several States which may be included within this Union, according to their respective Numbers, which shall be determined by adding to the whole Number of free Persons, including those bound to Service for a Term of Years, and excluding Indians not taxed, three fifths of all other Persons. The actual Enumeration shall be made within three Years after the first Meeting of the Congress of the United States, and within every subsequent Term of ten Years, in such Manner as they shall by Law direct. The Number of Representatives shall not exceed one for every thirty thousand, but each State shall have at least one Representative. . . .

ARTICLE I, SECTION 4

The Times, Places and Manner of holding Elections for Senators and Representatives, shall be prescribed in each State by the Legislature thereof; but the Congress may at any time by Law make or alter such Regulations, except as to the Place of Chusing Senators. . . .

AMENDMENT XIV

(Ratified July 28, 1868)

Section 2. Representatives shall be apportioned among the several States according to their respective numbers, counting the whole number of persons in each State, excluding Indians not taxed. But when the right to vote at any election for the choice of electors for President and Vice President of the United States, Representatives in Congress, the Executive and Judicial officers of a State, or the members of the Legislature thereof, is denied to any of the male inhabitants of such State, being twenty-one years of age, and citizens of the United States, or in any way abridged, except for participation in rebellion, or other crime, the basis of representation therein shall be reduced in the proportion which the number of such male citizens shall bear to the whole number of male citizens twenty-one years of age in such State.

Convention. The occasion was Madison's defense of Article I, Section 4, of the proposed Constitution, giving Congress the power to override state regulations on "the times . . . and manner" of holding elections for members of Congress. Madison's argument related to the fact that many state legislatures of the time were badly malapportioned: "The inequality of the representation in the legislatures of particular states would produce a like inequality in their representation in the national legislature, as it was presumable that the counties having the power in the former case would secure it to themselves in the latter." [6]

The implication was that states would create congressional districts and that unequal districting was undesirable and should be prevented.

Madison made this interpretation even more clear in his contributions to *The Federalist Papers*. Arguing in favor of the relatively small size of the projected House of Representatives, he wrote in No. 56: "Divide the largest state into ten or twelve districts and it will be found that there will be no peculiar local interests . . . which will not be within the knowledge of the Representative of the district."

In the same paper Madison said, "The Representatives of each state will not only bring with them a considerable knowledge of its laws, and a local knowledge of their respective districts, but will probably in all cases have been members, and may even at the very time be members, of the state legislature, where all the local information and interests of the state are assembled, and from whence they may easily be conveyed by a very few hands into the legislature of the United States." Finally, in *The Federalist* No. 57 Madison stated that "each Representative of the United States will be elected by five or six thousand citizens." In making these arguments, Madison seems to have assumed that all or most representatives would be elected by districts, not at large.[7]

In the states' ratifying conventions, the grant to Congress by Article I, Section 4, of ultimate jurisdiction over the "Times, Places and Manner of holding Elections" (except the places of choosing senators) held the attention of many delegates. There were differences over the merits of this section but no justification of unequal districts was prominently used to attack the grant of power. Further evidence that individual districts were the intention of the Founders was given in the New York ratifying convention when Alexander Hamilton said, "The natural and proper mode of holding elections will be to divide the state into districts in proportion to the number to be elected. This state will consequently be divided at first into six." [8]

From his study of the sources relating to the question of congressional districting, Hacker concluded:

> There is, then, a good deal of evidence that those who framed and ratified the Constitution intended that the House of Representatives have as its constituency a public in which the votes of all citizens were of equal weight. . . . The House of Representatives was designed to be a popular chamber, giving the same electoral power to all who had the vote. And the concern of Madison . . . that districts be equal in size was an institutional step in the direction of securing this democratic principle.[9]

REAPPORTIONMENT: THE NUMBER OF SEATS

The Constitution made the first apportionment, which was to remain in effect until the first census was taken. No reliable figures on the population were available at the time. The Constitution's apportionment yielded a sixty-five member House. The seats were allotted among the thirteen states as follows: Virginia, ten; Massachusetts and Pennsylvania, eight; Maryland and New York, six; Connecticut, North Carolina, and South Carolina, five; New Jersey, four; Georgia and New Hampshire, three; and Delaware and Rhode Island and Providence Plantations, one. This apportionment remained in effect during the First and Second Congresses (1789–1793).

Apparently realizing that apportionment of the House was likely to become a major bone of contention, the First Congress submitted to the states a proposed constitutional amendment containing a formula to be used in future reapportionments. The amendment provided that following the taking of a decennial census one representative would be allotted for every thirty thousand people until the House membership reached one hundred. Once that level was reached, there would be one representative for every forty thousand people until the House membership reached two hundred, when there would be one representative for every fifty thousand people.

First Apportionment by Congress

The states, however, refused to ratify the reapportionment-formula amendment, which forced Congress to enact apportionment legislation after the first census was taken in 1790. The first apportionment bill was sent to the president in March 1792. President George Washington sent the bill back to Congress without his signature—the first presidential veto.

The bill had incorporated the constitutional minimum of thirty thousand as the size of each district. But the population of each state was not a simple multiple of thirty thousand; significant fractions were left over. For example, Vermont was found to be entitled to 2.85 representatives, New Jersey to 5.98, and Virginia to 21.02. A formula had to be found that would deal in the fairest possible manner with unavoidable variations from exact equality.

Accordingly, Congress proposed in the first apportionment bill to distribute the members on a fixed ratio of one representative for each thirty thousand inhabitants and to give an additional member to each state with a fraction exceeding one-half. Washington's veto was based on the belief that eight states would receive more than one representative for each thirty thousand people under this formula.

A motion to override the veto was unsuccessful. A new bill meeting the president's objections, approved in April 1792, provided for a ratio of one member for every thirty-three thousand inhabitants and fixed the exact number of representatives to which each state was entitled. The total membership of the House was to be 105. In dividing the population of the various states by thirty-three thousand, all remainders were to be disregarded. Thomas Jefferson devised the solution, known as the method of rejected fractions.

A method of reapportionment devised by Thomas Jefferson resulted in great inequalities among states. This method was in use until 1840.

Jefferson's Method

Jefferson's method of reapportionment resulted in great inequalities among districts. A Vermont district would contain 42,766 inhabitants, a New Jersey district 35,911, and a Virginia district only 33,187. Jefferson's method emphasized what was considered to be the ideal size of a congressional district instead of what the size of the House ought to be.

The reapportionment act based on the census of 1800 continued the ratio of 33,000, which provided a House of 141 members. The third apportionment bill, enacted in 1811, fixed the ratio at 35,000, yielding a House of 181 members. Following the 1820 census Congress set the ratio at 40,000 inhabitants per district, which produced a House of 213 members. The act of May 22, 1832, fixed the ratio at 47,700, resulting in a House of 240 members.

Dissatisfaction with inequalities produced by the method of rejected fractions grew. Launching a vigorous attack against it, Daniel Webster urged adoption of a method that would assign an additional representative to each state with a large fraction. Webster outlined his reasoning in a report he submitted to Congress in 1832.

> The Constitution, therefore, must be understood not as enjoining an absolute relative equality—because that would be demanding an impossibility—but as requiring of Congress to make the apportionment of Representatives among the several states according to their respective numbers, *as near as may be.* That which cannot be done perfectly must be done in a manner as near perfection as can be. . . . In such a case approximation becomes a rule.[10]

Following the 1840 census Congress adopted a reapportionment method similar to that advocated by Webster. The method fixed a ratio of one representative for every 70,680 people. This figure was reached by deciding on a fixed size of the House in advance (223), dividing that figure into the total national representative population, and using the result (70,680) as the fixed ratio. The population of each state was then divided by this ratio to find the number of its representatives, and the states were assigned an additional representative for each fraction more than one-half. Under this method the size of the House dropped. *(See Table 5-1, p. 113.)*

The modified reapportionment formula adopted by Congress in 1842 was more satisfactory than the previous method, but another change was made following the census of 1850. Proposed by Rep. Samuel F. Vinton of Ohio, the new system became known as the Vinton method.

Vinton Apportionment Formula

Under the Vinton formula Congress first fixed the size of the House and then distributed the seats. The total qualifying population of the country was divided by the desired number of representatives, and the resulting number became the ratio of population to each representative. The population of each state was divided by this ratio, and each state received the number of representatives equal to the whole number in the quotient for that state. Then, to reach the required size of the House, additional representatives were assigned based on the remaining fractions, beginning with the state having the largest fraction. This procedure differed from the 1842 method only in the last step, which assigned one representative to every state having a fraction larger than one-half.

Proponents of the Vinton method pointed out that it had the distinct advantage of fixing the size of the House in advance and taking into account at least the largest fractions. The concern of the House turned from the ideal size of a congressional district to the ideal size of the House itself.

Under the 1842 reapportionment formula, the exact size of the House could not be fixed in advance. If every state with a fraction more than one-half were given an additional representative, the House might wind up with a few more or a few less than the desired number. However, under the Vinton method, only states with the largest fractions were given additional House members and only up to the desired total size of the House.

Vinton Apportionments

Six reapportionments were carried out under the Vinton method. The 1850 census act contained three provisions not included in any previous law. First, it required reapportionment not only after the census of 1850 but also after all the subsequent censuses. Second, it purported to fix the size of the House permanently at 233 members. Third, it provided in advance for an automatic apportionment by the secretary of the interior under the method prescribed in the act.

Following the census of 1860 an automatic reapportionment was to be carried out by the Interior Department. However, because the size of the House was to remain at the 1850 level, some states faced loss of representation and others were to gain fewer seats than they expected. To avert that possibility, an act was approved in 1862 increasing the size of the House to 241 and giving an extra representative to eight states—Illinois, Iowa, Kentucky, Minnesota, Ohio, Pennsylvania, Rhode Island, and Vermont.

Apportionment legislation following the 1870 census contained several new provisions. The act fixed the size of the House at 283, with the proviso that the number should be increased if new states were admitted. A supplemental act assigned one additional representative each to Alabama, Florida, Indiana, Louisiana, New Hampshire, New York, Pennsylvania, Tennessee, and Vermont.

With the Reconstruction era at its height in the South, the reapportionment legislation of 1872 reflected the desire of Congress to enforce Section 2 of the new Fourteenth Amendment. That section attempted to protect the right of blacks to vote by providing for reduction of representation in the House of a state that interfered with the exercise of that right. The number of representatives of such a state was to be reduced in proportion to the number of inhabitants of voting age whose right to go to the polls was denied or abridged. The reapportionment bill repeated the language of Section 2, but the provision never was put into effect because of the difficulty of determining the exact number of people whose right to vote was being abridged.

The reapportionment act of 1882 provided for a House of 325 members, with additional members for any new states admitted to the Union. No new apportionment provisions were added. The acts of 1891 and 1901 were routine as far as apportionment was concerned. The 1891 measure provided for a House of 356 members, and the 1901 statute increased the number to 386.

Problems with Vinton Method

Despite the apparent advantages of the Vinton method, certain difficulties revealed themselves as the formula was applied. Zechariah Chafee Jr. of the Harvard Law School summarized these problems in an article in the *Harvard Law Review* in 1929. The method, he pointed out, suffered from what he called the "Alabama paradox." Under that aberration, an increase in the total size of the House might be accompanied by an actual loss of a seat by some states, even though there had been no corresponding change in population. This phenomenon first appeared in tables prepared for Congress in 1881, which gave Alabama eight members in a House of 299 but only seven members in a House of 300. It could even happen that the state that lost a seat was the one state that had expanded in population, while all the others had fewer people.

Chafee concluded from his study of the Vinton method:

> Thus, it is unsatisfactory to fix the ratio of population per Representative before seats are distributed. Either the size of the House comes out haphazard, or, if this be determined in advance, the absurdities of the "Alabama paradox" vitiate the apportionment. Under present conditions, it is essential to determine the size of the House in advance; the problem thereafter is to distribute the required number of seats among the several states as nearly as possible in proportion to their respective populations so that no state is treated unfairly in comparison with any other state.[11]

Maximum Membership of House

In 1911 the membership of the House was fixed at 433. Provision was made for the addition of one representative each from Arizona and New Mexico, which were expected to become states in the near future. Thus, the size of the House reached 435, where it has remained with the exception of a brief period, 1959–1963, when the admission of Alaska and Hawaii raised the total temporarily to 437. In 2007 the

TABLE 5-1 **Congressional Apportionment, 1789–2000**

	U.S. Constitution[a]	Year of census[b]																				
	(1789)	1790	1800	1810	1820	1830	1840	1850	1860	1870	1880	1890	1900	1910	1930[c]	1940	1950	1960	1970	1980	1990	2000
Ala.				1[d]	3	5	7	7	6	8	8	9	9	10	9	9	9	8	7	7	7	7
Alaska																	1[d]	1	1	1	1	1
Ariz.														1[d]	1	2	2	3	4	5	6	8
Ark.						1[d]	1	2	3	4	5	6	7	7	7	7	6	4	4	4	4	4
Calif.							2[d]	2	3	4	6	7	8	11	20	23	30	38	43	45	52	53
Colo.										1[d]	1	2	3	4	4	4	4	4	5	6	6	7
Conn.	5	7	7	7	6	6	4	4	4	4	4	4	5	5	6	6	6	6	6	6	6	5
Del.	1	1	1	2	1	1	1	1	1	1	1	1	1	1	1	1	1	1	1	1	1	1
Fla.							1[d]	1	1	2	2	2	3	4	5	6	8	12	15	19	23	25
Ga.	3	2	4	6	7	9	8	8	7	9	10	11	11	12	10	10	10	10	10	10	11	13
Hawaii																	1[d]	2	2	2	2	2
Idaho											1[d]	1	1	2	2	2	2	2	2	2	2	2
Ill.				1[d]	1	3	7	9	14	19	20	22	25	27	27	26	25	24	24	22	20	19
Ind.				1[d]	3	7	10	11	11	13	13	13	13	13	12	11	11	11	11	10	10	9
Iowa							2[d]	2	6	9	11	11	11	11	9	8	8	7	6	6	5	5
Kan.									1	3	7	8	8	8	7	6	6	5	5	5	4	4
Ky.		2	6	10	12	13	10	10	9	10	11	11	11	11	9	9	8	7	7	7	6	6
La.				1[d]	3	3	4	4	5	6	6	6	7	8	8	8	8	8	8	8	7	7
Maine				7[d]	7	8	7	6	5	5	4	4	4	4	3	3	3	2	2	2	2	2
Md.	6	8	9	9	9	8	6	6	5	6	6	6	6	6	6	6	7	8	8	8	8	8
Mass.	8	14	17	13[e]	13	12	10	11	10	11	12	13	14	16	15	14	14	12	12	11	10	10
Mich.						1[d]	3	4	6	9	11	12	12	13	17	17	18	19	19	18	16	15
Minn.								2[d]	2	3	5	7	9	10	9	9	9	8	8	8	8	8
Miss.				1[d]	1	2	4	5	5	6	7	7	8	8	7	7	6	5	5	5	5	4
Mo.					1	2	5	7	9	13	14	15	16	16	13	13	11	10	10	9	9	9
Mont.											1[d]	1	1	2	2	2	2	2	2	2	1	1
Neb.									1[d]	1	3	6	6	6	5	4	4	3	3	3	3	3
Nev.									1[d]	1	1	1	1	1	1	1	1	1	1	2	2	3
N.H.	3	4	5	6	6	5	4	3	3	3	2	2	2	2	2	2	2	2	2	2	2	2
N.J.	4	5	6	6	6	6	5	5	5	7	7	8	10	12	14	14	14	15	15	14	13	13
N.M.														1[d]	1	2	2	2	2	3	3	3
N.Y.	6	10	17	27	34	40	34	33	31	33	34	34	37	43	45	45	43	41	39	34	31	29
N.C.	5	10	12	13	13	13	9	8	7	8	9	9	10	10	11	12	12	11	11	11	12	13
N.D.											1[d]	1	2	3	2	2	2	2	1	1	1	1
Ohio			1[d]	6	14	19	21	21	19	20	21	21	21	22	24	23	23	24	23	21	19	18
Okla.													5[d]	8	9	8	6	6	6	6	6	5
Ore.								1[d]	1	1	1	2	2	3	3	4	4	4	4	5	5	5
Pa.	8	13	18	23	26	28	24	25	24	27	28	30	32	36	34	33	30	27	25	23	21	19
R.I.	1	2	2	2	2	2	2	2	2	2	2	2	2	3	2	2	2	2	2	2	2	2
S.C.	5	6	8	9	9	9	7	6	4	5	7	7	7	7	6	6	6	6	6	6	6	6
S.D.											2[d]	2	2	3	2	2	2	2	2	1	1	1
Tenn.		1	3	6	9	13	11	10	8	10	10	10	10	10	9	10	9	9	8	9	9	9
Texas							2[d]	2	4	6	11	13	16	18	21	21	22	23	24	27	30	32
Utah												1[d]	1	2	2	2	2	2	2	3	3	3
Vt.		2	4	6	5	5	4	3	3	3	2	2	2	2	1	1	1	1	1	1	1	1
Va.	10	19	22	23	22	21	15	13	11	9	10	10	10	10	9	9	10	10	10	10	11	11
Wash.											1[d]	2	3	5	6	6	7	7	7	8	9	9
W.Va.										3	4	4	5	6	6	6	6	5	4	4	3	3
Wis.							2[d]	3	6	8	9	10	11	11	10	10	10	10	9	9	9	8
Wyo.											1[d]	1	1	1	1	1	1	1	1	1	1	1
TOTAL	65	106	142	186	213	242	232	237	243	293	332	357	391	435	435	435	437[f]	435	435	435	435	435

NOTES: a. The original apportionment was provided for in the Constitution, pending the first census. b. Apportionment was effective with the congressional election held two years after the census. c. No apportionment was made in 1920. d. These figures are not based on any census but indicate the provisional representation accorded newly admitted states by Congress, pending the next census. e. Twenty members were assigned to Massachusetts, but seven of these were credited to Maine when that area became a state. f. Although the total had been set at 435, Congress temporarily increased it by two seats when Alaska and Hawaii became states.

SOURCES: *Biographical Directory of the American Congress*; and the Bureau of the Census.

House passed a bill that would give the District of Columbia a full voting member of the House and add another seat, most likely a fourth seat for Utah, which would raise the total to 437 once again. President George W. Bush threatened to veto the measure, which by summer 2007 had not been taken up in the Senate.

Limiting the size of the House amounted to recognition that the body soon would expand to unmanageable proportions if Congress continued the practice of adding new seats every ten years to match population gains without depriving any state of its existing representation. Agreement on a fixed number made the task of reapportionment even more difficult when the population not only increased but also became much more mobile. Population shifts brought Congress up hard against the politically painful necessity of taking seats away from slow-growing states to give the fast-growing states adequate representation.

A new mathematical calculation was adopted for the reapportionment following the 1910 census. Devised by W. F. Willcox of Cornell University, the new system established a priority list that assigned seats progressively, beginning with the first seat above the constitutional minimum of at least one seat for each state. When there were forty-eight states, this method was used to assign the forty-ninth member, the fiftieth member, and so on, until the agreed upon size of the House was reached. The method was called major fractions and was used after the censuses of 1910, 1930, and 1940. There was no reapportionment after the 1920 census.

1920s Struggle

The results of the fourteenth decennial census were announced in December 1920, just after the short session of the 66th Congress convened. The 1920 census showed that for the first time in history most Americans were urban residents. This came as a profound shock to people accustomed to emphasizing the nation's rural traditions and the virtues of life on farms and in small towns as Jefferson had. He once wrote:

> Those who labor in the earth are the chosen people of God, if ever He had a chosen people, whose breasts He had made His peculiar deposit for substantial and genuine virtue. . . . The mobs of great cities add just as much to the support of pure government as sores do to the strength of the human body. . . . I think our governments will remain virtuous for many centuries as long as they are chiefly agricultural: and this shall be as long as there shall be vacant lands in any part of America. When they get piled up upon one another in large cities as in Europe, they will become corrupt as in Europe.[12]

As their power waned throughout the latter part of the nineteenth century and the early part of the twentieth, farmers clung to the Jeffersonian belief that somehow they were more virtuous than the growing number of urban residents. When faced with the fact that they were in the minority, these country residents put up a strong rearguard action to prevent the inevitable shift of congressional districts to the cities. They succeeded in postponing reapportionment legislation for almost a decade.

Rural representatives insisted that, because the 1920 census was taken as of January 1, the farm population had been undercounted. In support of this contention, they argued that many farm laborers were seasonally employed in the cities at that time of year. Furthermore, midwinter road conditions probably had prevented enumerators from visiting many farms, they said, and other farmers were said to have been uncounted because they were absent on winter vacation trips. The change of the census date to January 1 in 1920 had been made to conform to recommendations of the U.S. Department of Agriculture, which had asserted that the census should be taken early in the year if an accurate statistical picture of farming conditions was to be obtained.

Another point raised by rural legislators was that large numbers of unnaturalized aliens were congregated in northern cities, with the result that these cities gained at the expense of constituencies made up mostly of citizens of the United States. Rep. Homer Hoch, R-Kan., submitted a table showing that, in a House of 435 representatives, exclusion from the census count of people not naturalized would have altered the allocation of seats in sixteen states. Southern and western farming states would have retained the number of seats allocated to them in 1911 or would have gained, while northern industrial states and California would have lost or at least would have gained fewer seats.

A constitutional amendment to exclude all aliens from the enumeration for purposes of reapportionment was proposed during the 70th Congress (1927–1929) by Hoch, Sen. Arthur Capper, R-Kan., and others. But nothing further came of the proposals.

Reapportionment Bills Opposed

The first bill to reapportion the House according to the 1920 census was drafted by the House Census Committee early in 1921. Proceeding on the principle that no state should have its representation reduced, the committee proposed to increase the total number of representatives from 435 to 483. But the House voted 267–76 to keep its membership at 435. The bill then was blocked by a Senate committee, where it died when the 66th Congress expired March 4, 1921.

Early in the 67th Congress, the House Census Committee again reported a bill, this time fixing the total membership at 460, an increase of 25. Two states—Maine and Massachusetts—would have lost one representative each and sixteen states would have gained. On the House floor an unsuccessful attempt was made to fix the number at the existing 435, and the House sent the bill back to committee.

During the 68th Congress (1923–1925), the House Census Committee failed to report any reapportionment bill. In April 1926, midway through the 69th Congress (1925–1927), it became apparent that the committee would not produce a reapportionment measure. A motion to discharge a reapportionment bill from the committee failed, however, and the matter once again was put aside.

Coolidge Intervention

President Calvin Coolidge, who previously had made no reference to reapportionment in his communications to Congress, announced in January 1927 that he favored passage of a new apportionment bill during the short session of the 69th Congress, which would end in less than two months. The House Census Committee refused to act. Its chair, Rep. E. Hart Fenn, R-Conn., therefore moved in the House to suspend the rules and pass a bill he had introduced authorizing the secretary of commerce to reapportion the House immediately after the 1930 census. The motion was voted down 183–197.

The Fenn bill was rewritten early in the 70th Congress (1927–1929) to give Congress itself a chance to act before the proposed reapportionment by the secretary of commerce should go into effect. The House passed an amended version of the Fenn bill in January 1929, and it was quickly reported by the Senate Commerce Committee. Repeated efforts to bring it up for floor action ahead of other bills failed. Its supporters gave up the fight when it became evident that senators from states slated to lose representation were ready to carry on a filibuster that would have blocked not only reapportionment but also all other measures.

Hoover Intervention

President Herbert Hoover listed provision for the 1930 census and reapportionment as "matters of emergency legislation" that should be acted on in the special session of the 71st Congress, which was convened on April 15, 1929. In response to this urgent request, the Senate on June 13 passed, 48–37, a combined census-reapportionment bill that had been approved by voice vote of the House two days earlier.

The 1929 law established a permanent system of reapportioning the 435 House seats following each census. It provided that immediately after the convening of the 71st Congress for its short session in December 1930, the president was to transmit to Congress a statement showing the population of each state together with an apportionment of representatives to each state based on the existing size of the House. Failing enactment of new apportionment legislation, that apportionment would go into effect without further action and would remain in effect for ensuing elections to the House of Representatives until another census had been taken and another reapportionment made.

Because two decades had passed between reapportionments, a greater shift than usual took place following the 1930 census. California's House delegation was almost doubled, rising from eleven to twenty. Michigan gained four seats; Texas, three; and New Jersey, New York, and Ohio, two each. Twenty-one states lost a total of twenty-seven seats. Missouri lost three seats, and Georgia, Iowa, Kentucky, and Pennsylvania each lost two.

To test the fairness of two allocation methods—the familiar major fractions and the new equal proportions system—the 1929 act required the president to report the distribution of seats by both methods. But, pending legislation to the contrary, the method of major fractions was to be used.

CONGRESS AND REDISTRICTING

In the post–World War II period, Congress considered several proposals regarding redistricting. Only one of these efforts was successful—enactment of a measure barring at-large elections in states with more than one House seat.

In January 1951 President Harry S. Truman asked for a ban on gerrymandering, an end to at-large seats in states having more than one representative, and a sharp reduction in the huge differences in size among congressional districts within most states. On behalf of the administration, Emanuel Celler, D-N.Y., chair of the House Judiciary Committee, introduced a bill reflecting these requests but the committee took no action.

Celler regularly introduced such legislation throughout the 1950s and early 1960s, but it made no headway until the U.S. Supreme Court handed down the *Wesberry v. Sanders* decision in 1964. The House passed a version of the Celler bill in 1965, largely to discourage the Supreme Court from imposing even more rigid criteria. The Senate, however, took no action and the measure died.

In 1967, after defeating a conference report that would have prevented the courts from ordering a state to redistrict or to hold at-large elections until after the 1970 census, Congress approved a measure to ban at-large elections in all states entitled to more than one representative. Exceptions were made for Hawaii and New Mexico, which had a tradition of electing their representatives at large. Both states, however, soon passed districting laws—New Mexico for the 1968 elections and Hawaii for 1970.

Bills to increase the size of the House to prevent states from losing seats as a result of population shifts have been introduced after most recent censuses, but Congress has given little consideration to any of them.

In 2005 Rep. John Tanner, D-Tenn., introduced the Fairness and Independence in Redistricting Act, which proposed the establishment of five-member independent commissions to draw each state's congressional district map only once every decade and sought to render the redistricting process less political. Rep. F. James Sensenbrenner Jr., R-Wis., had proposed the same concept when he authored the Congressional Districting Reform Act of 1989. Neither bill became law.

The two methods gave an identical distribution of seats based on 1930 census figures. However, in 1940 the two methods gave different results. Under major fractions, Michigan would gain a seat lost by Arkansas; under equal proportions, no change would occur in either state. The automatic reapportionment provisions of the 1929 act went into effect in January 1941. But the House Census Committee moved to reverse the result, favoring the method of equal proportions and the certain Democratic seat in Arkansas over a possible Republican gain if the seat were shifted to Michigan. The Democratic-controlled Congress went along, adopting equal proportions as the method to be used in reapportionment calculations after the 1950 and subsequent censuses and making this action retroactive to January 1941 to save Arkansas its seat.

While politics doubtless played a part in the timing of the action taken in 1941, the method of equal proportions had come to be accepted as the best available. It had been worked out by Edward V. Huntington of Harvard University in 1921. At the request of the Speaker of the House, all known methods of apportionment were considered in 1929 by the National Academy of Sciences Committee on Apportionment. The committee expressed its preference for equal proportions.

Method of Equal Proportions

The method of equal proportions involves complicated mathematical calculations. In brief, each of the fifty states is initially assigned the one seat to which it is entitled by the Constitution. Then priority numbers for states to receive second seats, third seats, and so on are calculated by dividing the state's population by the square root of $n(n-1)$, where n is the number of seats for that state. The priority numbers are then lined up in order and the seats given to the states with priority numbers until 435 are awarded.

The method is designed to make the proportional difference in the average district size in any two states as small as possible. After the 1990 reapportionment, for example, Montana's single district was the most populous, with 803,655 residents, while Wyoming's single district was the least populous, with 453,588 people. The average population per district nationwide was about 572,500. In 2000 the average population per district increased to 647,000. Montana's single district remained the most populous with 902,195 people; Wyoming's single district remained the least populous with 493,782 residents.

Questioning the Count in the 1980s and 1990s

While the method of equal proportions came to be accepted as the best way to apportion House seats among the states, the 1980s and 1990s brought heated debate over a more fundamental issue: the accuracy of the census itself. Members of Congress as well as state and local officials have a keen interest in an accurate population count. In addition to being the basis for reapportionment and redistricting, the census is used to determine the allocation of funding for many federal aid programs.

Concern about the census undercount grew after 1980, when the Census Bureau estimated that it counted about 99 percent of the white population but only about 94 percent of the African American population. Democrats, especially those representing inner-city districts where the undercount was comparatively high, argued unsuccessfully for a statistical adjustment to compensate for undercounting.

The controversy over the 1990 count began even before the census was taken, when the Commerce Department, the parent agency to the Census Bureau, announced in 1987 that it would not statistically adjust the 1990 data. New York City, along with other cities, states, and civil rights organizations, pressed a case in court to force the Census Bureau to make a statistical adjustment to account for people who were missed, including sizable numbers of blacks, Hispanics, and Native Americans. In 1996 the Supreme Court rejected adjusting the census.

But by then, the White House had passed from Republican to Democratic hands, and Commerce Department officials were laying plans to have the Census Bureau use statistical sampling techniques that they said would enhance the accuracy of the 2000 census. The Republican majority in Congress gave statistical sampling a cold eye, worrying that it might lead to politically motivated manipulating of the census. *(See box, How Should the Census Count the Population, p. 118.)*

The same issue arose after the 2000 census. Advocates for minority groups, fearing that many persons of their race or ethnic background were missed in the new count, argued vocally for a statistical adjustment to the actual head count in the census. But by the time the issue was to be resolved in early 2001, the White House and both houses of Congress were under Republican control, making a decision to statistically adjust the count unlikely. Moreover, in an unexpected development, Census Bureau officials announced on March 1, 2001, that the actual count turned out to be more reliable than expected and warned that the use of the statistical adjustment methods available could make the count less accurate. Their recommendation against adjustment diffused the politics surrounding the issue.

REDISTRICTING: DRAWING THE LINES

Although the Constitution contained provisions for the apportionment of U.S. House seats among the states, it was silent about how the members should be elected. From the beginning most states divided their territory into geographic districts, permitting only one member of Congress to be elected from each district.

But some states allowed would-be House members to run at large, with voters able to cast as many votes as there were seats to be filled. Still other states created what were known as multimember districts, in which a single geographic unit would elect two or more members of the House. At various times, some states used combinations of these methods. For example, a state might elect ten representatives from ten individual districts and two at large.

In the first few elections to the House, Georgia, New Hampshire, New Jersey, and Pennsylvania elected their representatives at large, as did Delaware and Rhode Island, the two states with only a single representative. Districts were used in Maryland, Massachusetts, New York, North Carolina, South Carolina, and Virginia. In Connecticut a preliminary election was held to nominate three times as many people as the number of representatives to be chosen at large in the subsequent election. In 1840, twenty-two of the thirty-one states elected their representatives by districts. Alabama, Georgia, Mississippi, Missouri, New Hampshire, and New Jersey, with a combined representation of thirty-three House seats, elected their representatives at large. Three states, Arkansas, Delaware, and Florida, had only one representative each.

Those states that used congressional districts quickly developed what came to be known as the gerrymander. The term refers to the practice of drawing district lines so as to maximize the advantage of a political party or interest group. The name originated from a salamander-shaped congressional district created by the Massachusetts Legislature in 1812 when Elbridge Gerry was governor. *(See box, Origins of the Gerrymander, p. 121.)*

Constant efforts were made during the early 1800s to lay down national rules, by means of a constitutional amendment, for congressional districting. The first resolution proposing a mandatory division of each state into districts was introduced in Congress in 1800. In 1802 the legislatures of Vermont and North Carolina adopted resolutions in support of such action. From 1816 to 1826 twenty-two states adopted resolutions proposing the election of representatives by districts.

Sen. Mahlon Dickerson, R-N.J., proposed such an amendment regularly almost every year from 1817 to 1826. It was adopted by the Senate three times, in 1819, 1820, and 1822, but each time it failed to reach a vote in the House. Although the constitutional amendment was unsuccessful, a law passed in 1842 required contiguous single-member congressional districts. That law required representatives to be "elected by districts composed of contiguous territory equal in number to the representatives to which said state may be entitled, no one district electing more than one Representative."

The districting provisions of the 1842 act were not repeated in the legislation that followed the 1850 census. But in 1862 an act separate from the reapportionment act revived the provisions of the act of 1842 requiring districts to be composed of contiguous territory.

The 1872 reapportionment act again repeated the districting provisions and went even further by adding that districts should contain "as nearly as practicable an equal number of inhabitants." Similar provisions were included in the acts of 1881 and 1891. In the act of 1901, the words "compact territory" were added, and the clause then read "contiguous and compact territory and containing as nearly as practicable an equal number of inhabitants." This requirement appeared also in the legislation of 1911. The "contiguous and compact" provisions of the act subsequently lapsed, and Congress has never replaced them.

Several unsuccessful attempts were made to enforce redistricting provisions. Despite the districting requirements enacted in 1842, Georgia, Mississippi, Missouri, and New Hampshire elected their representatives at large that autumn. When the new House convened for its first session, on December 4, 1843, objection was made to seating the representatives of the four states.

The House debated the matter in February 1844. With the Democratic Party holding a majority of more than sixty, and with eighteen of the twenty-one challenged members being Democrats, the House decided to seat the members. However, by 1848 all four states had come around to electing their representatives by districts.

The next challenge a representative encountered over federal districting laws occurred in 1901. A charge was leveled that the existing Kentucky redistricting law did not comply with the reapportionment law of 1901. The charge was aimed at preventing the seating of Democratic representative George G. Gilbert of Kentucky's Eighth District. The committee assigned to investigate the matter turned aside the challenge, asserting that the federal act was not binding on the states. The reasons given were practical and political.

> Your committee are therefore of opinion that a proper construction of the Constitution does not warrant the conclusion that by that instrument Congress is clothed with power to determine the boundaries of Congressional districts, or to revise the acts of a State Legislature in fixing such boundaries; and your committee is further of opinion that even if such power is to be implied from the language of the Constitution, it would be in the last degree unwise and intolerable that it should exercise it. To do so would be to put into the hands of Congress the ability to disfranchise, in effect, a large body of the electors. It would give Congress the power to apply to all the States, in favor of one party, a general system of gerrymandering. It is true that the same method is to a large degree resorted to by the several states, but the division of political power is so general and diverse that notwithstanding the inherent vice of the system of gerrymandering, some kind of equality of distribution results.[13]

HOW SHOULD THE CENSUS COUNT THE POPULATION?

Counting the number of people in the United States has never been as easy as one, two, three, and that is not just because of logistical problems. When it comes to the decennial census, the political stakes are huge, as is the interest in how the count is conducted. The constitutionally mandated census not only provides crucial information for reapportioning U.S. House seats among the states but also supplies the data for drawing district boundaries for state and local public officials and for determining how billions in federal spending is distributed through dozens of grant programs, including Medicaid, educational assistance to poor children, community development block grants, and job training.

Questions about the accuracy of the census are as old as the Republic. A 1998 report issued by the General Accounting Office said, "The census has never counted 100 percent of those it should, in part, because American sensibilities would probably not tolerate more foolproof census-taking methods." For instance, the census could be made more precise if people were required to register with the government. But even proposing such a mandate would stir a huge public fuss.

Disputes over the accuracy of the census have intensified since 1911, when Congress fixed the number of representatives at 435. Since then, a gain of representation in any one state can come only at the loss of representation in another. After the 1920 census showed for the first time that the majority of Americans lived in cities, rural interests objected that the farm population had been undercounted. They pressed their case with such tenacity that legislation reapportioning House seats for the 1920s never passed. In 1941 concerns about the accuracy of the census arose when the number of men turning out for the wartime draft was considerably higher than expectations based on the 1940 census.

In the latter years of the twentieth century, intense controversy arose over the undercounting of certain groups, especially minorities. It became more difficult for government census-takers to make an accurate population count in crowded inner-city neighborhoods and in some sparsely settled rural areas. The undercount issue became a particular concern for major cities and for the Democrats who tended to represent them. They were in the forefront of an effort to persuade the Census Bureau to use a statistical method to adjust the census for the undercount.

The Census Bureau estimated that it did not count 1.4 percent of the total population in 1980, including roughly 5.9 percent of the nation's blacks. In 1991 Commerce secretary Robert A. Mosbacher, serving in the administration of Republican president George H. W. Bush, said that he would not adjust the 1990 census, even though a postcensus survey found that blacks were undercounted by 4.8 percent, Native Americans by 5 percent, and Hispanics by 5.2 percent. Mosbacher said he was "deeply troubled" by the disproportionate undercount of minorities but decided that sticking with the head count would be "fairest for all Americans."

Several states and cities pursued the matter in court, pressing a suit requesting a statistical adjustment of the census to compensate for the undercount. A 1996 U.S. Supreme Court ruling went against them.

By then, though, Democrat Bill Clinton was in the White House, and the Census Bureau was laying the groundwork for a 2000 census that bureau officials said would produce a more accurate count by combining traditional head-tallying methods with large-scale use of statistical sampling techniques. Their plan was to count at least 90 percent of the people in each census tract by tabulating surveys returned in the mail and sending census-takers to interview those who did not respond by mail. Then the remaining population would be estimated by statistically extrapolating the demographics of 750,000 randomly selected homes nationwide.

However, this proposal met with fierce resistance in the Republican-controlled Congress. The GOP majority complained that sampling was unconstitutional and open to political manipulation. "Our Constitution calls for an 'actual enumeration' of citizens, not just an educated guess by Washington bureaucrats," Rep. John A. Boehner, R-Ohio, said. Democrats in Congress retorted that conservatives opposed statistical sampling because they feared it would cost the GOP seats in

In 1908 the Virginia Legislature transferred Floyd County from the Fifth District to the Sixth District. As a result, the population of the Fifth was reduced from 175,579 to 160,191 and that of the Sixth was increased from 181,571 to 196,959. The average for the state was 185,418. The newly elected representative from the Fifth District, Democrat Edward W. Saunders, was challenged by his opponent in the election on the ground that the Virginia law of 1908 was null and void because it did not conform with the federal reapportionment law of 1901 or with the constitution of Virginia. Had the district included the counties that were a part of it before enactment of the 1908 state legislation, Saunders's opponent would have had a majority of the votes.

The majority of the congressional investigating committee upheld the challenge and recommended that Saunders's opponent be seated. For the first time, it appeared that the districting legislation would be enforced, but the House did not take action on the committee's report and Saunders was seated.

Who Draws the House District Lines?

Drawing congressional district boundaries following a decennial census has traditionally been a political event under the control of state legislatures, usually with the participation of the state's governor. A few states use a commission or another type of procedure, usually with an eye toward reducing the partisan political calculations behind the map-drawing. In addition, courts have been asserted into the process in some states where divided control of legislative houses and the governor's office prevented creating a final plan. In those cases, courts imposed their own plan.

Both parties largely accepted this system for decades. The party controlling a state legislature would draw congressional and state legislative districts favorable to their candi-

the House. "They believe not counting certain minorities and the poor is to their political advantage," said Rep. Carolyn B. Maloney, D-N.Y.

With the Republican House and the Democratic White House at a standoff on allowing statistical sampling in the 2000 census, the dispute headed to the courts. When the Supreme Court heard arguments on the case in late 1998, justices expressed reluctance to get involved in what looked essentially like a partisan fight.

In January 1999 in *Department of Commerce v. House of Representatives,* the Court issued an equivocal 5–4 ruling that seemed likely to spur further litigation. Pleasing Republicans, the Court majority said that amendments to the Census Act added in 1976 forbade "the use of sampling in calculating the population for purposes of apportionment." House Speaker J. Dennis Hastert, R-Ill., declared, "The administration should abandon its illegal and risky polling scheme and start preparing for a true head count."

But Democrats took some solace in the Court majority's position that the Census Act "required" that sampling be used for other purposes (such as establishing the population formulas used to distribute some federal grant monies) if the Census Bureau and the secretary of commerce deem it "feasible."

The ruling led the Clinton administration to plot a course to produce two sets of numbers in the 2000 census—a count based on traditional methods to be used for reapportionment and an adjusted count to be used for distributing federal money and other purposes, possibly including redistricting within the states. That decision drew a harsh response from Republicans in Congress. Rep. Dan Miller, R-Fla., chair of the House Census Committee, said, "It will absolutely be a disaster if we have a two-number census. . . . If we try to divide the census, we'll have two failed censuses." Democrats, and racial and ethnic minority groups, pressed hard for the Census Bureau to statistically adjust the numbers of the 2000 count for purposes of redistricting within states but were not optimistic that the White House—by then back in the control of Republicans—would do this. But in early March 2001 Census Bureau professionals unexpectedly said they could not guarantee that an adjusted number for redistricting would be any better than the actual head count Republicans favored using. The professionals said unresolved issues in using statistical adjustment could not be solved before the legal deadline of April 1, 2001, to release redistricting data to the states.

ILLEGAL ALIENS

Members of Congress and other public officials also have taken a strong interest in the traditional inclusion of illegal aliens in the census. Some complain that the Census Bureau's effort to count all people living in the United States has unfair political ramifications.

The Fourteenth Amendment states that "representatives shall be apportioned among the several states according to their respective numbers, counting the whole number of persons in each state, excluding Indians not taxed." The Census Bureau has never attempted to exclude illegal aliens from the census—a policy troubling to states that fear losing House seats and clout to states with large numbers of illegal aliens.

The Census Bureau does not have a method for excluding illegal aliens, although it has studied some alternatives. Some supporters of the current policy say that any questions used to separate out illegal aliens could discourage others from responding, thus undermining the accuracy of the census.

OVERSEAS PERSONNEL

For the 1990 census the Commerce Department reversed a long-standing policy and counted military personnel and dependents stationed overseas. "Historically we have not included them because the census is based on the concept of usual residence," said Charles Jones, associate director of the Census Bureau. "People overseas have a 'usual residence' overseas." An exception was made once in 1970 during the Vietnam War. This policy was continued in the 2000 census. For the purposes of reapportionment, overseas personnel were assigned to the state each individual considered home.

dates that were then fixed for the next five elections. Some legislatures would seek configurations likely to increase their party's numbers; others would draw lines principally to protect incumbents of both parties. Rarely were the mapmakers concerned with increasing political competition through districts with partisan balance and the potential for frequent turnover in seats.

By the 2000 census the process was increasingly in disarray. A number of factors contributed to this development.

- An unmistakable decline in competitive races became evident in much of the country as most incumbents were returned to office.
- Hard-ball political efforts were made in a few states to redraw district lines—mid-decade redistricting—to enhance a party's chances of winning elections.
- The narrow divisions between the two major political parties in federal elections dramatically raised the stakes of winning congressional seats to achieve a majority in the U.S. House.
- Increasingly sophisticated methods involving high-powered computers were used to tailor district lines with an exactness never before possible that in effect allowed politicians to select the voters they wanted in their districts.

By 2005 these trends were bringing together a loosely knit aggregation of citizen groups, disenchanted politicians, scholars, and others who pushed for reform of districting procedures.

California

Perhaps the most significant development after the 2000 census redistricting was the unexpected proposal by California's Republican governor, Arnold Schwarzenegger, in January 2005 to give the map-making job—for both con-

TABLE 5-2 **State Population Totals, House Seat Changes in the 2000s**

	1990 population[a]	2000 population[a]	Percent change	1992 to 2000 seats	2002 to 2010 seats	Seat changes in 2000s
Ala.	4,040,587	4,447,100	10.1	7	7	0
Alaska	550,043	626,932	14.0	1	1	0
Ariz.	3,665,228	5,130,632	40.0	6	8	+2
Ark.	2,350,725	2,673,400	13.7	4	4	0
Calif.	29,760,021	33,871,648	13.8	52	53	+1
Colo.	3,294,394	4,301,261	30.6	6	7	+1
Conn.	3,287,116	3,405,565	3.6	6	5	−1
Del.	666,168	783,600	17.6	1	1	0
D.C.[b]	606,900	572,059	−5.7	—	—	
Fla.	12,937,926	15,982,378	23.5	23	25	+2
Ga.	6,478,216	8,186,453	26.4	11	13	+2
Hawaii	1,108,229	1,211,537	9.3	2	2	0
Idaho	1,006,749	1,293,953	28.5	2	2	0
Ill.	11,430,602	12,419,293	8.6	20	19	−1
Ind.	5,544,159	6,080,485	9.7	10	9	−1
Iowa	2,776,755	2,926,324	5.4	5	5	0
Kan.	2,477,574	2,688,418	8.5	4	4	0
Ky.	3,685,296	4,041,769	9.7	6	6	0
La.	4,219,973	4,468,976	5.9	7	7	0
Maine	1,227,928	1,274,923	3.8	2	2	0
Md.	4,781,468	5,296,486	10.8	8	8	0
Mass.	6,016,425	6,349,097	5.5	10	10	0
Mich.	9,295,297	9,938,444	6.9	16	15	−1
Minn.	4,375,099	4,919,479	12.4	8	8	0
Miss.	2,573,216	2,844,658	10.5	5	4	−1
Mo.	5,117,073	5,595,211	9.3	9	9	0
Mont.	799,065	902,195	12.9	1	1	0
Neb.	1,578,385	1,711,263	8.4	3	3	0
Nev.	1,201,833	1,998,257	66.3	2	3	+1
N.H.	1,109,252	1,235,786	11.4	2	2	0
N.J.	7,730,188	8,414,350	8.9	13	13	0
N.M.	1,515,069	1,819,046	20.1	3	3	0
N.Y.	17,990,455	18,976,457	5.5	31	29	−2
N.C.	6,628,637	8,049,313	21.4	12	13	+1
N.D.	638,800	642,200	0.5	1	1	0
Ohio	10,847,115	11,353,140	4.7	19	18	−1
Okla.	3,145,585	3,450,654	9.7	6	5	−1
Ore.	2,842,321	3,421,399	20.4	5	5	0
Pa.	11,881,632	12,281,054	3.4	21	19	−2
R.I.	1,003,464	1,048,319	4.5	2	2	0
S.C.	3,486,703	4,012,012	15.1	6	6	0
S.D.	696,004	754,844	8.5	1	1	0
Tenn.	4,877,185	5,689,283	16.7	9	9	0
Texas	16,986,510	20,851,820	22.8	30	32	+2
Utah	1,722,850	2,233,169	29.6	3	3	0
Vt.	562,758	608,827	8.2	1	1	0
Va.	6,187,358	7,078,515	14.4	11	11	0
Wash.	4,866,692	5,894,121	21.1	9	9	0
W.Va.	1,793,477	1,808,344	0.8	3	3	0
Wis.	4,891,769	5,363,675	9.6	9	8	−1
Wyo.	453,588	493,782	8.9	1	1	0
TOTAL[c]	**248,709,862**	**281,421,906**	**13.2**	**435**	**435**	**12**

NOTES: a. For comparative purposes, the 1990 and 2000 figures do not include citizens living overseas. b. The District of Columbia, which has one nonvoting delegate to the House, is not included in the determination of apportionment. c. Total population for 1990 and 2000 includes the District of Columbia.

gressional and legislative seats in his state—to a panel of retired judges. The governor said that the 2004 election results showed that not one of the 153 seats in the California Legislature and the U.S. House delegations changed political hands. "What kind of a democracy is that?" he asked. "The current system is rigged to benefit the interests of those in office and not those who put them there." His analysis of California was all but indisputable. As with most states after the 2000 census, the California Legislature drew the new lines to keep the status quo to the extent possible: the first order of business was protecting incumbents. Democrats controlling the legislature did the work, but Republicans acquiesced in fear that opposition would push Democrats to draw lines harming GOP candidates.

Schwarzenegger's California plan took on special importance in part because the charismatic film actor and governor made it a high priority of his agenda. After compromise with the state legislature failed, Schwarzenegger succeeded, after court challenges, in placing the measure on the ballot in a special election held in November 2005. Many viewed the outcome of the vote as important because California—the largest state with a House delegation of fifty-three members—had a reputation for leading-edge social, cultural, and political developments that presaged actions elsewhere in the nation. California voters, however, threw cold water on the reform plan by defeating the initiative, with 59 percent of voters casting ballots against the measure.

Schwarzenegger's proposal, dramatic as it was because of its source, was not without precedent. Judges were often called on to draw lines in states when political parties could not agree. A few states had institutionalized procedures that isolated the process from politicians, even when not entirely blocking their influence, and vested it in commissions. One state (Iowa) had a unique process that reformers sometimes pointed to as an exemplary way to draw district lines, and another (Arizona) used an even more politically insulated method approved in a ballot initiative by voters.

ORIGINS OF THE GERRYMANDER

The practice of gerrymandering—the excessive manipulation of the shape of a legislative district to benefit certain persons or groups—is probably as old as the Republic, but the name originated in 1812.

In that year the Massachusetts Legislature carved out of Essex County a district that historian John Fiske said had a "dragonlike contour." When the painter Gilbert Stuart saw the misshapen district, he penciled in a head, wings, and claws and exclaimed: "That will do for a salamander!"—to which editor Benjamin Russell replied: "Better say a Gerrymander"—after Elbridge Gerry, then governor of Massachusetts.

By the 1990s the term had broadened to include the modern-day practice of drawing maps to benefit racial and ethnic groups, so-called racial gerrymandering. In the past the term was applied largely to districts drawn to benefit incumbents or political parties.

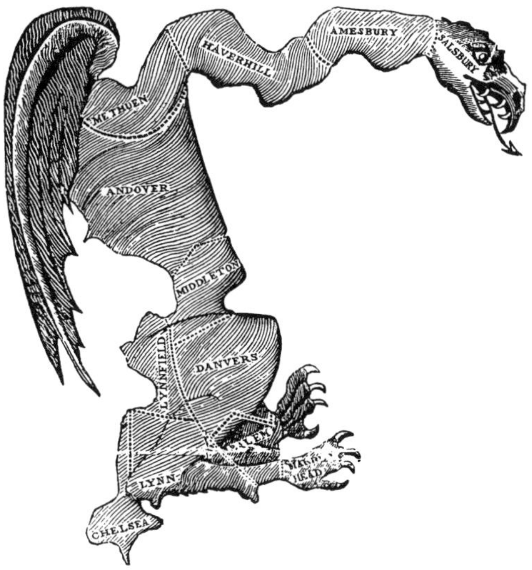

Independent Commissions

In 2000, six states used commissions for drawing federal congressional districts, while twice as many used commissions for state legislative redistricting. A few states maintained backup commissions—one of which in Connecticut was used in 2001 for congressional districts.

The six states in 2000 that used commissions for drawing U.S. House seats were Arizona, Hawaii, Idaho, Montana, New Jersey, and Washington. Arizona and Idaho were the most recent additions to the list, using a commission for the first time in the 2000 redistricting process. Procedures varied in these states, but generally they involved appointments made by legislative leaders, thereby retaining some connection to the basic political process used in most states. Indiana employed a system using legislative leaders but allowed the governor to set lines if the parties could not agree.

A proposed amendment to the Ohio constitution in 2005 would have added it to the list of states with independent commissions. The proposal put to the Ohio electorate would have empanelled a five-member redistricting commission, composed of two members selected by the two most tenured judges from different parties on the Ohio state courts of appeals and three additional members chosen by the first two commission appointees from a pool of applicants, with party officials, officerholders, candidates, and

FIGURE 5-1 **Reapportionment Gainers and Losers**

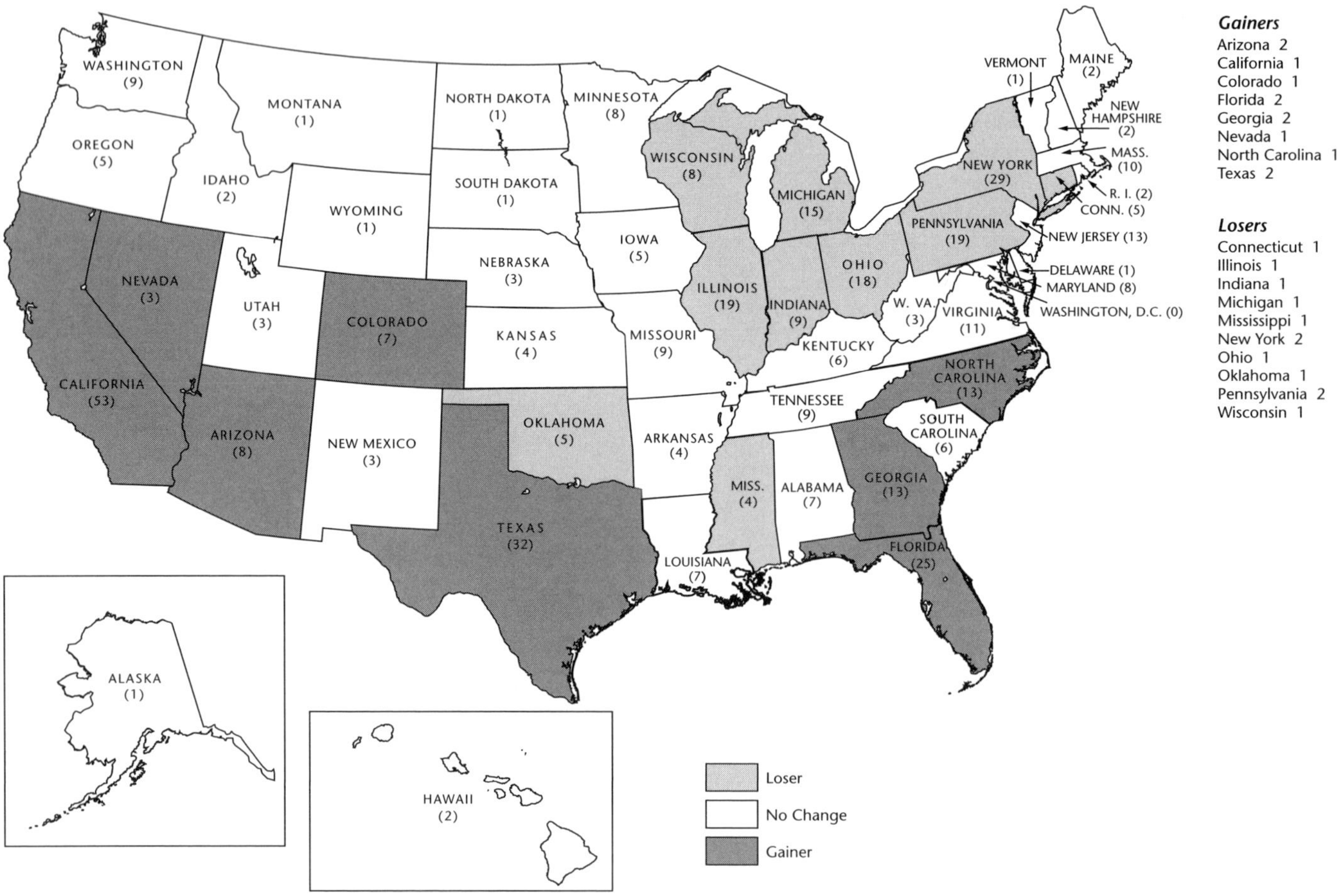

NOTE: Number in parentheses indicates state's House seats under 2000 reapportionment.

lobbyists being ineligible for selection. Ohio voters, like those in California, overwhelmingly voted against the measure, 71 percent against and only 21 percent in favor.

Iowa was technically not a commission state, but it used a procedure unlike any other. In Iowa the redistricting task was given to neither the legislature nor a commission. Instead a nonpartisan legislative staff (the Legislative Service Bureau of the general assembly) developed a redistricting plan for the legislature to accept or reject. If the first plan is rejected, a second one is submitted. If that is rejected, a third is submitted but that one, unlike the earlier two, could be amended by the legislators. At that point the normal play of politics could, theoretically, came into play. The Iowa redistricting for both the state legislature and the U.S. House was done without any political data or information about incumbents. Iowa law specified that districts could not be drawn to favor a political party, incumbent, or any other person or group. Iowa law provided that counties could not be split for the congressional seats and must be contiguous. The Iowa code also defined a compact district as those "which are square, rectangular, or hexagonal in shape to the extent permitted by natural or political boundaries."

Reformers point to these exacting standards as models for other states. Other observers, although admiring Iowa's approach, note that the state is small (it had only five House seats) and had a homogeneous population in which minorities were not a significant consideration as they were in many other locations, particularly southern states, where provisions of the Voting Rights Act were important.

Arizona voters in 2000 approved Proposition 106, which set up the Arizona Independent Redistricting Commission (AIRC). The AIRC quickly became for reformers an even brighter poster child for redistricting reform because, unlike Iowa, it attempted to permanently remove the redistricting process from politicians and place it in the hands of a citizens' commission. The AIRC consisted of five members, selected from a list of twenty-five applicants—reviewed by the state supreme court—that had ten Democrats and ten Republicans. Another five from minor parties or independent registered voters were on the list also. The AIRC tightly restricted the political activities of any candidate for the three years before a commission was established. Four commission members were selected by the majority and minority leaders of the state house and senate, and the four commissioners then selected a chair from the list of five minor or independent persons on the list.

The AIRC instructions to the members were exact: draw lines that satisfied the federal Voting Rights Act and created districts of equal populations that were compact and contiguous. Proposition 106 went on to delineate a number of other factors including respecting communities of interest, following geographic features as much as possible, and, to the extent practicable, creating competitive districts. The first use of the AIRC after the 2000 census produced congressional seats without difficulty. But the legislative districts ran into many challenges and had to be redone three times.

Competitiveness and Incumbency

The widely noted tendency in elections after the 2000 redistricting of returning incumbents to office, often by large margins, became a rallying cry for reformers pushing for changes in the system of drawing lines. The two concepts were closely linked, and few denied that much of the 2000 redistricting effort was aimed at enhancing incumbency and thereby diminishing competitiveness. The much-publicized successful effort in Texas to redraw lines for the 2004 election originally ordered by the court so that the delegation better reflected the GOP orientation in the state was made to strengthen the position of Republicans. By contrast, the unsuccessful attempt in Colorado to redraw court-ordered lines was a hard-ball Republican effort to increase the reelection chances of a Republican who barely won in 2002. Both

GERRYMANDERING: THE SHAPE OF THE HOUSE

Gerrymanders come in three basic types. One is the partisan gerrymander, in which a single party draws the lines to its advantage. Another is the proincumbent (sometimes called the bipartisan or sweetheart) gerrymander, in which the lines are drawn to protect incumbents, with any gains or losses in the number of seats shared between the two parties. When control of the state government is divided, proincumbent gerrymanders are common.

A third form of gerrymandering is race-based. Lines are drawn to favor the election of candidates from particular racial or ethnic groups. Initially, racial redistricting referred to the practice of drawing lines to scatter minority voters across several districts so they would not have a dominant influence in any of them. But the 1965 Voting Rights Act and numerous court rulings produced a new version of racial gerrymandering: designing constituencies to concentrate minority voters. These majority-minority districts were more likely to elect a minority candidate.

Sweetheart gerrymandering rarely attracted much attention, but it significantly affected the House. "Districts get more Democratic for Democrats and more Republican for Republicans. Competition is minimized," said Bernard Grofman, a political scientist at the University of California at Irvine. Incumbent reelection rates were high for most elections after World War II, in part because a proincumbent spin in much of the line-drawing diminished the prospects for dramatic change in the House's membership.

Still, redistricting at least increased the possibility of turnover because most states must redraw their districts to accommodate population shifts within the state as well as the gain or loss of any seats. Typically, some House members would retire to avoid having to stand for election in redesigned districts.

Partisan gerrymanders did not always achieve their goals. Indiana Republicans redrew their map in 1981 with the hope that it would turn the Democrats' congressional majority into a 7–3 Republican edge. Instead, by the end of the decade Democrats held a 7–3 advantage. But Texas Republicans in 2003—in the second redistricting of the decade—redrew a number of districts with the specific aim of defeating seven Democratic incumbents and succeeded in all but one race.

But without question, gerrymandering during redistricting is an important determinant of which party controls the House. Many political analysts predicted that the 1980 reapportionment would alter the political makeup of the House, because most of the states that lost seats tended to favor liberal Democrats, while the states that gained seats were more likely to favor Republicans or conservative Democrats. But in part because of Democrats' gerrymandering successes in the state redistricting battles, their party remained in control of the House throughout the 1980s.

In the 1990 reapportionment, the shift of House seats to more conservative areas in the South and West continued but successful gerrymandering by Democrats helped the party hold its House majority in 1992. Finally in 1994 a broad surge of support for Republican candidates helped the GOP take control of the House, which they held through the 2004 elections. Population changes recorded in the 2000 census showed a continuing trend toward states that have voted more Republican than Democratic in recent years, some of which received additional House members under the 2000 reapportionment. *(See Table 5-2, p. 120.)*

As a result, the redistricting following the 2000 census—particularly within Republican-leaning states—was expected to be a highly contentious exercise. As it turned out, in the initial round of redistricting Democrats and Republicans tacitly agreed that their primary interest was in protecting incumbents. As a result, much of the drawing of lines focused on creating districts incumbents could hold. There was less emphasis on designing districts for competitive party advantage. The end result was that incumbents were protected—96 percent won reelection in 2002 and 98 percent won their seats back in 2004.

But there were exceptions. After a second round of redistricting, a Texas remap brought huge gains for the GOP in 2004. Another remap in Colorado was rejected by the state's supreme court in 2003. By 2005 other states where control of the legislature changed hands, such as Georgia, were looking at opportunities to redraw lines to bolster party fortunes. *(See "Mid-Decade Redistricting and Partisan Gerrymandering," p. 134.)*

actions, however, drew unexpected and unwanted attention to many of the conditions that reformers said needed fixing. *(See "Mid-Decade Redistricting and Partisan Gerrymandering," p. 134.)*

Most reformers, however, agreed that achieving competitiveness in drawing district lines was difficult, particularly when other important values such as equal population and meeting voting rights standards had to be considered. In addition many noncompetitive districts simply reflected the political preferences of the population in the area. Still critics, such as Schwarzenegger in California, pointed to the election returns as evidence that legislatures that drew new congressional district lines had all but obliterated meaningful challenges in House races.

In the 2004 elections, only thirteen seats in the House (3 percent of all 435 seats) switched parties and just seven incumbents were defeated in the general election. Another two went down in primaries. Only ten of the House contestants won with margins under 5 percent. Only thirty-two contestants won with 55 percent or less of the total vote. More than 85 percent of House incumbents won with majorities greater than 60 percent, a number most experts consider a landslide. Some sixty-two members were elected without major-party opposition. All of these figures supported critics' contentions that districts were largely configured to prevent a serious contest even when both parties were well represented in an area.

Historical numbers also supported the argument that incumbents were coming back to Washington, D.C., in unprecedented numbers after the 2000 redistricting. For comparable elections (the first after a decennial census), the percentage of incumbents seeking reelection was 93.6 percent in 1972. It dropped to 90.1 percent in 1982 and to 88.3 percent in 1992. It then jumped to 96 percent in 2002. (The 2002 election was the first since 1990 that the reelection rate for House and Senate incumbents both surpassed 95 percent.) For 2004, 99.2 percent of non-Texas incumbents who sought reelection won. When Texas was included, 98.2 percent of incumbents won. Numbers at this level were not uncommon in the half-century before 2000, but high incumbency victory rates usually occurred four to five election cycles after a redistricting—when members had become better known to the electorate.

The partisan lineup in House districts was reflected in another emerging phenomenon: increasing congruency in presidential and House voting in congressional districts. By one count, only fifty-nine districts in 2004 produced a split result with one party winning the presidential vote and the other party the House vote—the lowest number of split districts since at least 1952. One major contributor to this trend was the emergence of Republican control in many of the southern states. The South had been moving to the Republican presidential column for several decades, but until late in the twentieth century the region still voted for Democratic representatives. As the latter changed and the GOP increasingly took House seats, the voting patterns for president and representatives became better aligned.

The 2006 midterm congressional elections, however, which shifted the majority in both chambers from the Republicans to the Democrats in the 110th Congress, showed that even high-tech redistricting techniques can be overcome by unforeseen political earthquakes, as demonstrated by the twenty-two House Republicans who lost their reelection bids in the backlash against Republican rule. Nevertheless, even in this unusual election cycle in which Democrats gained a net of thirty seats in the House and six in the Senate, 94 percent of all House incumbents who sought reelection won, and most by a margin greater than 55 percent.

MAJOR SUPREME COURT CASES ON REDISTRICTING

After the long and desultory battle over reapportionment in the 1920s, those who were unhappy over the inaction of Congress and the state legislatures began taking their cases to court. At first, the protesters had no luck. But as the population disparities grew in both federal and state legislative districts and the Supreme Court began to show a tendency to intervene, the objectors were more successful.

Finally, in a series of decisions beginning in 1962 with *Baker v. Carr*, the Court exerted great influence over the redistricting process, ordering that congressional districts as well as state and local legislative districts be drawn so that their populations would be as nearly equal as possible.

Supreme Court's 1932 Decision

Baker v. Carr essentially reversed the direction the Court had taken in 1932. *Wood v. Broom* was a case challenging the constitutionality of a Mississippi redistricting law because it violated the standards of the 1911 federal redistricting act. The question was whether the federal act was still in effect. That law, which required that districts be separate, compact, contiguous, and equally populated, had been neither specifically repealed nor reaffirmed in the 1929 reapportionment act.

Speaking for the Court, Chief Justice Charles Evans Hughes ruled that the 1911 act, in effect, had expired with the approval of the 1929 apportionment act and that the standards of the 1911 act therefore were no longer applicable. The Court reversed the decision of a lower federal court, which had permanently enjoined elections under the new Mississippi redistricting act.

That the Supreme Court upheld a state law that failed to provide for districts of equal population was almost less important than the minority opinion that the Court should not have heard the case. Justices Louis D. Brandeis, Harlan F.

Stone, Owen J. Roberts, and Benjamin N. Cardozo, while concurring in the majority opinion, said they would have dismissed the *Wood* case for "want of equity." The "want-of-equity" phrase in this context suggested a policy of judicial self-limitation with respect to the entire question of judicial involvement in essentially political questions.

"Political Thicket"

Not until 1946, in *Colegrove v. Green,* did the Court again rule in a significant case dealing with congressional redistricting. The case was brought by Kenneth Colegrove, a political science professor at Northwestern University, who alleged that congressional districts in Illinois, which varied between 112,116 and 914,053 in population, were so unequal that they violated the Fourteenth Amendment's guarantee of equal protection of the laws. A seven-member Supreme Court divided 4–3 in dismissing the suit.

Justice Felix Frankfurter gave the opinion of the Court, speaking for himself and Justices Stanley F. Reed and Harold H. Burton. Frankfurter's opinion cited *Wood v. Broom* to indicate that Congress had deliberately removed the standard set by the 1911 act. He also said that he, Reed, and Burton agreed with the minority that the Court should have dismissed the case. The issue, Frankfurter said, was of

> a peculiarly political nature and therefore not meant for judicial interpretation. . . . The short of it is that the Constitution has conferred upon Congress exclusive authority to secure fair representation by the states in the popular House and has left to that House determination whether states have fulfilled their responsibility. If Congress failed in exercising its powers, whereby standards of fairness are offended, the remedy lies ultimately with the people. . . . To sustain this action would cut very deep into the very being of Congress. Courts ought not to enter this political thicket. The remedy for unfairness in districting is to secure state legislatures that will apportion properly, or to invoke the ample powers of Congress.

Frankfurter also said that the Court could not affirmatively remap congressional districts and that elections at large would be politically undesirable.

In a dissenting opinion Justice Hugo L. Black, joined by Justices William O. Douglas and Frank Murphy, maintained that the district court did have jurisdiction over congressional redistricting. The three justices cited as evidence a section of the U.S. Code that allowed district courts to redress deprivations of constitutional rights occurring through action of the states. Black's opinion also rested on an earlier case in which the Court had indicated that federal constitutional questions, unless frivolous, fall under the jurisdiction of the federal courts. Black asserted that the appellants had standing to sue and that the population disparities violated the Equal Protection Clause of the Fourteenth Amendment.

With the Court split 3–3 on whether the judiciary had or should exercise jurisdiction, Justice Wiley B. Rutledge cast the deciding vote in *Colegrove v. Green.* On the question of justiciability, Rutledge agreed with Black, Douglas, and Murphy that the issue could be considered by the federal courts. Thus a majority of the Court participating in the *Colegrove* case felt that congressional redistricting cases were justiciable.

Yet on the question of granting relief in this specific instance, Rutledge agreed with Frankfurter, Reed, and Burton that the case should be dismissed. He pointed out that four of the nine justices in *Wood v. Broom* had felt that dismissal should be for want of equity. Rutledge saw a want-of-equity situation in *Colegrove v. Green* as well. "I think the gravity of the constitutional questions raised [is] so great, together with the possibility of collision [with the political departments of the government], that the admonition [against an avoidable constitutional decision] is appropriate to be followed here," Rutledge said. Jurisdiction, he thought, should be exercised "only in the most compelling circumstances." He thought that "the shortness of time remaining [before the forthcoming election] makes it doubtful whether action could or would be taken in time to secure for petitioners the effective relief they seek." Rutledge warned that congressional elections at large would deprive citizens of representation by districts, "which the prevailing policy of Congress demands." In the case of at-large elections, he said, "the cure sought may be worse than the disease." For all these reasons he concluded that the case was "one in which the Court may properly, and should, decline to exercise its jurisdiction."

Changing Views

In the ensuing years, law professors, political scientists, and other commentators increasingly criticized the *Colegrove* doctrine and grew impatient with the Supreme Court's reluctance to intervene in redistricting disputes. At the same time, the membership of the Court was changing, and the new members were more inclined toward judicial action on redistricting.

In the 1950s the Court decided two cases that laid some groundwork for its subsequent reapportionment decisions. The first was *Brown v. Board of Education,* the historic school desegregation case, in which the Court decided that an individual citizen could assert a right to equal protection of the laws under the Fourteenth Amendment, contrary to the "separate but equal" doctrine of public facilities for white and black citizens.

By 1962 only three members of the Court that decided *Colegrove* remained: Justices Black and Douglas, dissenters in that case, and Justice Frankfurter, aging spokesperson for restraint in the exercise of judicial power.

By then it was clear that malapportionment within the states no longer could be ignored. By 1960 not a single state legislative body existed in which there was not at least a two-to-one population disparity between the most and the least heavily populated districts. For example, the disparity was 242–1 in the Connecticut House, 223–1 in the Nevada Senate, 141–1 in the Rhode Island Senate, and 9–1 in the Georgia Senate. Studies of the effective vote of large and small counties in state legislatures between 1910 and 1960 showed that the effective vote of the most populous counties had slipped while their percentage of the national population had more than doubled. The most lightly populated counties, meanwhile, advanced from a position of slight overrepresentation to one of extreme overrepresentation, holding almost twice as many seats as they would be entitled to by population size alone. Predictably, the rural-dominated state legislatures resisted every move toward reapportioning state legislative districts to reflect new population patterns.

Population imbalance among congressional districts was substantially lopsided but by no means so gross. In Texas the 1960 census showed the most heavily populated district had four times as many inhabitants as the most lightly populated. Arizona, Maryland, and Ohio each had at least one district with three times as many inhabitants as the least populated. In most cases rural areas benefited from the population imbalance in congressional districts. As a result of the postwar population movement out of central cities to the surrounding areas, the suburbs were the most underrepresented.

Baker v. Carr

Against this background a group of Tennessee city-dwellers successfully broke the long-standing precedent against federal court involvement in legislative apportionment problems. For more than half a century, since 1901, the Tennessee Legislature had refused to reapportion itself, even though a decennial reapportionment based on population was specifically required by the state's constitution. In the meantime, Tennessee's population had grown and shifted dramatically to urban areas. By 1960 the House legislative districts ranged from 3,454 to 36,031 in population, while the Senate districts ranged from 39,727 to 108,094. Appeals by urban residents to the rural-controlled Tennessee Legislature proved

DRAWING DISTRICTS

Drawing congressional and legislative district boundaries evolved since 1970 from a primitive task of a few specialists to a highly sophisticated art form in which anyone with a few thousand dollars, a modicum of knowledge about databases, and lots of discipline could participate.

Even with the quasi-democratization of the process, the task was largely left to a handful of experts working in the shadow of political party stakeholders, a multitude of court decisions, and—increasingly—citizen activists who alleged the entire system needed reform.

ADVANCE OF TECHNOLOGY

The development and plunging costs of technology tools since the 1970s was at the center of advanced methods of drawing lines with a diamond-like precision that came to full flower in the 1990s and after the 2000 census.

Before that, the job of redrawing districts was a manual affair involving huge paper maps of census information (practitioners preferred two-story offices with high ceilings and lots of wall space) often overlaid with layer upon layer of acetate on which to draw lines. Computers, to the extent they were used, were mainframes often owned by corporations and banks that would lend map-drawers calculating time overnight.

Personal computers, still a rarity in the early 1980s when redistricting occurred for that decade, did not become part of the mapmakers arsenal until the 1990s. Such software as was available to help with placing district lines was extremely expensive. Programs in the 1980s could cost as much as $75,000. By the 1990s costs were down to the $20,000 range and ten years later for as little as $3,000. When married to modern personal computers with great speed and vast memory costing less than $3,000, remapping opened up to many more participants.[1]

But the march of technology was much more than powerful laptop computers and relatively inexpensive programs. The precise line-drawing that later emerged depended on development of geographic information systems (GIS) programs, which is computer software that integrates geography and demographic data from the Census Bureau with state-specific numbers such as election results collected at extremely small levels, usually the precinct. This information then may be distributed to the even smaller block level by use of an algorithm related to voting-age population and demographics. A key part of the evolution was the Census Bureau's creation in the 1980s, in preparation for the 1990 census, of a mapping system called Topologically Integrated Geographic Encoding and Referencing (TIGER), which produced a uniform map of the United States. This gave an accurate picture of the location of people, geography (including roads, buildings, rivers, and lakes), and concentrations of groups. When used with databases of political information, the redistricting business crossed over from a specialized cottage industry into a sophisticated business that gave politicians an unprecedented power to select the voters they preferred to have in their districts, both in Congress and state legislatures.

PARTISAN CONSIDERATIONS

The power of technology gave mapmakers the ability to draw almost any district configuration they were asked to provide. But experts who did the drawing emphasized that their computers and databases were little more than tools. They typically would give a litany of considerations that circumscribed their activities. At the top of any list was the partisan interest—or party agenda—of an organization seeking a particular district realignment. Closely related was the interest of a member, especially the concerns of an incumbent to have a district in which he could reasonably expect to be given continued employment by the voters.

fruitless. A suit brought in the state courts to force reapportionment was rejected on grounds that the courts should stay out of legislative matters.

City-dwellers then appealed to the federal courts, stating that they had no redress. The legislature had refused to act for more than half a century, the state courts had refused to intervene, and Tennessee had no referendum or initiative laws. They charged that there was "a debasement of their votes by virtue of the incorrect, obsolete and unconstitutional apportionment" to such an extent that they were being deprived of their right to equal protection of the laws under the Fourteenth Amendment.

The Supreme Court on March 26, 1962, handed down its historic decision in *Baker v. Carr,* ruling 6–2 in favor of the Tennessee city-dwellers. In the majority opinion, Justice William J. Brennan Jr. emphasized that the federal judiciary had the power to review the apportionment of state legislatures under the Fourteenth Amendment's Equal Protection Clause. "The mere fact that a suit seeks protection as a political right," Brennan wrote, "does not mean that it presents a political question" that the courts should avoid.

In a vigorous dissent, Justice Frankfurter said the majority decision constituted "a massive repudiation of the experience of our whole past" and was an assertion of "destructively novel judicial power." He contended that the lack of any clear basis for relief "catapults the lower courts" into a "mathematical quagmire." Frankfurter insisted that "there is not under our Constitution a judicial remedy for every political mischief." Appeal for relief, Frankfurter maintained, should not be made in the courts but "to an informed civically militant electorate."

The Court had abandoned the view that malapportionment questions were outside its competence. But it stopped there and in *Baker v. Carr* did not address the merits of the challenge to the legislative districts, stating only that federal courts had the power to resolve constitutional challenges to maldistribution of voters among districts.

Gray v. Sanders

The one-person, one-vote rule was set out by the Court almost exactly one year after its decision in *Baker v. Carr.* But

Legal requirements also played a huge role in drawing lines. For more than forty years, the courts—especially the U.S. Supreme Court—laid down rules that confined the shape and composition of districts. Most important were the earliest rules that districts have equal population (for congressional districts) or only slight deviations in numbers (for legislative districts). Later came decisions on redistricting action that limited the opportunities for minority groups to gain increased representation. Congress played an important role in this regard with the 1965 Voting Rights Act. Originally redistricting was not part of the law's legal underpinnings but over time courts expanded its logic to the shape and nature of districts. Other traditional considerations in redistricting also shaped the way mapmakers went about their tasks. These included such factors as compactness, contiguity, preservation of political subdivisions (such as a county), and sometimes a community of interest that—when it could be defined—showed a relationship among the inhabitants. A few states mentioned competitiveness as a value to be considered, but this was not a major element in most districting.

WHAT MAPMAKERS DO

Given the power of technology and the array of restrictions and considerations that constrain line-drawing, the persons who do the district configurations usually work under a set of tools or approaches that guide their activities.[2]

- *Pairing.* This assigns more than one incumbent to a district that elects just one. Pairing is a technique used by a party controlling redistricting against the other party.
- *Packing.* This puts large numbers of an incumbent's supporters in a single district, more than needed to—in effect—waste the votes.
- *Cracking.* This scatters an incumbent's supporters into two or more districts to dilute his support. It was seen in raw form in the 2003 Texas redistricting engineered by Republicans that was designed to defeat as many as seven Democrats.
- *Dislocation.* This shifts key parts of an incumbent's district to another location. It can be a small or large change.
- *Populating.* This is a device characteristic of legislative redistricting because congressional districts, under Supreme Court decisions, must be almost exactly equal in population, although even in these cases some jumbling of numbers can influence outcomes because a person in the census sense is not necessarily a voter. When it is done for state legislatures it involves putting many of a party's voters in a district or districts while providing a disproportionately smaller number in districts for the other party. If done artfully it can produce more district majorities for the smaller population groupings.
- *Contiguity or Layout.* This technique draws a district in a way that a candidate must cover a large territory, often involving an array of subdivisions such as counties or partial counties, cities, and towns. It makes for weird-shaped districts and can significantly increase the difficulty and cost of campaigning.

1. Kimball Brace and Clark Bensen, "Competition, Partisanship, and Congressional Redistricting," paper presented at the Brookings Institution and Institute of Governmental Studies Conference "The Impact of Technology," Washington, D.C., April 16, 2004.
2. Clark Bensen, "Substantial Political Consequences: A Practitioner's Perspective on Redistricting," *Extensions: A Journal of the Carl Albert Congressional Research and Studies Center* (Fall 2004): 5.

the case in which the announcement came did not involve congressional districts.

In *Gray v. Sanders* the Court found that Georgia's county-unit primary system for electing state officials—a system that weighted votes to give advantage to rural districts in statewide primary elections—denied voters equal protection of the laws. All votes in a statewide election must have equal weight, the Court held:

> How then can one person be given twice or 10 times the voting power of another person in a statewide election merely because he lives in a rural area or because he lives in the smallest rural county? Once the geographical unit for which a representative is to be chosen is designated, all who participate in the election are to have an equal vote—whatever their race, whatever their sex, whatever their occupation, whatever their income, and wherever their home may be in that geographical unit. This is required by the Equal Protection Clause of the Fourteenth Amendment. The concept of "we the people" under the Constitution visualizes no preferred class of voters but equality among those who meet the basic qualification. The idea that every voter is equal to every other voter in his State, when he casts his ballot in favor of one of several competing candidates, underlies many of our decisions. . . . The conception of political equality from the Declaration of Independence to Lincoln's Gettysburg Address, to the Fifteenth, Seventeenth, and Nineteenth Amendments can mean only one thing—one person, one vote.

The Rule Applied

The Court's rulings in *Baker* and *Gray* concerned the equal weighting and counting of votes cast in state elections. In 1964, deciding the case of *Wesberry v. Sanders,* the Court applied the one-person, one-vote principle to congressional districts and set equality as the standard for congressional redistricting.

Shortly after the *Baker* decision was handed down, James P. Wesberry Jr., an Atlanta resident and a member of the Georgia Senate, filed suit in federal court in Atlanta claiming that gross disparity in the population of Georgia's congressional districts violated Fourteenth Amendment rights of equal protection of the laws. At the time, Georgia districts ranged in population from 272,154 in the rural Ninth District in the northeastern part of the state to 823,860 in the Fifth District in Atlanta and its suburbs. District lines had not been changed since 1931. The state's number of House seats remained the same in the interim, but Atlanta's district population—already high in 1931 compared with the others—had more than doubled in thirty years, making a Fifth District vote worth about one-third that of a vote in the Ninth.

In June 1962 the three-judge federal court divided 2–1 in dismissing Wesberry's suit. The majority reasoned that the precedent of *Colegrove* still controlled in congressional district cases. The judges cautioned against federal judicial interference with Congress and against "depriving others of the right to vote" if the suit should result in at-large elections. They suggested that the Georgia Legislature (under court order to reapportion itself) or the U.S. Congress might better provide relief. Wesberry then appealed to the Supreme Court.

On February 17, 1964, the Supreme Court ruled in *Wesberry v. Sanders* that congressional districts must be substantially equal in population. The Court, which upheld Wesberry's challenge by a 6–3 decision, based its ruling on the history and wording of Article I, Section 2, of the Constitution, which states that representatives shall be apportioned among the states according to their respective numbers and be chosen by the people of the several states. This language, the Court stated, meant that "as nearly as is practicable, one man's vote in a congressional election is to be worth as much as another's."

The majority opinion, written by Justice Black and supported by Chief Justice Earl Warren and Justices Brennan, Douglas, Arthur J. Goldberg, and Byron R. White, said: "While it may not be possible to draw congressional districts with mathematical precision, that is no excuse for ignoring our Constitution's plain objective of making equal representation for equal numbers of people the fundamental goal for the House of Representatives."

In a strongly worded dissent, Justice John M. Harlan asserted that the Constitution did not establish population as the only criterion of congressional districting but left the matter to the discretion of the states, subject only to the supervisory power of Congress. "The constitutional right which the Court creates is manufactured out of whole cloth," Harlan concluded.

The *Wesberry* opinion established no precise standards for districting beyond declaring that districts must be as nearly equal in population "as is practicable." In his dissent Harlan suggested that a disparity of more than 100,000 between a state's largest and smallest districts would "presumably" violate the equality standard enunciated by the majority. On that basis, Harlan estimated, the districts of thirty-seven states with 398 representatives would be unconstitutional, "leaving a constitutional House of 37 members now sitting."

The Court's decision also did not make any reference to gerrymandering, because it discussed only the population, not the shape of districts. In a separate opinion handed down the same day as *Wesberry,* the Court dismissed a challenge to congressional districts in New York City, which had been brought by voters who charged that Manhattan's "silk-stocking" Seventeenth District had been gerrymandered to exclude blacks and Puerto Ricans.

Strict Equality

Five years elapsed between *Wesberry* and the Court's next application of constitutional standards to congressional districting. In 1967 the Court hinted at the strict stance it would adopt two years later. With two unsigned opinions, the Court sent back to Indiana and Missouri for revision those two states' congressional redistricting plans because they allowed variations of as much as 20 percent from the average district population.

Two years later Missouri's revised plan returned to the Court for full review. By a 6–3 vote, the Court rejected the plan. It was unacceptable, the Court held in *Kirkpatrick v. Preisler,* because it allowed a variation of as much as 3.1 percent from perfectly equal population districts. Thus the Court made clear its stringent application of the one-person, one-vote rule to congressional districts.

A Census enumerator talks with a man about the 2000 census.

There was no "fixed numerical or percentage population variance small enough to be considered *de minimis* and to satisfy without question the 'as nearly as practicable' standard," Justice Brennan wrote for the Court. "Equal representation for equal numbers of people is a principle designed to prevent debasement of voting power and diminution of access to elected Representatives. Toleration of even small deviations detracts from these purposes."

The only permissible variances in population, the Court ruled, were those that were unavoidable despite the effort to achieve absolute equality or those that could be legally justified. The variances in Missouri could have been avoided, the Court said.

None of Missouri's arguments for the plan qualified as "legally acceptable" justifications. The Court rejected the argument that population variance was necessary to allow representation of distinct interest groups. It said that acceptance of such variances to produce districts with specific interests was "antithetical" to the basic purpose of equal representation.

Justice White dissented from the majority opinion, which he characterized as "an unduly rigid and unwarranted application of the Equal Protection Clause which will unnecessarily involve the courts in the abrasive task of drawing district lines." White added that some "acceptably small" population variance could be established. He indicated that considerations of existing political boundaries and geographical compactness could justify to him some variation from "absolute equality" of population.

Justice Harlan, joined by Justice Potter Stewart, dissented, saying that "whatever room remained under this Court's prior decisions for the free play of the political process in matters of reapportionment is now all but eliminated by today's Draconian judgments."

PRACTICAL RESULTS OF COURT'S RULINGS

As a result of the Supreme Court's decisions of the 1960s, nearly every state was forced to redraw its congressional district lines—sometimes more than once. By the end of the decade, thirty-nine of the forty-five states with more than one representative had made the necessary adjustments.

However, the effect of the one-person, one-vote standard on congressional districts did not bring about immediate population equality in districts. Most of the new districts were far from equal in population because the only official population figures came from the 1960 census. Massive population shifts during the decade rendered most post-*Wesberry* efforts to achieve equality useless.

But redistricting based on the 1970 census resulted in districts that differed only slightly in population from the state average. Among House members elected in 1972, 385 of 435 represented districts that varied by less than 1 percent from the state average district population.

By contrast, only 9 of the districts in the 88th Congress (elected in 1962) deviated less than 1 percent from the state average; 81, from 1 to 5 percent; 87, from 5 to 10 percent; and 236, 10 percent or greater. Twenty-two House members were elected at large.

The Supreme Court made only one major ruling concerning congressional districts during the 1970s. In 1973 the Court declared the Texas congressional districts, as redrawn in 1971, unconstitutional because of excessive population variance among districts. The variance between the largest and smallest districts was 4.99 percent. The Court returned the case to a three-judge federal panel, which adopted a new congressional district plan.

GEOGRAPHICAL PATTERNS IN REAPPORTIONMENT, 1790–2000

The history of reapportionment and redistricting is, in reality, a history of the geographic reallocation of political power in the United States. Because the U.S. Constitution requires that representation in the U.S. House of Representatives be based on population, the decennial census report of population location, growth, and decline is the basis of the reassignment of seats. To a great extent the geography of population theoretically and realistically determines the geography of internal American political power.

The reallocation of seats in the House occurs at four spatial scales: local, intrastate, intraregional, and between regions. For example, in a large urban area seats are reallocated locally when an inner-city declines in population while the suburbs expand. Within states, seats are reallocated when one portion of the state declines, such as farm areas, while others increase, such as metropolitan areas. In certain instances seats are adjusted between states but remain in the same region, such as what happened in the mid-twentieth century with population movement from New York City across the Hudson River into northern New Jersey.

While all the above types of movement are politically important, the loss and gain of House seats from one distant region to another is a critical phenomenon in understanding the political history of the United States. The regional reallocation of House seats is in actuality the reallocation of state and sectional power. Because the differences in regional issues, political parties, and ideology tend to be more pronounced than the differences in local or state issues, the reallocation of power has had a profound effect on U.S. politics and elections. Four major demographic and apportionment areas had a long-term effect on American history.[1]

WESTWARD EXPANSION: ORIGINAL AND NEW STATES

The population of the United States has expanded westward since the origin of the country. At the first census in 1790 virtually all of the population was east of the Appalachian Mountains in the original thirteen states. In fact, the 1790 congressional reapportionment put only the two Kentucky representatives, of the 105 total, in the "Trans Appalachian West." As population steadily migrated into Ohio, Kentucky, Tennessee, and Louisiana, these states became eligible for statehood and representation in the House. As this process continued into the early nineteenth century, more and more new western states entered the Union.

For the original coastal states, the new western states evoked two political concerns. The first question was the theoretical size a nation could be and still be a democracy. This was an important matter because the United States was the first experiment of a large democratic society. The second question was of a more immediate and practical level. It concerned the loss of influence and political power by the original states to the western states. In the 1790 census less than 2 percent of the House seats were in the west, but by 1850, 43 percent of the House's seats were in the west. In addition, this was not just a sheer loss of power but also a political concern in that some of the major issues of the area were in conflict with the more established coastal regions. For example, in the early nineteenth century to encourage settlement the western states, both in the northern and southern parts of the region, lobbied for low-priced public land sales. Because public land sales were the major source of government revenue at this time, the original states in the North and South favored high-priced public land sales. The nation in the early nineteenth century slowly became divided, not simply by North-South issues, but North-South-West issues, especially in certain areas of public policy.

SLAVERY: FREE AND SLAVE STATES

In the framing of the Constitution and in the first seventy years of U.S. history, slavery was the single most important and divisive issue. By the late 1780s slavery was banned in the northern states while permissible and expanding in the southern states. As western states entered the Union, the northern states adopted antislavery constitutions while the southern states allowed slavery. The nation was regionally divided on moral, ethical, and economic lines with respect to the institution of slavery.

This significant division was the centerpiece of the allocation of power in Congress. In the Senate a careful equilibrium of admittance of free states and slave states was conducted to sustain a balance of sectional political power. However, the allocation of power in the House of Representatives could not be controlled and manipulated in this way. The soil and general farming conditions in the northern states of Illinois, Indiana, Iowa, and Ohio far exceeded the conditions in the westward expanding southern states. In the agricultural Midwest a dense farm settlement and expanding population grew westward along the north tier.

At the first census in 1790 approximately half (46 percent) of the House seats were allocated to southern slave states. By the eve of the Civil War, the 1860 census House allocation was approximately one-third (35 percent) to the slave states. Northern interests were in control of the U.S. House, not only with respect to slavery issues, but also other public policy concerns such as internal improvements and tariff policy. Perhaps even more profoundly important than control of the House was the shift in power of the electoral college and election of the president. Because the electoral college allocates votes to each state based on the number of senators plus representatives, a shift of power in the U.S. House means a shift of power in electing the president. At the beginning of the nation there was a rough balance in population, and therefore of electoral votes, between the North and the South. However, because of the geographic change in population growth and settlement, northerner Abraham Lincoln was elected president in 1860 without carrying a single Deep South or border state.

Precise Equality

Following the 1980 census, several federal courts accepted or imposed redistricting maps that achieved population equality but were drawn for blatant partisan purposes. In Missouri a federal court accepted the Democrats' remap proposal over the Republican plan because its districts were more nearly equal in population. The Democratic map obtained population equality by dismantling a district in a part of the state where population was growing and preserving a district in inner-city St. Louis that had been losing population. The plan cost one Republican incumbent his seat.

Michigan's map for the 1980s offered an extreme example of fealty to precise population equality. In 1982 a court-imposed redistricting plan created sixteen congressional districts with exactly equal populations—514,560. The state's two other districts each had a population of just

URBANIZATION: RURAL, URBAN, AND SUBURBAN PLACES

Urbanization, the process of people moving from rural areas to urban places, has been a significant feature of American population geography throughout the nation's history. As incredible as it may seem today, the 1870 census reported no urban place in the United States greater than one million in population. The period of rapid urbanization, 1870–1930, coincides with the period of rapid industrialization of America. This industrialization has a specific regional geography. The first textile manufacturing and later the development of the iron and steel industry and heavy manufacturing began in the North and Northeast. In the corridor from Baltimore to Boston and extending westward to the industrial cities of the Erie Canal and lower Great Lakes, northern urban manufacturing areas boomed while other regions did not have the same rapid development. The population concentration of the North and Northeast became so dominant that William McKinley carried the electoral college in 1896 with little support from the South, Great Plains, and interior West. Large foreign immigration to northern cities in the late nineteenth and early twentieth centuries was supplemented by large internal migration of blacks and whites from the rural South, especially in the period from 1914 to the 1960s.

The rural to urban shift in power in the United States reached its psychological climax in the famous census report of 1920. For the first time in American history the Census Bureau enumerated more people in cities than in rural areas. The nation was changing from its agrarian roots, and shockwaves were felt in farm states and rural congressional districts. So profound was the emotional impact of this census report that, for the first and only time in U.S. history, Congress did not reapportion the House after a census count. *(See "1920s Struggle," p. 114.)*

At the height of high-density, urban industrial America, in the 1920s and 1930s, approximately one-fourth (26 percent) of congressional districts were extremely small with a high concentration of urban working-class and other population. Since the end of World War II, the American urban landscape has changed once again, with the sprawl and suburbanization of population and congressional districts. This change has lessoned the power of inner-city representatives and has heightened the level of more suburban issues and perhaps has even changed the political party makeup and political ideology of some districts.

MODERN ERA: SUN BELT AND THE SNOW BELT

The United States was the dominant world industrial power in the post–World War II era of the late 1940s and 1950s. In the 1960s America began the transition from an industrial to postindustrial society. Manufacturing declined or became less tied to the specific geographic locations of such items as iron ore and coal. In addition to economic changes, the structure of the U.S. population changed to a more mature, mobile, and affluent society. As the American economy and demography changed, profound differences were taking place in regional population growth, decline, and movement.

The census reports of 1960 through 2000 show a significant shift of population from the North and Northeast to the South and Southwest. Demographers have termed this the rise of the Sun Belt or the Snow Belt-to-Sun Belt migration. The causes of this change are many and complex. As the name implies, there is a weather and climate aspect to the movement. However, the climate explanation is tied to a number of technological changes such as the widespread growth and development of air-conditioning, which have made large areas of the South and desert Southwest pleasantly habitable year-round. The mobility of manufacturing in the postindustrial society saw movement of employment from the high-cost-of-living and high-cost-of-labor North to the relatively cheaper South. The growth of retirement, tourism, and high-tech industries seems to benefit the warmer and more scenic regions of the United States.

The Sun Belt population revolution has caused an incredible shift in American political power. Table 5-3 lists the states in order of their gain and loss of representation in the House from 1960 to 2000. Sixteen states gained power in the House during this period, all of which are in the southern tier of states, that is, the Sun Belt. Three states have gained significant political power, the so-called growth pole states of California, Florida, and Texas. Twenty-six states lost representation in this period, with virtually all of these in the North, Midwest, and Great Plains. Significantly, the largest losers are the old northern industrial states of Illinois, Massachusetts, New York, Ohio, and Pennsylvania. In all, seventy-five seats (17 percent of the House) have been shifted from one section of the country to another in recent decades. Figure 5-1 maps the 2000 reapportionment and clearly indicated the Sun Belt era reallocation geography of House seats.

The recent shift of House seats from the North to the South and West is symbolic of the continuing change of regional power throughout U.S. history. In the Sun Belt era, as in previous eras, political party support, political ideology, and many political issues have a specific regional or geographic context. For example, the political ideology and recent political party support in national elections is different in New York than in Texas. In the current Sun Belt–Snow Belt demographic era, some political parties and some issue areas gain and others lose in importance. Recent demographic trend analysis by the Census Bureau shows a continuation of the current Sun Belt movement for the 2010 census and congressional reapportionment.

1. Extensive discussion of each demographic political era and each decennial apportionment is found in Kenneth C. Martis and Gregory Elmes, *The Historical Atlas of State Power in Congress, 1790–1900* (Washington, D.C.: Congressional Quarterly Press, 1993).

one person fewer—514,559. To achieve that equality, however, the line for many districts cut through many small cities and towns, dividing their residents between two or three different districts.

Although maps such as these raised the question whether partisan gerrymandering was also a violation of an individual's voting rights, the Supreme Court in 1983 appeared to make it even more difficult to challenge a redistricting map on grounds other than population deviation. In a 5–4 decision, the Court ruled in *Karcher v. Daggett* that states must adhere as closely as possible to the one-person, one-vote standard and bear the burden of proving that deviations from precise population equality were made in pursuit of a legitimate goal. The decision overturned New Jersey's congressional map because the variation between the most populated and the least populated districts was 0.69 percent.

Brennan, who wrote the Court's opinion in *Baker* and *Kirkpatrick,* also wrote the opinion in *Karcher,* contending that population differences between districts "could have been avoided or significantly reduced with a good-faith effort to achieve population equality." "Adopting any standard other than population equality, using the best census data available, would subtly erode the Constitution's ideal of equal representation," Brennan wrote. "In this case, appellants argue that a maximum deviation of approximately 0.7 percent should be considered *de minimis.* If we accept that argument, how are we to regard deviations of 0.8 percent, 0.95 percent, 1.0 percent or 1.1 percent? . . . To accept the legitimacy of unjustified, though small population deviations in this case would mean to reject the basic premise of *Kirkpatrick* and *Wesberry.*"

Brennan said that "any number of consistently applied legislative policies might justify" some population variation. These included "making districts compact, respecting municipal boundaries, preserving the cores of prior districts, and avoiding contests between incumbent Representatives." However, he cautioned, the state must show "with some specificity that a particular objective required the specific deviations in its plan, rather than simply relying on general assertions."

In his dissent Justice White criticized the majority for its "unreasonable insistence on an unattainable perfection in the equalizing of congressional districts." He warned that the decision would invite "further litigation of virtually every congressional redistricting plan in the nation."

Partisan Gerrymandering

In *Karcher* the Court did not address the underlying political issue in the New Jersey case, which was that its map had been drawn to serve Democratic interests. As a partisan gerrymander, the map had few peers, boasting some of the most oddly shaped districts in the country. One constituency, known as the "fishhook" by its detractors, twisted through central New Jersey's industrial landscape, picking up Democratic voters along the way. Another stretched from the suburbs of New York to the fringes of Trenton.

In separate dissents Justices Lewis F. Powell Jr. and John Paul Stevens broadly hinted that they were willing to hear constitutional challenges to instances of partisan gerrymandering. "A legislator cannot represent his constituents properly—nor can voters from a fragmented district exercise the ballot intelligently—when a voting district is nothing more than an artificial unit divorced from, and indeed often in conflict with, the various communities established in the State," wrote Powell.

The Court's opportunity to address that issue came in *Davis v. Bandemer.* On June 30, 1986, the Court ruled that political gerrymanders are subject to constitutional review by federal courts, even if the disputed districts meet the one-person, one-vote test. The case arose from a challenge by Indiana Democrats who argued that the Republican-drawn map so heavily favored the Republican Party that Democrats were denied appropriate representation. But the Court rejected the Democrats' challenge to the alleged gerrymander, saying that one election was insufficient to prove unconstitutional discrimination. Left unclear were what standards the Court would use to find a partisan gerrymander legally unacceptable.

National Republicans expressed delight with the *Bandemer* decision. The GOP had long held that Democratic control over most state legislatures had allowed them to draw congressional and legislative districts to their partisan advantage. In particular, Republicans expressed confidence that the *Bandemer* decision lay the groundwork for overturning California's congressional district map, created by Democratic Rep. Phillip Burton in the early 1980s.

Widely recognized as a classic example of a partisan gerrymander, the map featured a number of oddly shaped districts, drawn neither compactly nor with respect to community boundaries, but all with nearly equal populations. As one commentator described it, "Burton carefully stretched districts from one Democratic enclave to another—sometimes joining them with nothing but a bridge, a stretch of harbor, or a spit of land . . . —avoiding Republicans block for block and household for household." Before the 1982 elections, Democrats held twenty-two congressional districts; Republicans, twenty-one. With the Burton map in place for the 1982 elections, Democrats held twenty-eight seats; Republicans, only seventeen.

Republican representative Robert E. Badham filed a lawsuit against the Burton plan in federal district court in 1983. In the wake of the *Bandemer* decision, that court held a hearing on *Badham v. Eu* but dismissed the Republican complaint by a 2–1 vote. The court in essence ruled that a party seeking to overturn a gerrymandered map must show a general pattern of exclusion from the political process, which the California Republican Party, in control of the governorship, a Senate seat, and 40 percent of the House seats, could not do. The Republicans appealed to the Supreme Court, but the Court refused to become involved, voting 6–3 in 1989 to reaffirm the lower court's decision without comment.

But with the law largely settled on population and racial issues in redistricting, partisan gerrymandering appeared by 2005 to be taking the spotlight. The *Bandemer* decision, with its exceptionally difficult standard to prove a partisan drawing of lines, still was the controlling law and remained so when the Court in 2004, in *Vieth v. Jubelirer,* rejected a claim under it to districts in Pennsylvania that Democrats said were constitutionally invalid. In that case the swing vote on the Court came from Anthony M. Kennedy, who agreed that the Pennsylvania Democrats had not shown enough to meet the framework for partisan gerrymandering set out in *Bandemer.* But Kennedy also said that because no adequate standard to measure partisan gerrymandering had yet emerged did not mean that it would never evolve in the future.[14] *(See "Pennsylvania," p. 137.)*

Two instances of partisan gerrymandering were prominent after the 2000 census. In Colorado, Republicans sought to tweak district lines to enhance the reelection chances of an incumbent who barely won in 2002. On December 1, 2003, the state supreme court, however, ruled a second redistricting in the decade was impermissible under the state's constitution. The U.S. Supreme Court in 2004 declined to review the decision.

In Texas, however, Republicans orchestrated a major redrawing of some district lines with the goal of defeating as many as seven incumbents who had won in 2002 under a court-ordered redistrict plan. After their second remap of the decade was passed, six of the seven lost in the new districts in 2004. Democrats charged the action was unconstitutional, but courts did not accept their contention. Initially, the Supreme Court in 2004 sent the case back to a Texas court with the instructions to reconsider the issue in light of its decision in *Vieth v. Jubelirer.* When the case returned to the Court in 2006, the justices upheld the mid-decade partisan gerrymander because the Texas Democrats failed to offer a workable standard for constitutional review. At the same time they struck down a small part of the remap on grounds that it violated the Voting Rights Act's provisions protecting against the dilution of minority voting strength. *(See "Texas," p. 137.)*

Minority Representation

One form of gerrymandering is expressly forbidden by law: redistricting for the purpose of racial discrimination. The Voting Rights Act of 1965, extended in 1970, 1975, and 1982, banned redistricting that diluted the voting strength of black communities. Other minorities, including Hispanics, Asian

TABLE 5-3 **Interstate Transfer of House Seats by Census and Senate, 1960–2000**

	Seat change					
	1960	**1970**	**1980**	**1990**	**2000**	**1960–2000**
California	+8	+5	+2	+7	+1	+23
Florida	+4	+3	+4	+4	+2	+17
Texas	+1	+1	+3	+3	+2	+10
Arizona	+1	+1	+1	+1	+2	+6
Colorado		+1	+1		+1	+3
Georgia				+1	+2	+3
Hawaii	+2					+2
Nevada			+1		+1	+2
Washington			+1	+1		+2
Alaska	+1					+1
Maryland	+1					+1
New Mexico			+1			+1
North Carolina	−1			+1	+1	+1
Oregon			+1			+1
Utah			+1			+1
Virginia				+1		+1
Tennessee		−1	+1			0
Connecticut					−1	−1
Louisiana				−1		−1
Maine	−1					−1
Minnesota	−1					−1
Montana				−1		−1
Nebraska	−1					−1
New Jersey	+1		−1	−1		−1
North Dakota		−1				−1
Oklahoma					−1	−1
South Dakota			−1			−1
Alabama	−1	−1				−2
Arkansas	−2					−2
Indiana			−1		−1	−2
Kansas	−1			−1		−2
Kentucky	−1			−1		−2
Mississippi	−1				−1	−2
Missouri	−1		−1			−2
Wisconsin		−1			−1	−2
Iowa	−1	−1		−1		−3
Michigan	+1		−1	−2	−1	−3
West Virginia	−1	−1		−1		−3
Massachusetts	−2		−1	−1		−4
Ohio	+1	−1	−2	−2	−1	−5
Illinois	−1		−2	−2	−1	−6
Pennsylvania	−3	−2	−2	−2	−2	−11
New York	−2	−2	−5	−3	−2	−14
TOTAL	**21**	**11**	**17**	**19**	**12**	**75[1]**

NOTES: This table lists the forty-three states that have lost or gained seats in the House of Representatives in one or more of the past five census reapportionments. Seven of the fifty states have kept the same number of seats from 1960 through 2000. Delaware, Vermont, and Wyoming have kept the minimum required one seat; Idaho, New Hampshire, and Rhode Island have kept two seats; and South Carolina has kept six seats.

1. Net transfer for 1960 to 2000 for the entire United States.

SOURCES: Data for 1960, 1970, and 1980 from Kenneth C. Martis, *The Historical Atlas of Political Parties in the United States Congress: 1789–1989* (New York: Macmillan, 1989). Data for 1990 and 2000 from "House History, Congressional Apportionment," Office of the Clerk, United States House of Representatives, Washington, D.C., available at http://clerk.house.gov/art_history/house_history/congApp.html.

Americans, American Indians, and native Alaskans, subsequently were brought under the protection of the law.

In 1980 the Supreme Court for the first time narrowed the reach of the Voting Rights Act in the case of *Mobile v. Bolden,* a challenge to the at-large system of electing city commissioners used in Mobile, Alabama. By a vote of 6–3, the Court ruled that proof of discriminatory intent by the commissioners was necessary before a violation could be found. The fact that no African American had ever been elected under the challenged system was not proof enough.

The *Mobile* decision set off an immediate reaction on Capitol Hill. In extending the Voting Rights Act in 1982, Congress amended it to outlaw any practice that has the effect of discriminating against blacks or other minorities—regardless of the lawmakers' intent.

The Justice Department later adopted a similar "results test" for another part of the act (Section 5), which requires certain states and localities with a history of discrimination to have their electoral plans "precleared" by the department. In 1986 the Supreme Court applied this test in *Thornburg v. Gingles,* ruling that six of North Carolina's multimember legislative districts impermissibly diluted black voting strength. Sharply departing from *Mobile,* the Court held that because few blacks had been elected from these districts, the system must be in violation of the law.

The Court also used the *Thornburg* decision to develop three criteria that, if met, should lead to the creation of a minority legislative district: the minority group must be large and geographically compact enough to constitute a majority in a single-member electoral district; the group must be politically cohesive; and the white majority must vote as a bloc to the degree that it usually can defeat candidates preferred by the minority.

Thus, within a period of ten years the burden of proof was shifted from minorities, who had been required to show that lines were being drawn to dilute their voting strength, to lawmakers, who had to show that they had done all they could to maximize minority voting strength.

But maps drawn for the 1990s that went to extraordinary lengths to elect minorities came quickly under scrutiny by the Supreme Court. In a 1993 ruling on districts in North Carolina, *Shaw v. Reno,* Justice Sandra Day O'Connor wrote for the Court majority that any map that groups people "who may have little in common with one another but the color of their skin bears an uncomfortable resemblance to political apartheid." The ruling reinstated a suit by five white North Carolinians who contended that the state's congressional district map, which created two oddly shaped majority-minority districts, violated their right to equal protection under law by diluting their votes.

In 1995 the Court ruled in *Miller v. Johnson,* a case involving districts in Georgia, that using race as "the predominant factor" in drawing districts is presumed to be unconstitutional, unless it serves a compelling government interest. The decision struck down a redistricting plan that created three black-majority districts.

Those two rulings represented a speedy swing of the judicial pendulum away from the 1986 *Gingles* doctrine of maximizing minority voting strength in redistricting. As the 1990s unfolded, the constitutionality of majority-minority districts was widely challenged, and eventually, federal courts ordered a number of states—including Florida, Georgia, Louisiana, New York, North Carolina, Texas, and Virginia—to redraw districts that were adjudged to be unconstitutional racial gerrymanders.

But the Supreme Court did not make sweeping determinations affecting all majority-minority districts. In Illinois, a majority-minority district was allowed to stand after the state argued successfully that it had a "compelling state interest" in giving Chicago's large Hispanic population the opportunity to elect one representative of its own. In a 1999 North Carolina case, *Hunt v. Cromartie,* the Court unanimously ruled that mapmakers could create a district with a "supermajority" of black Democrats as long as the primary reason for doing so was political, not racial.

Even though numerous majority-minority districts were redrawn in the 1990s to reduce minority populations, nearly all those districts retained members of minority groups as their representatives by the end of the twentieth century. Nevertheless, the mapmakers following the 2000 census devised many bizarrely shaped districts, some for racial reasons but many for incumbent-protection purposes. The North Carolina Twelfth District, a serpentine majority-minority creation in the 1990s that was the focus of the Supreme Court's actions, survived in a roughly similar configuration in 2001. But in Illinois mapmakers outdid even North Carolina in creating the Seventeenth District, one of the strangest in the nation taking in nine full counties and parts of fourteen others for the purpose of protecting a Democratic incumbent.

MID-DECADE REDISTRICTING AND PARTISAN GERRYMANDERING

The always contentious act of drawing boundaries for House districts in Congress took on a new flavor—and controversy—in the years following the 2000 census. For the first time in more than a century politicians in a few states sought to enhance their party's power by redrawing district lines outside the long-accepted window of about two years following a decennial census. Although only a few states had moved in that direction, the prospect of widespread mid-decade redistricting threatened even more intense partisan conflict in the period before the 2010 census and raised questions about the value of settled political divisions within a once widely accepted time period.

FIGURE 5-2 **Redistricting in North Carolina**

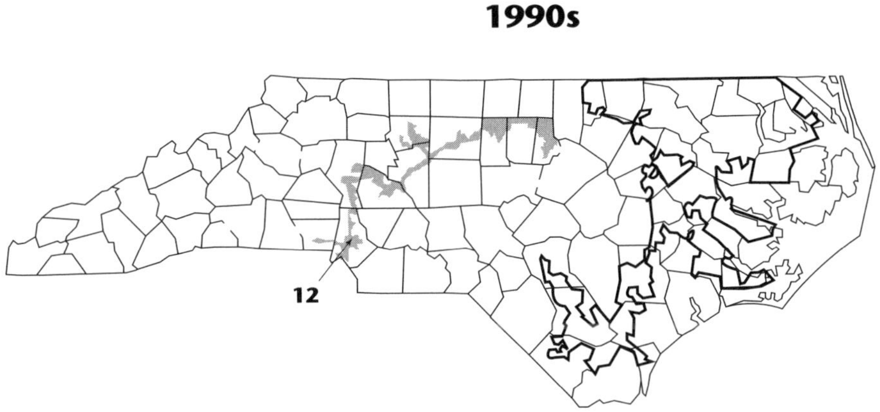

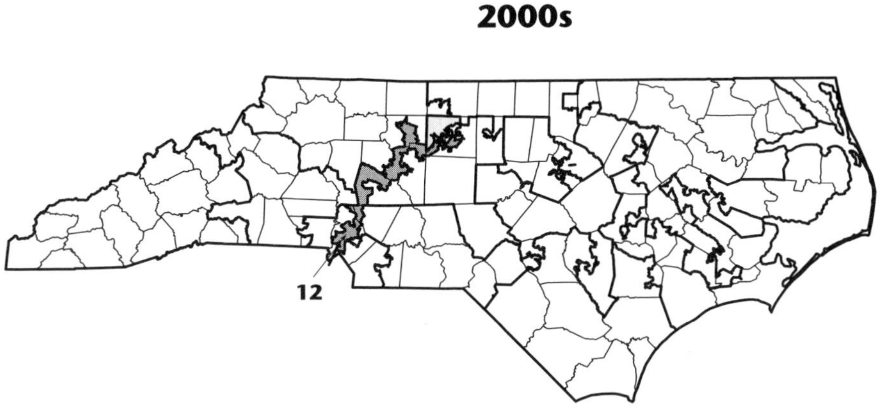

House redistricting in some states after the 1990 census sought to create so-called majority-minority districts that were likely to elect a person from a minority group, usually an African American. The effort resulted in unusually shaped districts such as North Carolina's Twelfth District. The Supreme Court in a series of rulings cast doubt on these configurations, and mapmakers after the 2000 census focused on other concerns, particularly protection of incumbents. Nevertheless, North Carolina's Twelfth District in 2002 (above, bottom) looked similar to the 1990s version (above, top). States with large minority populations continued efforts after the 2000 count to make sure district configurations provided representation in the House for minority groups.

The redistricting efforts that followed the original post–2000 census redistricting were driven to boost the fortunes of major parties and to redress the division of House seats that their advocates argued did not reflect twenty-first century political alignments in each state. These efforts—in Colorado, Georgia, and Texas—had their roots in each state's recent shifting patterns of partisan competition, but taken together they appeared also to have a collateral effect on a growing national movement to alter the manner in which House district lines were drawn. The advocates of change were arguing for removing the redistricting power from state legislators and governors and investing it in independent commissions, as was already done in a small number of states. This movement, which was at most embryonic as states were redrawing lines after 2000, had other causes, most particularly a growing national belief that districting as normally practiced contributed to largely noncompetitive races in which most House incumbents were returned to Washington with little difficulty. A number of self-styled good government groups, Common Cause in particular, seized on the redistricting issue as—in their view—a major impediment to representative, competitive Houses elections. However, many noncompetitive elections were often seen as highly representative of the voter preferences in a geographic region. *(See "Competitiveness and Incumbency," p. 123.)*

FIGURE 5-3 **Redistricting in Illinois**

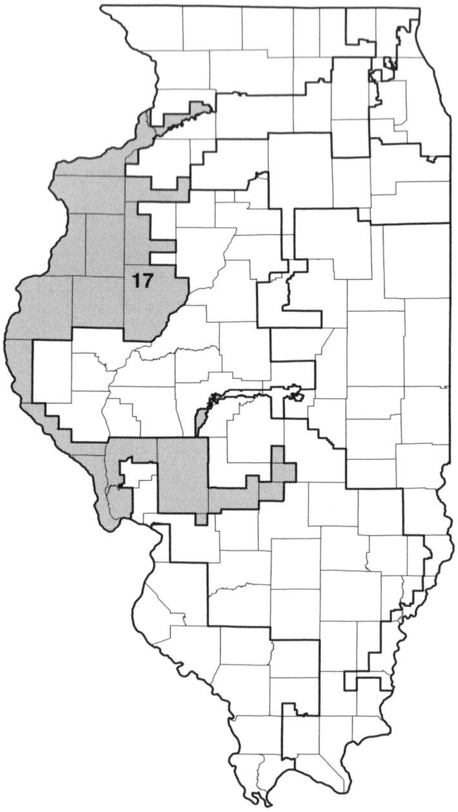

Following the 2000 census, Democrats and Republicans were particularly interested in drawing new House districts that protected incumbents and were less concerned about creating new districts that benefited their party—although a good deal of that went on also. One of the most striking examples of a bizarrely shaped district that was drawn to ensure the reelection of an incumbent was the Seventeenth District in Illinois. The Seventeenth covered nine full counties and parts of fourteen others.

Further complicating the redistricting controversy was an effort by some aggrieved voters to challenge district boundaries on judicial grounds of partisan gerrymandering. This legal attack had not won favor in the courts and was, under existing legal theories, exceedingly difficult to prove. The Supreme Court in 2004 rejected such a claim in a case that came from Pennsylvania but left standing an earlier decision that said such claims might in time be proven, thereby leaving open the opportunity to litigate on partisan gerrymandering.

Two of the mid-decade redistricting efforts, Colorado and Texas, arose originally from the special circumstances of court-ordered plans following the 2000 census. But both also were overlaid with partisan efforts, Republican in both cases, to enlarge the GOP's majority in Congress. In Georgia the original House district lines were drawn after 2000 by a Democratic majority in the state. But by 2005 Republicans were in control and saw an opportunity to redraw the lines to their party's advantage. For both Georgia and Texas, Republicans argued that the redistricting they wanted to put in place was no more than a natural reflection of the emerging political orientation of each state away from Democratic and toward Republican majorities. In Colorado, the motives were seen mainly as a Republican effort to simply improve reelection chances of one of its GOP members. Still, regardless of the background to these actions, all raised the possibility that other states where legislative control had changed hands between the parties would undertake similar bare-knuckles redrawing of lines for partisan gains.

Redrawing of district lines beyond the normal window following a census was not unprecedented in U.S. history. Instances occurred in the late nineteenth century. But the mid-decade redistricting efforts after 2000 were the first in modern times outside of legal decisions that required new lines. The most important came in 1964 when the U.S. Supreme Court first applied a one-person, one-vote standard to the drawing of congressional maps. In the following decades some states, mostly in the South, had to redistrict—some more than once—under court orders that grew from efforts to draw lines enhancing opportunities for minorities to win election, creating the majority-minority districts.

Whether unprecedented or not, mid-decade redistricting introduces a potential flaw in the logic underpinning redrawing of the legislative district boundaries, which are supposed to be based on the decennial census. The census is an actual enumeration of the population. And yet, the U.S. population is not static. In fact, the census counts are out of date as soon as they are compiled and published because of the constant migration of people from one place to another. So even with the availability of periodic Census Bureau population reestimates following the decennial enumeration, a redrawing of boundaries using these estimated results would not be based on an actual count at that time. Moreover, the accuracy of that actual count, if used as the basis for drawing maps three, five, or even seven years out from the enumeration, is open to challenge.[15]

Colorado

The Republican-controlled Colorado General Assembly on May 7, 2003, cleared legislation redrawing the state's seven House districts. Republican Gov. Bill Owens signed the law two days later. The new map was designed to enhance the GOP leanings of two potentially competitive districts held by Republicans in the 108th Congress: the Third District, which covered the western half of the state, and the Seventh District, in suburban Denver. In the latter, a Republican won in 2002 by the closest margin of any House race—121 votes out of 172,879 cast. The legal premise for the legislature acting was similar to the situation in Texas. Colorado gained one seat in reapportionment after the 2000 census, but the state house and senate, then held by the Republicans and Democrats, respectively, in 2001, failed to agree on a map. Instead, the map used in the 2002 election had been adopted by a state district court judge.

On December 1, 2003, however, the Colorado Supreme Court struck down the new map created by the state legislature, ruling that it violated the state constitution. That document "limits redistricting to once per census, and nothing in state or federal law negates this limitation," Chief Justice Mary Mullarkey wrote for a 5–2 majority. "Having failed to redistrict when it should have, the General Assembly has lost its chance to redistrict until after the 2010 federal census." In dissent, Justice Rebecca Love Kourlis wrote that "courts cannot be lawmakers under Article V" of the state constitution, which said that after each census the legislature "shall divide the state into congressional districts accordingly." In 2004 the U.S. Supreme Court rejected a request from Colorado Republicans to review the Colorado Supreme Court ruling.

The case came back to the U.S. Supreme Court after four Colorado voters brought suit seeking to overturn the court-ordered redistricting plan on grounds that it violated the Elections Clause of the U.S. Constitution because the judiciary and not the legislature had fashioned the redistricting plan. On May 5, 2007, the Court, in *Lance v. Coffman,* issued a unanimous per curiam decision that held that the voters had no standing to bring the lawsuit. The Court ruled that the voters had "no particularized stake" because their grievance was an "undifferentiated, generalized" one, different in character from injuries alleged in voting rights cases. *(See box, Constitutional Provisions, p. 109.)*

Pennsylvania

The Pennsylvania case, *Vieth v. Jubelirer,* grew from allegations by state Democrats who argued that the congressional map used in the 2002 elections unconstitutionally benefited the GOP. Legislation setting those boundaries was written by a Republican-majority Pennsylvania General Assembly and signed in early 2002 by Republican Gov. Mark Schweiker. The aim was to guarantee that the party would gain House seats even after Pennsylvania lost two seats in the reapportionment following the 2000 census. Republicans had won eleven of the state's twenty-one seats in 2000. After the remap, which paired six Democratic incumbents in three districts, the party won twelve of the remaining nineteen seats in 2002 in a state that Democratic presidential candidate Al Gore carried in 2000 and Democrat Edward G. Rendell won in the 2002 gubernatorial race.

Democrats maintained that several of the meandering districts in the new map failed to adequately reflect communities of interest by, for example, hewing to county boundaries. Republicans maintained that the map complied with legal precedents.

The U.S. Supreme Court in 2004 ruled against the Democrats in a 5–4 decision but did not—as several justices wanted—overrule a 1986 decision, on which the Pennsylvania case was based, that said political gerrymandering could be a subject of legal action.

The case marked the Court's first review of a partisan gerrymandering case. The 1986 ruling *Davis v. Bandemer* said that successful challengers to a map on partisan grounds had to "prove both intentional discrimination against an identifiable political group and an actual discriminatory effect on that group." It also held that political gerrymandering suits could be brought under the Equal Protection Clause of the Fourteenth Amendment. No state or congressional redistricting plan had been invalidated under the *Bandemer* standard.

Because no standard to judge political gerrymandering had been formed, the most conservative justices, led by Antonin Scalia, wanted to overturn *Bandemer.* But five other justices were loath to dismiss the possibility of valid future claims to unconstitutional political gerrymandering. Writing for the majority, Justice Anthony Kennedy said: "That a workable standard for measuring a gerrymander's burden on representational rights has not yet emerged does not mean that none will emerge in the future."

Texas

Texas presented a situation similar to Colorado in some respects, but the outcome was different. The original map for Texas congressional districts during the 2000s was drawn in 2001 by a three-judge federal panel after the Democratic state house and Republican state senate could not agree on new lines. The map was designed principally to protect incumbents, as was the case in many other states. In 2002 the state elected fifteen Republicans and seventeen Democrats to the House for the 108th Congress.

Texas Republicans, led by House Majority Leader Tom DeLay, the most influential Texan in the state's congressional delegation, contended that the court redistricting did not reflect the new political realities in the state: the GOP was the dominant party in Texas, which, as with most of the southern states, was becoming increasingly Republican. In 2003, for example, all twenty-nine of the statewide elected officeholders were Republicans. Moreover, Republicans by 2003 were in control of both houses in the state legislature for the first time since Reconstruction.

DeLay became the driving force that eventually led to redrawing of the lines but only after a bizarre series of events that drew national attention—and considerable ridicule—to the state. Getting a plan approved required three special sessions of the legislature, made all the more colorful by Democratic lawmakers fleeing the state—in what late-night

Democratic Texas state senators referred to as the "Texas 11" discuss their experiences fleeing the state to avoid a special session of the legislature to approve a redistricting plan favorable to Republicans.

comedians compared with episodes out of the Old West—to deny Republicans enough members present to conduct business. They first decamped to Oklahoma and later to New Mexico before deciding the effort was futile and returned to their jobs as legislators.

As a result on October 12, 2003, the Republican-majority legislature cleared a bill drawing a new congressional district map and Republican Gov. Rick Perry signed it into law the next day. The comprehensive redrawing of the lines was designed to produce as many as seven additional GOP House members after the 2004 elections. The state, which had gained two more seats following the 2000 census, had the second-largest congressional delegation, after California.

As everyone expected, litigation followed. The Justice Department on December 19, 2003, endorsed, or precleared, the new map. Texas was one of sixteen mostly southern states required under the Voting Rights Act to obtain a determination from the Justice Department or the U.S. District Court for the District of Columbia that any proposed voting change "does not have the purpose and will not have the effect of denying or abridging the right to vote" of protected minority groups. A congressional map in those states could be legally enforced only after it had been precleared.

Notwithstanding that, Texas Democrats and African American and Hispanic advocacy groups filed suit in federal court, alleging that the map would unconstitutionally dilute the political strength of blacks and Hispanics by spreading their numbers among GOP districts. The Democrats also maintained that the map disenfranchised ethnic minorities in Texas by threatening the reelection of white Democratic incumbents who were overwhelmingly their candidates of choice. Republicans responded candidly that their motivations were entirely political, not racial. Their main aim was to undercut the prospects of Democrats and to bolster the prospects of Republicans, in concert with the changed partisan political landscape of the state.

On January 6, 2004, a three-judge federal panel upheld the map. "The allegation that the minority voting strength in these districts has been diluted is in truth no more than a claim that these districts have been drawn to add Republican voting strength to overcome the election advantage that the current Democrat incumbents hold," wrote Judge Patrick E. Higginbotham of the Fifth Circuit Court of Appeals and District Court Judge Lee H. Rosenthal. All three judges ruled against Democratic arguments that the new map was an unconstitutional political gerrymander and that the legislature was not permitted to substitute a new map for the court-drawn plan. Neither the Texas constitution nor the U.S. Constitution explicitly bars redrawing lines more than once per decade, they said.

Ten days later, the U.S. Supreme Court denied the Democrats' request to stay the ruling in the case, *Jackson v. Perry.* That seemed to end the matter, but in 2004 the Court sent the case back to the lower court, suggesting the judges should consider the matter again in light of the justices' decision on the Pennsylvania case that involved political gerrymandering.

On election day 2004 the new remap was a smashing success for the Republicans. The GOP picked up six of the seven seats they targeted. One of the targeted Democrats retired and a second switched to the Republican Party. In the other four districts, Republicans defeated Democratic incumbents. Only one Democrat, one of the most conservative members of his party in the House, survived.

In March 2006 the refashioned lawsuit, now dubbed *League of United Latin American Citizens et al. v. Perry,* was back before the Supreme Court for a full hearing on whether the Democrat's challenge to the Texas mid-decade redistricting plan presented, in Justice Anthony Kennedy's words, any "manageable, reliable measure of fairness for determining whether a partisan gerrymander" is unconstitutional. The case also raised questions about whether several of the new districts violated a provision of the Voting Rights Act by diluting minority voting strength. The first issue touched on the precedents in *Bandemer* and *Vieth v. Jubelirer*—whether partisan gerrymanders presented justiciable issues with workable constitutional standards that would keep courts out of the thorniest parts of the political thicket. The second issue raised a claim along the line of cases dealing with racial gerrymandering in which the Court had demonstrated less deference to mapmaking by state legislatures.

The Supreme Court issued its ruling on June 28, 2006, at the end of the 2005–2006 term. With two new justices—Chief Justice John G. Roberts Jr. and Associate Justice Samuel A. Alito Jr.—a new Court had the opportunity to reverse *Bandemer* and *Vieth* or fashion a new standard for striking down unfair partisan gerrymanders, thus bringing some clarity to the ambiguities of the two precedents. The decision proved disappointing to advocates of either position. In a fractured ruling in which justices both joined and dissented in so many parts of one another's opinions that observers were left scratching their heads, Justice Kennedy wrote the opinion of the Court upholding the mid-decade redistricting in general but striking down the district map in District 23 as a violation of the Section 2 of the Voting Rights Act. The Court passed on the opportunity to ban mid-decade redistricting as an unfair political gerrymander by a vote of 7–2 and in so doing opened the door to rolling redistricting as a partisan strategy whenever state legislatures change partisan hands. While not condoning this practice, a majority of the justices could find no clear statutory or constitutional prohibition of it and no "manageable, reliable measure of fairness" to embolden courts to enter the political thicket and strike it down.

The decision required a new map to rectify the Voting Rights Act violation in Texas House District 23, which a lower federal court fashioned by August. The March 7, 2006, Texas primary results for the affected districts were voided by this action, and the November 7, 2006, general election ballots in these districts listed all candidates, regardless of party, on a single ballot, with runoff elections to be held if no candidate received a majority vote. Henry Bonilla, the Republican incumbent from District 23, ultimately lost the seat to Democrat Ciro Rodriguez when the final results were tallied.

Georgia

The situation in Georgia was strictly partisan. District lines following the 2000 census were drawn by the legislature under Democratic control. The effort produced some of the oddest shaped districts of any in the United States. By 2005 Republicans had won control of the state legislature so they created a new plan aimed at getting the GOP nine of the state's thirteen House seats. Under the Democratic plan Republicans held seven of the seats to six for the Democrats. As with Texas, Republicans argued that the previous district configuration did not reflect the political realities in Georgia that by mid-decade were increasingly Republican. Legal challenges to the plan were unsuccessful, and the 2006 congressional election was contested under the redrawn maps. The election results, however, frustrated the partisan ambitions behind the mid-decade redistricting as Democrats retained all six House seats. But for two of the incumbents, the margin of victory was razor-thin. Even before the election, Georgia Gov. Sonny Perdue, a Republican, appointed a task force to consider ways to remove the boundary line drawing part of the redistricting process from the legislature and give it to an independent commission before the next decennial census in 2010.

NOTES

1. Ronald D. Elving, "Redistricting: Drawing Power with a Map," *Editorial Research Reports,* February 15, 1991, 99.
2. Congressional Quarterly, *Congressional Districts in the 2000s: A Portrait of America* (Washington, D.C.: CQ Press, 2003), 11, 18.
3. Robert Luce, *Legislative Principles* (New York: DaCapo Press, 1971), 342.
4. Thomas Jefferson, *The Portable Thomas Jefferson,* ed. Merrill D. Peterson, Part 3: *Notes on the State of Virginia* (New York: Viking, 1965), 163.
5. Andrew Hacker, *Congressional Districting: The Issue of Equal Representation,* rev. ed. (Washington, D.C.: Brookings Institution, 1964), 6–7.
6. Max Farrand, ed., *The Records of the Federal Convention of 1787* (New Haven, Conn.: Yale University Press, 1911, 1966), vol. 2, 241.
7. James Madison, Alexander Hamilton, and John Jay, *The Federalist Papers,* with an introduction by Clinton Rossiter (New York: New American Library, 1961), 347–348, 354.
8. Quoted in Laurence F. Schmeckebier, *Congressional Apportionment* (Washington, D.C.: Brookings Institution, 1941), 131.
9. Hacker, *Congressional Districting,* 14.

10. Quoted in Schmeckebier, *Congressional Apportionment,* 113.

11. Zechariah Chafee Jr., "Congressional Reapportionment," *Harvard Law Review* (1929): 1015–1047.

12. Jefferson, *Notes on the State of Virginia,* 217.

13. Schmeckebier, *Congressional Reapportionment,* 137.

14. Gregory L. Giroux, "High Court Draws No Bright Lines to Limit Political Gerrymandering," *CQ Weekly,* May 1, 2004, 1019.

15. Steve Blankenship, *Lines in the Sand: Congressional Redistricting in Texas and the Downfall of Tom DeLay* (Austin: University of Texas Press, 2007), 318–322.

SELECTED BIBLIOGRAPHY

Baker, Gordon E. *The Reapportionment Revolution: Representation, Political Power, and the Supreme Court.* New York: Random House, 1966.

Bickerstaff, Steve. *Lines in the Sand: Congressional Redistricting in Texas and the Downfall of Tom DeLay.* Austin: University of Texas Press, 2007.

Bositis, David A., ed. *Voting Rights and Minority Representation: Redistricting, 1992–2002.* Lanham, Md.: University Press of America, 2006.

Buchman, Jeremy. *Drawing Lines in Quicksand: Courts, Legislatures, and Redistricting.* New York: P. Lang, 2003.

Butler, David, and Bruce Cain. *Congressional Redistricting: Comparative and Theoretical Perspectives.* New York: Macmillan, 1992.

Canon, David T. *Race, Redistricting, and Representation: The Unintended Consequences of Black Majority Districts.* Chicago: University of Chicago Press, 1999.

Congressional Districts in the 2000s: A Portrait of America. Washington, D.C.: CQ Press, 2003.

Cortner, Richard C. *The Apportionment Cases.* Knoxville: University of Tennessee Press, 1970.

Cox, Gary W., and Jonathan N. Katz. *Elbridge Gerry's Salamander: The Electoral Consequences of the Reapportionment Revolution.* New York: Cambridge University Press, 2002.

Cunningham, Maurice T. *Maximization, Whatever the Cost: Race, Redistricting, and the Department of Justice.* Westport, Conn.: Praeger, 2001.

Davidson, Chandler, ed. *Minority Vote Dilution.* Washington, D.C.: Howard University Press, 1984.

Ehrenhalt, Alan. "Reapportionment and Redistricting." In *The American Elections of 1982,* edited by Thomas E. Mann and Norman J. Ornstein. Washington, D.C.: American Enterprise Institute, 1983.

Engstrom, Erik J. "Stacking the States, Stacking the House: The Partisan Consequences of Congressional Redistricting in the 19th Century." *American Political Science Review* 100 (August 2006): 419–427.

Farrand, Max, ed. *The Records of the Federal Convention of 1787.* 4 vols. New Haven, Conn.: Yale University Press, 1966.

Fenno, Richard F. *Congress at the Grassroots: Representational Change in the South, 1970–1998.* Chapel Hill: University of North Carolina Press, 2000.

Galderisi, Peter F., ed. *Redistricting in the New Millennium.* Lanham, Md.: Lexington Books, 2005.

Grofman, Bernard, ed. *Race and Redistricting in the 1990s.* New York: Agathon Press, 1998.

Hacker, Andrew. *Congressional Districting: The Issue of Equal Representation.* Rev. ed. Washington, D.C.: Brookings Institution, 1964.

Hamilton, Alexander, James Madison, and John Jay. *The Federalist Papers with Letters of Brutus.* Introduction by Terence Ball. New York: Cambridge University Press, 2003.

Hamilton, Howard D. *Legislative Apportionment: Key to Power.* New York: Harper and Row, 1964.

Hanson, Royce. *The Political Thicket: Reapportionment and Constitutional Democracy.* Englewood Cliffs, N.J.: Prentice-Hall, 1966.

Herrnson, Paul S. *Congressional Elections: Campaigning at Home and in Washington.* 4th ed. Washington, D.C.: CQ Press, 2004.

Jigsaw Politics: Shaping the House after the 1990 Census. Washington, D.C.: CQ Press, 1990.

Krousser, J. Morgan. *Colorblind Justice: Minority Voting Rights and the Undoing of the Second Reconstruction.* Chapel Hill: University of North Carolina Press, 1999.

Lee, Frances E., and Bruce I. Oppenheimer. *Sizing Up the Senate: The Unequal Consequences of Equal Representation.* Chicago: University of Chicago Press, 1999.

Lublin, David. *The Paradox of Representation: Racial Gerrymandering and Minority Interests in Congress.* Princeton, N.J.: Princeton University Press, 1997.

Luce, Robert. *Legislative Principles.* Boston: Houghton Mifflin, 1930. Reprint. New York: Da Capo Press, 1971.

Mann, Thomas E., and Bruce E. Cain, eds. *Party Lines: Competition, Partisanship, and Congressional Redistricting.* Washington, D.C.: Brookings Institution Press, 2005.

Mayhew, David R. *Electoral Realignments: A Critique of an American Genre.* New Haven, Conn.: Yale University Press, 2002.

McDonald, Michael P., and John Samples, eds. *The Marketplace of Democracy: Electoral Competition and American Politics.* Washington, D.C.: Cato Institute, Brookings Institution Press, 2006.

Overby, L. Marvin, and Kenneth M. Cosgrove. "Unintended Consequences? Racial Redistricting and the Representation of Minority Interests." *Journal of Politics* 58 (May 1996): 540–558.

Pacelle, Richard L., Jr. *Between Law and Politics: The Solicitor General and the Structuring of Race, Gender, and Reproductive Rights Litigation.* College Station: Texas A&M University Press, 2003.

Parker, Frank R. *Black Votes Count: Political Empowerment in Mississippi after 1965.* Chapel Hill: University of North Carolina Press, 1990.

Peacock, Anthony, ed. *Affirmative Action and Representation:* Shaw v. Reno *and the Future of Voting Rights.* Durham, N.C.: Carolina Academic Press, 1997.

Rush, Mark. *Does Redistricting Make a Difference? Partisan Representation and Electoral Behavior.* Lanham, Md.: Lexington Books, 2000.

Scher, Richard K., Jon L. Mills, and John J. Hotaling. *Voting Rights and Democracy: The Law and Politics of Districting.* Chicago: Nelson-Hall, 1997.

Schmeckebier, Laurence F. *Congressional Apportionment.* Washington, D.C.: Brookings Institution, 1941. Reprint. Westport, Conn.: Greenwood Press, 1976.

Schubert, Glendon, ed. *Reapportionment.* New York: Scribner, 1965.

Schwab, Larry M. *The Impact of Congressional Reapportionment and Redistricting.* Lanham, Md.: University Press of America, 1988.

Streb, Matthew J. *Law and Election Politics: The Rules of the Game.* Boulder, Colo.: Lynne Rienner Publishers, 2005.

Swain, Carol M. *Black Faces, Black Interests: The Representation of African Americans in Congress.* Enl. ed. Lanham, Md.: University Press of America, 2006.

Thernstrom, Abigail M. *Whose Votes Count? Affirmative Action and Minority Voting Rights.* Cambridge: Harvard University Press, 1987.

Thompson, Dianne T. *Congressional Redistricting in North Carolina: Reconsidering Traditional Criteria.* New York: LFB Scholarly Publications, 2002.

Yarbrough, Tinsley E. *Race and Redistricting: The Shaw-Cromartie Cases.* Lawrence: University Press of Kansas, 2002.

APPENDIX

Political Party Affiliations in Congress and the Presidency, 1789–2007	143
Election Results, Congress and the Presidency, 1860–2006	146
Women Members of Congress, 1917–2007	148
African American Members of Congress, 1870–2007	151
Hispanic Members of Congress, 1877–2007	153
Congressional Information on the Internet	154
Constitution of the United States	156

POLITICAL PARTY AFFILIATIONS IN CONGRESS AND THE PRESIDENCY, 1789–2007

Affiliations are as of the beginning of the Congress.

		House		Senate		
Year	Congress	Majority party	Principal minority party	Majority party	Principal minority party	President
1789–1791	1st	AD-38	Op-26	AD-17	Op-9	F (Washington)
1791–1793	2nd	F-37	DR-33	F-16	DR-13	F (Washington)
1793–1795	3rd	DR-57	F-48	F-17	DR-13	F (Washington)
1795–1797	4th	F-54	DR-52	F-19	DR-13	F (Washington)
1797–1799	5th	F-58	DR-48	F-20	DR-12	F (J. Adams)
1799–1801	6th	F-64	DR-42	F-19	DR-13	F (J. Adams)
1801–1803	7th	DR-69	F-36	DR-18	F-13	DR (Jefferson)
1803–1805	8th	DR-102	F-39	DR-25	F-9	DR (Jefferson)
1805–1807	9th	DR-116	F-25	DR-27	F-7	DR (Jefferson)
1807–1809	10th	DR-118	F-24	DR-28	F-6	DR (Jefferson)
1809–1811	11th	DR-94	F-48	DR-28	F-6	DR (Madison)
1811–1813	12th	DR-108	F-36	DR-30	F-6	DR (Madison)
1813–1815	13th	DR-112	F-68	DR-27	F-9	DR (Madison)
1815–1817	14th	DR-117	F-65	DR-25	F-11	DR (Madison)
1817–1819	15th	DR-141	F-42	DR-34	F-10	DR (Monroe)
1819–1821	16th	DR-156	F-27	DR-35	F-7	DR (Monroe)
1821–1823	17th	DR-158	F-25	DR-44	F-4	DR (Monroe)
1823–1825	18th	DR-187	F-26	DR-44	F-4	DR (Monroe)
1825–1827	19th	AD-105	J-97	AD-26	J-20	DR (J. Q. Adams)
1827–1829	20th	J-119	AD-94	J-28	AD-20	DR (J. Q. Adams)
1829–1831	21st	D-139	NR-74	D-26	NR-22	DR (Jackson)
1831–1833	22nd	D-141	NR-58	D-25	NR-21	D (Jackson)
1833–1835	23rd	D-147	AM-53	D-20	NR-20	D (Jackson)
1835–1837	24th	D-145	W-98	D-27	W-25	D (Jackson)
1837–1839	25th	D-108	W-107	D-30	W-18	D (Van Buren)
1839–1841	26th	D-124	W-118	D-28	W-22	D (Van Buren)
1841–1843	27th	W-133	D-102	W-28	D-22	W (W. H. Harrison) W (Tyler)
1843–1845	28th	D-142	W-79	W-28	D-25	W (Tyler)
1845–1847	29th	D-143	W-77	D-31	W-25	D (Polk)
1847–1849	30th	W-115	D-108	D-36	W-21	D (Polk)
1849–1851	31st	D-112	W-109	D-35	W-25	W (Taylor) W (Fillmore)
1851–1853	32nd	D-140	W-88	D-35	W-24	W (Fillmore)
1853–1855	33rd	D-159	W-71	D-38	W-22	D (Pierce)
1855–1857	34th	R-108	D-83	D-40	R-15	D (Pierce)
1857–1859	35th	D-118	R-92	D-36	R-20	D (Buchanan)
1859–1861	36th	R-114	D-92	D-36	R-26	D (Buchanan)
1861–1863	37th	R-105	D-43	R-31	D-10	R (Lincoln)
1863–1865	38th	R-102	D-75	R-36	D-9	R (Lincoln)
1865–1867	39th	U-149	D-42	U-42	D-10	R (Lincoln) R (A. Johnson)
1867–1869	40th	R-143	D-49	R-42	D-11	R (A. Johnson)
1869–1871	41st	R-149	D-63	R-56	D-11	R (Grant)
1871–1873	42nd	R-134	D-104	R-52	D-17	R (Grant)
1873–1875	43rd	R-194	D-92	R-49	D-19	R (Grant)
1875–1877	44th	D-169	R-109	R-45	D-29	R (Grant)
1877–1879	45th	D-153	R-140	R-39	D-36	R (Hayes)
1879–1881	46th	D-149	R-130	D-42	R-33	R (Hayes)

Year	Congress	House: Majority party	House: Principal minority party	Senate: Majority party	Senate: Principal minority party	President
1881–1883	47th	R-147	D-135	R-37	D-37	R (Garfield)
						R (Arthur)
1883–1885	48th	D-197	R-118	R-38	D-36	R (Arthur)
1885–1887	49th	D-183	R-140	R-43	D-34	D (Cleveland)
1887–1889	50th	D-169	R-152	R-39	D-37	D (Cleveland)
1889–1891	51st	R-166	D-159	R-39	D-37	R (B. Harrison)
1891–1893	52nd	D-235	R-88	R-47	D-39	R (B. Harrison)
1893–1895	53rd	D-218	R-127	D-44	R-38	D (Cleveland)
1895–1897	54th	R-244	D-105	R-43	D-39	D (Cleveland)
1897–1899	55th	R-204	D-113	R-47	D-34	R (McKinley)
1899–1901	56th	R-185	D-163	R-53	D-26	R (McKinley)
1901–1903	57th	R-197	D-151	R-55	D-31	R (McKinley)
						R (T. Roosevelt)
1903–1905	58th	R-208	D-178	R-57	D-33	R (T. Roosevelt)
1905–1907	59th	R-250	D-136	R-57	D-33	R (T. Roosevelt)
1907–1909	60th	R-222	D-164	R-61	D-31	R (T. Roosevelt)
1909–1911	61st	R-219	D-172	R-61	D-32	R (Taft)
1911–1913	62nd	D-228	R-161	R-51	D-41	R (Taft)
1913–1915	63rd	D-291	R-127	D-51	R-44	D (Wilson)
1915–1917	64th	D-230	R-196	D-56	R-40	D (Wilson)
1917–1919	65th	D-216	R-210	D-53	R-42	D (Wilson)
1919–1921	66th	R-240	D-190	R-49	D-47	D (Wilson)
1921–1923	67th	R-301	D-131	R-59	D-37	R (Harding)
1923–1925	68th	R-225	D-205	R-51	D-43	R (Coolidge)
1925–1927	69th	R-247	D-183	R-56	D-39	R (Coolidge)
1927–1929	70th	R-237	D-195	R-49	D-46	R (Coolidge)
1929–1931	71st	R-267	D-167	R-56	D-39	R (Hoover)
1931–1933	72nd	D-220	R-214	R-48	D-47	R (Hoover)
1933–1935	73rd	D-310	R-117	D-60	R-35	D (F. D. Roosevelt)
1935–1937	74th	D-319	R-103	D-69	R-25	D (F. D. Roosevelt)
1937–1939	75th	D-331	R-89	D-76	R-16	D (F. D. Roosevelt)
1939–1941	76th	D-261	R-164	D-69	R-23	D (F. D. Roosevelt)
1941–1943	77th	D-268	R-162	D-66	R-28	D (F. D. Roosevelt)
1943–1945	78th	D-218	R-208	D-58	R-37	D (F. D. Roosevelt)
1945–1947	79th	D-242	R-190	D-56	R-38	D (F. D. Roosevelt)
	–					D (Truman)
1947–1949	80th	R-245	D-188	R-51	D-45	D (Truman)
1949–1951	81st	D-263	R-171	D-54	R-42	D (Truman)
1951–1953	82nd	D-234	R-199	D-49	R-47	D (Truman)
1953–1955	83rd	R-221	D-211	R-48	D-47	R (Eisenhower)
1955–1957	84th	D-232	R-203	D-48	R-47	R (Eisenhower)
1957–1959	85th	D-233	R-200	D-49	R-47	R (Eisenhower)
1959–1961	86th	D-283	R-153	D-64	R-34	R (Eisenhower)
1961–1963	87th	D-263	R-174	D-65	R-35	D (Kennedy)
1963–1965	88th	D-258	R-177	D-67	R-33	D (Kennedy)
						D (L. B. Johnson)
1965–1967	89th	D-295	R-140	D-68	R-32	D (L. B. Johnson)
1967–1969	90th	D-247	R-187	D-64	R-36	D (L. B. Johnson)
1969–1971	91st	D-243	R-192	D-57	R-43	R (Nixon)
1971–1973	92nd	D-254	R-180	D-54	R-44	R (Nixon)
1973–1975	93rd	D-239	R-192	D-56	R-42	R (Nixon)
						R (Ford)
1975–1977	94th	D-291	R-144	D-60	R-37	R (Ford)
1977–1979	95th	D-292	R-143	D-61	R-38	D (Carter)

		House		Senate		
Year	Congress	Majority party	Principal minority party	Majority party	Principal minority party	President
1979–1981	96th	D-276	R-157	D-58	R-41	D (Carter)
1981–1983	97th	D-243	R-192	R-53	D-46	R (Reagan)
1983–1985	98th	D-269	R-165	R-54	D-46	R (Reagan)
1985–1987	99th	D-252	R-182	R-53	D-47	R (Reagan)
1987–1989	100th	D-258	R-177	D-55	R-45	R (Reagan)
1989–1991	101st	D-259	R-174	D-55	R-45	R (G. H. W. Bush)
1991–1993	102nd	D-267	R-167	D-56	R-44	R (G. H. W. Bush)
1993–1995	103rd	D-258	R-176	D-57	R-43	D (Clinton)
1995–1997	104th	R-230	D-204	R-53	D-47	D (Clinton)
1997–1999	105th	R-227	D-207	R-55	D-45	D (Clinton)
1999–2001	106th	R-222	D-211	R-55	D-45	D (Clinton)
2001–2003	107th	R-221	D-212	R-50	D-50	R (G. W. Bush)
2003–2005	108th	R-229	D-205	R-51	D-48	R (G. W. Bush)
2005–2007	109th	R-232	D-202	R-55	D-44	R (G. W. Bush)
2007–2009	110th	D-233	R-202	D-49	R-49	R (G. W. Bush)

NOTES: Figures are for the beginning of the first session of each Congress. Key to abbreviations: AD—Administration; AM—AntiMasonic; D—Democratic; DR—Democratic-Republican; F—Federalist; J—Jacksonian; NR—National Republican; Op—Opposition; R—Republican; U—Unionist; W—Whig.

SOURCES: U.S. Bureau of the Census, *Historical Statistics of the United States: Colonial Times to 1970* (Washington, D.C.: Government Printing Office, 1975); U.S. Congress, Joint Committee on Printing, *Official Congressional Directory* (Washington, D.C.: Government Printing Office, 1967–); and *CQ Weekly,* selected issues.

ELECTION RESULTS, CONGRESS AND THE PRESIDENCY, 1860–2006

		House					*Senate*					*Presidency*	
		Members elected			*Gains/losses*		*Members elected*			*Gains/losses*		*Popular vote*	
Election year	*Congress*	*Dem.*	*Rep.*	*Misc.*	*Dem.*	*Rep.*	*Dem.*	*Rep.*	*Misc.*	*Dem.*	*Rep.*	*Elected*	*Plurality*
1860	37th	42	106	28	–59	–7	11	31	7	–27	+5	Lincoln (R)	485,706
1862	38th	80	103		+38	–3	12	39		+1	+8		
1864	39th	46	145		–34	+42	10	42		–2	+3	Lincoln (R)	405,581
1866	40th	49	143		+3	–2	11	42		+1	0	A. Johnson (R)	
1868	41st	73	170		+24	+27	11	61		0	+19	Grant (R)	304,906
1870	42nd	104	139		+31	–31	17	57		+6	–4		
1872	43rd	88	203		–16	+64	19	54		+2	–3	Grant (R)	763,474
1874	44th	181	107	3	+93	–96	29	46		+10	–8		
1876	45th	156	137		–25	+30	36	39	1	+7	–7	Hayes (R)	–254,235
1878	46th	150	128	14	–6	–9	43	33		+7	–6		
1880	47th	130	152	11	–20	+24	37	37	2	–6	+4	Garfield (R)	1,898
1882	48th	200	119	6	+70	–33	36	40		–1	+3	Arthur (R)	
1884	49th	182	140	2	–18	+21	34	41		–2	+2	Cleveland (D)	25,685
1886	50th	170	151	4	–12	+11	37	39		+3	–2		
1888	51st	156	173	1	–14	+22	37	47		0	+8	B. Harrison (R)	–90,596
1890	52nd	231	88	14	+75	–85	39	47	2	+2	0		
1892	53rd	220	126	8	–11	+38	44	38	3	+5	–9	Cleveland (D)	372,639
1894	54th	104	246	7	–116	+120	30	44	5	–5	+6		
1896	55th	134	206	16	+30	–40	34	46	10	–5	+2	McKinley (R)	596,985
1898	56th	163	185	9	+29	–21	26	53	11	–8	+7		
1900	57th	153	198	5	–10	+13	29	56	3	+3	+3	McKinley (R)	859,694
1902	58th	178	207		+25	+9	32	58		+3	+2	T. Roosevelt (R)	
1904	59th	136	250		–42	+43	32	58		0	0	T. Roosevelt (R)	2,543,695
1906	60th	164	222		+28	–28	29	61		–3	–3		
1908	61st	172	219		+8	–3	32	59		+3	–2	Taft (R)	1,269,457
1910	62nd	228	162	1	+56	–57	42	49		+10	–10		
1912	63rd	290	127	18	+62	–35	51	44	1	+9	–5	Wilson (D)	2,173,945
1914	64th	231	193	8	–59	+66	56	39	1	+5	–5		
1916	65th	210	216	9	–21	+23	53	42	1	–3	+3	Wilson (D)	579,511
1918	66th	191	237	7	–19	+21	47	48	1	–6	+6		
1920	67th	132	300	1	–59	+63	37	59		–10	+11	Harding (R)	7,020,023
1922	68th	207	225	3	+75	–75	43	51	2	+6	–8	Coolidge (R)	
1924	69th	183	247	5	–24	+22	40	54	1	–3	+3	Coolidge (R)	7,333,217
1926	70th	195	237	3	+12	–10	47	48	1	+7	–6		
1928	71st	167	267	1	–28	+30	39	56	1	–8	+8	Hoover (R)	6,429,579
1930	72nd	220	214	1	+53	–53	47	48	1	+8	–8		
1932	73rd	313	117	5	+97	–101	59	36	1	+12	–12	F. D. Roosevelt (D)	7,068,817
1934	74th	322	103	10	+9	–14	69	25	2	+10	–11		
1936	75th	333	89	13	+11	–14	75	17	4	+6	–8	F. D. Roosevelt (D)	11,073,102
1938	76th	262	169	4	–71	+80	69	23	4	–6	+6		
1940	77th	267	162	6	+5	–7	66	28	2	–3	+5	F. D. Roosevelt (D)	4,964,561
1942	78th	222	209	4	–45	+47	57	38	1	–9	+10		

		House					*Senate*					*Presidency*	
		Members elected			*Gains/losses*		*Members elected*			*Gains/losses*		*Popular vote*	
Election year	*Congress*	*Dem.*	*Rep.*	*Misc.*	*Dem.*	*Rep.*	*Dem.*	*Rep.*	*Misc.*	*Dem.*	*Rep.*	*Elected*	*Plurality*
1944	79th	243	190	2	+21	–19	57	38	1	0	0	F. D. Roosevelt (D)	3,594,993
1946	80th	188	246	1	–55	+56	45	51		–12	+13	Truman (D)	
1948	81st	263	171	1	+75	–75	54	42		+9	–9	Truman (D)	2,188,054
1950	82nd	234	199	2	–29	+28	48	47	1	–6	+5		
1952	83rd	213	221	1	–21	+22	47	48	1	–1	+1	Eisenhower (R)	6,621,242
1954	84th	232	203		+19	–18	48	47	1	+1	–1		
1956	85th	234	201		+2	–2	49	47		+1	0	Eisenhower (R)	9,567,720
1958	86th	283	154		+49	–47	64	34		+17	–13		
1960	87th	263	174		–20	+20	64	36		–2	+2	Kennedy (D)	118,574[a]
1962	88th	258	176	1[b]	–4	+2	67	33		+4	–4		
1964	89th	295	140		+38	–38	68	32		+2	–2	L. B. Johnson (D)	15,951,378
1966	90th	248	187		–47	+47	64	36		–3	+3		
1968	91st	243	192		–4	+4	58	42		–5	+5	Nixon (R)	510,314
1970	92nd	255	180		+12	–12	55	45		–4	+2		
1972	93rd	243	192		–12	+12	57	43		+2	–2	Nixon (R)	17,999,528
1974	94th	291	144		+43	–43	61	38		+3	–3		
1976	95th	292	143		+1	–1	62	38		0	0	Carter (D)	1,682,970
1978	96th	277	158		–11	+11	59	41		–3	+3		
1980	97th	243	192		–33	+33	47	53		–12	+12	Reagan (R)	8,420,270
1982	98th	269	166		+26	–26	46	54		0	0		
1984	99th	253	182		–14	+14	47	53		+2	–2	Reagan (R)	16,877,890
1986	100th	258	177		+5	–5	55	45		+8	–8		
1988	101st	259	174		+2	–2	55	45		+1	–1	G. H. W. Bush (R)	7,077,023
1990	102nd	267	167	1	+9	–8	56	44		+1	–1		
1992	103rd	258	176	1	–9	+9	57	43		+1	–1	Clinton (D)	5,805,444
1994	104th	204	230	1	–52	+52	47	53		–8	+8[c]		
1996	105th	207	227	1	+3	–3	45	55		–2	+2	Clinton (D)	8,203,602
1998	106th	211	223	1	+5	–5	45	55		0	0		
2000	107th	212	221	2	+1	–2	50	50		+4	–4	G. W. Bush (R)	537,179
2002	108th	205	229	1	–6	+6	48	51	1	–1	+1		
2004	109th	202	232	1	–3	+3	44	55	1	–4	+4	G. W. Bush (R)	3,012,171
2006	110th	233	202		+31	–30	49	49	2	+5	–6		

NOTES: The seat totals reflect general election results for the House and Senate. Special elections that shifted party ratios between elections are not noted. a. Includes divided Alabama elector slate votes. b. Vacancy—Rep. Clem Miller, D-Calif., died Oct. 6, 1962, but his name remained on the ballot and he received a plurality. c. Sen. Richard Shelby of Alabama switched from the Democratic to the Republican Party the day after the election, bringing the total Republican gain to nine.

SOURCES: *Guide to U.S. Elections,* 5th ed. (Washington, D.C.: CQ Press, 2005), 1635–1637; and *CQ Weekly,* selected issues.

WOMEN MEMBERS OF CONGRESS, 1917–2007

As of January 2007, a total of 239 women had been elected or appointed to Congress. Of the 236 women who served (2 others were elected to fill vacancies when Congress was not in session and may never have been sworn in, and another resigned her seat the day after she was sworn in), 203 served in the House only, 26 in the Senate only, and 7—Maine Republicans Margaret Chase Smith and Olympia J. Snowe, Maryland Democrat Barbara A. Mikulski, California Democrat Barbara Boxer, Arkansas Democrat Blanche Lincoln, Washington Democrat Maria Cantwell, and Michigan Democrat Debbie Stabenow—in both chambers. Following is a list of the women members, their political affiliations and states, and the years in which they served. In the table, a single year without a dash indicates the person's term began and ended within that year. In addition, Mary E. Farrington, R-Hawaii (1954–1957), Eleanor Holmes Norton, D-D.C. (1991–), and Donna M. C. Christensen, D-V.I. (1997–), served as delegates.

SENATE

Rebecca L. Felton, Ind. D-Ga.[a]	1922
Hattie W. Caraway, D-Ark.	1931–1945
Rose McConnell Long, D-La.	1936–1937
Dixie Bibb Graves, D-Ala.	1937–1938
Gladys Pyle, R-S.D.[b]	1938–1939
Vera C. Bushfield, R-S.D.	1948
Margaret Chase Smith, R-Maine	1949–1973
Hazel H. Abel, R-Neb.	1954
Eva K. Bowring, R-Neb.	1954
Maurine B. Neuberger, D-Ore.	1960–1967
Elaine S. Edwards, D-La.	1972
Maryon Pittman Allen, D-Ala.	1978
Muriel Buck Humphrey, D-Minn.	1978
Nancy Landon Kassebaum, R-Kan.	1978–1997
Paula Hawkins, R-Fla.	1981–1987
Barbara Mikulski, D-Md.	1987–
Jocelyn B. Burdick, D-N.D.	1992
Dianne Feinstein, D-Calif.	1992–
Barbara Boxer, D-Calif.	1993–
Kay Bailey Hutchison, R-Texas	1993–
Carol Moseley-Braun, D-Ill.	1993–1999
Patty L. Murray, D-Wash.	1993–
Olympia J. Snowe, R-Maine	1995–
Sheila Frahm, R-Kan.	1996
Susan Collins, R-Maine	1997–
Mary L. Landrieu, D-La.	1997–
Blanche Lincoln, D-Ark.	1999–
Debbie Stabenow, D-Mich.	2001–
Hillary Rodham Clinton, D-N.Y.	2001–
Maria Cantwell, D-Wash.	2001–
Jean Carnahan, D-Mo.	2001–2002
Lisa Murkowski, R-Alaska	2002–
Elizabeth Dole, R-N.C.	2003–
Amy Klobuchar, D-Minn.	2007–
Claire McCaskill, D-Mo.	2007–

HOUSE

Jeannette Rankin, R-Mont.	1917–1919; 1941–1943
Alice M. Robertson, R-Okla.	1921–1923
Winnifred S. M. Huck, R-Ill.	1922–1923
Mae E. Nolan, R-Calif.	1923–1925
Florence P. Kahn, R-Calif.	1925–1937
Mary T. Norton, D-N.J.	1925–1951
Edith N. Rogers, R-Mass.	1925–1960
Katherine G. Langley, R-Ky.	1927–1931
Ruth H. McCormick, R-Ill.	1929–1931
Pearl P. Oldfield, D-Ark.	1929–1931
Ruth B. Owen, D-Fla.	1929–1933
Ruth S. B. Pratt, R-N.Y.	1929–1933
Effiegene Locke Wingo, D-Ark.	1930–1933
Willa M. B. Eslick, D-Tenn.	1932–1933
Marian W. Clarke, R-N.Y.	1933–1935
Virginia E. Jenckes, D-Ind.	1933–1939
Kathryn O'Loughlin McCarthy, D-Kan.	1933–1935
Isabella S. Greenway, D-Ariz.	1933–1937
Caroline L. G. O'Day, D-N.Y.	1935–1943
Nan W. Honeyman, D-Ore.	1937–1939
Elizabeth H. Gasque, D-S.C.[b]	1938–1939
Clara G. McMillan, D-S.C.	1939–1941
Jessie Sumner, R-Ill.	1939–1947
Frances P. Bolton, R-Ohio	1940–1969
Florence R. Gibbs, D-Ga.	1940–1941
Margaret Chase Smith, R-Maine	1940–1949
Katherine E. Byron, D-Md.	1941–1943
Veronica G. Boland, D-Pa.	1942–1943
Clare Boothe Luce, R-Conn.	1943–1947
Winifred C. Stanley, R-N.Y.	1943–1945
Willa L. Fulmer, D-S.C.	1944–1945
Emily Taft Douglas, D-Ill.	1945–1947
Helen G. Douglas, D-Calif.	1945–1951
Chase G. Woodhouse, D-Conn.	1945–1947; 1949–1951
Helen D. Mankin, D-Ga.	1946–1947
Eliza J. Pratt, D-N.C.	1946–1947
Georgia L. Lusk, D-N.M.	1947–1949
Katharine P. C. St. George, R-N.Y.	1947–1965
Reva Z. B. Bosone, D-Utah	1949–1953
Cecil M. Harden, R-Ind.	1949–1959
Edna F. Kelly, D-N.Y.	1949–1969
Vera D. Buchanan, D-Pa.	1951–1955
Marguerite S. Church, R-Ill.	1951–1963
Maude E. Kee, D-W.Va.	1951–1965
Ruth Thompson, R-Mich.	1951–1957
Gracie B. Pfost, D-Idaho	1953–1963
Leonor K. Sullivan, D-Mo.	1953–1977
Iris F. Blitch, D-Ga.	1955–1963
Edith Starrett Green, D-Ore.	1955–1975
Martha W. Griffiths, D-Mich.	1955–1974
Coya G. Knutson, DFL-Minn.	1955–1959
Kathryn E. Granahan, D-Pa.	1956–1963
Florence P. Dwyer, R-N.J.	1957–1973
Catherine D. May, R-Wash.	1959–1971
Edna O. Simpson, R-Ill.	1959–1961
Jessica McCullough Weis, R-N.Y.	1959–1963

Julia B. Hansen, D-Wash.	1960–1974
Catherine D. Norrell, D-Ark.	1961–1963
Louise G. Reece, R-Tenn.	1961–1963
Corinne B. Riley, D-S.C.	1962–1963
Charlotte T. Reid, R-Ill.	1963–1971
Irene B. Baker, R-Tenn.	1964–1965
Patsy T. Mink, D-Hawaii	1965–1977; 1990–2002
Lera M. Thomas, D-Texas	1966–1967
Margaret M. Heckler, R-Mass.	1967–1983
Shirley A. Chisholm, D-N.Y.	1969–1983
Bella S. Abzug, D-N.Y.	1971–1977
Ella T. Grasso, D-Conn.	1971–1975
Louise Day Hicks, D-Mass.	1971–1973
Elizabeth B. Andrews, D-Ala.	1972–1973
Yvonne B. Burke, D-Calif.	1973–1979
Marjorie Sewell Holt, R-Md.	1973–1987
Elizabeth Holtzman, D-N.Y.	1973–1981
Barbara C. Jordan, D-Texas	1973–1979
Patricia Schroeder, D-Colo.	1973–1997
Corinne "Lindy" Boggs, D-La.	1973–1991
Cardiss R. Collins, D-Ill.	1973–1997
Marilyn Lloyd, D-Tenn.	1975–1995
Millicent Fenwick, R-N.J.	1975–1983
Martha E. Keys, D-Kan.	1975–1979
Helen S. Meyner, D-N.J.	1975–1979
Virginia Smith, R-Neb.	1975–1991
Gladys Noon Spellman, D-Md.	1975–1981
Shirley N. Pettis, R-Calif.	1975–1979
Barbara A. Mikulski, D-Md.	1977–1987
Mary Rose Oakar, D-Ohio	1977–1993
Beverly Byron, D-Md.	1979–1993
Geraldine Ferraro, D-N.Y.	1979–1985
Olympia J. Snowe, R-Maine	1979–1995
Bobbi Fiedler, R-Calif.	1981–1987
Lynn M. Martin, R-Ill.	1981–1991
Marge Roukema, R-N.J.	1981–2003
Claudine Schneider, R-R.I.	1981–1991
Jean Spencer Ashbrook, R-Ohio	1982–1983
Barbara B. Kennelly, D-Conn.	1982–1999
Katie Beatrice Hall, D-Ind.	1982–1985
Sala Burton, D-Calif.	1983–1987
Barbara Boxer, D-Calif.	1983–1993
Nancy L. Johnson, R-Conn.	1983–2007
Marcy Kaptur, D-Ohio	1983–
Barbara Farrell Vucanovich, R-Nev.	1983–1997
Helen Delich Bentley, R-Md.	1985–1995
Jan Meyers, R-Kan.	1985–1997
Cathy Long, D-La.	1985–1987
Constance A. Morella, R-Md.	1987–2003
Elizabeth J. Patterson, D-S.C.	1987–1993
Patricia Saiki, R-Hawaii	1987–1991
Louise M. Slaughter, D-N.Y.	1987–
Nancy Pelosi, D-Calif.	1987–
Nita M. Lowey, D-N.Y.	1989–
Jolene Unsoeld, D-Wash.	1989–1995
Jill L. Long, D-Ind.	1989–1995
Ileana Ros-Lehtinen, R-Fla.	1989–
Susan Molinari, R-N.Y.	1990–1997
Barbara-Rose Collins, D-Mich.	1991–1997
Rosa DeLauro, D-Conn.	1991–
Joan Kelly Horn, D-Mo.	1991–1993
Maxine Waters, D-Calif.	1991–
Eva M. Clayton, D-N.C.	1992–2003
Corrine Brown, D-Fla.	1993–
Leslie L. Byrne, D-Va.	1993–1995
Maria Cantwell, D-Wash.	1993–1995
Pat Danner, D-Mo.	1993–2001
Jennifer B. Dunn, R-Wash.	1993–2005
Karan English, D-Ariz.	1993–1995
Anna G. Eshoo, D-Calif.	1993–
Tillie Fowler, R-Fla.	1993–2001
Elizabeth Furse, D-Ore.	1993–1999
Jane F. Harman, D-Calif.	1993–1999; 2001–
Eddie Bernice Johnson, D-Texas	1993–
Blanche Lincoln, D-Ark.	1993–1997
Carolyn B. Maloney, D-N.Y.	1993–
Cynthia Ann McKinney, D-Ga.	1993–2003; 2005–2007
Carrie P. Meek, D-Fla.	1993–2003
Marjorie Margolies-Mezvinsky, D-Pa.	1993–1995
Deborah Pryce, R-Ohio	1993–
Lucille Roybal-Allard, D-Calif.	1993–
Lynn Schenk, D-Calif.	1993–1995
Karen Shepherd, D-Utah	1993–1995
Karen L. Thurman, D-Fla.	1993–2003
Nydia M. Velázquez, D-N.Y.	1993–
Lynn Woolsey, D-Calif.	1993–
Helen Chenoweth-Hage, R-Idaho	1995–2001
Barbara Cubin, R-Wyo.	1995–
Sheila Jackson-Lee, D-Texas	1995–
Sue W. Kelly, R-N.Y.	1995–2007
Zoe Lofgren, D-Calif.	1995–
Karen McCarthy, D-Mo.	1995–2005
Sue Myrick, R-N.C.	1995–
Lynn N. Rivers, D-Mich.	1995–2003
Andrea Seastrand, R-Calif.	1995–1997
Linda Smith, R-Wash.	1995–1999
Enid Greene Waldholtz, R-Utah	1995–1997
Juanita Millender-McDonald, D-Calif.	1996–2007
Jo Ann Emerson, R-Mo.	1996–
Julia Carson, D-Ind.	1997–
Diana DeGette, D-Colo.	1997–
Kay Granger, R-Texas	1997–
Darlene Hooley, D-Ore.	1997–
Carolyn Cheeks Kilpatrick, D-Mich.	1997–
Carolyn McCarthy, D-N.Y.	1997–
Anne M. Northup, R-Ky.	1997–2007
Loretta Sanchez, D-Calif.	1997–
Debbie Stabenow, D-Mich.	1997–2001
Ellen O. Tauscher, D-Calif.	1997–
Mary Bono, R-Calif.	1998–
Lois Capps, D-Calif.	1998–
Barbara Lee, D-Calif.	1998–
Heather A. Wilson, R-N.M.	1998–
Tammy Baldwin, D-Wis.	1999–
Shelley Berkley, D-Nev.	1999–
Judy Biggert, R-Ill.	1999–
Stephanie Tubbs Jones, D-Ohio	1999–
Grace F. Napolitano, D-Calif.	1999–
Jan Schakowsky, D-Ill.	1999–
Jo Ann Davis, R-Va.	2001–

Shelley Moore Capito, R-W.Va.	2001–	Melissa Bean, D-Ill.	2005–
Susan A. Davis, D-Calif.	2001–	Jean Schmidt, R-Ohio	2005–
Betty McCollum, D-Minn.	2001–	Cathy McMorris, R-Wash.	2005–
Hilda L. Solis, D-Calif.	2001–	Gwen Moore, D-Wis.	2005–
Diane Watson, D-Calif.	2001–	Allyson Y. Schwartz, D-Pa.	2005–
Melissa A. Hart, R-Pa.	2001–2007	Debbie Wasserman-Schultz, D-Fla.	2005–
Marsha Blackburn, R-Tenn.	2003–	Shelley Sekula Gibbs, R-Texas	2006–2007
Ginny Brown-Waite, R-Fla.	2003–	Nancy E. Boyda, D-Kan.	2007–
Candice S. Miller, R-Mich.	2003–	Kathy Castor, D-Fla.	2007–
Marilyn Musgrave, R-Colo.	2003–	Yvette D. Clarke, D-N.Y.	2007–
Linda T. Sanchez, D-Calif.	2003–	Gabrielle Giffords, D-Ariz.	2007–
Denise L. Majette, D-Ga.	2003–2005	Mary Fallin, R-Okla.	2007–
Katherine Harris, R-Fla.	2003–2007	Michelle Marie Bachmann, R-Minn.	2007–
Stephanie Herseth, D-S.D.	2004–	Kirsten E. Gillibrand, D-N.Y.	2007–
Thelma Drake, R-W.Va.	2005–	Mazie K. Hirono, D-Hawaii	2007–
Virginia Foxx, R-N.C.	2005–	Carol Shea-Porter, D-N.H.	2007–
Doris Matsui, D-Calif.	2005–	Betty Sue Sutton, D-Ohio	2007–

NOTES: a. Rebecca L. Felton was sworn in Nov. 21, 1922, to fill the vacancy created by the death of Thomas E. Watson, D. The next day she gave up her seat to Walter F. George, D, the elected candidate for the vacancy. b. *The Biographical Directory of the United States Congress* documents that Gladys Pyle was elected Nov. 8, 1938, to fill a vacancy caused by a death and served from Nov. 9, 1938, until Jan. 3, 1939. However, because Congress was not in session between the election and the expiration of term on Jan. 3, other sources indicate that she was never sworn in. The *Directory* lists Elizabeth H. Gasque as elected to fill a vacancy but does not indicate that she served.

SOURCES: Commission on the Bicentenary of the U.S. House of Representatives, *Women in Congress, 1917–1990* (Washington, D.C.: Government Printing Office, 1991); *Biographical Directory of the American Congress, 1774–1996* (Alexandria, Va.: CQ Staff Directories, 1997); *CQ Weekly,* selected issues; "Biographical Directory of the United States Congress," http://bioguide.congress.gov/biosearch/biosearch.asp; and U.S. Senate, http://www.senate.gov/artandhistory/history/common/briefing/women_senators.htm.

AFRICAN AMERICAN MEMBERS OF CONGRESS, 1870–2007

As of January 2007, 115 African Americans had served in Congress; 5 in the Senate and 110 in the House. Following is a list of the African American members, their political affiliations and states, and the years in which they served. In addition, John W. Menard, R-La., won a disputed election in 1868 but was not permitted to take his seat in Congress. In addition to those listed below, Walter E. Fauntroy, D-D.C. (1971–1991), Melvin Evans, R-V.I. (1979–1981), Eleanor Holmes Norton, D-D.C. (1991–), Victor O. Frazer, I-V.I. (1995–1997), and Donna M. C. Christensen, D-V.I. (1997–), served as delegates.

SENATE

Hiram R. Revels, R-Miss.	1870–1871
Blanche K. Bruce, R-Miss.	1875–1881
Edward W. Brooke III, R-Mass.	1967–1979
Carol Moseley-Braun, D-Ill.	1993–1999
Barack Obama, D-Ill.	2005–

HOUSE

Joseph H. Rainey, R-S.C.	1870–1879
Jefferson F. Long, R-Ga.	1870–1871
Robert C. De Large, R-S.C.	1871–1873
Robert B. Elliott, R-S.C.	1871–1874
Benjamin S. Turner, R-Ala.	1871–1873
Josiah T. Walls, R-Fla.	1871–1876
Richard H. Cain, R-S.C.	1873–1875; 1877–1879
John R. Lynch, R-Miss.	1873–1877; 1882–1883
Alonzo J. Ransier, R-S.C.	1873–1875
James T. Rapier, R-Ala.	1873–1875
Jeremiah Haralson, R-Ala.	1875–1877
John A. Hyman, R-N.C.	1875–1877
Charles E. Nash, R-La.	1875–1877
Robert Smalls, R-S.C.	1875–1879; 1882–1883; 1884–1887
James E. O'Hara, R-N.C.	1883–1887
Henry P. Cheatham, R-N.C.	1889–1893
John M. Langston, R-Va.	1890–1891
Thomas E. Miller, R-S.C.	1890–1891
George W. Murray, R-S.C.	1893–1895; 1896–1897
George H. White, R-N.C.	1897–1901
Oscar S. De Priest, R-Ill.	1929–1935
Arthur W. Mitchell, D-Ill.	1935–1943
William L. Dawson, D-Ill.	1943–1970
Adam Clayton Powell Jr., D-N.Y.	1945–1967; 1969–1971
Charles C. Diggs Jr., D-Mich.	1955–1980
Robert N. C. Nix, D-Pa.	1958–1979
Augustus F. Hawkins, D-Calif.	1963–1991
John Conyers Jr., D-Mich.	1965–
Shirley A. Chisholm, D-N.Y.	1969–1983
William L. Clay, D-Mo.	1969–2001
Louis Stokes, D-Ohio	1969–1999
George W. Collins, D-Ill.	1970–1972
Ronald V. Dellums, D-Calif.	1971–1998
Ralph H. Metcalfe, D-Ill.	1971–1978
Parren J. Mitchell, D-Md.	1971–1987
Charles B. Rangel, D-N.Y.	1971–
Yvonne B. Burke, D-Calif.	1973–1979
Cardiss Collins, D-Ill.	1973–1997
Barbara C. Jordan, D-Texas	1973–1979
Andrew J. Young Jr., D-Ga.	1973–1977
Harold E. Ford, D-Tenn.	1975–1997
Julian C. Dixon, D-Calif.	1979–2000
William H. Gray III, D-Pa.	1979–1991
George T. Leland, D-Texas	1979–1989
Bennett McVey Stewart, D-Ill.	1979–1981
George W. Crockett Jr., D-Mich.	1980–1991
Mervyn M. Dymally, D-Calif.	1981–1993
Gus Savage, D-Ill.	1981–1993
Harold Washington, D-Ill.	1981–1993
Katie B. Hall, D-Ind.	1982–1985
Charles A. Hayes, D-Ill.	1983–1993
Major R. Owens, D-N.Y.	1983–2007
Edolphus Towns, D-N.Y.	1983–
Alan D. Wheat, D-Mo.	1983–1995
Alton R. Waldon Jr., D-N.Y.	1986–1987
Mike Espy, D-Miss.	1987–1993
Floyd H. Flake, D-N.Y.	1987–1997
John Lewis, D-Ga.	1987–
Kweisi Mfume, D-Md.	1987–1996
Donald M. Payne, D-N.J.	1989–
Craig A. Washington, D-Texas	1990–1995
Barbara-Rose Collins, D-Mich.	1991–1997
Gary A. Franks, R-Conn.	1991–1997
William J. Jefferson, D-La.	1991–
Maxine Waters, D-Calif.	1991–
Lucien E. Blackwell, D-Pa	1991–1995
Eva Clayton, D-N.C.	1992–2003
Sanford D. Bishop Jr., D-Ga.	1993–
Corrine Brown, D-Fla.	1993–
James E. Clyburn, D-S.C.	1993–
Cleo Fields, D-La.	1993–1997
Alcee L. Hastings, D-Fla.	1993–
Earl F. Hilliard, D-Ala.	1993–2003
Eddie Bernice Johnson, D-Texas	1993–
Cynthia McKinney, D-Ga.	1993–2003; 2005–2007
Carrie P. Meek, D-Fla.	1993–2003
Melvin J. Reynolds, D-Ill.	1993–1995
Bobby L. Rush, D-Ill.	1993–
Robert C. Scott, D-Va.	1993–
Bennie Thompson, D-Miss.	1993–
Walter R. Tucker III, D-Calif.	1993–1995
Melvin Watt, D-N.C.	1993–
Albert R. Wynn, D-Md.	1993–
Chaka Fattah, D-Pa.	1995–
Jesse L. Jackson Jr., D-Ill.	1995–
Sheila Jackson-Lee, D-Texas	1995–
J. C. Watts Jr., R-Okla.	1995–2003
Elijah E. Cummings, D-Md.	1996–
Juanita Millender-McDonald, D-Calif.	1996–2007
Julia Carson, D-Ind.	1997–
Danny K. Davis, D-Ill.	1997–

Harold E. Ford Jr., D-Tenn.	1997–
Carolyn Cheeks Kilpatrick, D-Mich.	1997–
Barbara Lee, D-Calif.	1998–
Gregory W. Meeks, D-N.Y.	1998–
Stephanie Tubbs Jones, D-Ohio	1999–
William Lacy Clay, D-Mo.	2001–
Diane Watson, D-Calif.	2001–
Artur Davis, D-Ala.	2003–
Kendrick B. Meek, D-Fla.	2003–
David Scott, D-Ga.	2003–
Frank W. Ballance Jr., D-N.C.	2003–2004
Denise L. Majette, D-Ga.	2003–2005
G. K. Butterfield Jr., D-N.C.	2004–
Emanuel Cleaver II, D-Mo.	2005–
Al Green, D-Texas	2005–
Gwen Moore, D-Wis.	2005–
Yvette D. Clarke, D-N.Y.	2007–
Keith Ellison, D-Minn.	2007–
Hank Johnson, D-Ga.	2007–

SOURCES: Maurine Christopher, *America's Black Congressmen* (Crowell, 1971); *Biographical Directory of the American Congress, 1774–1996* (Alexandria, Va.: CQ Staff Directories, 1997); and *CQ Weekly,* selected issues.

HISPANIC MEMBERS OF CONGRESS, 1877–2007

As of January 2007, forty-eight Hispanics had served in Congress. Of those members, forty-two served in the House only, three in the Senate only, and three—Dennis Chavez, Joseph M. Montoya, and Robert Menendez—in both chambers. Following is a list of the Hispanic members, their political affiliations and states, and the years in which they served. Not included are Hispanics who served as territorial delegates, resident commissioners of Puerto Rico, or delegates of Guam or the Virgin Islands.

SENATE

Octaviano Larrazolo	1928–1929
Dennis Chavez, D-N.M.	1935–1962
Joseph M. Montoya, D-N.M.	1964–1977
Mel Martinez, R-Fla.	2005–
Ken Salazar, D-Colo.	2005–
Robert Menendez, D-N.J.	1993–2006

HOUSE

Romualdo Pacheco, R-Calif.	1877–1878; 1879–1883
Ladislas Lazaro, D-La.	1913–1927
Benigno Cardenas Hernandez, R-N.M.	1915–1917; 1919–1921
Nestor Montoya, R-N.M.	1921–1923
Dennis Chavez, D-N.M.	1931–1935
Joachim Octave Fernandez, D-La.	1931–1941
Antonio Manuel Fernandez, D-N.M.	1943–1956
Joseph M. Montoya, D-N.M.	1957–1964
Henry B. Gonzalez, D-Texas	1961–1999
Edward R. Roybal, D-Calif.	1963–1993
E. "Kika" de la Garza II, D-Texas	1965–1997
Manuel Lujan Jr., R-N.M.	1969–1989
Herman Badillo, D-N.Y.	1971–1977
Robert Garcia, D-N.Y.	1978–1990
Anthony Lee Coelho, D-Calif.	1979–1989
Matthew G. Martinez, D-Calif.	1982–2001
Solomon P. Ortiz, D-Texas	1983–
William B. Richardson, D-N.M.	1983–1997
Esteban E. Torres, D-Calif.	1983–1999
Albert G. Bustamante, D-Texas	1985–1993
Ileana Ros-Lehtinen, R-Fla.	1989–
José E. Serrano, D-N.Y.	1990–
Ed Pastor, D-Ariz.	1991–
Xavier Becerra, D-Calif.	1993–
Henry Bonilla, R-Texas	1993–2007
Lincoln Diaz-Balart, R-Fla.	1993–
Luis V. Gutierrez, D-Ill.	1993–
Robert Menendez, D-N.J.	1993–2006; 2007–
Lucille Roybal-Allard, D-Calif.	1993–
Frank Tejeda, D-Texas	1993–1997
Nydia M. Velázquez, D-N.Y.	1993–
Rubén Hinojosa, D-Texas	1997–
Silvestre Reyes, D-Texas	1997–
Ciro D. Rodriguez, D-Texas	1997–2005; 2007–
Loretta Sanchez, D-Calif.	1997–
Joe Baca, D-Calif.	1999–
Charlie Gonzalez, D-Texas	1999–
Grace F. Napolitano, D-Calif.	1999–
Hilda L. Solis, D-Calif.	2001–
Mario Diaz-Balart, D-Fla.	2003–
Raúl M. Grijalva, D-Ariz.	2003–
Linda T. Sanchez, D-Calif.	2003–
John Salazar, D-Colo.	2005–
Henry Cuellar, D-Texas	2005–
Albio Sires, D-N.J.	2006–

SOURCES: *Biographical Directory of the American Congress, 1774–1996* (Alexandria, Va.: CQ Staff Directories, 1997); Congressional Hispanic Caucus; and *CQ Weekly,* selected issues.

CONGRESSIONAL INFORMATION ON THE INTERNET

A huge array of congressional information is available for free at Internet sites operated by the federal government, colleges and universities, and commercial firms. The sites offer the full text of bills introduced in the House and Senate, voting records, campaign finance information, transcripts of selected congressional hearings, investigative reports, and much more.

THOMAS

The most important site for congressional information is THOMAS *(http://thomas.loc.gov)*, which is named for Thomas Jefferson and operated by the Library of Congress. THOMAS's highlight is its databases containing the full text of all bills introduced in Congress since 1989 (101st Congress), the full text of the *Congressional Record* since 1989, and the status and summary information for all bills introduced since 1973 (93rd Congress).

THOMAS also offers special links to bills that have received or are expected to receive floor action during the current week and newsworthy bills that are pending or that have recently been approved. Finally, THOMAS has selected committee reports, answers to frequently asked questions about accessing congressional information, publications titled *How Our Laws Are Made* and *Enactment of a Law*, and links to many other congressional Web sites.

HOUSE OF REPRESENTATIVES

The U.S. House of Representatives site *(http://www.house.gov)* offers the schedule of bills, resolutions, and other legislative issues the House is to consider in the current week. It also has updates about current proceedings on the House floor and a list of the next day's meeting of House committees. Other highlights include a database that helps users identify their representative, a directory of House members and committees, the House ethics manual, links to Web pages maintained by House members and committees, a calendar of congressional primary dates and candidate-filing deadlines for ballot access, the full text of all amendments to the U.S. Constitution that have been ratified and those that have been proposed but not ratified, and information about Washington, D.C., for visitors.

Another key House site is the Office of the Clerk On-line Information Center *(http://clerk.house.gov)*, which has records of all roll-call votes taken since 1990 (101st Congress). The votes are recorded by bill. The site also has lists of committee assignments, a telephone directory for members and committees, mailing label templates for members and committees, rules of the current Congress, election statistics from 1920 to the present, biographies of Speakers of the House, biographies of women who have served since 1917, information on public disclosure, and a virtual tour of the House chamber.

The site operated by the House Committee on Rules *(http://www.rules.house.gov)* has posted dozens of Congressional Research Service reports about the legislative process. Some of the available titles include *Legislative Research in Congressional Offices: A Primer; Hearings in the House of Representatives: A Guide for Preparation and Conduct; How Measures Are Brought to the House Floor: A Brief Introduction; House and Senate Rules of Procedure: A Comparison;* and *Presidential Vetoes 1789–1996: A Summary Overview*

The office of the Law Revision Counsel operates a site *(http://uscode.house.gov)* that has a searchable version of the U.S. Code, which contains the text of public laws enacted by Congress, and a tutorial for searching the Code.

SENATE

The Senate is not as active in the Internet world as the House. Its main Web site *(http://www.senate.gov)* has records of all roll-call votes taken since 1989 (101st Congress, arranged by bill), brief descriptions of all bills and joint resolutions introduced in the Senate during the past week, and a calendar of upcoming committee hearings. The site also provides the standing rules of the Senate, a directory of senators and their committee assignments, lists of nominations that the president has submitted to the Senate for approval, links to Web pages operated by senators and committees, information on the history and art of the Senate, and a virtual tour of the Senate.

GENERAL REFERENCE

Information about the membership, jurisdiction, and rules of each congressional committee is available at the U.S. Government Printing Office site *(http://www.gpoaccess.gov/congress/index.html)*. It also has transcripts of selected congressional hearings, the full text of selected House and Senate reports, and the House and Senate rules manuals.

The U.S. Government Accountability Office (GAO, which changed its name in 2004 from General Accounting Office), the investigative arm of Congress, operates a site *(http://www.gao.gov)* that provides the full text of its reports from October 1995 to the present. The reports cover a wide range of topics: aviation safety, combating terrorism, counternarcotics efforts in Mexico, defense contracting, electronic warfare, food assistance programs, hurricane preparedness, health insurance, illegal aliens, information technology, long-term care, mass transit, Medicare, military readiness, money laundering, national parks, nuclear waste, organ donation, student loan defaults, and prescription drugs, among others.

GAO e-mail updates are excellent current awareness tools. Electronic mailing lists distribute daily and monthly lists of reports and testimony released by the GAO. Subscriptions are available by filling out a form and identifying topic interests at *http://www.gao.gov/subtest/subscribe.php*.

Current budget and economic projections are provided at the Congressional Budget Office (CBO) Web site *(http://www.cbo.gov)*. The site also has reports about the economic and budget outlook for the next decade, the president's budget proposals, federal civilian employment, Social Security privatization, cost analyses of war operations, tax reform, water use conflicts in the west, marriage and the federal income tax, and the role of foreign aid in development, among other topics. Additional highlights include monthly budget updates, historical budget data, cost estimates for bills reported by congressional committees, and transcripts of congressional testimony by CBO officials.

The congressional Office of Technology Assessment (OTA) was eliminated in 1995, but every report it ever issued is available at The OTA Legacy *(http://www.wws.princeton.edu:80/~ota)*, a site operated by the Woodrow Wilson School of Public and International Affairs at Princeton University. The site has more than 100,000 pages of detailed reports about aging, agricultural technology, arms control, biological research, cancer, computer security, defense technology, economic development, education, environmental protection, health and health technology, information technology, space, transportation, and many other subjects. The reports are organized in alphabetical, chronological, and topical lists.

CAMPAIGN FINANCE

Several Internet sites provide detailed campaign finance data for congressional elections. The official site is operated by the Federal Election Commission (FEC, *http://www.fec.gov)*, which regulates political spending. The site's highlight is its database of campaign reports filed from May 1996 to the present by House and presidential candidates, political action committees, and political party committees. Senate reports are not included because they are filed with the secretary of the Senate. The reports in the FEC's database are scanned images of paper reports filed with the commission.

The FEC site also has summary financial data for House and Senate candidates in the current election cycle, abstracts of court decisions pertaining to federal election law from 1976 to 2007, and a directory of national and state agencies that are responsible for releasing information about campaign financing, candidates on the ballot, election results, lobbying, and other issues. Another useful feature is a collection of brochures about federal election law, public funding of presidential elections, the ban on contributions by foreign nationals, independent expenditures supporting or opposing a candidate for federal office, contribution limits, filing a complaint, researching public records at the FEC, and other topics. Finally, the site provides the FEC's legislative recommendations, its annual report, a report about its first thirty years in existence, the FEC's monthly newsletter, several reports about voter registration, election results for the most recent presidential and congressional elections, and campaign guides for corporations and labor organizations, congressional candidates and committees, political party committees, and nonconnected committees.

Another online source for campaign finance data is CQ Money Line (*http://moneyline.cq.com,* formerly politicalmoneyline.com and FECinfo.com) from Congressional Quarterly. Its searchable databases provide extensive itemized information about receipts and expenditures by federal candidates and political action committees from 1980 to the present. The detailed data are obtained from the FEC. For example, candidates contributions can be searched by Zip code. The site also has data on soft-money contributions, lists of the top political action committees in various categories, lists of the top contributors from each state, and much more.

More campaign finance data are available from the Center for Responsive Politics *(http://www.opensecrets.org)*, a public interest organization. The center provides a list of all soft-money donations to political parties of $100,000 or more in the current election cycle and data about leadership political action committees associated with individual politicians. Other databases at the site provide information about travel expenses that House members received from private sources for attending meetings and other events, activities of registered federal lobbyists, and activities of foreign agents who are registered in the United States.

CONSTITUTION OF THE UNITED STATES

The United States Constitution was written at a convention that Congress called on February 21, 1787, for the purpose of recommending amendments to the Articles of Confederation. Every state but Rhode Island sent delegates to Philadelphia, where the convention met that summer. The delegates decided to write an entirely new constitution, completing their labors on September 17. Nine states (the number the Constitution itself stipulated as sufficient) ratified by June 21, 1788.

We the People of the United States, in Order to form a more perfect Union, establish Justice, insure domestic Tranquility, provide for the common defence, promote the general Welfare, and secure the Blessings of Liberty to ourselves and our Posterity, do ordain and establish this Constitution for the United States of America.

ARTICLE I

Section 1. All legislative Powers herein granted shall be vested in a Congress of the United States, which shall consist of a Senate and House of Representatives.

Section 2. The House of Representatives shall be composed of Members chosen every second Year by the People of the several States, and the Electors in each State shall have the Qualifications requisite for Electors of the most numerous Branch of the State Legislature.

No Person shall be a Representative who shall not have attained to the age of twenty five Years, and been seven Years a Citizen of the United States, and who shall not, when elected, be an Inhabitant of that State in which he shall be chosen.

[Representatives and direct Taxes shall be apportioned among the several States which may be included within this Union, according to their respective Numbers, which shall be determined by adding to the whole Number of free Persons, including those bound to Service for a Term of Years, and excluding Indians not taxed, three fifths of all other Persons.][1] The actual Enumeration shall be made within three Years after the first Meeting of the Congress of the United States, and within every subsequent Term of ten Years, in such Manner as they shall by Law direct. The Number of Representatives shall not exceed one for every thirty Thousand, but each State shall have at Least one Representative; and until such enumeration shall be made, the State of New Hampshire shall be entitled to chuse three, Massachusetts eight, Rhode-Island and Providence Plantations one, Connecticut five, New-York six, New Jersey four, Pennsylvania eight, Delaware one, Maryland six, Virginia ten, North Carolina five, South Carolina five, and Georgia three.

When vacancies happen in the Representation from any State, the Executive Authority thereof shall issue Writs of Election to fill such Vacancies.

The House of Representatives shall chuse their Speaker and other Officers; and shall have the sole Power of Impeachment.

Section 3. The Senate of the United States shall be composed of two Senators from each State, [chosen by the Legislature thereof,][2] for six Years; and each Senator shall have one Vote.

Immediately after they shall be assembled in Consequence of the first Election, they shall be divided as equally as may be into three Classes. The Seats of the Senators of the first Class shall be vacated at the Expiration of the second Year, of the second Class at the Expiration of the fourth Year, and of the third Class at the Expiration of the sixth Year, so that one third may be chosen every second Year; [and if Vacancies happen by Resignation, or otherwise, during the Recess of the Legislature of any State, the Executive thereof may make temporary Appointments until the next Meeting of the Legislature, which shall then fill such Vacancies.][3]

No Person shall be a Senator who shall not have attained to the Age of thirty Years, and been nine Years a Citizen of the United States, and who shall not, when elected, be an Inhabitant of that State for which he shall be chosen.

The Vice President of the United States shall be President of the Senate, but shall have no Vote, unless they be equally divided.

The Senate shall chuse their other Officers, and also a President pro tempore, in the Absence of the Vice President, or when he shall exercise the Office of President of the United States.

The Senate shall have the sole Power to try all Impeachments. When sitting for that Purpose, they shall be on Oath or Affirmation. When the President of the United States is tried, the Chief Justice shall preside: And no Person shall be convicted without the Concurrence of two thirds of the Members present.

Judgment in Cases of Impeachment shall not extend further than to removal from Office, and disqualification to hold and enjoy any Office of honor, Trust or Profit under the United States: but the Party convicted shall nevertheless be liable and subject to Indictment, Trial, Judgment and Punishment, according to Law.

Section 4. The Times, Places and Manner of holding Elections for Senators and Representatives, shall be prescribed in each State by the Legislature thereof; but the Congress may at any time by Law make or alter such Regulations, except as to the Places of chusing Senators.

The Congress shall assemble at least once in every Year, and such Meeting shall [be on the first Monday in December],[4] unless they shall by Law appoint a different Day.

Section 5. Each House shall be the Judge of the Elections, Returns and Qualifications of its own Members, and a Majority of each shall constitute a Quorum to do Business; but a smaller Number may adjourn from day to day, and may be authorized to compel the Attendance of absent Members, in such Manner, and under such Penalties as each House may provide.

Each House may determine the Rules of its Proceedings, punish its Members for disorderly Behaviour, and, with the Concurrence of two thirds, expel a Member.

Each House shall keep a Journal of its Proceedings, and from time to time publish the same, excepting such Parts as may in their Judgment require Secrecy; and the Yeas and Nays of the Members of either House on any question shall, at the Desire of one fifth of those Present, be entered on the Journal.

Neither House, during the Session of Congress, shall, without the Consent of the other, adjourn for more than three days, nor to any other Place than that in which the two Houses shall be sitting.

Section 6. The Senators and Representatives shall receive a Compensation for their Services, to be ascertained by Law, and paid out of the Treasury of the United States. They shall in all

Cases, except Treason, Felony and Breach of the Peace, be privileged from Arrest during their Attendance at the Session of their respective Houses, and in going to and returning from the same; and for any Speech or Debate in either House, they shall not be questioned in any other Place.

No Senator or Representative shall, during the Time for which he was elected, be appointed to any civil Office under the Authority of the United States, which shall have been created, or the Emoluments whereof shall have been encreased during such time; and no Person holding any Office under the United States, shall be a Member of either House during his Continuance in Office.

Section 7. All Bills for raising Revenue shall originate in the House of Representatives; but the Senate may propose or concur with Amendments as on other Bills.

Every Bill which shall have passed the House of Representatives and the Senate, shall, before it become a Law, be presented to the President of the United States; If he approve he shall sign it, but if not he shall return it, with his Objections to that House in which it shall have originated, who shall enter the Objections at large on their Journal, and proceed to reconsider it. If after such Reconsideration two thirds of that House shall agree to pass the Bill, it shall be sent, together with the Objections, to the other House, by which it shall likewise be reconsidered, and if approved by two thirds of that House, it shall become a Law. But in all such Cases the Votes of both Houses shall be determined by yeas and Nays, and the Names of the Persons voting for and against the Bill shall be entered on the Journal of each House respectively. If any Bill shall not be returned by the President within ten Days (Sundays excepted) after it shall have been presented to him, the Same shall be a Law, in like Manner as if he had signed it, unless the Congress by their Adjournment prevent its Return, in which Case it shall not be a Law.

Every Order, Resolution, or Vote to which the Concurrence of the Senate and House of Representatives may be necessary (except on a question of Adjournment) shall be presented to the President of the United States; and before the Same shall take Effect, shall be approved by him, or being disapproved by him, shall be repassed by two thirds of the Senate and House of Representatives, according to the Rules and Limitations prescribed in the Case of a Bill.

Section 8. The Congress shall have Power To lay and collect Taxes, Duties, Imposts and Excises, to pay the Debts and provide for the common Defence and general Welfare of the United States; but all Duties, Imposts and Excises shall be uniform throughout the United States;

To borrow Money on the credit of the United States;

To regulate Commerce with foreign Nations, and among the several States, and with the Indian Tribes;

To establish an uniform Rule of Naturalization, and uniform Laws on the subject of Bankruptcies throughout the United States;

To coin Money, regulate the Value thereof, and of foreign Coin, and fix the Standard of Weights and Measures;

To provide for the Punishment of counterfeiting the Securities and current Coin of the United States;

To establish Post Offices and post Roads;

To promote the Progress of Science and useful Arts, by securing for limited Times to Authors and Inventors the exclusive Right to their respective Writings and Discoveries;

To constitute Tribunals inferior to the supreme Court;

To define and punish Piracies and Felonies committed on the high Seas, and Offences against the Law of Nations;

To declare War, grant Letters of Marque and Reprisal, and make Rules concerning Captures on Land and Water;

To raise and support Armies, but no Appropriation of Money to that Use shall be for a longer Term than two Years;

To provide and maintain a Navy;

To make Rules for the Government and Regulation of the land and naval Forces;

To provide for calling forth the Militia to execute the Laws of the Union, suppress Insurrections and repel Invasions;

To provide for organizing, arming, and disciplining, the Militia, and for governing such Part of them as may be employed in the Service of the United States, reserving to the States respectively, the Appointment of the Officers, and the Authority of training the Militia according to the discipline prescribed by Congress;

To exercise exclusive Legislation in all Cases whatsoever, over such District (not exceeding ten Miles square) as may, by Cession of particular States, and the Acceptance of Congress, become the Seat of the Government of the United States, and to exercise like Authority over all Places purchased by the Consent of the Legislature of the State in which the Same shall be, for the Erection of Forts, Magazines, Arsenals, dock-Yards, and other needful Buildings;—And

To make all Laws which shall be necessary and proper for carrying into Execution the foregoing Powers, and all other Powers vested by this Constitution in the Government of the United States, or in any Department or Officer thereof.

Section 9. The Migration or Importation of such Persons as any of the States now existing shall think proper to admit, shall not be prohibited by the Congress prior to the Year one thousand eight hundred and eight, but a Tax or duty may be imposed on such Importation, not exceeding ten dollars for each Person.

The Privilege of the Writ of Habeas Corpus shall not be suspended, unless when in Cases of Rebellion or Invasion the public Safety may require it.

No Bill of Attainder or ex post facto Law shall be passed.

No Capitation, or other direct, Tax shall be laid, unless in Proportion to the Census or Enumeration herein before directed to be taken.[5]

No Tax or Duty shall be laid on Articles exported from any State.

No Preference shall be given by any Regulation of Commerce or Revenue to the Ports of one State over those of another; nor shall Vessels bound to, or from, one State, be obliged to enter, clear, or pay Duties in another.

No Money shall be drawn from the Treasury, but in Consequence of Appropriations made by Law; and a regular Statement and Account of the Receipts and Expenditures of all public Money shall be published from time to time.

No Title of Nobility shall be granted by the United States: And no Person holding any Office of Profit or Trust under them, shall, without the Consent of the Congress, accept of any present, Emolument, Office, or Title, of any kind whatever, from any King, Prince, or foreign State.

Section 10. No State shall enter into any Treaty, Alliance, or Confederation; grant Letters of Marque and Reprisal; coin

Money; emit Bills of Credit; make any Thing but gold and silver Coin a Tender in Payment of Debts; pass any Bill of Attainder, ex post facto Law, or Law impairing the Obligation of Contracts, or grant any Title of Nobility.

No State shall, without the Consent of the Congress, lay any Imposts or Duties on Imports or Exports, except what may be absolutely necessary for executing it's inspection Laws: and the net Produce of all Duties and Imposts, laid by any State on Imports or Exports, shall be for the Use of the Treasury of the United States; and all such Laws shall be subject to the Revision and Controul of the Congress.

No State shall, without the Consent of Congress, lay any Duty of Tonnage, keep Troops, or Ships of War in time of Peace, enter into any Agreement or Compact with another State, or with a foreign Power, or engage in War, unless actually invaded, or in such imminent Danger as will not admit of delay.

ARTICLE II

Section 1. The executive Power shall be vested in a President of the United States of America. He shall hold his Office during the Term of four Years, and, together with the Vice President, chosen for the same Term, be elected, as follows

Each State shall appoint, in such Manner as the Legislature thereof may direct, a Number of Electors, equal to the whole Number of Senators and Representatives to which the State may be entitled in the Congress: but no Senator or Representative, or Person holding an Office of Trust or Profit under the United States, shall be appointed an Elector.

[The Electors shall meet in their respective States, and vote by Ballot for two Persons, of whom one at least shall not be an Inhabitant of the same State with themselves. And they shall make a List of all the Persons voted for, and of the Number of Votes for each; which List they shall sign and certify, and transmit sealed to the Seat of the Government of the United States, directed to the President of the Senate. The President of the Senate shall, in the Presence of the Senate and House of Representatives, open all the Certificates, and the Votes shall then be counted. The Person having the greatest Number of Votes shall be the President, if such Number be a Majority of the whole Number of Electors appointed; and if there be more than one who have such Majority, and have an equal Number of Votes, then the House of Representatives shall immediately chuse by Ballot one of them for President; and if no Person have a Majority, then from the five highest on the list the said House shall in like Manner chuse the President. But in chusing the President, the Votes shall be taken by States, the Representation from each State having one Vote; A quorum for this Purpose shall consist of a Member or Members from two thirds of the States, and a Majority of all the States shall be necessary to a Choice. In every Case, after the Choice of the President, the Person having the greatest Number of Votes of the Electors shall be the Vice President. But if there should remain two or more who have equal Votes, the Senate shall chuse from them by Ballot the Vice President.][6]

The Congress may determine the Time of chusing the Electors, and the Day on which they shall give their Votes; which Day shall be the same throughout the United States.

No Person except a natural born Citizen, or a Citizen of the United States, at the time of the Adoption of this Constitution, shall be eligible to the Office of President; neither shall any Person be eligible to that Office who shall not have attained to the Age of thirty five Years, and been fourteen Years a Resident within the United States.

In Case of the Removal of the President from Office, or of his Death, Resignation, or Inability to discharge the Powers and Duties of the said Office,[7] the Same shall devolve on the Vice President, and the Congress may by Law provide for the Case of Removal, Death, Resignation or Inability, both of the President and Vice President, declaring what Officer shall then act as President, and such Officer shall act accordingly, until the Disability be removed, or a President shall be elected.

The President shall, at stated Times, receive for his Services, a Compensation, which shall neither be encreased nor diminished during the Period for which he shall have been elected, and he shall not receive within that Period any other Emolument from the United States, or any of them.

Before he enter on the Execution of his Office, he shall take the following Oath or Affirmation:—"I do solemnly swear (or affirm) that I will faithfully execute the Office of President of the United States, and will to the best of my Ability, preserve, protect and defend the Constitution of the United States."

Section 2. The President shall be Commander in Chief of the Army and Navy of the United States, and of the Militia of the several States, when called into the actual Service of the United States; he may require the Opinion, in writing, of the principal Officer in each of the executive Departments, upon any Subject relating to the Duties of their respective Offices, and he shall have Power to grant Reprieves and Pardons for Offences against the United States, except in Cases of Impeachment.

He shall have Power, by and with the Advice and Consent of the Senate, to make Treaties, provided two thirds of the Senators present concur; and he shall nominate, and by and with the Advice and Consent of the Senate, shall appoint Ambassadors, other public Ministers and Consuls, Judges of the supreme Court, and all other Officers of the United States, whose Appointments are not herein otherwise provided for, and which shall be established by Law: but the Congress may by Law vest the Appointment of such inferior Officers, as they think proper, in the President alone, in the Courts of Law, or in the Heads of Departments.

The President shall have Power to fill up all Vacancies that may happen during the Recess of the Senate, by granting Commissions which shall expire at the End of their next Session.

Section 3. He shall from time to time give to the Congress Information of the State of the Union, and recommend to their Consideration such Measures as he shall judge necessary and expedient; he may, on extraordinary Occasions, convene both Houses, or either of them, and in Case of Disagreement between them, with Respect to the Time of Adjournment, he may adjourn them to such Time as he shall think proper; he shall receive Ambassadors and other public Ministers; he shall take Care that the Laws be faithfully executed, and shall Commission all the Officers of the United States.

Section 4. The President, Vice President and all civil Officers of the United States, shall be removed from Office on Impeachment for, and Conviction of, Treason, Bribery, or other high Crimes and Misdemeanors.

ARTICLE III

Section 1. The judicial Power of the United States, shall be vested in one supreme Court, and in such inferior Courts as the Congress may from time to time ordain and establish. The Judges, both of the supreme and inferior Courts, shall hold their Offices during good Behaviour, and shall, at stated Times, receive for their Services, a Compensation, which shall not be diminished during their Continuance in Office.

Section 2. The judicial Power shall extend to all Cases, in Law and Equity, arising under this Constitution, the Laws of the United States, and Treaties made, or which shall be made, under their Authority; —to all Cases affecting Ambassadors, other public Ministers and Consuls; —to all Cases of admiralty and maritime Jurisdiction; —to Controversies to which the United States shall be a Party; —to Controversies between two or more States; —between a State and Citizens of another State; —between Citizens of different States; —between Citizens of the same State claiming Lands under Grants of different States, and between a State, or the Citizens thereof, and foreign States, Citizens or Subjects.[8]

In all Cases affecting Ambassadors, other public Ministers and Consuls, and those in which a State shall be Party, the supreme Court shall have original Jurisdiction. In all the other Cases before mentioned, the supreme Court shall have appellate Jurisdiction, both as to Law and Fact, with such Exceptions, and under such Regulations as the Congress shall make.

The Trial of all Crimes, except in Cases of Impeachment, shall be by Jury; and such Trial shall be held in the State where the said Crimes shall have been committed; but when not committed within any State, the Trial shall be at such Place or Places as the Congress may by Law have directed.

Section 3. Treason against the United States, shall consist only in levying War against them, or in adhering to their Enemies, giving them Aid and Comfort. No Person shall be convicted of Treason unless on the Testimony of two Witnesses to the same overt Act, or on Confession in open Court.

The Congress shall have Power to declare the Punishment of Treason, but no Attainder of Treason shall work Corruption of Blood, or Forfeiture except during the Life of the Person attainted.

ARTICLE IV

Section 1. Full Faith and Credit shall be given in each State to the public Acts, Records, and judicial Proceedings of every other State. And the Congress may by general Laws prescribe the Manner in which such Acts, Records and Proceedings shall be proved, and the Effect thereof.

Section 2. The Citizens of each State shall be entitled to all Privileges and Immunities of Citizens in the several States.

A Person charged in any State with Treason, Felony, or other Crime, who shall flee from Justice, and be found in another State, shall on Demand of the executive Authority of the State from which he fled, be delivered up, to be removed to the State having Jurisdiction of the Crime.

[No Person held to Service or Labour in one State, under the Laws thereof, escaping into another, shall, in Consequence of any Law or Regulation therein, be discharged from such Service or Labour, but shall be delivered up on Claim of the Party to whom such Service or Labour may be due.][9]

Section 3. New States may be admitted by the Congress into this Union; but no new State shall be formed or erected within the Jurisdiction of any other State; nor any State be formed by the Junction of two or more States, or Parts of States, without the Consent of the Legislatures of the States concerned as well as of the Congress.

The Congress shall have Power to dispose of and make all needful Rules and Regulations respecting the Territory or other Property belonging to the United States; and nothing in this Constitution shall be so construed as to Prejudice any Claims of the United States, or of any particular State.

Section 4. The United States shall guarantee to every State in this Union a Republican Form of Government, and shall protect each of them against Invasion; and on Application of the Legislature, or of the Executive (when the Legislature cannot be convened) against domestic Violence.

ARTICLE V

The Congress, whenever two thirds of both Houses shall deem it necessary, shall propose Amendments to this Constitution, or, on the Application of the Legislatures of two thirds of the several States, shall call a Convention for proposing Amendments, which, in either Case, shall be valid to all Intents and Purposes, as Part of this Constitution, when ratified by the Legislatures of three fourths of the several States, or by Conventions in three fourths thereof, as the one or the other Mode of Ratification may be proposed by the Congress; Provided [that no Amendment which may be made prior to the Year One thousand eight hundred and eight shall in any Manner affect the first and fourth Clauses in the Ninth Section of the first Article; and][10] that no State, without its Consent, shall be deprived of its equal Suffrage in the Senate.

ARTICLE VI

All Debts contracted and Engagements entered into, before the Adoption of this Constitution, shall be as valid against the United States under this Constitution, as under the Confederation.

This Constitution, and the Laws of the United States which shall be made in Pursuance thereof; and all Treaties made, or which shall be made, under the Authority of the United States, shall be the supreme Law of the Land; and the Judges in every State shall be bound thereby, any Thing in the Constitution or Laws of any State to the Contrary notwithstanding.

The Senators and Representatives before mentioned, and the Members of the several State Legislatures, and all executive and judicial Officers, both of the United States and of the several States, shall be bound by Oath or Affirmation, to support this Constitution; but no religious Test shall ever be required as a Qualification to any Office or public Trust under the United States.

ARTICLE VII

The Ratification of the Conventions of nine States, shall be sufficient for the Establishment of this Constitution between the States so ratifying the Same.

Done in Convention by the Unanimous Consent of the States present the Seventeenth Day of September in the Year of our Lord one thousand seven hundred and Eighty seven and of the Independence of the United States of America the Twelfth. IN WITNESS whereof We have hereunto subscribed our Names,

George Washington,
President and deputy from Virginia.

New Hampshire:
John Langdon
Nicholas Gilman
Massachusetts:
Nathaniel Gorham
Rufus King
Connecticut:
William Samuel Johnson
Roger Sherman
New York:
Alexander Hamilton
New Jersey:
William Livingston
David Brearley
William Paterson
Jonathan Dayton
Pennsylvania:
Benjamin Franklin
Thomas Mifflin
Robert Morris
George Clymer
Thomas FitzSimons
Jared Ingersoll
James Wilson
Gouverneur Morris

Delaware:
George Read
Gunning Bedford Jr.
John Dickinson
Richard Bassett
Jacob Broom
Maryland:
James McHenry
Daniel of St. Thomas Jenifer
Daniel Carroll
Virginia:
John Blair
James Madison Jr.
North Carolina:.
William Blount
Richard Dobbs Spaight
Hugh Williamson
South Carolina:
John Rutledge
Charles Cotesworth Pinckney
Charles Pinckney
Pierce Butler
Georgia:
William Few
Abraham Baldwin

[The language of the original Constitution, not including the Amendments, was adopted by a convention of the states on September 17, 1787, and was subsequently ratified by the states on the following dates: Delaware, December 7, 1787; Pennsylvania, December 12, 1787; New Jersey, December 18, 1787; Georgia, January 2, 1788; Connecticut, January 9, 1788; Massachusetts, February 6, 1788; Maryland, April 28, 1788; South Carolina, May 23, 1788; New Hampshire, June 21, 1788.

Ratification was completed on June 21, 1788.

The Constitution subsequently was ratified by Virginia, June 25, 1788; New York, July 26, 1788; North Carolina, November 21, 1789; Rhode Island, May 29, 1790; and Vermont, January 10, 1791.]

AMENDMENTS

Amendment I (First ten amendments ratified December 15, 1791.)

Congress shall make no law respecting an establishment of religion, or prohibiting the free exercise thereof; or abridging the freedom of speech, or of the press; or the right of the people peaceably to assemble, and to petition the Government for a redress of grievances.

Amendment II

A well regulated Militia, being necessary to the security of a free State, the right of the people to keep and bear Arms, shall not be infringed.

Amendment III

No Soldier shall, in time of peace be quartered in any house, without the consent of the Owner, nor in time of war, but in a manner to be prescribed by law.

Amendment IV

The right of the people to be secure in their persons, houses, papers, and effects, against unreasonable searches and seizures, shall not be violated, and no Warrants shall issue, but upon probable cause, supported by Oath or affirmation, and particularly describing the place to be searched, and the persons or things to be seized.

Amendment V

No person shall be held to answer for a capital, or otherwise infamous crime, unless on a presentment or indictment of a Grand Jury, except in cases arising in the land or naval forces, or in the Militia, when in actual service in time of War or public danger; nor shall any person be subject for the same offence to be twice put in jeopardy of life or limb; nor shall be compelled in any criminal case to be a witness against himself, nor be deprived of life, liberty, or property, without due process of law; nor shall private property be taken for public use, without just compensation.

Amendment VI

In all criminal prosecutions, the accused shall enjoy the right to a speedy and public trial, by an impartial jury of the State and district wherein the crime shall have been committed, which district shall have been previously ascertained by law, and to be informed of the nature and cause of the accusation; to be confronted with the witnesses against him; to have compulsory process for obtaining witnesses in his favor, and to have the Assistance of Counsel for his defence.

Amendment VII

In Suits at common law, where the value in controversy shall exceed twenty dollars, the right of trial by jury shall be preserved, and no fact tried by a jury, shall be otherwise re-examined in any Court of the United States, than according to the rules of the common law.

Amendment VIII

Excessive bail shall not be required, nor excessive fines imposed, nor cruel and unusual punishments inflicted.

Amendment IX

The enumeration in the Constitution, of certain rights, shall not be construed to deny or disparage others retained by the people.

Amendment X

The powers not delegated to the United States by the Constitution, nor prohibited by it to the States, are reserved to the States respectively, or to the people.

Amendment XI (Ratified February 7, 1795)

The Judicial power of the United States shall not be construed to extend to any suit in law or equity, commenced or prosecuted against one of the United States by Citizens of another State, or by Citizens or Subjects of any Foreign State.

Amendment XII (Ratified June 15, 1804)

The Electors shall meet in their respective states and vote by ballot for President and Vice-President, one of whom, at least, shall not be an inhabitant of the same state with themselves; they shall name in their ballots the person voted for as President, and in distinct ballots the person voted for as Vice-President, and they shall make distinct lists of all persons voted for as President, and of all persons voted for as Vice-President, and of the number of votes for each, which lists they shall sign and certify, and transmit sealed to the seat of the government of the United States, directed to the President of the Senate; — The President of the Senate shall, in the presence of the Senate and House of Representatives, open all the certificates and the votes shall then be counted; — The person having the greatest number of votes for President, shall be the President, if such number be a majority of the whole number of Electors appointed; and if no person have such majority, then from the persons having the highest numbers not exceeding three on the list of those voted for as President, the House of Representatives shall choose immediately, by ballot, the President. But in choosing the President, the votes shall be taken by states, the representation from each state having one vote; a quorum for this purpose shall consist of a member or members from two-thirds of the states, and a majority of all the states shall be necessary to a choice. [And if the House of Representatives shall not choose a President whenever the right of choice shall devolve upon them, before the fourth day of March next following, then the Vice-President shall act as President, as in the case of the death or other constitutional disability of the President. —][11] The person having the greatest number of votes as Vice-President, shall be the Vice-President, if such number be a majority of the whole number of Electors appointed, and if no person have a majority, then from the two highest numbers on the list, the Senate shall choose the Vice-President; a quorum for the purpose shall consist of two-thirds of the whole number of Senators, and a majority of the whole number shall be necessary to a choice. But no person constitutionally ineligible to the office of President shall be eligible to that of Vice-President of the United States.

Amendment XIII (Ratified December 6, 1865)

Section 1. Neither slavery nor involuntary servitude, except as a punishment for crime whereof the party shall have been duly convicted, shall exist within the United States, or any place subject to their jurisdiction.

Section 2. Congress shall have power to enforce this article by appropriate legislation.

Amendment XIV (Ratified July 9, 1868)

Section 1. All persons born or naturalized in the United States, and subject to the jurisdiction thereof, are citizens of the United States and of the State wherein they reside. No State shall make or enforce any law which shall abridge the privileges or immunities of citizens of the United States; nor shall any State deprive any person of life, liberty, or property, without due process of law; nor deny to any person within its jurisdiction the equal protection of the laws.

Section 2. Representatives shall be apportioned among the several States according to their respective numbers, counting the whole number of persons in each State, excluding Indians not taxed. But when the right to vote at any election for the choice of electors for President and Vice President of the United States, Representatives in Congress, the Executive and Judicial officers of a State, or the members of the Legislature thereof, is denied to any of the male inhabitants of such State, being twenty-one years of age,[12] and citizens of the United States, or in any way abridged, except for participation in rebellion, or other crime, the basis of representation therein shall be reduced in the proportion which the number of such male citizens shall bear to the whole number of male citizens twenty-one years of age in such State.

Section 3. No person shall be a Senator or Representative in Congress, or elector of President and Vice President, or hold any office, civil or military, under the United States, or under any State, who, having previously taken an oath, as a member of Congress, or as an officer of the United States, or as a member of any State legislature, or as an executive or judicial officer of any State, to support the Constitution of the United States, shall have engaged in insurrection or rebellion against the same, or given aid or comfort to the enemies thereof. But Congress may by a vote of two-thirds of each House, remove such disability.

Section 4. The validity of the public debt of the United States, authorized by law, including debts incurred for payment of pensions and bounties for services in suppressing insurrection or rebellion, shall not be questioned. But neither the United States nor any State shall assume or pay any debt or obligation incurred in aid of insurrection or rebellion against the United States, or any claim for the loss or emancipation of any slave; but all such debts, obligations and claims shall be held illegal and void.

Section 5. The Congress shall have power to enforce, by appropriate legislation, the provisions of this article.

Amendment XV (Ratified February 3, 1870)

Section 1. The right of citizens of the United States to vote shall not be denied or abridged by the United States or by any State on account of race, color, or previous condition of servitude.

Section 2. The Congress shall have power to enforce this article by appropriate legislation.

Amendment XVI (Ratified February 3, 1913)

The Congress shall have power to lay and collect taxes on incomes, from whatever source derived, without apportionment among the several States, and without regard to any census or enumeration.

Amendment XVII (Ratified April 8, 1913)

The Senate of the United States shall be composed of two Senators from each State, elected by the people thereof, for six years; and each Senator shall have one vote. The electors in each State shall have the qualifications requisite for electors of the most numerous branch of the State legislatures.

When vacancies happen in the representation of any State in the Senate, the executive authority of such State shall issue writs of election to fill such vacancies: *Provided,* That the legislature of any State may empower the executive thereof to make temporary appointments until the people fill the vacancies by election as the legislature may direct.

This amendment shall not be so construed as to affect the election or term of any Senator chosen before it becomes valid as part of the Constitution.

Amendment XVIII (Ratified January 16, 1919)

Section 1. After one year from the ratification of this article the manufacture, sale, or transportation of intoxicating liquors within, the importation thereof into, or the exportation thereof from the United States and all territory subject to the jurisdiction thereof for beverage purposes is hereby prohibited.

Section 2. The Congress and the several States shall have concurrent power to enforce this article by appropriate legislation.

Section 3. This article shall be inoperative unless it shall have been ratified as an amendment to the Constitution by the legislatures of the several States, as provided in the Constitution, within seven years from the date of the submission hereof to the States by the Congress.][13]

Amendment XIX (Ratified August 18, 1920)

The right of citizens of the United States to vote shall not be denied or abridged by the United States or by any State on account of sex.

Congress shall have power to enforce this article by appropriate legislation.

Amendment XX (Ratified January 23, 1933)

Section 1. The terms of the President and Vice President shall end at noon on the 20th day of January, and the terms of Senators and Representatives at noon on the 3d day of January, of the years in which such terms would have ended if this article had not been ratified; and the terms of their successors shall then begin.

Section 2. The Congress shall assemble at least once in every year, and such meeting shall begin at noon on the 3d day of January, unless they shall by law appoint a different day.

Section 3.[14] If, at the time fixed for the beginning of the term of the President, the President elect shall have died, the Vice President elect shall become President. If a President shall not have been chosen before the time fixed for the beginning of his term, or if the President elect shall have failed to qualify, then the Vice President elect shall act as President until a President shall have qualified; and the Congress may by law provide for the case wherein neither a President elect nor a Vice President elect shall have qualified, declaring who shall then act as President, or the manner in which one who is to act shall be selected, and such person shall act accordingly until a President or Vice President shall have qualified.

Section 4. The Congress may by law provide for the case of the death of any of the persons from whom the House of Representatives may choose a President whenever the right of choice shall have devolved upon them, and for the case of the death of any of the persons from whom the Senate may choose a Vice President whenever the right of choice shall have devolved upon them.

Section 5. Sections 1 and 2 shall take effect on the 15th day of October following the ratification of this article.

Section 6. This article shall be inoperative unless it shall have been ratified as an amendment to the Constitution by the legislatures of three-fourths of the several States within seven years from the date of its submission.

Amendment XXI (Ratified December 5, 1933)

Section 1. The eighteenth article of amendment to the Constitution of the United States is hereby repealed.

Section 2. The transportation or importation into any State, Territory, or possession of the United States for delivery or use therein of intoxicating liquors, in violation of the laws thereof, is hereby prohibited.

Section 3. This article shall be inoperative unless it shall have been ratified as an amendment to the Constitution by conventions in the several States, as provided in the Constitution, within seven years from the date of the submission hereof to the States by the Congress.

Amendment XXII (Ratified February 27, 1951)

Section 1. No person shall be elected to the office of the President more than twice, and no person who has held the office of President, or acted as President, for more than two years of a term to which some other person was elected President shall be elected to the office of the President more than once. But this Article shall not apply to any person holding the office of President when this Article was proposed by the Congress, and shall not prevent any person who may be holding the office of President, or acting as President, during the term within which this Article becomes operative from holding the office of President or acting as President during the remainder of such term.

Section 2. This article shall be inoperative unless it shall have been ratified as an amendment to the Constitution by the legislatures of three-fourths of the several States within seven years from the date of its submission to the States by the Congress.

Amendment XXIII (Ratified March 29, 1961)

Section 1. The District constituting the seat of Government of the United States shall appoint in such manner as the Congress may direct:

A number of electors of President and Vice President equal to the whole number of Senators and Representatives in Congress to which the District would be entitled if it were a State, but in no event more than the least populous State; they shall be in addition to those appointed by the States, but they shall be considered, for the purposes of the election of President and Vice President, to be electors appointed by a State; and they shall meet in the District and perform such duties as provided by the twelfth article of amendment.

Section 2. The Congress shall have power to enforce this article by appropriate legislation.

Amendment XXIV (Ratified January 23, 1964)

Section 1. The right of citizens of the United States to vote in any primary or other election for President or Vice President, for electors for President or Vice President, or for Senator or Representative in Congress, shall not be denied or abridged by the United States or any State by reason of failure to pay any poll tax or other tax.

Section 2. The Congress shall have power to enforce this article by appropriate legislation.

Amendment XXV (Ratified February 10, 1967)

Section 1. In case of the removal of the President from office or of his death or resignation, the Vice President shall become President.

Section 2. Whenever there is a vacancy in the office of the Vice President, the President shall nominate a Vice President who shall take office upon confirmation by a majority vote of both Houses of Congress.

Section 3. Whenever the President transmits to the President pro tempore of the Senate and the Speaker of the House of Representatives his written declaration that he is unable to discharge the powers and duties of his office, and until he transmits to them a written declaration to the contrary, such powers and duties shall be discharged by the Vice President as Acting President.

Section 4. Whenever the Vice President and a majority of either the principal officers of the executive departments or of such other body as Congress may by law provide, transmit to the President pro tempore of the Senate and the Speaker of the House of Representatives their written declaration that the President is unable to discharge the powers and duties of his office, the Vice President shall immediately assume the powers and duties of the office as Acting President.

Thereafter, when the President transmits to the President pro tempore of the Senate and the Speaker of the House of Representatives his written declaration that no inability exists, he shall resume the powers and duties of his office unless the Vice President and a majority of either the principal officers of the executive departments or of such other body as Congress may by law provide, transmit within four days to the President pro tempore of the Senate and the Speaker of the House of Representatives their written declaration that the President is unable to discharge the powers and duties of his office. Thereupon Congress shall decide the issue, assembling within forty-eight hours for that purpose if not in session. If the Congress, within twenty-one days after receipt of the latter written declaration, or, if Congress is not in session, within twenty-one days after Congress is required to assemble, determines by two-thirds vote of both Houses that the President is unable to discharge the powers and duties of his office, the Vice President shall continue to discharge the same as Acting President; otherwise, the President shall resume the powers and duties of his office.

Amendment XXVI (Ratified July 1, 1971)

Section 1. The right of citizens of the United States, who are eighteen years of age or older, to vote shall not be denied or abridged by the United States or by any State on account of age.

Section 2. The Congress shall have power to enforce this article by appropriate legislation.

Amendment XXVII (Ratified May 7, 1992)

No law varying the compensation for the services of the Senators and Representatives shall take effect, until an election of Representatives shall have intervened.

NOTES: 1. The part in brackets was changed by section 2 of the Fourteenth Amendment. 2. The part in brackets was changed by the first paragraph of the Seventeenth Amendment. 3. The part in brackets was changed by the second paragraph of the Seventeenth Amendment. 4. The part in brackets was changed by section 2 of the Twentieth Amendment. 5. The Sixteenth Amendment gave Congress the power to tax incomes. 6. The material in brackets was superseded by the Twelfth Amendment. 7. This provision was affected by the Twenty-fifth Amendment. 8. These clauses were affected by the Eleventh Amendment. 9. This paragraph was superseded by the Thirteenth Amendment. 10. Obsolete. 11. The part in brackets was superseded by section 3 of the Twentieth Amendment. 12. See the Nineteenth and Twenty-sixth Amendments. 13. This amendment was repealed by section 1 of the Twenty-first Amendment. 14. See the Twenty-fifth Amendment.

SOURCE: U.S. Congress, House, Committee on the Judiciary, *The Constitution of the United States of America, as Amended,* 100th Cong., 1st sess., 1987, H Doc 100–94.

★ ILLUSTRATION CREDITS AND ACKNOWLEDGMENTS

1. WHO ELECTS CONGRESS

9 Library of Congress
12 AP Images
18 Library of Congress

2. POLITICAL PARTIES AND ELECTIONS

26 Scott J. Ferrell, Congressional Quarterly
30 Wood engraving in *Harper's Weekly*, May 19, 1860, Library of Congress
34 Scott J. Ferrell, Congressional Quarterly
37 Dorothea Lange, Library of Congress

3. WHO GETS ELECTED

49 Scott J. Ferrell, Congressional Quarterly
49 Scott J. Ferrell, Congressional Quarterly
50 Scott J. Ferrell, Congressional Quarterly
57 Scott J. Ferrell, Congressional Quarterly

4. CAMPAIGN FINANCING

68 AP Images
75 Scott J. Ferrell, Congressional Quarterly
84 Library of Congress
95 Library of Congress.

5. REAPPORTIONMENT AND REDISTRICTING

111 AP Images
121 Library of Congress
129 U.S. Census Bureau
138 AP Images

INDEX

Note: This index is sorted word-by-word. Page numbers in *italics* indicate an illustration.

A
Abernethy, Thomas G., 41
Abramoff, Jack,
influence-peddling scandal, 78, 82
Adams, John
party development, 29
Adams, John Quincy
House-Senate shifts, 17
Adolescents and youth
minimum voting age, 19
Aero Club of America, 17
African American Members of Congress, 54–55
African American Members of Congress, 1870–2007, 151–152 (list)
African Americans
census undercount, 116
members of Congress
in House leadership, 53–55
list, 53
Reconstruction era, 9
voting by, 7–8
Age Structure of Congress, 1949–2007, 47 (table)
Agricultural interest groups, 31
Agriculture Committee, House, 52
Alabama
poll taxes, 10
population totals, 120 (table)
seat transfer, 133 (table)
voting requirements, 9, 19
"Alabama paradox," 112
Alaska
population totals, 120 (table)
seat transfer, 133 (table)
voting requirements, 9–10
Alaskan natives' voting rights, 14
Aldrich, Nelson W.
party leadership, 30
Alexander, Herbert, 88–89
Alito, Samuel A.
Supreme Court
redistricting, 139
Allison, William B.
leadership style, 30
party development, 30–31
service record, 62 (table)
Allwright, S. S., 11
American, industrialization of, 131
American Civil Liberties Union (ACLU), 103
American Federation of Labor-Congress of Industrial Organizations (AFL-CIO)
issue advocacy ads, 82
PACs, 71, 103
American (Know-Nothing) Party, 27 (graph)
American National Election Studies (ANES), 5, 32, 34–35
American Political Parties, 1789–2004, 27 (graph)
American Samoa
representation in Congress, 2, 60–61 (box)
An American Dilemma (Myrdal), 9
Anthony, Susan B., 17
Anti-Mason Party, 27 (graph)
Anti-Masonic Party, 26
Apportionment of the House of Representatives
Alabama paradox, 112
apportionment by state, 112
changes, population totals, 115–116
constitutional provisions, 107, 109 (box)
equal proportions system, 112, 116
fixed ratio method, 110–111
House history, 8 (box), 108–110
major fractions method, 116
original apportionment, 110
rejected fractions method, 38, 111
Vinton method, 111–112
Appropriations Committee, House
subcommittees, 52
Appropriations Committee, Senate
subcommittees, 52
Arizona
independent commission, 121
population totals, 120 (table)
redistricting, 122–123
seat transfer, 133
voting requirements, 14, 20
women's suffrage, 17
Arizona Independent Redistricting Commission (AIRC), 122–123
Arkansas
poll taxes, 10
population totals, 120 (table)
seat transfer, 133 (table)
Armed Services Committee, House
history, 54
Ashcroft, John, 8 (box)
Asian Americans
voting rights, 14

B
Badham, Robert E., 132–133
Ballot Access News
voter affiliation, 5–6
Baptists
in Congress, 49
voting rights, 1
Begich, Nick, 8 (box)
Belmont, Perry, 85
Berman, Howard L., 74–75
Bilingual voting materials, 14
Bipartisan Campaign Reform Act of 2002 (BCRA), 46 (box), 97 (box), 102
soft money, 67, 69–70
Black, Hugo L.
on redistricting, 125, 128
Black codes, 8
Blacks in Congress, 1947–2007, 53 (table)
Blaz, Ben, 42
Boggs, Hale, 8 (box)
Boggs, Lindy, 8
Bonilla, Henry, 139
Bono, Mary, 51
Bono, Sonny, 51
Bordallo, Madeleine Z., 61 (box)
Boxer, Barbara, 52, 74
Bradley, Bill
television costs, 74
Brandeis, Louis D., 124–125
Brennan, William J., Jr., 128, 129
Brennan Center for Justice, 75
Bribery and corruption
Abscam scandal, 69, 72
Teapot Dome scandal, 86
Brooke, Edward W., 53
Brownell, Herbert, Jr., 88
Bruce, Blanche Kelso, 9, 53
Bryan, William Jennings, 85
Buchanan, Vern, 21
Buckley, James L., 94–95, *95*
Bull Moose-Progressive Party, 27 (graph)
Bull Moose Progressives, 31
Burke, Yvonne Brathwaite, 54
Burton, Harold H.
redistricting, 125
Burton, Phillip
redistricting, 132
Bush, George Herbert Walker
census undercount, 118–119 (box)
elections and politics
campaign finance reform, 78, 99
divided government, 32, 58
Bush, George W.
divided government, 36–37
election of 2000, 3
presidential election of 2000, 82
veto threat, 114
Business and industry
issue advertising, 82, 88
political contributions, 87–88
Byrd, Robert C.
campaign finance, 65, 78, 99
service record, 62 (table)

C
California
population totals, 120 (table)
seat transfer, 133 (table)
voting restrictions, 14
women's suffrage, 17
Campaign finance
ceilings, 87
coordinated expenditures, 72
costs
television costs, 74–75
disclosure mandate, 94
federal candidate promotion, 80–81
historical development, 85–86
limits, 93 (table), 95–96
overview, 84–85
public funding for, 78, 94
public opinion of, 47
soft money
campaign finance role, 46–47, 73, 80 (graph), 102–103
party contributions, 72
sources
bundling, 46 (box), 66 (box), 69, 73, 84, 87
candidate wealth, 73–74

electioneering communication, 66 (box)
independent expenditures, 69, 71
individual contributions, 70, 78, 87
leadership PACs, 71, 72
"millionaire's amendment," 73–74, 102–103
party contributions, 72, 80
political action committees (PACs), 70–71
public funding, 78
Campaign financing glossary, 46 (box)
Campbell, Ben Nighthorse, 59
Cannon, Howard W., 39–40
Cannon, Joseph G.
on filibusters, 31
party development, 31
as Reed aide, 30
service record, 62 (table)
as Speaker, 30
Canon, David T., 47
Cantor, Joseph E., 76, 81–82
Capper, Arthur, 114
Capps, Lois, 51
Capps, Walter, 51
Caraway, Hattie W., 51
Cardozo, Benjamin, 10, 125
Carnahan, Jean, 8 (box), 51
Carnahan, Mel, 8 (box), 51
Carson, Julia, 54
Carter, Jimmy
congressional relations
foreign policy, 32
elections and politics
campaign finance law, 98
voter registration, 20
Iran hostages, 32
Caucuses
party discipline, 31
presidential candidate selection, 25
Celler, Emanuel, 115
service record, 62 (table)
Census, *129*
accuracy, 116
aliens, 114
farm laborers, 114
House apportionment, 8 (box), 57, 114–116, 115 (box), 119 (box)
methodology, 118 (box)
overseas personnel, 119 (box)
voter turnout, 3, 4 (box), 19
Census Committee, House, 115, 116
Center for Responsive Politics, 76, 77
Center for Responsive Politics website, 155
Center for the Study of the American Electorate at the American University
voter turnout, 4 (box)
Chafee, Zechariah, Jr., 112
Chamberlain, George, 37
Chavez, Dennis, 56
Cheney, Dick
as vice president
relations with Congress, 60
China
U.S. campaign finance scandal, 100
Chipman, Norton P., 60 (box)
Chisholm, Shirley, 52, 54
Christensen, Donna M. C., 54, 61 (box)
Churches and religious groups
campaign contributions, 59
characteristics of members of Congress, 48–49
Citizens Party, 27 (graph)
Citizens' Research Foundation, 88
Civil Rights Act of 1957, 11
Civil Rights Act of 1964
extensions, 14–15
voting rights, 11, 35
Civil Rights Commission, U.S., 11, 14
Civil rights interest groups, 14
Civil Service Reform Act of 1883, 85
Clay, Henry
House-Senate shifts, 62
Clay, William L., 54
Clerk of the House
campaign finance law, 90
Clinton, Bill
congressional relations
divided government, 31
midterm campaigning, 59
elections and politics
campaign finance, 100
fund-raising, 69, 100
popular, electoral vote, 59
voting rights, 20
health care proposals, 31, 59
impeachment
House role, 36
partisanship, 36
Senate role, 36
presidential election of 1996, 3
Clinton, Hillary Rodham
campaign expenditures, 76
as senator of New York, 8 (box), 51
Clinton, William Jefferson (Bill). *See* Clinton, Bill
Clyburn, James E.
as majority whip, 55
Cochran, Thad, 102
Coelho, Tony
campaign finance, 71
Colby, Bainbridge, 18
Colegrove, Kenneth, 125
Collins, Cardiss, 54
Collins, George W., 54
Colmer, William M., 41
Colorado
population totals, 120 (table)
redistricting, 135, 136–137
school elections, 17
seat transfer, 133 (table)
term limits, 58 (box)
women's suffrage, 17
Combined Insurance Co. of America, 91
Committee of Detail, 1
Committee on Committees, 30
Committee on Expenditures in the Executive Departments, 54
Committee on Privileges and Elections, 39
Common Cause
campaign finance reform, 79, 81, 90, 97
redistricting, 135
Watergate scandal, 91, 92
Wright ethics case, 69
Communist Party, 27 (graph)
Congress, members of
African Americans, 16, 17, 46, 52–55, 53 (table)
age, 46–47, 47 (table)
characteristics
age, 46–47
law practice, 47
race, 46
religious affiliation, 48–49
Hispanics, 46
occupations, 48 (table)
service records
chamber shifts, 62
length, 62 (table)
tems of office, 62 (table)
veterans, 48, *49* (caption)
women, 46, 147–149
Congress, U.S.
criticisms of, 45
internal organization, 26, 28
party control history, 34 (table)
party organization, influence, 26
public skepticism of, 45
Senate
election deadlocks/disputes, 36
size, 110
Congressional Apportionment, 1789–2000, 113 (table)
Congressional Budget Office (CBO), 154
Congressional Districting (Hacker), 109
Congressional Districting Reform Act of 1989, 115 (box)
Congressional districts
at-large seats, 117
contiguous requirement, 117
drawing, 126–127 (box)
single member districts, 117
Congressional election chronology
1980
turnover, 57
1990
turnover, 58
1992
Hispanic candidates, 16–17
House bank scandal, 1
turnover, 58
women candidates, 50
1994
divided government, 32, 46
turnover, 59
1996
turnover, 59
1998
turnover, 59
2000, turnover, 60
2002, turnover, 60
2004, turnover, 60
2006, turnover, 60
Congressional elections
Congressional Candidates' Campaign Spending by Election Year, 1980–2006, 76 (graph)
contested elections
House controversies, 38–39, 41–42
Senate controversies, 39–40
ticket-splitting, 33 (table), 35 (table)
turnover in membership, 56–62, 79
voters
minimum voting age, 19
turnout trends, 2 (table)
Congressional electoral anomalies, 8 (box)
Congressional-judicial relations
redistricting, 115
Congressional Quarterly Weekly Report, 32, 71
Congressional Research Service
campaign costs report, 74
Conkling, Roscoe, 30
Connecticut
population totals, 120 (table)
seat transfer, 133 (table)
voting restrictions, 9
Constituent service
Keating Five scandal, 100

Constitution, U.S.
complete text, 156–163
Congress
size, 110
congressional elections
term of office, 38
political parties, 28
Constitutional amendments
Founders' debate, 36
proposed amendments
term limits, 58 (box)
Constitutional Union Party, 27 (graph)
Continental Congress
consent of the governed philosophy, 109
structure, 36
Contract with America
as partisan trends, 35–36
Contribution Limits for 2007–2008, 93 (table)
Conyers, John, Jr., 54–55
service record, 62 (table)
Cook, Rhodes
turnout rate, 4
voter dissatisfaction, 7
Coolidge Calvin
congressional relations
House apportionment, 115
Cornell, Robert J., 48
Corrado, Anthony, 80, 101
Corzine, Jon S., 56, 75
Cotton, Norris, 39
Council for a Livable World, 84
CQ Money Line website, 155
Cranston, Alan
Keating Five scandal, 69
Crist, Charlie, 21
Curtis, Charles, 59
Customs service, 85

D

D'Alesandro Thomas J., Jr., 52
Daschle, Tom
campaign finance, 77
Davidson, Roger H.
on incumbents' advantage, 46, 78
Dawson, William L., 53, 54
De Priest, Oscar, 53
Declaration of Principles (Stanton), 17
DeConcini, Dennis
Keating Five scandal, *48*, (caption)
Degetau, Federico, 61 (box)
Delaware, election deadlock, 36
DeLay, Tom
redistricting, 137–139
Deleware, population totals, 120 (table)
Dellums, Ronald V., 54
Democracy in America (de Tocqueville), 45
Democratic Congressional Campaign Committee
campaign finance, 35, 71
Democratic National Committee
campaign finance scandal, 100–101
fund-raising, 69, 87
Democratic Party, 27 (graph)
2006 midterm elections, 25
Congress membership turnover, 31, 60
historic development, 25, 29
leadership, 31
white primaries, 10–11
Democratic-Republican Party (Jeffersonians), 27 (graph)
presidential election of 1800, 29
Democratic Senatorial Campaign Committee, 35, 72
Democrats for Nixon, 92
Dempsey, John T., 41
Devine, Annie, 41
Diaz-Balart, Lincoln, 56
Diaz-Balart, Mario, 56
Dickerson, Mahlon, 117
Diggs, Charles C., Jr., 53
Dingell, John D.
service record, 62 (table)
Disclosure laws, 91–92
Discrimination
intent to discriminate, 14
District of Columbia
introduction of legislation, 60 (box)
polulation totals, 120 (table)
representation in Congress, 19, 60 (box)
voting rights, 2, 18, 114
District of Columbia Committee, House
delegate, 2, 60
Dole, Bob
majority leader, 51
presidential election of 1996, 3
Dole, Elizabeth, 51
Dornan, Robert K., 42
Douglas, Emily Taft, 51
Douglas, Paul H., 51
Douglas, William O.
redistricting, 125, 128
Drinan, Robert F., 48
Due process clause (14th Amendment), 8
Durkin, John A., 39–40

E

Earmarking, 73
Ehrenhalt, Alan, 32
Eisenhower, Dwight D.
congressional relations
divided government, 32
minimum voting age, 19
Election Assistance Commission, 21
Election Results, Congress and the Presidency, 1860–2006, 145–146 (table)
Electoral anomalies
in congressional elections, 8 (box)
Electors
choosing, 1
Eligible Voter Turnout Rates, 2 (table)
Ellison, Keith, *49* (caption)
Elving, Ron
on reapportionment, 107
Emancipation Proclamation, 8
Emerson, Bill, 51
Emerson, Jo Ann, 51
EMILY's List, 84
Enron Corp. collapse, 102
Episcopalians, in Congress, 49
Equal protection clause
civil rights, 8
redistricting, 125
Espy, Mike, 54

F

Fairness and Independence in Redistricting Act, 115 (box)
Faleomavaega, Eni F. H., 61 (box)
Faulkner, Gen. Walter, 35
Fauntroy, Walter E., 60 (box)
Federal Contested Elections Act of 1969, 39
Federal Corrupt Practices Act of 1910, 85–86, 87, 89, 91
Federal Corrupt Practices Act of 1925, Teapot Dome scandal, 67, 86
Federal Election Campaign Act Amendments of 1974
FEC enforcement, 89–90
provisions, 46 (box)
soft money, 46, 46 (box)
Watergate effect, 65, 68, 80
Federal Election Campaign Act Amendments of 1976, 96–97
Federal Election Campaign Act Amendments of 1979, 98–99
Federal Election Campaign Act (FECA) of 1971, limits, disclosure, 89–90
Federal Election Campaign Act (FECA) of 1974, 93–94
Federal Election Commission (FEC)
business PACs, 59
campaign finance reports, 68
contribution limits, 94, 104
federal candidate limits, 94
Internet communications exemption, 84
presidential campaign limits, 94, 101
soft money, 46 (box), 46–47, 81
structure, 94
SunPac decision, 97
Federal Election Commission website, 155
Federal employees, political fund-raising, 86
The Federalist papers
foreign policy powers, 28
House apportionment, 109–110
political parties, factions, 28
Federalist Party, 27 (graph)
history, 28
Feingold, Russell, 103, 104
campaign finance reform, *75* (caption), 97 (box)
Feinstein, Dianne, 52
Felony exemption, 2
Felton, Rebecca L., 50
Fenn, E. Hart, 115
Ferraro, Geraldine, 52
Fifteenth Amendment
minority voting rights, 2, 8, 9
Filibusters
history
campaign finance reform, 99, 101–102
Finance Committee for the Reelection of the President, 91
First Amendment
campaign finance limits, 95, 98
First Congress
House apportionment, 110–111
size, 110
Flake, Floyd H., 58 (box)
Flanigan, William H., 34
Florida
2002 election, 21
poll taxes, 10
population totals, 120 (table)
redistricting, 16, 134
seat transfer, 133 (table)
Foley, Thomas S.
as Speaker
defeat, 58 (box)
Ford, Gerald R.
absentee voting, 20
campaign finance law, 94, 97
Ford, Harold E., 52, 54
Fortuno, Luis, 55, 61 (box)
Foster, Mike, 40
Fourteenth Amendment
citizenship definition, 1–2

discrimination remedy, 8
aliens, 119 (box)
House apportionment, 112
minority voting rights, 8, 9
women's voting rights, 17–19
Frankfurter, Felix
redistricting, 125
Franking privilege
constituent relations, 78–79
Franks, Gary, 53
Free Soil Party, 27 (graph), 29

G
Gamache, Murielle E., 75
Gans, Curtis, 6
Gardner, John, 91
Garfield, James A.
assassination
civil service reform, 85
Garner, John Nance, 8 (box)
as Speaker, 8
General Accountability Office (GAO), website, 154
General Accounting Office (GAO), 90. *See* General Accountability Office (GAO)
General Motors (GM), 76
Geographical Patterns in Reapportionment, 1790–2000, 130–131 (box)
George, Walter F., 50
George Wallace/American Independent Party, 27 (graph)
Georgia
poll taxes, 10
population totals, 120 (table)
redistricting, 134, 135, 139
seat transfer, 133 (table)
voting requirements, 9
Gephardt, Richard
contested elections, 42
House leadership, 52
Gerry, Elbridge
gerrymanders, 117, 121 (box)
Gerrymanders
origins, 117
partisan gerrymanders, 108, 115 (box), 123 (box), 132–133, 137
racial gerrymanders, 54, 108, 123 (box), 139
majority-minority districts, 16, 55
"sweetheart" gerrymanders, 123 (box)
Gilbert, George G., 117
Gingrich, Newt
congressional-executive relations
midterm elections, 59
as Speaker, 59
Giuliani, Rudy
campaign expenditures, 76
Glenn, John
Keating Five scandal, *48* (caption)
Goldberg, Arthur J., 128
Gore, Al
2000 election, 137
campaign fund-raising, 69, 100
Governing Magazine, 32
Government Operations Committee, 54
Government Printing Office website, 154
"Grand Old Party" designation, 29
Grandfather clauses, 9
Grant, Ulysses, S.
election, 8
Grassroots lobbying, 82
Gray, Virginia, 41
Gray, William H., III
leadership positions, 54
Great Compromise (Constitutional Convention), 36
Green Party, 27 (graph)
Greenback Party, 27 (graph)
Greene, Harold H.
on D.C. voting rights, 61 (box)
Grofman, Bernard, 123
Grundy, Joseph R., 39
Guam
contested elections, 42
representative in Congress, 2, 19, 60–61 (box)

H
Hacker, Andrew, 109–110
Haldeman, H. R., 91
Hall, Katie, 54
Hamer, Fannie L., 41
Hamilton, Alexander
on constitutional issues
central government, 28
Federalist papers, 28, 110
Revolutionary War debt assumption, 28
Hanna, Marcus A. (Mark), 85
Hansen, George V., 42
Harlan, John Marshall, 128
Harris, Thomas E., 80
Hartke, Vance, 88
Hastert, J. Dennis. *See also* Republican Party
census accuracy, 119 (box)
Hastie, William H., 11
Hatch Act of 1939, 87
Hawaii
independent commission, 121
population totals, 120 (table)
seat transfer, 133 (table)
voting requirements, 9–10
Hawkins, Augustus F., 54
Hawkins, Paula, 52
Hayden, Carl
service record, 62 (table)
Health care policy
universal health care proposals, 59
Heard, Alexander, 88, 89
Help America Vote Act of 2000, 20
Help America Vote Act of 2002, 20
Henry Wallace Progressive Party, 27 (graph)
Hermandad Mexicana Nacional, 42
Herrnson, Paul S.
on Republican Party fundraising, 72
Higginbotham, Patrick E., 138
Highton, Benjamin, 4–5
Hill, Anita F., 50
Hill, Lister, 62 (table)
Hispanic Americans
census undercount, 116
civil rights interest groups, 46
Hispanics in Congress, 1947–2007, 56 (table)
members of Congress, 57
redistricting, 55
Hispanic Members of Congress, 1877–2007, 153 (list)
Hoch, Homer, 114
Hollings, Ernest F.
television costs, 74
Homeland security, 55
Homestead law proposal, 29
Hoover, Herbert
House apportionment, 115–116
House Administration [Oversight] Committee
contested elections, 42
House Bank scandal, 31
House Committee on Expenditures (Post Office Department), 52
House Committee on Woman Suffrage, 17
House Judiciary Committee, 115 (box)
House of Representatives, U.S.
elections
campaign costs, 65, 77, 90
constitutional provisions, 13 (box)
first, 107
framers intent, 109–110
maximum membership, 112, 114
party control, 34 (table)
seat changes, 120 (table)
size and apportionment, 38, 107
terms, 37
House of Representatives website, 154
Hoyer, Steny, 52
Hruska, Roman L., 88
Huffington, Michael, 74
Hughes, Charles Evans
redistricting, 124
Hughes, Howard, 91
Human Events, 94–95
Huntington, Edward V., 116
Hyde, Henry
term limits, 58 (box)

I
Idaho
independent commission, 121
population totals, 120 (table)
voting requirements/restrictions, 14
Illegal aliens, 119 (box)
Illinois
population totals, 120 (table)
redistricting, 16–17, *136* (caption), *136* (map)
seat transfer, 133 (table)
Immigration
census count of aliens, 119 (box)
Import taxes
tariff policy history, 29
Income taxes
campaign finance checkoff, 68, 90
16th Amendment, 31
Incumbency Advantage in Reelection, 1946–2006, 79 (graph)
Incumbents
PACs role, 71
reelection advantage
House, Senate percentages, 59 (graph), 79 (graph)
public opinion, 45–46
turnover rate, 60
Indentured servants
franchise expansion, 1
Independent commissions
federal congressional districts, 121–123
Independent expenditures, 46 (box), 83
Indiana
gerrymandering, 123 (box)
population totals, 120 (table)
seat transfer, 133 (table)
Inouye, Daniel K.
service record, 62 (table)
Insanity exemption, 2
Interior Department, U.S.
American Samoa, 61 (box)

Internal Revenue Service
campaign finance law, 101–102
Internet
congressional information on, 154–155
Interstate Transfer of House Seats by Census and Senate, 1960–2000, 133 (table)
Iowa
population totals, 120 (table)
redistricting, 122
seat transfer, 133 (table)
Iran
hostage rescue attempt, 32
Iraq
Iraq War of 2002, 4, 46
Issue advocacy advertising, 46 (box), 81, 82

J
Jackson, Andrew
presidential election of 1828, 25, 26, 29
presidential election of 1832, 25
Jackson, Henry M.
service record, 62 (table)
Jackson, Jesse, Jr., 54
Jackson, Jesse, Sr., 54
Jacobs, Andrew, 51, 54
Jacobson, Gary, 77
Jay, John
Federalist papers, 110
Jaybird Club, 11
Jefferson, Thomas
on constitutional issues
House apportionment, 38, 111, *111*
party development, 28
on political parties, 28
states rights, 28
Jefferson, William J., 54
Jeffords, James M., 32, 52, 60
Jenkins, Louis "Woody," 40
Jennings W. Pat, 88
Jennings,Christine, 21
Jews
in Congress, 49
voting rights, 1
Johnson, Andrew
chamber shift, 62
Johnson, Hank, 55
Johnson, Lyndon B.
civil rights, 12
congressional relations
House terms extension, 38
on term extension, 38
Johnson, Norma Holloway, 104
Joint Center for Political Studies, 14
Jones, Charles, 119 (box)
Jones, Stephanie Tubbs, 52, 54, 55
Jordan, Barbara C., 54
Judiciary Committee, House
term limits, 58 (box)
Justice Department, U.S.
campaign finance, enforcement, 92

K
Kalmbach, Herbert, 91
Kansas
seat transfer, 133 (table)
women's suffrage, 17
Kansas, population totals, 120 (table)
Kaptur, Marcy, 52
Kassebaum, Nancy Landon, 51, 52
Keating, Charles H., Jr., 69
Keating Five scandal, 100
Kennedy, Anthony M.
redistricting, 16, 133
Kennedy, Edward M.
D.C. representation, 60 (box)
service record, 62 (table)
Kennedy, John F.
campaign finance reform, 88–89
Kentucky
franchise enhancement, 19
redistricting, 117
school elections, 17
Kentucky
migration to, 120 (table)
seat transfer, 133 (table)
Key, V. O., 26
Keys, Martha, 51
Kilpatrick, Carolyn Cheeks, 54
King, Martin Luther, Jr.
"Walk for Freedom," 12
Kohl, Herb, 103
Kourlis, Rebecca Love, 137

L
La Follette, Robert M., Sr.
direct primaries, 26
La Follette Progressive Party, 27 (graph)
Labor and Human Resources Committee, Senate, 52
Labor-Management Relations Act of 1947, 87
Labor unions
campaign finance reform, 90
political contributions, 79, 88, 90
LaMont, Ned, 74
Landrieu, Mary L., 40, 52
Larrazolo, Octaviano, 56
Leadership
positions held by women, 52
Leadership Conference on Civil Rights, 12
Leadership PACs, 66 (box), 72
Legislative Principles (Luce), 109
Levin, Carl, 73, 102
Lewinson, Paul, 9
Lewis, John, *12,* (caption), 54
Liberal Republican Party, 27 (graph)
Libertarian Party, 27 (graph)
Liberty Party, 27 (graph)
Lieberman, Joseph I., 25, *34,* 74
Lincoln, Abraham, 30
black voting rights, 8
Literacy barriers to voting, 9–10, 12, 14, 53
Lloyd, Marilyn, 51
Lobbyists and lobbying
disclosure rules, 85
history of, 36
Longworth, Nicholas, 8 (box)
Lorimer, William, 39
Los Angeles Times study
campaign television costs, 74
Lott, Trent
campaign finance reform, 104
Louisiana
migration to, 120 (table)
poll taxes, 10
population totals, 120 (table)
redistricting, 16, 134
seat transfer, 133 (table)
voting requirements, 9, 19
Luce, Robert, 109
Lutherans, in Congress, 49

M
Madison, James
on constitutional issues
factions, 28
Federalist papers, 109
House terms, 38
Magleby, David, 78, 82
Magnuson, Warren G.
service record, 62 (table)
Mahon, George H.
service record, 62 (table)
Maine
population totals, 120 (table)
presidential electors, 114
seat transfer, 133 (table)
Majority leaders, Senate
scheduling, 26
Majority-minority districts
African American Members of Congress, 54
minority voting rights, 16
redistricting, 55
Maloney, Carolyn B., 119 (box)
Mann, Thomas E., 83, 97
Mansfield, Mike
contested elections, 39–40
Mapmakers, 127 (box)
Margolis-Mezvinsky, Marjorie, 51
Marshall, John
campaign finance limits, 95–96
Marshall, Thurgood
voting rights, 11
Martinez, Mel, 56, 57
Maryland
population totals, 120 (table)
seat transfer, 133 (table)
voting requirements, 19
Massachusetts
population totals, 120 (table)
school elections, 17
seat transfer, 133 (table)
voting requirements, 9
Matsui, Doris, 51
McCain, John
campaign finance reform, *75* (caption), 97 (box), 104
Keating Five scandal, 68
McCain-Feingold bill, 101–102
McCarthy, Eugene J., 94–95
McCaskill, Claire, 73
McCloskey, Frank, 41
McConnell, Mitch
campaign reform bill, 103
McCormack, John W.
contested elections, 41
McDonald, Michael P., 3, 4
McGovern, George, 84, 88
McIntyre, Richard D., 41
McKernan, John R., 51
McKinley, William
campaign finance, 85
presidential election, 131 (box)
McKinney, Cynthia, 55
Meehan, Martin, *75* (caption), 84, 97 (box), 101, 104
Mellman, Mark, 3
Mellon, Andrew W., 87
Members' Occupations, 110th Congress, 48 (table)
Menard, John W., 52
Menendez, Robert, 42, 56
Merchant Marine and Fisheries Committee, House, 52
Methodists, in Congress, 49
Metzenbaum, Howard M.
campaign finance, 89
Meyers, Jan, 52

Mezvinsky, Edward, 51
Michel, Robert H.
D.C. voting rights challenge, 61 (box)
Michigan
population totals, 120 (table), 131–132
school elections, 17
seat transfer, 133 (table)
Mikulski, Barbara A., 52
Military Construction Appropriations Subcommittee, House, 52
Millender-McDonald, Juanita, 52, 55
Miller, Dan, 119 (box)
Minnesota
election-day registration, 20–21
population totals, 120 (table)
school elections, 17
seat transfer, 133 (table)
Minorities
census undercount, 116
Minority voting rights
barriers, 9–11
civil rights movement, 11–12, 13
franchise expansion, 1–2, 14–15
indentured servant status, 7–8
judicial support, 15
majority-minority districts, 16
Reconstruction era, 8–9
Supreme Court decisions, 13 (box), 16–17
Mississippi
poll taxes, 10
seat transfer, 133 (table)
voting requirements, 9, 19
Mississippi Five, 41
Mississippi Freedom Democratic Party, 41
Missouri
population totals, 120 (table)
redistricting, 129
seat transfer, 133 (table)
Mitchell, Arthur W., 53
Molinari, Guy, 51
Molinari, Susan, 51
Money
campaign laundering of, 91–92
Montana
independent commission, 121
population totals, 120 (table)
seat transfer, 133 (table)
women's suffrage, 17
Montoya, Joseph, 56
Morrill, Justin S.
service record, 62 (table)
Morris, Dwight, 74, 75
Mosbacher, Robert A., 118 (box)
Moseley-Braun, Carol, 52, 53, 54, 59
Motor-voter registration, 19, 20
Mott, Stewart, 92
Moveon.org, 104
Muckrakers, 85
Mullarkey, Mary, 137
Murphy, Frank
redistricting, 125
Murphy, Patrick J., 48, *48*
Murray, Patty, 52
Muskie, Edmund
campaign finance, 88
Muslims, in Congress, *49* (caption)
Mutch, Robert, 84, 85
Myrdal, Gunnar, 9, 11

N
Nast, Thomas, *84*
National Academy of Sciences Committee on Apportionment, 116
National Association for the Advancement of Colored People (NAACP), 11
National Bank, 28, 29
National Committee for an Effective Congress, 90
National Democratic Party, 27 (graph)
National Party Soft Money Receipts, 1993–2002, 80 (graph)
National Policy Forum, 100
National Publicity Law Organization, 85
National Republican Campaign Committee (NRCC), 35
National Republican Congressional Committee, 72
National Republican Party, 27 (graph), 29
National Republican Senatorial Committee
campaign finance, 72
National Rifle Association (NRA), 59, 103
National Unity Party, 27 (graph)
National Voter Registration Act of 1993, 20
The Nation's Voters, 1980–2004, 6 (table)
Native Americans
census undercount, 116
voting rights, 14
Natural Law Party, 27 (graph)
Nebraska
population totals, 120 (table)
seat transfer, 133 (table)
Nelson, Candice, 78
Nethercutt, George, 58 (box)
Neuberger, Maurine B., 52
Nevada
seat transfer, 133 (table)
women's suffrage, 17
New Alliance Party, 27 (graph)
New Hampshire
population totals, 120 (table)
school elections, 17
New Jersey
independent commission, 121
population totals, 120 (table)
seat transfer, 133 (table)
New Mexico
population totals, 120 (table)
seat transfer, 133 (table)
New York
population totals, 120 (table)
redistricting, 16
seat transfer, 133 (table)
voting requirements, 9–10, 14, 19
women's suffrage, 17
New York Civil Liberties Union, 94
Nineteenth Amendment, 2, 3, *18*
Nix, Robert N. C., 53
Nixon, L. A., 10
Nixon, Richard M.
divided government, draft, 32
elections and politics
campaign finance law, 89, 91
minimum voting age, 19
resignation, 32, 91
Nofziger, Lyn
influence peddling scandal, 102
Nolan, Mae Ella, 52
Nominations and appointments
early practices, 25–26
Nonvoting delegates
District of Columbia, 60
Norbeck, Peter, 51
North American Free Trade Agreement (NAFTA)
president's lobbying, 59
North Carolina
majority-minority districts, 16
poll taxes, 10
population totals, 120 (table)
redistricting, 134, 135 (map)
seat transfer, 133 (table)
voting requirements, 9
North Dakota, seat transfer, 133 (table)
Norton, Eleanor Holmes, 61 (box)

O
Obama, Barack
senatorial election, 46, 53
O'Connor, Sandra Day
majority-minority districts, 16, 134
Office of Technology Assessment (OTA), 155
Ohio
migration to, 120 (table)
population totals, 120 (table)
seat transfer, 133 (table)
Oklahoma
population totals, 120 (table)
seat transfer, 133 (table)
voting requirements, 9
Oleszek, Walter, J.
on incumbents' advantage, 46, 78
One person, one-vote rulings, 53, 108, 132
Oregon
mail voting, 21
population totals, 120 (table)
seat transfer, 133 (table)
voting requirements, 14
women's suffrage, 17
"Oregon System," 37
Ottinger, Richard L., 89
Owens, Bill, 136–137

P
Pacheco, Romualdo, 56
Packwood, Bob
campaign finance reform, 99
Partisanship
partisan identification, 1952–2004, 7 (graph)
party unity trends, 28
presidential election of 2000, 3
September 11, 2001, attacks, 4
Party loyalty and discipline
maintaining, 30
Patman, Wright
service record, 62 (table)
Paxon, Bill, 51
Pearlman, Marian, 92
Pelosi, Nancy
as minority leader, 52
as Speaker, *49*, 50, 52
Pendleton Act of 1883, 85
Pennsylvania
partisan districts dispute, 108
population totals, 120 (table)
redistricting, 137
seat transfer, 133 (table)
voting requirements, 19
Perdue, Sonny, 139
Perot, H. Ross
presidential election of 1992, 3
Perry, Rick, 138
Pinchback, P. B. S., 9
Political action committees (PACs)
campaign finance role
costs, 65
incumbents advantage, 78–79
use of, 65, 70

  definition, 46 (box)
  independent expenditures, 69
  leadership PACs, 46 (box)
  limits, 98
  personal PACs, 46 (box)
  reforms, 99–100
Political advertising
  campaign costs, 80
  FECA media lists, 90
  television limits, 93
Political Money Line, 71
Political parties
  campaign finance
    independent expenditures, 69, 83, *84*
  defined, 25
  divided government
    control of presidency and Congress, 33 (table), 34 (table)
  functions, 25–28
  major parties, 27 (graph)
  party name confusion, 29 (box)
  spoils system, 84–85
  third parties, 27 (graph)
  two party model, 30–31
  voter affiliation, 5, 32
  whip functions, 26
Political Party Affiliations in Congress and the Presidency, 1789–2007, 142–144 (table)
Politics, Parties, and Pressure (Key), 26
Poll taxes, 9, 10, 53–54
Populist Party, 27 (graph)
  poll-tax barriers, 10
  as reform force, 31
Post Office and Civil Service Committee, 54
Powell, Adam Clayton, Jr.
  African Americans in Congress, 53
  Education and Labor Committee, 64
Powell, Lewis F., Jr., 132
Presbyterians, in Congress, 49
Presidential Election Campaign Fund, 89
Presidential election chronology
  1792, electors, 29
  1796, electors, 29
  1972
    divided government, 32
    minimum voting age, 3
  1980, divided government, 32
  1988, 58
  1992
    Congress membership turnover, 58
    voter participation, 3
  2000, 3, 60
  2004, 4, 20, 60
  2006, 4, 60
Presidential elections
  campaign finance
    public funding, 78
    tax checkoff, 68–69, 89
  divided government, 32
  voting
    residency requirements, 2
    ticket-splitting, 33 (table), 35 (table)
    turnout trends, 2–3
President's Commission on Campaign Costs, 88–89
Price, David E.
  on campaign finance, 77–78
Price, Melvin, 62 (table)
PricewaterhouseCoopers lobbyists, 97 (box)
Primary elections
  direct primaries, 26
  early primaries, 26, 87
  jurisdiction of, 86
  white primaries, 10–11
Principles of Legislative Organization and Administration (Willoughby), 41
Proctor & Gamble, 76
Progressive (Bull Moose) Party, 25
Progressive movement
  direct election of senators, 26
  Senate history, 31
  women's voting rights, 17
Prohibition Party, 27 (graph)
Property ownership requirement, 1, 37
Publicity Act of 1910, 85
Puerto Rico
  representation in Congress, 60–61 (box)
  status, 61 (box)
  voting rights, 2, 15
Pyle, Gladys, 51

Q

Quakers, voting rights, 1

R

Race, Class and Party (Lewinson), 9
Rainey, Henry T., 53
Rangel, Charles B., 54
Rankin, Jeanette, 50
Rayburn, Sam
  service record, 62 (table)
Reagan, Ronald
  civil rights policies, 14
Reapportionment Act of 1882, 112
Reapportionment Gainers and Losers, *122* (map)
Rebozo, Bebe, 91
Reconstruction Act of 1867, 8–9
Reconstruction governments, 9
Redistricting
  Congress membership turnover, 31, 57, 59
  historic development, 57, 108
  legislative proposals, 116
  mid-decade, 134–136
  minority representation
    African American Members of Congress, 17, 54
    Hispanics, 17
    majority-minority districts, 16
  Supreme Court decisions, 16, 126–128, 133–134
Redistricting in Illinois, *136* (map)
Redistricting in North Carolina, *135* (caption), *135* (map)
Reed, Stanley F.
  redistricting, 125
Reed, Thomas Brackett
  as strong Speaker
    caucus role, 30
"Reed Rules," 30–31
Reid, Charlotte T., 51
Remonstrance (journal)
  on women's suffrage, 17
Rendell, Edward G., 137
Reno, Janet, 100–101
Republican Conference, House
  history, 59
  seniority, 28
Republican Conference, Senate
  history, 25
Republican Congressional Campaign Committee, 35
Republican National Committee
  fund-raising, 87
Republican Party, 27 (graph)
  Congress membership turnover, 60
  Farm Belt Republicans, 8 (box)
  founding of, 29
  historical development, 29, 31
  political conventions, *30*
Republicans for Clean Air, 82–83
Residence requirements
  for voters, 19–20
Revels, Hiram R., 9, 52–53
Revenue Act of 1971, 89–90
Revenue Act of 1972, 89
Revolutionary War
  state debt assumption, 28
Rhode Island
  population totals, 120 (table)
  voting requirements, 19
Richard, (Father) Gabriel, 48
Riddick, Floyd M.
  The United States Congress: Organization and Procedure, 38
Roberts, John G., Jr.
  redistricting, 139
  Supreme Court
    political speech, 103
Roberts, Owen, 125
Rockefeller, John D., IV, 87
Rodriguez, Ciro, 139
Rogan, James E., 77
Rogers, Edith Nourse, 51
Rogers, Will, 76
Roman Catholics
  in Congress, 1
  voting rights, 1
Roosevelt, Franklin D.
  seniority system growth, 28
Roosevelt, Theodore
  campaign finance law, 67
  party development, 85
Rosenthal, Lee H., 138
Ross Perot Reform Party, 27 (graph)
Roybal, Lucille, 51–52
Rules and Administration Committee, Senate
  contested elections, 39–40
Russell, Benjamin, 121 (box)
Rutledge,Wiley B.
  redistricting, 125
Ryan, William F., 41

S

Sabath, Adolph J., 62 (table)
Sabato, Larry, 79
Salazar, John, 56
Salazar, Ken, 56
Sanchez, Linda, 56
Sanchez, Loretta, 42, 56
Sanders, Bernard, 25, *26,* 59
Saunders, Edward W., 118
Savings and loan associations
  Keating Five scandal, 69 (box), 100
Saxby, William B., 88
Scaife, Richard, 91
Scammon, Richard, 3
Schiff, Adam, 77
Schwarzenegger, Arnold
  redistricting proposal, 119, 121
Schweiker, Richard S., 88, 137
Secretary of the Senate
  campaign finance law, 90
Section 501 (c) political funding, 83, 101
Section 527 organizations, 66, 67, 82–83, 101–102, 104

Senate, U.S.
elections, 36–37, 59
campaign costs, 65, 76–77, 78
constitutional provisions, 13 (box)
history
early Senate, 36
media coverage, 90
party control, 34 (table)
turnover, 57, 58–61
Senate Government Affairs Committee, 100
Senate Republican Caucus, 30
Senate Watergate Committee, 91, 92–93
Senate website, 154
Seniority
in committee system
assignments, 28
Sensenbrenner, F. James, 115 (box)
Separation of powers
FEC operations, 96–97 (box)
Sestak, Joe, 48
Seventeenth Amendment
adoption, 37
impetus for, 39
as Progressive reform, 31
provisions, 86
Senate history, 39
Senate turnover, 56
Shays, Christopher, *75* (caption), *84*, 97 (box), 101, 104
Shays-Meehan campaign finance laws, 101, 102
Shelby, Richard C., 59
Shepherd, Alexander, 60 (box)
Simon, Donald, 97 (box)
Slaughter, Louis M., 52
Slavery and slaves
Constitution compromises
Fourteenth Amendment, 38
House apportionment, 8 (box)
disenfranchisement, 8, 130
franchise expansion, 1
minority voting rights, 1
Small Business Committee, House, 52
Smith, Frank L., 86
Smith, Lonnie E., 11
Smith, Margaret Chase, 49, 51
Smith-Connally Act, 87
Snowe, Olympia, 51, 52, 103–104
Socialist Labor Party, 27 (graph)
Socialist Party, 27 (graph)
Socialist Workers Party, 27 (graph)
Sorauf, Frank J.
on bundling, 84
on campaign finance reform, 65
on candidate fund-raising, 77
on independent expenditures, 71
South Carolina
electoral vote counts, 8 (box)
poll taxes, 10
population totals, 120 (table)
voting requirements, 9, 19
South Dakota, seat transfer, 133 (table)
Southern Democrat Party, 27 (graph)
Spanish-American War, 61 (box)
Special elections
representatives death or disability, 8 (box)
Special interest groups
grassroots lobbying, 82
Spoils system, 84
Stallings, Richard H., 42
Standards of Official Conduct Committee, House
membership, 52
Stanton, Elizabeth Cady, 17
State legislatures
redistricting, 117
State Population Totals, House Seat Changes in the 2000s, 120 (table)
States' Rights Democratic Party, 27 (graph)
Steering and policy committees
Senate, 30
Stennis, John C., 88
Select Committee on Standards and Conduct
chairmanship
service record, 62 (table)
Stevens, John Paul
redistricting, 132
Stewart, Potter, 16
Stokes, Louis
majority whip, 54
Stone, Harlan Fiske, 11, 124–125
Stone, W. Clement, 91
Stuart, Gilbert, 121 (box)
Sullivan, Leonor K., 52
Sun Oil Co. (SunPAC), 71, 97
Sunbelt, 131 (box)
Supreme Court, U.S.
2000 election, 3
Supreme Court cases
Badham v. Eu, 132–133
Baker v. Carr, 124, 126–127, 132
Beer v. United States, 15
Brown v. Board of Education, 125
Bryant v. Hill, 58 (box)
Buckley v. Valeo, 69, 73, 78, 94–95, 96–97 (box)
Burroughs and Cannon v. United States, 86
Bush v. Vera, 16
Colegrove v. Green, 125, 128
Colorado Republican Federal Campaign Committee v. Federal Election Commission, 72, 83
Davis v. Bandemer, 108, 132, 133, 137, 139
Department of Commerce v. House of Representatives, 119 (box)
Dunn v. Blumstein, 20
FEC v. NRA Political Victory Fund, 96 (box)
Federal Election Commission v. Wisconsin Right to Life, 82, 103
Gaston County v. United States, 15
Gray v. Sanders, 127–128
Grovey v. Townsend, 10–11
Hunt v. Cromartie, 134
Jackson v. Perry, 138–139
Karcher v. Daggett, 132
Kirkpatrick v. Preisler, 129, 132
Lance v. Coffman, 137
League v. United States et al. v. Perry, 139
McConnell v. Federal Election Commission, 73, 82, 103
Miller v. Johnson, 16, 55, 134
Mobile v. Bolden, 16, 134
Newberry v. United States, 10, 87
Nixon v. Herndon, 10
Oregon v. Mitchell, 19
Pennsylvania v. Wheeling and Belmont Bridge Co., 108
Richmond v. United States, 15
Shaw v. Hunt, 16
Shaw v. Reno, 55, 134
Smith v. Allwright, 11, 87
Terry v. Adams, 11
Thornburg v. Gingles, 16, 108, 134
United Jewish Organizations of Williamsburgh v. Cary, 15
U.S. Term Limits, Inc. v. Thornton, 58
U.S. v. Classic., 11, 87
U.S. v. Louisiana, 11–12
U.S. v. Mississippi, 11–12
U.S. v. Raines, 11
U.S. v. Reese, 9
Vieth v. Jubelirer, 108, 133, 137, 139
Wesberry v. Sanders, 107–108, 115 (box), 128
Wood v. Brown, 124, 125
Supreme Court decisions
Congress
redistricting, 15
voting rights
minimum voting age, 19
residency requirements, 2
Survey Research Center, 87
Swift Boat Verterans for Truth, 104

T

Taft-Hartley Act of 1947, 87
Talent, Jim, 73
Tanner, John
redistricting proposal, 115
Task forces, 41
Teapot Dome scandal, 47, 86
Television
political ads, 74–75, 89
Tennessee
electoral vote counts, 8 (box)
migration to, 120 (table)
poll taxes, 10
population totals, 120 (table)
representative at large, 38
seat transfer, 133 (table)
women's voting rights, 18
Term limits, 58 (box)
Territories, U.S.
District of Columbia, 60–61 (box)
Texas
gerrymandering, 123 (box)
poll taxes, 10
population totals, 120 (table)
redistricting, 16, 134, 135, 137–139
seat transfer, 133 (table)
voting requirements, 19
Texas 11, *138* (caption)
Thayer, George, 84
THOMAS website, 154
Thompson, Bennie, 55
Thornton, William, 58
Thurmond, Strom
service record, 62 (table)
Ticket-Splitting between Presidential and House Candidates, 1990–2004, 35 (table)
Tillman Act, 85
Tocqueville, Alexis de, 45
Topologically Integrated Geographic Encoding and Referencing (TIGER), 126 (box)
"Trans Appalachian West" designation, 130 (box)
Treaty of Berlin, 61 (box)
Treaty of Paris, 61 (box)
Truman, Harry S.
redistricting, 115 (box)
Twentieth Amendment
ratification, 38

Twenty-fourth Amendment
  blacks in Congress, 53–54
  ratification time, 10
Twenty-sixth Amendment
  adoption, 2
Twenty-third Amendment
  adoption, 2

U
Underwood, Oscar W.
  Democratic leadership, 25
Union Party, 27 (graph)
United Negro College Fund, 54
The United States Congress: Organization and Procedure (Riddick), 38
United States of Ambition (Ehrenhalt), 32
University of Pennsylvania's Annenberg Public Policy Center, 81–82
U.S. Taxpayers Party, 27 (graph)
Utah
  population totals, 120 (table)
  school elections, 17
  seat transfer, 133 (table)
  statehood, 2
  women's suffrage, 17

V
Valazquez, Nydia M., 52
Vare, William S., 39, 86
Ventura, Jesse, 20
Vermont
  population totals, 120 (table)
Vesco, Robert, 91
Vietnam War
  minimum voting age, 19
Vinson, Carl
  service record, 62 (table)
Vinton, Samuel F.
  apportionment formula, 111–112
Virgin Islands
  purchase treaties, 61 (box)
  representation in Congress, 2, 19, 54, 60–61 (box)
Virginia
  electoral vote counts, 8 (box)
  poll taxes, 10
  redistricting, 16, 134
  seat transfer, 133 (table)
  voting requirements, 9
Voter registration
  election-day sign-up, 20
  federal supervisors, 12–13
  independent voters, 32, 34
  motor-voter law, 20
  party affiliation, 5, 6 (graph)
  section 527 group funding, 82
  soft money in campaign finance, 81
  voter registration groups, 22, 80–81
Voter Turnout Rates, Presidential and Midterm Elections, 1789–2006, 5 (graph)
Voting
  absentee ballots, 21
  "early voting" option, 21
  electronic voting machines, 21
  exit polls, 15
  gender gap, 34
  mail-voting, 19
  methods, 117
  participation, 6 (table)
    elderly, 35
    Hispanic voters, 14
    measuring, 7 (box)
    turnout, 4, 15
    turnout trends, 5 (graph)
    young, 35
  poll workers/watchers, 21–22
  preregistration requirements, 6, 19, 20–21
  voting patterns, 15
  "voting referees," 11
Voting rights
  absentee ballots, 21
  District of Columbia, 61 (box)
  franchise expansion, 1–2, 17–18, 19
  literacy barriers, 2, 9
  minimum voting age, 19
  poll tax ban, 10
  property ownership, 37
  redistricting, 14
  residency requirements, 2, 19
  state constitutions, 9
  state legislative apportionment, 112, 113 (table)
Voting Rights Act Extension of 1982, 16, 56, 134
Voting Rights Act of 1965
  African American Members of Congress, 53
  contested House elections, 41
  extension, 14
  franchise expansion, 2, 14
  literacy test ban, 10
  racial gerrymanders, 54, 108, 139
Voting Rights Act of 1970, 19
Vucanovich, Barbara, 52

W
Walker, Prentiss, 41
Wall Street Journal, 71
Wallace, George C.
  presidential election of 1968, 32
"Want-of-equity," 125
War Labor Disputes Act of 1943, 87
Warner, John W., 40
Warren, Earl
  redistricting, 128
Washington
  independent commission, 121
  population totals, 120 (table)
  seat transfer, 133 (table)
Washington, George
  party development, 29
  political campaign, 84
  vetoes, 110
Washington (state)
  voting requirements, 9–10
  women's suffrage, 17
Watergate scandal
  campaign finance reforms, 68–69, 91
  Congress membership turnover, 32, 57
Waters, Maxine, 54
Watson, Thomas E., 50
Webster, Daniel
  House appointment, 111
Wertheimer, Fred, 92
Wesberry, James P., Jr., 128
West Virginia
  population totals, 120 (table)
  seat transfer, 133 (table)
Westward expansion, 130 (box)
Whig Party, 27 (graph), 29
Whips
  functions, 26
White, Byron R., 15–16, 95, 128
White, George Henry, 53
White primaries, 10–11
Whitten, Jamie L., 41
  service record, 62 (table)
Wilkins, Roy, 12
Willcox, W. F., 114
Williams, John Bell, 41
Willoughby, William F., 41
Wilson, Roger B., 8 (box)
Wilson, William B., 39
Wilson, Woodrow
  women's voting rights, 18
Winger, Richard, 5
Wisconsin
  population totals, 120 (table)
  seat transfer, 133 (table)
Wolfinger, Raymond E., 4–5
Women
  members of Congress, 148–150 (list)
  widow's mandate, 18, 51–52
Women's Rights Convention, 17
Women's voting rights
  franchise expansion, 17–19
  school elections, 17
  19th Amendment, 2, 18
  voting participation, 18
Won Pat, Antonio Borja, 42
Wood, Henry A. Wise, 17
Woodrow Wilson School of Public and International Affairs website, 155
World War I
  women's voting rights, 18
World War II
  minimum voting age, 19
Wright, Jim
  campaign finance reform, 69
Writers for McGovern, 92
Wyden, Ron, 21
Wyman, Louis C., 39
Wyoming
  population totals, 120 (table)
  women's suffrage, 17

Y
Young, Andrew, 54
Young, Jordan, 54

Z
Zingale, Nancy H., 34

45^{00}